Walter William Skeat, Frederic Madden, John Purvey, Josiah Forshall

The Books of Job, Psalms, Proverbs, Ecclesiastes

and the Song of Solomon according to the Wycliffite version

Walter William Skeat, Frederic Madden, John Purvey, Josiah Forshall

The Books of Job, Psalms, Proverbs, Ecclesiastes
and the Song of Solomon according to the Wycliffite version

ISBN/EAN: 9783337180515

Printed in Europe, USA, Canada, Australia, Japan

Cover: Foto ©Lupo / pixelio.de

More available books at **www.hansebooks.com**

JOB, PSALMS, PROVERBS, ECCLESIASTES, AND THE SONG OF SOLOMON

WYCLIFFE, HEREFORD, AND PURVEY

London

HENRY FROWDE

OXFORD UNIVERSITY PRESS WAREHOUSE

7 PATERNOSTER ROW

THE BOOKS OF

JOB, PSALMS, PROVERBS, ECCLESIASTES, AND THE SONG OF SOLOMON

ACCORDING TO THE

WYCLIFFITE VERSION

MADE BY

NICHOLAS DE HEREFORD
ABOUT A.D. 1381

AND REVISED BY

JOHN PURVEY
ABOUT A.D. 1388

FORMERLY EDITED BY

The Rev. JOSIAH FORSHALL, F.R.S., &c.
Late Fellow of Exeter College, Oxford

AND

SIR FREDERIC MADDEN, F.R.S., &c.
Keeper of the MSS. in the British Museum

And now reprinted

Oxford
AT THE CLARENDON PRESS
M DCCC LXXXI

INTRODUCTION.

The portion of the Old Testament printed in this volume is a reprint from the *later* of the two Wycliffite versions of the same, as exhibited in 'The Holy Bible, containing the Old and New Testaments, with the Apocryphal Books, in the earliest English Versions made from the Latin Vulgate by John Wycliffe and his followers: edited by the Rev. Josiah Forshall, F.R.S., &c., and Sir Frederic Madden, K.H., F.R.S., &c.; Oxford, at the University Press, 1850.' The later Wycliffite version of the New Testament was reprinted in 1879, with an Introduction which fully explains all that is most necessary to be known concerning these interesting Middle-English versions. To this the reader is referred for further information.

For the use of readers who may not possess a copy of that volume, some points most worthy of observation are here briefly recapitulated.

The Preface to the large quarto edition (in four volumes), by Forshall and Madden, of which the title is given above, is the chief source of our knowledge respecting the Wycliffite versions. The MSS. are there enumerated and described, and the whole subject is carefully investigated[1].

There are two distinct Wycliffite versions, known as the earlier and the later. The later version is a revised one, and better suited than the other for general reading. The earlier version is rougher and more literal, and contains, on the whole,

---

[1] See also The History of the English Bible, by the Rev. W. F. Moulton; chap. ii.

a larger number of unusual words, rendering it somewhat more valuable for purely philological purposes, but less eligible on other grounds. The earlier version is mainly the work of John Wycliffe and Nicholas de Hereford, about A.D. 1380–1383; the later version was revised by John Purvey, about A.D. 1388.

Both versions were made from MSS. of the Latin version known as the Vulgate. A few specimens, selected from the portion here reprinted, may be of service in shewing the nature of the renderings. It is well to remember that *both* versions are, not unfrequently, almost unintelligible in certain passages until the Latin version has been consulted.

Job xx. 22 (*Vulgate*). Cum satiatus fuerit, arctabitur, æstuabit, et omnis dolor irruet super eum[1].

Earlier Version (*N. de Hereford*). Whan he shal be fulfild, he shal be streyned, and brenne; and alle sorewe shall falle in-to hym.

Later Version (*Purvey*). Whanne he is fillid, he schal be maad streit; he schal be hoot, and alle sorewe schal falle in on hym.

Job xxxix. 13. Penna struthionis similis est pennis herodii, et accipitris. Quando derelinquit ova sua in terra, tu forsitan in pulvere calefacies ea?

Earlier Version. The fether of a strucioun is lic to the fetheris of a ierfakoun, and of a goshauk; that leueth hir eiren in the erthe, thou perauenture in pouder shalt make them hot.

Later Version. The fethere of an ostriche is lijk the fetheris of a gerfawcun and of an hauk; which *ostrige* forsakith hise eirun in the erthe, in hap thou schalt make tho hoot in the dust.

Psalm cii (ciii). 12. Quantum distat ortus ab occidente: longe fecit a nobis iniquitates nostras.

Earlier Version. Hou myche the rising stant fro the going doun; aferr he made fro vs oure wickidnessis.

Later Version. As myche as the eest is fer fro the west; he made fer oure wickidnessis fro vs.

---

[1] Quoted from 'Biblia Sacra vulgatae editionis, &c. Parisiis, apud A. Jouby, 7, Via Majorum Augustinianorum. MDCCCLXII.'

Psalm cvi (cvii). 5. Esurientes, et sitientes : anima eorum in ipsis defecit.

Earlier Version. Hungrende and thirstende; the soule of hem in hem failide.

Later Version. Thei *weren* hungri and thirsti ; her soule failide in hem.

In the last example, the difference between the close translation in the earlier version and the freer one in the later version, is well marked.

The necessity of consulting the Latin text may be illustrated from the version here printed, in the following instances:—

Job xiv. 9. It [a tree] schal make heer[1]; *Lat.* faciet comam.

Job xxi. 17. Flowing schal come on hem; *Lat.* superveniet eis inundatio.

Ps. ci (cii). 29. The seed of hem schal be dressid in-to the world; *Lat.* semen eorum in sæculum dirigetur.

Ps. cviii (cix). 18. He clothide cursing as a cloth; *Lat.* induit maledictionem sicut vestimentum.

Prov. xxx. 31. A cok gird the leendis; *Lat.* gallus succinctus lumbos.

A comparison with our Authorised Version is full of interest, especially in the renderings of the Psalms. Sometimes the likeness is very close, as in the following :—

Ps. iii. 4. With my vois Y criede to the Lord; and he herde me fro his hooli hil.

(A. V.) I cried unto the Lord with my voice, and he heard me out of his holy hill.

The text here reprinted is taken from MS. I. C. VIII. in the Old Royal Library in the British Museum, i. e. from the same MS. as that which contains the best copy of the later text of the New Testament. It is described in full in Forshall and Madden's preface, and their description is repeated in the Introduction to the late reprint of the New Testament, at p. xii.

As regards the later version, the large quarto edition not only

---

[1] i. e. hair.

gives the text from the above MS., but also records various readings from other MSS., besides numerous glosses or interpretations (printed in the margin) of the more difficult passages. Thus, in Job i. 5, the expression 'in-to the world' is glossed by 'that is, in the ende of the wouke[1].' These glosses, together with the various readings, are omitted in the present volume, to save space and expense. It may be noted here, that the names of the Hebrew letters prefixed to the various parts of Psalm cxviii (cxix). do not occur in the MS. from which the later version is printed, but are copied from the best MS. of the *earlier* version, in which they are duly inserted.

It will at once be observed that most of the Psalms are marked with a *double* numbering. The explanation is as follows. The editors of the quarto edition very properly followed the numbering of the Chapters (or Psalms) and Verses as given in the ordinary editions *of the Vulgate version*, as this is the one upon which the Wycliffite translations really depend. But this numbering does not always agree with that in our Authorised Version, and there is, in particular, a difference in the mode of numbering the Psalms which causes a difficulty in finding the place. In order to remedy this to some extent, the numbering of the Psalms as in the Authorised Version has been supplied within marks of parenthesis. Even then, there is frequently a discrepancy in the numbering of the verses; but, as this is a minor difficulty, it was not worth while to attempt to remove it. A double set of numbers in a long chapter or Psalm would, perhaps, have only tended to confuse. A short account of the nature of the discrepancies may here be useful.

The difficulty begins after verse 21 of Psalm ix., where the Vulgate version has the remark 'Psalmus x. secundum Hebræos,' with a fresh numbering of the remaining verses in the Psalm. The English version makes Psalm x. begin here. But the Vulgate version heads our Psalm xi. with the title: 'In finem, Psalmus David x.' This throws the whole numbering out

---

[1] i.e. week. The Vulgate has: 'Cumque *in orbem* transissent dies convivii.'

for a long way, down to the end of Psalm cxlvi.[1] Ps. cxlvii. has its verses numbered from 12 to 20, and agrees with the latter part of Ps. cxlvii. in the English version. The three last Psalms are the same in both versions.

In the book of Ecclesiastes there are also certain slight differences of numbering, which are due rather to the Latin MSS. used by the Wycliffite translators than to the ordinary numbering of the Vulgate version. They cause no particular difficulty, as the numbering *of the verses* is clearly marked in the margin, and the English numbering of the chapters is inserted between marks of parenthesis, wherever any discrepancy exists.

REMARKS ON THE LANGUAGE, &C.

Remarks on the language of the Wycliffite versions are given in the Introduction to the reprint of the New Testament; see also the Introduction to Specimens of English, ed. Morris and Skeat, in the Clarendon Press Series. The following notes are thrown together in the briefest possible form.

Dialect.—The dialect of Purvey's version is Midland, resembling that of standard English.

Pronunciation.—The pronunciation of Middle-English differed widely from that now in use, especially in the vowel-sounds, which resembled those of modern Italian and German[2].

Spelling.—The spelling is *phonetic*, i.e. the words are written as they were then pronounced. The scribes occasionally miswrite a word, chiefly by adding a final *e* where it is not required by the grammar. Thus *wynde* in Job i. 19 should be *wynd*.

Capital letters, &c.—The editors have, in general, altered the capitals of the MS., so as to conform them to the modern use. Words printed in italics, such as *he is* in Job i. 8, are not in the original Latin.

---

[1] Psalms cxiii., cxiv., cxv. in the Vulgate are strangely divided. The first is our Psalms cxiv. and cxv.; the other two make up our Psalm cxvi.

[2] The Middle-English sounds are described in the Preface to Chaucer's Man of Law's Tale (Clarendon Press Series).

Punctuation.—The punctuation is due to the editors, the MS. not being punctuated.

Compound words.—The parts of compound words are written separately in the MS., and are so printed. Thus *in to* in Job i. 12, is the modern *into*. To save the reader trouble, the use of hyphens has been rather freely introduced into the present reprint [1], so that *with out* here commonly appears as *with-out*. Wherever they are omitted, the reader can easily supply them.

Alphabet.—The character 3 signifies *y* at the beginning of a word, and *gh* elsewhere. Thus *ri3tful* = *rightful*, Job i. 1; *3af*= *yaf*, old form of *gave*, Job i. 21. For words beginning with 3, see the *last* section of the Glossary.

The character *u* between two vowels is to be read as *v*. Thus *perauenture* = *peraventure*, Job i. 5. It is sometimes so to be read at the beginning of a syllable; thus *siluer* = *silver*, Job iii. 15. The use of *v* for *u* is not common, and only found at the beginning of words, as in *vs* (us), *vp* (up). Observe 3*yue* = *yyve* = *yive* = give, Job ii. 4.

Grammar.—The final *-e*, usually to be sounded as a distinct syllable, plays an important part in Middle-English grammar, representing several older inflections. Thus *allë* (dissyllabic) is the plural of *al* (all), and is rightly associated with *men*; Job i. 3. *Etë* (dissyllabic) is the infinitive mood, from A.S. *etan*; Job i. 4. *Biholdë* is short for *biholden*; Job i. 8. *For to tellë* is a gerund (A.S. *tó tellanne*); Job i. 15. *Fleddë* is the past tense of a weak verb; Job i. 19. See further in the Introductions to Chaucer's Prologue, &c. (Clarendon Press Series), and to Chaucer's Prioress's Tale (same series).

Vocabulary.—The vocabulary contains numerous French words. The following is a list of such words in Job i. Symple, possessioun, femal, meynee, feestis, feeste, passid, sacrifices, perauenture, present, cumpassid, seruaunt, veyn, catel, cumpas, encreeside, touche, face, gendrid, messanger, femal, touchid, ascapide, cumpenyes, assaileden, entride, suden, coost, desert, corneris, oppresside, pleside. Of these words, the difficult word *touch* is probably

---

[1] In the quarto edition they are very sparingly employed.

of Teutonic origin, according to Diez; the others are all various modifications of Latin words. *Camel* is an Oriental word, and so probably is *ass*. The rest of the words in the same chapter are, mostly, of the highest antiquity and of pre-historic origin; many of them first emerge into history in Anglo-Saxon forms. The word *offride* (offered), from A.S. *offrian*, to offer, is, however, merely borrowed from Lat. *offerre*.

Changes of meaning.—The meaning of many words has changed. Thus *cheer* can hardly now be used in the sense of 'countenance,' as in 'the li3t of thi *cheer*,' Ps. iv. 7; we still retain some remembrance of this old use in the phrase 'to be of good *cheer*.'

Imperfect translation.—In some places, especially in the book of Psalms, the translators have been content to retain Latin words and phrases, and even idioms, without any attempt to supply their place by English expressions. 'Thou schalt gouerne hem *in* an yrun 3erde' (Ps. ii. 9) is not, nor ever was, good English; it is simply due to retaining the Latin *in*, in the phrase 'Reges eos in virga ferrea.' *Singulerli* in Ps. iv. 10 is merely the Lat. *singulariter*. 'Lord, be thou conuertid' represents 'convertere, Domine;' Ps. vi. 5. In Ps. vii. 17, the Latin version has: 'Convertetur dolor ejus in caput ejus; et in verticem ipsius iniquitas ejus descendet.' The Wycliffite version is not a little curious, viz.: 'His sorewe schal be turnid in-to his heed; and his wickidnesse schal come doun in-to his necke.'

Glossarial Index.—For the explanation of unusual or obsolete words, see the Glossarial Index, partly compiled from the original glossary to the quarto edition made by the Rev. Josiah Forshall and Sir Frederic Madden. Several additions, however, have been made to this, and the glossary, as here printed, has been carefully prepared by Mr. W. E. Gabbett, B.A., of Lincoln College, Oxford, and subsequently revised by myself. I have also supplied an Index to the first words of the Latin psalms.

WALTER W. SKEAT.

CAMBRIDGE, *Nov.* 5, 1880.

J O B.

Cap. I.

1 A MAN, Joob bi name, was in the lond of Hus; and thilke man was symple, and riʒtful, and dredynge God,
2 and goynge awey fro yuel. And seuene sones and thre
3 douʒtris weren borun to hym; and his possessioun was seuene thousynde of scheep, and thre thousynde of camels, and fyue hundrid ʒockis of oxis, and fyue hundrid of femal assis, and ful myche meynee; and thilke man was grete
4 among alle men of the eest. And hise sones ʒeden, and maden feestis bi housis, ech man in his day; and thei senten, and clepiden her thre sistris, that thei schulden ete,
5 and drynke wiyn with hem. And whanne the daies of feeste hadden passid in to the world, Joob sente to hem, and halewide hem, and he roos eerli, and offride brent sacrifices bi alle. For he seide, Lest perauenture my sones do synne, and curse God in her hertis. Joob dide so in
6 alle daies. Forsothe in sum day, whanne the sones of God weren comun to be present bifor the Lord, also
7 Sathan cam among hem. To whom the Lord seide, Fro whennus comest thou? Which answeride, and seide, Y haue cumpassid the erthe, and Y haue walkid thorouʒ it.
8 And the Lord seide to hym, Whether thou hast biholde my seruaunt Joob, that noon in erthe is lyik hym; *he is* a symple man, and riʒtful, and dredynge God, and goynge

B

9 awei fro yuel? To whom Sathan answeride, Whether Joob
10 dredith God veynli? Whethir thou hast not cumpassid
hym, and his hows, and al his catel bi cumpas? Thou
hast blessid the werkis of hise hondis, and hise possessioun
11 encreesside in erthe. But stretche forth thin hond a litil,
and touche thou alle thingis whiche he hath in possessioun;
12 if he cursith not thee in the face, *bileue not to me*. Therfor
the Lord seide to Sathan, Lo! alle thingis, whiche he hath,
ben in thin hond; oneli stretche thou not forth thin hond
in to hym. And Sathan ȝede out fro the face of the Lord.
13 Sotheli whanne in sum dai hise sones and douȝtris eeten,
and drunken wiyn in the hows of her firste gendrid brothir,
14 a messanger cam to Job, whiche *messanger* seide, Oxis
15 eriden, and femal assis weren lesewid bisidis tho; and
Sabeis felden yn, and token awey alle thingis, and smytiden the children with swerd; and Y aloone ascapide for
16 to telle to thee. And whanne he spak ȝit, anothir cam,
and seide, Fier of God cam doun fro heuene, and wastide
scheep, and children touchid; and Y aloone ascapide for
17 to telle to thee. But ȝit the while he spak, also anothir
cam, and seide, Caldeis maden thre cumpenyes, and as-
sailiden the camels, and token tho awei, and thei smytiden
also the children with swerd; and Y aloone ascapide to
18 telle to thee. And ȝit he spak, and, lo! anothir entride,
and seide, While thi sones and douȝtris eeten, and drunken
19 wiyn in the hows of her firste gendrid brothir, a greet
wynde felde yn sudenli fro the coost of desert, and schook
foure corneris of the hows, which felde doun, and oppresside thi children, and thei ben deed; and Y aloone fledde
20 to telle to thee. Thanne Joob roos, and to-rente hise
clothis, and with pollid heed he felde doun on the erthe,
21 and worschipide *God*, and seide, Y ȝede nakid out of the
wombe of my modir, Y schal turne aȝen nakid thidur; the

Lord 3af, the Lord took awei; as it pleside the Lord, so
22 it is doon; the name of the Lord be blessid. In alle these
thingis Joob synnede not in hise lippis, nether spak ony
fonned thing a3ens God.

CAP. II.

1 FORSOTHE it was doon, whanne in sum dai the sones of
God weren comun, and stoden bifor the Lord, and Sathan
2 was comun among hem, and stood in his si3t, that the Lord
seide to Sathan, Fro whennus comest thou? Which answeride, and seide, Y haue cumpassid the erthe, and Y
3 haue go thur3 it. And the Lord seide to Sathan, Whethir
thou hast biholde my seruaunt Joob, that noon in erthe
is lijk hym; *he is* a symple man, and ri3tful, and dredynge
God, and goynge awei fro yuel, and 3it holdynge innocence? But thou hast moued me a3ens him, that Y schulde
4 turmente hym in veyn. To whom Sathan answeride, and
seide, A man schal 3yue skyn for skyn, and alle thingis
5 that he hath for his lijf; ellis sende thin hond, and touche
his boon and fleisch, and thanne thou schalt se, that he
6 schal curse thee in the face. Therfor the Lord seide to
Sathan, Lo! he is in thin hond; netheles kepe thou his
7 lijf. Therfor Sathan 3ede out fro the face of the Lord,
and smoot Joob with a ful wickid botche fro the sole of
8 the foot til to his top; which *Joob* schauyde the quytere
9 with a schelle, and sat in the dunghil. Forsothe his wijf
seide to hym, Dwellist thou 3it in thi symplenesse? Curse
10 thou God, and die. And Joob seide, Thou hast spoke as
oon of the fonned wymmen; if we han take goodis of
the hond of the Lord, whi forsothe suffren we not yuels?
11 In alle these thingis Joob synnede not in hise lippis. Therfor
thre frendis of Joob herden al the yuel, that hadde bifelde

to hym, and camen ech man fro his place, Eliphath Temanytes, and Baldach Suythes, and Sophar Naamathites; for thei hadden seide togidere to hem silf, that thei wolden 12 come togidere, and visite hym, and coumforte. And whanne thei hadden reisid afer her iȝen, thei knewen not hym; and thei crieden, and wepten, and to-renten her clothis, and 13 spreynten dust on her heed in to heuene. And thei saten with hym in the erthe seuene daies and seuene nyȝtis, and no man spak a word to hym; for thei sien, that his sorewe was greet.

Cap. III.

1 Aftir these thingis Joob openyde his mouth, and curside 2, 3 his dai, and seide, Perische the dai in which Y was borun, and the nyȝt in which it was seid, The man is conceyued. 4 Thilke dai be turnede in to derknessis; God seke not it aboue, and be it not in mynde, nethir be it liȝtned with 5 liȝt. Derknessis make it derk, and the schadewe of deeth and myist occupie it; and be it wlappid with bittirnesse. 6 Derk whirlwynde holde that niȝt; be it not rikynyd among the daies of the ȝeer, nethir be it noumbrid among the 7 monethes. Thilke nyȝt be soleyn, and not worthi of 8 preisyng. Curse thei it, that cursen the dai, that ben redi 9 to reise Leuyathan. Sterris be maad derk with the derknesse therof; abide it liȝt, and se it not, nethir the bigyn-10 nyng of the morwetid risyng vp. For it closide not the doris of the wombe, that bar me, nethir took awei yuels 11 fro min iȝen. Whi was not Y deed in the wombe? whi ȝede Y out of the wombe, and perischide not anoon? Whi 12 was Y takun on knees? whi was Y suclid with teetis? For 13 now Y slepynge schulde be stille, and schulde reste in my 14 sleep, with kyngis, and consuls of erthe, that bilden to hem 15 soleyn places; ethir with pryncces that han gold in posses-

16 sioun, and fillen her housis with siluer; ethir as a thing hid not borun Y schulde not stonde, ethir whiche con-
17 seyued sien not li3t. There wickid men ceessiden of noise,
18 and there men maad wery of strengthe restiden. And sum tyme boundun togidere with out disese thei herden not the
19 voys of the wrongful axere. A litil man and greet man be
20 there, and a seruaunt free fro his lord. Whi is li3t 3ouun to the wretche, and lijf to hem that ben in bitternesse of
21 soule? Whiche abiden deeth, and it cometh not; as men
22 diggynge out tresour and ioien greetly, whanne thei han
23 founde a sepulcre? *Whi is li3t 3ouun* to a man, whos weie is hid, and God hath cumpassid hym with derknessis?
24 Bifore that Y ete, Y si3he; and as of watir flowynge, so
25 is my roryng. For the drede, which Y dredde, cam to
26 me; and that, that Y schamede, bifelde. Whether Y dissymilide not? whether Y was not stille? whether Y restide not? and indignacioun cometh on me.

Cap. IV.

1, 2 Forsothe Eliphat Themanytes answeride, and seide, If we bigynnen to speke to thee, in hap thou schalt take it
3 heuyli; but who may holde a word conseyued? Lo! thou hast tau3t ful many men, and thou hast strengthid hondis
4 maad feynt. Thi wordis confermyden men doutynge, and
5 thou coumfortidist knees tremblynge. But now a wounde is comun on thee, and thou hast failid; it touchide thee, and
6 thou art disturblid. Where is thi drede, thi strengthe, and thi
7 pacience, and the perfeccioun of thi weies? Y biseche thee, haue thou mynde, what innocent man perischide euere, ethir
8 whanne ri3tful men weren doon awei? Certis rathir Y si3 hem, that worchen wickidnesse, and sowen sorewis, and
9 repen tho, to haue perischid bi God blowynge, and to be

10 wastid bi the spirit of his ire. The roryng of a lioun, and the vois of a lionesse, and the teeth of whelpis of liouns ben
11 al to-brokun. Tigris perischide, for sche hadde not prey;
12 and the whelpis of a lioun ben distried. Certis an hid word was seid to me, and myn eere took as theueli the veynes of
13 priuy noise therof. In the hidousnesse of nyʒtis siʒt, whanne
14 heuy sleep is wont to occupie men, drede and tremblyng
15 helde me; and alle my boonys weren aferd. And whanne the spirit ʒede in my presence, the heiris of my fleisch hadden
16 hidousnesse. Oon stood, whos chere Y knewe not, an ymage bifor myn iʒen; and Y herde a vois as of softe
17 wynd. Whether a man schal be maad iust in comparisoun of God? ethir whethir a man schal be clennere than his
18 Makere? Lo! thei that seruen hym ben not stidefast; and
19 he findeth schrewidnesse in hise aungels. Hou myche more thei that dwellen in housis of cley, that han an ertheli
20 foundement, schulen be wastyd as of a mouʒte. Fro morewtid til to euentid thei schulen be kit doun; and for no man vndurstondith, thei schulen perische with outen ende.
21 Sotheli thei, that ben residue, schulen be takun awei; thei schulen die, and not in wisdom.

Cap. V.

1 Therfor clepe thou, if ony is that schal answere thee,
2 and turne thou to summe of seyntis. Wrathfulnesse sleeth
3 a fonned man, and enuye sleeth a litil child. Y siʒ a fool
4 with stidefast rote, and Y curside his feirnesse anoon. Hise sones schulen be maad fer fro helthe, and thei schulen be defoulid in the ʒate, and noon schal be that schal delyuere
5 *hem.* Whos ripe corn an hungri man schal ete, and an armed man schal rauysche hym, and thei, that thirsten,
6 schulen drynke hise richessis. No thing is doon in erthe

with out cause, and sorewe schal not go out of the erthe.
7, 8 A man is borun to labour, and a brid to fliȝt. Wherfor
Y schal bisceche the Lord, and Y schal sette my spechc to
9 my God. That makith grete thingis, and that moun not
be souȝt out, and wondurful thingis with out noumbre.
10 Which ȝyueth reyn on the face of erthe, and moistith alle
11 thingis with watris. Which settith meke men an hiȝ, and
12 reisith with helthe hem that morenen. Which distrieth the
thouȝtis of yuel willid men, that her hondis moun not fille
13 tho thingis that thei bigunnen. Which takith cautelouse
men in the felnesse of hem, and distrieth the counsel of
14 schrewis. Bi dai thei schulen renne in to derknessis, and
15 as in nyȝt so thei schulen grope in myddai. Certis God
schal make saaf a nedi man fro the swerd of her mouth,
and a pore man fro the hond of the violent, *ethir raynour*.
16 And hope schal be to a nedi man, but wickidnesse schal
17 drawe togidere his mouth. Blessid is the man, which is
chastisid of the Lord; therfor repreue thou not the blam-
18 yng of the Lord. For he woundith, and doith medicyn;
19 he smytith, and hise hondis schulen make hool. In sixe
tribulaciouns he schal delyuere thee, and in the seuenthe
20 tribulacioun yuel schal not touche thee. In hungur he schal
delyuere thee fro deeth, and in batel fro the power of swerd.
21 Thou schalt be hid fro the scourge of tunge, and thou schalt
not drede myseiste, *ethir wretchidnesse*, whanne it cometh.
22 In distriyng *maad of enemyes* and in hungur thou schalt leiȝe,
23 and thou schalt not drede the beestis of erthe. But thi
couenaunt schal be with the stonys of erthe, and beestis of
24 erthe schulen be pesible to thee. And thou schalt wite,
that thi tabernacle hath pees, and thou visitynge thi fairnesse
25 schalt not do synne. And thou schalt wite also, that thi
seed schal be many fold, and thi generacioun schal be as
26 an erbe of erthe. In abundaunce thou schalt go in to the

27 sepulcre, as an heep of wheete is borun in his tyme. Lo! this is so, as we han souȝt; which thing herd, trete thou in minde.

Cap. VI.

1, 2 Forsothe Joob answeride, and seide, Y wolde, that my synnes, bi whiche Y desseruede ire, and the wretchidnesse 3 which Y suffre, weren peisid in a balaunce. As the grauel of the see, this wretchidnesse schulde appere greuousere; 4 wherfor and my wordis ben ful of sorewe. For the arowis of the Lord ben in me, the indignacioun of whiche drynkith vp my spirit; and the dredis of the Lord fiȝten aȝens me. 5 Whether a feeld asse schal rore, whanne he hath gras? Ethir whether an oxe schal lowe, whanne he stondith byfor 6 a ful cratche? Ether whethir a thing vnsauery may be etun, which is not maad sauery bi salt? Ether whether ony man may taaste a thing, which tastid bryngith deeth? For whi 7 to an hungri soule, ȝhe, bittir thingis semen to be swete; tho thingis whiche my soule nolde touche bifore, ben now 8 my meetis for angwisch. Who ȝyueth, that myn axyng 9 come; and that God ȝyue to me that, that Y abide? And he that bigan, al to-breke me; releesse he his hond, and 10 kitte me doun? And this be coumfort to me, that he turmente me with sorewe, and spare not, and that Y aȝenseie 11 not the wordis of the hooli. For whi, what is my strengthe, that Y suffre? ethir which is myn ende, that Y do pacientli? 12 Nethir my strengthe is the strengthe of stoonus, nether my 13 fleisch is of bras. Lo! noon help is to me in me; also my 14 meyneal frendis ȝeden awey fro me. He that takith awei 15 merci fro his frend, forsakith the drede of the Lord. My britheren passiden me, as a stronde *doith*, that passith rusch- 16 yngli in grete valeis. Snow schal come on hem, that dreden 17 frost. In the tyme wherynne thei ben scaterid, thei schulen

perische; and as thei ben hoote, thei schulen be vnknyt
18 fro her place. The pathis of her steppis ben wlappid; thei
19 schulen go in veyn, and schulen perische. Biholde ȝe the
pathis of Theman, and the weies of Saba; and abide ȝe
20 a litil. Thei ben schent, for Y hopide; and thei camen til
21 to me, and thei ben hilid with schame. Now ȝe ben comun,
22 and now ȝe seen my wounde, and dreden. Whether Y seide,
Brynge ȝe to me, and ȝiue ȝe of ȝoure catel to me? ethir,
23 Delyuere ȝe me fro the hond of enemy, and rauysche ȝe
24 me fro the hond of stronge men? Teche ȝe me, and Y
schal be stille; and if in hap Y vnknew ony thing, teche
25 ȝe me. Whi han ȝe depraued the wordis of trewthe? sithen
26 noon is of ȝou, that may repreue me. Ȝe maken redi spechis
oneli for to blame, and ȝe bryngen forth wordis in to wynde.
27 Ȝe fallen in on a fadirles child, and enforsen to peruerte
28 ȝoure frend. Netheles fille ȝe that, that ȝe han bigunne;
29 ȝyue ȝe the eere, and se ȝe, whether Y lie. Y biseche, answere ȝe with out strijf, and speke ȝe, and deme ȝe that, that
30 is iust. And ȝe schulen not fynde wickidnesse in my tunge,
nethir foli schal sowne in my chekis.

Cap. VII.

1 Knyȝthod is lijf of man on erthe, and his daies ben as
2 the daies of an hired man. As an hert desireth schadowe,
3 and as an hirede man abideth the ende of his werk; so and
Y hadde voide monethis, and Y noumbrede trauailous niȝtes
4 to me. If Y schal slepe, Y schal seie, Whanne schal Y
rise? and eft Y schal abide the euentid, and Y schal be
5 fillid with sorewis til to derknessis. Mi fleisch is clothid
with rot, and filthis of dust; my skyn driede vp, and is
6 drawun togidere. My daies passiden swiftliere thanne a
web is kit doun of a webstere; and tho daies ben wastid

7 with outen ony hope. *God,* haue thou mynde, for my lijf is wynde, and myn iȝe schal not turne aȝen, that it se goodis. 8 Nethir the siȝt of man schal biholde me; but thin iȝen ben 9 in me, and Y schal not be *in deedli lijf.* As a cloude is wastid, and passith, so he that goith doun to helle, schal 10 not stie; nether schal turne aȝen more in to his hows, 11 and his place schal no more knowe hym. Wherfor and Y schal not spare my mouth; Y schal speke in the tribulacioun of my spirit, Y schal talke togidere with the bitter-12 nesse of my soule. Whether Y am the see, ethir a whal, 13 for thou hast cumpassid me with prisoun? If Y seie, My bed schal coumfort me, and Y schal be releeuyd, spekynge 14 with me in my bed; thou schalt make me aferd bi dremys, and thou schalt schake me with orrour, *ethir hidousnesse,* bi 15 siȝtis. Wherfor my soule chees hangyng, and my boonys 16 *cheesiden* deth. Y dispeiride, now Y schal no more lyue; 17 Lord, spare thou me, for my daies ben nouȝt. What is a man, for thou magnifiest hym? ether what settist thou 18 thin herte toward hym? Thou visitist hym eerly, and sud-19 eynli thou preuest hym. Hou long sparist thou not me, 20 nether suffrist me, that Y swolowe my spotele? Y haue synned; A! thou kepere of men, what schal Y do to thee? Whi hast thou set me contrarie to thee, and Y am maad 21 greuouse to my silf? Whi doist thou not awei my sinne, and whi takist thou not awei my wickidnesse? Lo! now Y schal slepe in dust, and if thou sekist me eerli, Y schal not abide.

Cap. VIII.

1, 2 Sotheli Baldath Suytes answeride, and seide, Hou longe schalt thou speke siche thingis? The spirit of the word of 3 thi mouth is manyfold. Whether God supplauntith, *ethir disseyueth,* doom, and whether Almyȝti God distrieth that, that

4 is iust? ȝhe, thouȝ thi sones synneden aȝens hym, and he
5 lefte hem in the hond of her wickidnesse ; netheles, if thou
6 risist eerli to God, and bisechist Almyȝti God, if thou goist
clene and riȝtful, anoon he schal wake fulli to thee, and schal
7 make pesible the dwellyng place of thi ryȝtfulnesse ; in so
miche that thi formere thingis weren litil, and that thi laste
8 thingis be multiplied greetli. For whi, axe thou the formere
generacioun, and seke thou diligentli the mynde of fadris.
9 For we ben men of ȝistirdai, and kunnen not ; for oure daies
10 ben as schadewe on the erthe. And thei schulen teche thee,
thei schulen speke to thee, and of her herte thei schulen bring
11 forth spechis. Whether a rusche may lyue with out moys-
12 ture? ethir a spier may wexe with out watir? Whanne it is
ȝit in the flour, nethir is takun with hond, it wexeth drie bifor
13 alle erbis. So the weies of alle men, that forȝeten God ; and
14 the hope of an ypocrite schal perische. His cowardise schal
15 not plese hym, and his trist *schal be* as a web of yreyns. He
schal leene, *ether reste*, on his hows, and it schal not stonde ; he
16 schal vndursette it, and it schal not rise togidere. The rusche
semeth moist, bifor that the sunne come ; and in the risyng
17 of the sunne the seed therof schal go out. Rootis therof
schulen be maad thicke on an heep of stoonys, and it schal
18 dwelle among stoonys. If a man drawith it out of his place,
his place schal denye it, and schal seie, Y knowe thee not.
19 For this is the gladnesse of his weie, that eft othere ruschis
20 springe out of the erthe. Forsothe God schal not caste a wei
21 a symple man, nethir schal dresse hond to wickid men ; til
thi mouth be fillid with leiȝtir, and thi lippis with hertli song.
22 Thei that haten thee schulen be clothid with schenschip ; and
the tabernacle of wickid men schal not stonde.

Cap. IX.

1, 2 Joob answeride, and seide, Verili Y woot, that it is so, and that a man comparisound to God schal not be maad iust. 3 If he wole stryue with God, he may not answere to God oon 4 for a thousynde. He is wiys in herte, and strong in my3t; 5 who a3enstood hym, and hadde pees? Which bar hillis fro o place to anothir, and thei wisten not; whiche he distriede 6 in his strong veniaunce. Which stirith the erthe fro his place, and the pilers therof schulen be schakun togidere. 7 Which comaundith to the sunne, and it risith not; and he 8 closith the sterris, as vndur a signet. Which aloone stretchith 9 forth heuenes, and goith on the wawis of the see. Which makith Ariture, and Orionas, and Hiadas, *that is, seuene ster-* 10 *ris,* and the innere thingis of the south. Which makith grete thingis, and that moun not be sou3t out, and wondurful 11 thingis, of whiche is noon noumbre. If he cometh to me, *that is, bi his grace,* Y schal not se hym; if he goith awey, *that is, in withdrawynge his grace,* Y schal not vndurstonde. 12 If he axith sodeynli, who schal answere to hym? ethir who 13 may seie to hym, Whi doist thou so? God *is he,* whos wraththe no man may withstonde; and vndur whom thei ben 14 bowid, that beren the world. Hou greet am Y, that Y 15 answere to hym, and speke bi my wordis with hym? Which also schal not answere, thou3 Y haue ony thing iust; but Y 16 schal biseche my iuge. And whanne he hath herd me inwardli clepynge, Y bileue not, that he hath herd my vois. 17 For in a whirlewynd he schal al to-breke me, and he schal 18 multiplie my woundis, 3he, without cause. He grauntith not, that my spirit haue reste, and he fillith me with bittirnesses. 19 If strengthe is sou3t, he is moost strong; if equyte of doom o *is sou3t,* no man dar 3elde witnessynge for me. If Y wole

make me iust, my mouth schal dampne me; if Y schal schewe
21 me innocent, he schal preue me a schrewe. ȝhe, thouȝ Y am
symple, my soule schal not knowe this same thing; and it
22 schal anoye me of my lijf. O thing is, which Y spak, he
schal waste *bi deth* also the innocent and wickid man. If he
23 betith, sle he onys, and leiȝe *he* not of the peynes of innocent
24 men. The erthe is ȝouun in to the hondis of the wickid; he
hilith the face of iugis; that if he is not, who therfor is?
25 Mi daies weren swiftere than a corour; thei fledden, and sien
26 not good. Thei passiden as schippis berynge applis, as an
27 egle fleynge to mete. Whanne Y seie, Y schal not speke
so; Y chaunge my face, and Y am turmentid with sorewe.
28 Y drede alle my werkis, witynge that thou woldist not spare
29 the trespassour. Sotheli if Y am also thus wickid, whi haue
30 Y trauelid in veyn? Thouȝ Y am waischun as with watris of
snow, and thouȝ myn hondis schynen as moost cleene,
31 netheles thou schalt dippe me in filthis, and my clothis, *that*
32 *is, werkis*, schulen holde me abhomynable. Trewli Y schal
not answere a man, which is lijk me; nether that may be
33 herd euenli with me in doom. Noon is, that may repreue
34 euer eithir, and sette his hond in bothe. Do he awei his
35 ȝerde fro me, and his drede make not me aferd. Y schal
speke, and Y schal not drede hym; for Y may not answere
dredynge.

CAP. X.

1 YT anoieth my soule of my lijf; Y schal lete my speche
2 aȝens me, Y schal speke in the bitternesse of my soule. Y
schal seie to God, Nyle thou condempne me; schewe thou
3 to me, whi thou demest me so. Whether it semeth good to
thee, if thou falsli chalengist and oppressist me, the werk of
thin hondis; and if thou helpist the counsel of wickid men?
4 Whethir fleischli iȝen ben to thee, ethir, as a man seeth, also

5 thou schalt se? Whether thi daies *ben* as the daies of man, 6 and thi ʒeeris ben as mannus tymes; that thou enquere my 7 wickidnesse, and enserche my synne? And wite, that Y haue do no wickid thing; sithen no man is, that may delyuere 8 fro thin hond? Thin hondis han maad me, and han formed me al in cumpas; and thou castist me doun so sodeynli. 9 Y preye, haue thou mynde, that thou madist me as cley, and 10 schalt brynge me aʒen in to dust. Whether thou hast not mylkid me as mylk, and hast cruddid me togidere as cheese? 11 Thou clothidist me with skyn and fleisch; thou hast ioyned 12 me togidere with boonys and senewis. Thou hast ʒoue lijf 13 and mercy to me, and thi visiting hath kept my spirit. Thouʒ thou helist these thingis in thin herte, netheles Y woot, that 14 thou hast mynde of alle thingis. If Y dide synne, and thou sparidist me at an our; whi suffrist thou not me to be cleene 15 of my wickidnesse? And if Y was wickid, wo is to me; and if Y was iust, Y fillid with turment and wretchidnesse schal 16 not reise the heed. And *if Y reise the heed* for pride, thou schalt take me as a lionesse; and thou turnest aʒen, and 17 turmentist me wondirli. Thou gaderist in store thi witnessis aʒens me, and thou multipliest thin yre, *that is, veniaunce,* 18 aʒens me; and peynes holden knyʒthod in me. Whi hast thou led me out of the wombe? And Y wolde, that Y were 19 wastid, lest an iʒe schulde se me. That Y hadde be, as if Y were not, and were translatid, *ethir borun ouer*, fro the wombe 20 to the sepulcre. Whether the fewnesse of my daies schal not be endid in schort? Therfor suffre thou me, that Y biweile 21 a litil my sorewe, bifor that Y go, and turne not aʒen, to the derk lond, and hilid with the derknesse of deth, to the lond of 22 wrecchidnesse and of derknessis; where *is* schadewe of deeth, and noon ordre, but euerlastynge hidousnesse dwellith.

Cap. XI.

1 Forsothe Sophar Naamathites answeride, and seide,
2 Whether he, that spekith many thingis, schal not also here? ether whethir a man ful of wordis schal be maad iust?
3 Schulen men be stille to thee aloone; whanne thou hast scorned othere men, schalt thou not be ouercomun of ony
4 man? For thou seidist, My word is cleene, and Y am cleene
5 in thi si3t. And Y wolde, that God spak with thee, and
6 openyde hise lippis to thee; to schewe to thee the priuetees of wisdom, and that his lawe is manyfold, and thou schuldist vndurstonde, that thou art requirid of hym *to paie* myche lesse
7 thingis, than thi wickidnesse disserueth. In hap thou schalt comprehende the steppis of God, and thou schalt fynde
8 Almy3ti God til to perfeccioun. He is hi3ere than heuene, and what schalt thou do? he is deppere than helle, and
9 wherof schalt thou knowe? His mesure *is* lengere than
10 erthe, and brodere than the see. If he distrieth alle thingis, ethir dryueth streitli in to oon, who schal a3enseie hym?
11 Ethir who may seie to hym, Whi doest thou so? For he knowith the vanyte of men; and whether he seynge byholdith
12 not wickidnesse? A veyn man is reisid in to pride; and
13 gessith hym silf borun fre, as the colt of a wilde asse. But thou hast maad stidefast thin herte, and hast spred abrood
14 thin hondis to hym. If thou doest awei fro thee the wickidnesse, which is in thin hond, and vnri3tfulnesse dwellith not
15 in thi tabernacle, thanne thou schalt mowe reise thi face with out wem, and thou schalt be stidefast, and thou schalt not
16 drede. And thou schalt for3ete wretchidnesse, and thou
17 schalt not thenke *of it*, as of watris that han passid. And as myddai schynynge it schal reise to thee at euentid: and whanne thou gessist thee wastid, thou schalt rise vp as the

18 dai-sterre. And thou schalt haue trist, while hope schal be
19 set forth to thee; and thou biried schalt slepe sikurli. Thou
schalt reste, and noon schal be that schal make thee aferd;
20 and ful many men schulen bisechi thi face. But the iȝen of
wickid men schulen faile; and socour schal perische fro hem,
and the hope of hem schal be abhominacyioun of soule.

Cap. XII.

1, 2 Sotheli Joob answeride, and seide, Therfor ben ȝe men
3 aloone, that wisdom dwelle with ȝou? And to me is an herte,
as and to ȝou, and Y am not lowere than ȝe; for who
4 knowith not these thingis, whiche ȝe knowen? He that is
scorned of his frend, as Y am, schal inwardli clepe God, and
God schal here hym; for the symplenesse of a iust man is
5 scorned. A laumpe is dispisid at the thouȝtis of riche men,
6 and *the laumpe* is maad redi to a tyme ordeyned. The
tabernaclis of robberis ben plenteuouse, *ether ful of goodis ;*
and boldli thei terren God to wraththe, whanne he hath ȝoue
7 alle thingis in to her hondis. No wondur, ax thou beestis,
and tho schulen teche thee; and *axe thou* volatilis of the eir,
8 and tho schulen schewe to thee. Speke thou to the erthe,
and it schal answere thee; and the fischis of the see schulen
9 telle tho thingis. Who knowith not that the hond of the
10 Lord made alle these thingis? In whos hond the soule is of
ech lyuynge thing, and the spirit, *that is, resonable soule*, of
11 ech fleisch of man. Whether the eere demeth not wordis,
12 and the chekis of the etere *demen* sauour? Wisdom is in
13 elde men, and prudence is in myche tyme. Wisdom and
strengthe is at God; he hath counsel and vndurstondyng.
14 If he distrieth, no man is that bildith; if he schittith in a
15 man, noon is that openith. If he holdith togidere watris,
alle thingis schulen be maad drie; if he sendith out tho

16 watris, tho schulen distrie the erthe. Strengthe and wisdom is at God; he knowith bothe hym that disseyueth and hym
17 that is disseyued. And he bryngith conselours in to a fonned eende, and iugis in to wondryng, *ethir astonyíng*.
18 He vnbindith the girdil of kyngis, and girdith her reynes
19 with a coorde. He ledith her prestis with out glorie, and
20 he disseyueth the principal men, *ethir counselours;* and he chaungith the lippis of sothefast men, and takith awei
21 the doctrine of elde men. He schedith out dispisyng on
22 princes, and releeueth hem, that weren oppressid. Which schewith depe thingis fro derknessis; and bryngith forth in
23 to liȝt the schadewe of deeth. Which multiplieth folkis, and leesith hem, and restorith hem destried in to the hool.
24 Which chaungith the herte of princes of the puple of erthe; and disseyueth hem, that thei go in veyn out of the weie.
25 Thei schulen grope, as in derknessis, and not in liȝt; and he schal make hem to erre as drunken men.

Cap. XIII.

1 Lo! myn iȝe siȝ alle thingis, and myn eere herde; and Y
2 vndurstood alle thingis. Euene with ȝoure kunnyng also Y
3 kan, and Y am not lowere than ȝe. But netheles Y schal speke to Almyȝti God, and Y coueite to dispute with God;
4 and firste Y schewe ȝou makeris of leesyng, and louyeris of
5 weyward techyngis. And Y wolde that ȝe weren stille, that
6 ȝe weren gessid to be wise men. Therfor here ȝe my chas-
7 tisyngis; and perseyue ȝe the doom of my lippis. Whether God hath nede to ȝoure leesyng, that ȝe speke gilis for hym?
8 Whether ȝe taken his face, and enforsen to deme for God?
9 Ethir it schal plese hym, fro whom no thing mai be hid? Whether he as a man schal be disseyued with ȝoure fals-
10 nessis? He schal repreue ȝou; for ȝe taken his face in

11 hiddlis. Anoon as he schal stire hym, he schal disturble
12 ȝou; and his drede schal falle on ȝou. Ȝoure mynde schal
be comparisound to aische; and ȝoure nollis schulen be
13 dryuun in to clei. Be ȝe stille a litil, that Y speke, what
14 euer thing the mynde hath schewid to me. Whi to-rende
Y my fleischis with my teeth, and bere my lijf in myn
15 hondis? Ȝhe, thouȝ God sleeth me, Y schal hope in hym;
16 netheles Y schal preue my weies in his siȝt. And he schal
be my sauyour; for whi ech ypocrite schal not come in his
17 siȝt. Here ȝe my word, and perseyue ȝe with ecris derke
18 and harde figuratif spechis. Yf Y schal be demed, Y woot
19 that Y schal be foundun iust. Who is he that is demed with
20 me? Come he; whi am Y stille, and am wastid? Do thou
not to me twei thingis oneli; and thanne Y schal not be hid
21 fro thi face. Make thin hond fer fro me; and thi drede
22 make not me aferd. Clepe thou me, and Y schal answere
thee; ethir certis Y schal speke, and thou schalt answere
23 me. Hou grete synnes and wickidnessis haue Y? Schewe
24 thou to me my felonyes, and trespassis. Whi hidist thou
25 thi face, and demest me thin enemy? Thou schewist thi
myȝt aȝens a leef, which is rauyschid with the wynd; and
26 thou pursuest drye stobil. For thou writist bitternessis aȝens
me; and wolt waste me with the synnes of my ȝong wex-
27 ynge age. Thou hast set my foot in a stok, and thou hast
kept alle my pathis; and thou hast biholde the steppis of
28 my feet. And Y schal be wastid as rot, and as a cloth,
which is etun of a mouȝte.

CAP. XIV.

1 A MAN *is* borun of a womman, and lyueth schort tyme,
2 and is fillid with many wretchidnessis. Which goith out,
and is defoulid as a flour; and fleeth as schadewe, and

JOB, XIV.

3 dwellith neuere perfitli in the same staat. And gessist thou it worthi to opene thin iȝen on siche a man; and to brynge 4 hym in to doom with thee? Who may make *a man* clene conseyued of vnclene seed? Whether not thou, which art 5 aloone? The daies of man ben schorte, the noumbre of his monethis is at thee; thou hast set, *ethir ordeyned*, hise termes, 6 whiche moun not be passid. Therfor go thou awey fro hym a litil, *that is, by withdrawyng of bodili lijf*, that he haue reste; til the *meede* coueitid come, and his dai is as the dai of an 7 hirid man. A tree hath hope, if it is kit doun; and eft it wexith 8 greene, and hise braunches spreden forth. If the roote therof is eeld in the erthe, and the stok therof is nyȝ deed in dust; 9 it schal buriowne at the odour of watir, and it schal make 10 heer, as whanne it was plauntid first. But whanne a man is deed, and maad nakid, and wastid; Y preye, where is he? 11 As if watris goen awei fro the see, and a ryuer maad voide 12 wexe drie, so a man, whanne he hath slept, *that is, deed*, he schal not rise aȝen, til heuene be brokun, *that is, be maad newe;* he schal not wake, nether he schal ryse togidere fro 13 his sleep. Who ȝiueth this to me, that thou defende me in helle, and that thou hide me, til thi greet veniaunce passe; and thou sette to me a tyme, in which thou haue mynde on 14 me? Gessist thou, whethir a deed man schal lyue aȝen? In alle the daies, in whiche Y holde knyȝthod, now Y abide, 15 til my chaungyng come. Thou schalt clepe me, and Y schal answere thee; thou schalt dresse the riȝt half, *that is, blis*, to 16 the werk of thin hondis. Sotheli thou hast noumbrid my 17 steppis; but spare thou my synnes. Thou hast seelid as in a bagge my trespassis, but thou hast curid my wickidnesse. 18 An hil fallynge droppith doun, and a rooche of stoon is 19 borun ouer fro his place. Watris maken stoonys holowe, and the erthe is wastid litil and litil bi waischyng awey of watir; and therfor thou schalt leese men in lijk maner.

20 Thou madist a man strong a litil, that he schulde passe with outen ende; thou schalt chaunge his face, and schalt sende
21 hym out. Whether hise sones ben noble, ether vnnoble,
22 he schal not vndurstonde. Netheles his fleisch, while he lyueth, schal haue sorewe, and his soule schal morne on hym silf.

Cap. XV.

1, 2 Forsothe Eliphat Themanytes answeride, and seide, Whether a wise man schal answere, as spekynge aȝens the wynd,
3 and schal fille his stomac with brennyng, *that is, ire?* For thou repreuest hym bi wordis, which is not lijk thee, and
4 thou spekist that, that spedith not to thee. As myche as is in thee, thou hast avoidid drede; and thou hast take awey
5 preyeris bifor God. For wickidnesse hath tauȝt thi mouth,
6 and thou suest the tunge of blasfemeris. Thi tunge, and not Y, schal condempne thee, and thi lippis schulen answere
7 thee. Whether thou art borun the firste man, and art formed
8 bifor alle little hillis? Whether thou herdist the counsel of
9 God, and his wisdom is lower than thou? What thing knowist thou, whiche we knowen not? What thing vndur-
10 stondist thou, whiche we witen not? Bothe wise men and
11 elde, myche eldre than thi fadris, ben among vs. Whether it is greet, that God coumforte thee? But thi schrewid
12 wordis forbeden this. What reisith thin herte thee, and thou
13 as thenkynge grete thingis hast iȝen astonyed? What bolneth thi spirit aȝens God, that thou brynge forth of thi mouth
14 siche wordis? What is a man, that he be with out wem,
15 and that he borun of a womman appere iust? Lo! noon among hise seyntis is vnchaungable, and heuenes ben not
16 cleene in his siȝt. How myche more a man abhomynable
17 and vnprofitable, that drynkith wickidnesse as water? I schal schewe to thee, here thou me; Y schal telle to thee that,

18 that Y siȝ. Wise men knoulechen, and hiden not her fadris.
19 To whiche aloone the erthe is ȝouun, and an alien schal not
20 passe bi hem. A wickid man is proud in alle hise daies;
and the noumbre of hise ȝeeris and of his tirauntrie is vncer-
21 teyn. The sown of drede is euere in hise eeris, and whanne
22 pees is, he supposith euere tresouns. He bileueth not that
he may turne aȝen fro derknessis to liȝt; and biholdith
23 aboute on ech side a swerd. Whanne he stirith hym to seke
breed, he woot, that the dai of derknessis is maad redi in
24 his hond. Tribulacioun schal make hym aferd, and angwisch schal cumpas hym, as a kyng which is maad redi to
25 batel. For he helde forth his hond aȝens God, and he was
26 maad strong aȝens Almyȝti God. He ran with neck reisid
27 aȝens God, and he was armed with fat nol. Fatnesse, *that is,
pride comyng forth of temporal aboundaunce,* hilide his face,
that is, the knowyng of vndurstondyng, and outward fatnesse
28 hangith doun of his sidis. He schal dwelle in desolat citees,
and in deseert, *ethir forsakun,* housis, that ben turned in to
29 biriels. He schal not be maad riche, nether his catel schal
dwelle stidefastli; nether he schal sende his roote in the
30 erthe, nether he schal go awei fro derknessis. Flawme schal
make drie hise braunchis, and he schal be takun a wey bi
31 the spirit of his mouth. Bileue he not veynli disseyued bi
32 errour, that he schal be aȝenbouȝt bi ony prijs. Bifor that
hise daies ben fillid, he schal perische, and hise hondis
33 schulen wexe drye; he schal be hirt as a vyne in the firste
flour of his grape, and as an olyue tre castinge awei his
34 flour. For the gaderyng togidere of an ipocrite is bareyn,
and fier schal deuoure the tabernaclis of hem, that taken
35 ȝiftis wilfuli. He conseyuede sorewe, and childide wickidnesse, and his wombe makith redi tretcheries.

Cap. XVI.

1, 2 Forsothe Joob answeride, and seide, Y herde ofte siche
3 thingis; alle ȝe ben heuy coumfortouris. Whether wordis
  ful of wynd schulen haue an ende? ether ony thing is
4 diseseful to thee, if thou spekist? Also Y myȝte speke
  thingis lijk to ȝou, and Y wolde, that ȝoure soule were for
5 my soule; and Y wolde coumfort ȝou by wordis, and Y
6 wolde moue myn heed on ȝou; Y wolde make ȝou stronge
  bi my mouth, and *Y wolde* moue lippis as sparynge ȝou.
7 But what schal Y do? If Y speke, my sorewe restith not;
8 and if Y am stille, it goith not awei fro me. But now my
  sorewe hath oppressid me, and alle my lymes ben dryuun
9 in to nouȝt. My ryuelyngis seien witnessyng aȝens me, and
  a fals spekere is reisid aȝens my face, and aȝenseith me.
10 He gaderide togidere his woodnesse in me, and he manaasside me, and gnastide aȝens me with his teeth; myn
11 enemye bihelde me with ferdful iȝen. Thei openyden her
  mouthis on me, and thei seiden schenschip, and smytiden
12 my cheke; and thei ben fillid with my peynes. God hath
  closid me togidere at the wickid, and hath ȝoue me to the
13 hondis of wickid men. Y thilke riche man and famouse
  sum tyme, am al to-brokun sudeynli; he helde my nol;
14 he hath broke me, and hath set me as in to a signe. He
  hath cumpasside me with hise speris, he woundide togidere
  my leendis; he sparide not, and schedde out myn entrails
15 in to the erthe. He beet me with wounde on wounde;
16 he as a giaunt felde in on me. Y sewide togidere a sak
17 on my skyn; and Y hilide my fleisch with aische. My
  face bolnyde of wepynge, and myn iȝeliddis wexiden derke.
18 Y suffride these thingis with out wickidnesse of myn hond,
19 *that is, werk,* whanne Y hadde cleene preieris to God. Erthe,

hile thou not my blood, and my cry fynde not in thee a
20 place of hidyng. For, lo! my witnesse is in heuene; and
21 the knowere of my conscience is in hiȝe places. A! my
22 frendis, ful of wordis, myn iȝe droppith to God. And Y
wolde, that a man were demed so with God, as the sone
23 of man is·demed with his felowe. For lo! schorte ȝeeris
passen, and Y go a path, bi which Y schal not turne aȝen.

Cap. XVII.

1 Mɪ spirit schal be maad feble; my daies schulen be maad
2 schort, and oneli the sepulcre is left to me. Y have not
3 synned, and myn iȝe dwellith in bittirnessis. Lord, delyuere
thou me, and sette thou me bisidis thee; and the hond of
4 ech fiȝte aȝens me. Thou hast maad the herte of hem fer
fro doctryn, *ethir knowyng of treuthe;* therfor thei schulen
5 not be enhaunsid. He bihetith prey to felowis, and the
6 iȝen of hise sones schulen faile. He hath set as in to a
prouerbe of the comyn puple, and his saumple bifor hem.
7 Myn iȝe dasewide at indignacioun; and my membris ben
8 dryuun as in to nouȝt. Iust men schulen wondre on this
thing; and an innocent schal be reisid aȝens an ypocrite.
9 And a iust man schal holde his weie, and he schal adde
10 strengthe to clene hondis. Therfor alle ȝe be conuertid,
and come ȝe; and Y schal not fynde in ȝou ony wiys man.
11 My daies ben passid; my thouȝtis ben scaterid, turment-
12 ynge myn herte. Tho han turned the nyȝt in to day; and
13 eft aftir derknessis hope liȝt. If Y susteyne, *ether suffre
paciently,* helle is myn hous; and Y haue arayede my bed
14 in derknessis. Y seide to rot, Thou art my fadur; and
15 to wormes, ȝe ben my modir and my sister. Therfor where
16 is now myn abidyng? and who biholdith my pacience? Alle
my thingis schulen go doun in to deppeste helle; gessist
thou, whether reste schal be to me, nameli there.

Cap. XVIII.

1, 2 Forsothe Baldach Suythes answeride, and seide, Til to what ende schalt thou booste with wordis? Vndurstonde 3 thou first, and so speke we. Whi ben we arettid as beestis, 4 and han we be foule bifor thee? What leesist thou thi soule in thi woodnes? Whether the erthe schal be forsakun for thee, and hard stoonys schulen be borun ouer fro her place? 5 Whethir the liȝt of a wickid man schal not be quenchid; 6 and the flawme of his fier schal not schyne? Liȝt schal wexe derke in his tabernacle; and the lanterne, which is 7 on hym, schal be quenchid. The steppis of his vertu schulen be maad streit; and his counsel schal caste hym 8 doun. For he hath sent hise feet in to a net; and he 9 goith in the meschis thereof. His foot schal be holdun 10 with a snare; and thirst schal brenne out aȝens hym. The foot trappe of hym is hid in the erthe, and his snare on 11 the path. Dredis schulen make hym aferd on ech side, 12 and schulen biwlappe hise feet. His strengthe be maad 13 feble bi hungur; and pouert asaile hise ribbis. Deuoure it the fairnesse of his skyn; the firste gendrid deth waste 14 hise armes. His trist be takun awei fro his tabernacle; 15 and perischyng, as a kyng, aboue trede on hym. The felowis of hym that is not, dwelle in his tabernacle; brymston 16 be spreynt in his tabernacle. The rootis of hym be maad drie bynethe; sotheli his ripe corn be al to-brokun aboue. 17 His mynde perische fro the erthe; and his name be not 18 maad solempne in stretis. He schal put hym out fro liȝt in to derknessis; and he schal bere hym ouer fro the 19 world. Nethir his seed nether kynrede schal be in his 20 puple, nether ony relifs in hise cuntreis. The laste men schulen wondre in hise daies; and hidousnesse schal asaile

21 the firste men. Therfor these ben the tabernaclis of a wickid man; and this is the place of hym, that knowith not God.

CAP. XIX.

1, 2 FORSOTHE Joob answeride, and seide, Hou long turmente 3 ȝe my soule, and al to-breken me with wordis? Lo! ten sithis ȝe schenden me, and ȝe ben not aschamed, oppres- 4 synge me. Forsothe and if Y koude not, myn vnkynnyng 5 schal be with me. And ȝe ben reisid aȝens me, and re- 6 preuen me with my schenschipis. Nameli now vndurstonde ȝe, that God hath turmentid me not bi euene doom, and 7 hath cumpassid me with hise betyngis. Lo! Y suffrynge violence schal crye, and no man schal here; Y schal crye 8 loude, and noon is that demeth. He bisette aboute my path, and Y may not go; and he settide derknessis in my 9 weie. He hath spuylid me of my glorye, and hath take 10 awey the coroun fro myn heed. He hath distried me on ech side, and Y perischide; and he hath take awei myn 11 hope, as fro a tree pullid vp bi the roote. His stronge veniaunce was wrooth aȝens me; and he hadde me so as 12 his enemye. Hise theues camen togidere, and maden to hem a wei bi me; and besegiden my tabernacle in cumpas. 13 He made fer my britheren fro me; and my knowun as 14 aliens ȝeden awei fro me. My neiȝboris forsoken me; and 15 thei that knewen me han forȝete me. The tenauntis of myn hows, and myn handmaydis hadden me as a straunger; and 16 Y was as a pilgrym bifor her iȝen. Y clepide my seruaunt, and he answeride not to me; with myn owne mouth Y 17 preiede hym. My wijf wlatide my breeth; and Y preiede 18 the sones of my wombe. Also foolis dispisiden me; and whanne Y was goon awei fro hem, thei bacbitiden me. 19 Thei, that weren my counselouris sum tyme, hadden ab-

homynacioun of me; and he, whom Y louede moost, was
20 aduersarie to me. Whanne fleischis weren wastid, my boon
cleuyde to my skyn; and oneli lippis ben left aboute my
21 teeth. Haue ȝe merci on me, haue ȝe merci on me, nameli,
ȝe my frendis; for the hond of the Lord hath touchid me.
22 Whi pursuen ȝe me, as God *pursueth;* and ben fillid with
23 my fleischis? Who ȝyueth to me, that my wordis be writun?
24 Who ȝyueth to me, that tho be writun in a book with an
yrun poyntil, ethir with a plate of leed; ethir with a chisel
25 be grauun in a flynt? For Y woot, that myn aȝenbiere
26 lyueth, and in the laste dai Y schal rise fro the erthe; and
eft Y schal be cumpassid with my skyn, and in my fleisch
27 Y schal se God, my sauyour. Whom Y my silf schal se,
and myn iȝen schulen biholde, and not an other man. This
28 myn hope is kept in my bosum. Whi therfor seien ȝe now,
Pursue we hym, and fynde we the roote of a word aȝens
29 hym? Therfor fle ȝe fro the face of the swerd; for the
swerd is the vengere of wickidnessis, and wite ȝe, that doom
schal be.

Cap. XX.

1, 2 Forsothe Sophar Naamathites answeride, and seide, Therfor my thouȝtis dyuerse comen oon aftir anothir; and the
3 mynde is rauyischid in to dyuerse thingis. Y schal here
the techyng, bi which thou repreuest me; and the spirit
4 of myn vndurstondyng schal answere me. Y woot this fro
5 the bigynnyng, sithen man was set on erthe, that the preisyng of wickid men is schort, and the ioie of an ypocrite
6 *is* at the licnesse of a poynt. Thouȝ his pride sticth in to
7 heuene, and his heed touchith the cloudis, he schal be lost
in the ende, as a dunghil; and, thei that sien hym, schulen
8 seie, Where is he? As a dreem fleynge awei he schal not
9 be foundun; he schal passe as a nyȝtis siȝt. The iȝe that

siȝ hym schal not se; and his place schal no more biholde
10 him. Hise sones schulen be al to-brokun with nedynesse;
11 and hise hondis schulen ȝelde to hym his sorewe. Hise
boonys schulen be fillid with the vices of his ȝong wexynge
12 age; and schulen slepe with hym in dust. For whanne yuel
13 was swete in his mouth, he hidde it vndur his tunge. He
schal spare it, and schal not forsake it; and schal hide in
14 his throte. His breed in his wombe schal be turned in to
15 galle of snakis withynne. He schal spue out the richessis,
whiche he deuouride; and God schal drawe tho ritchessis
16 out of his wombe. He schal souke the heed of snakis;
17 and the tunge of an addre schal sle hym. Se he not the
stremys of the flood of the stronde, of hony, and of botere.
18 He schal suffre peyne for alle thingis whiche he hath do,
netheles he schal not be wastid; aftir the multitude of his
19 fyndyngis, so and he schal suffre. For he brake, and made
nakid the hows of a pore man; he rauyschide, and bildide
20 it not. And his wombe was not fillid; and whanne he hath
21 that, that he couetide, he may not holde in possessioun. No
thing lefte of his mete; and therfor no thing schal dwelle
22 of his goodis. Whanne he is fillid, he schal be maad streit;
he schal be hoot, and alle sorewe schal falle in on hym.
23 Y wolde, that his wombe be fillid, that he sende out in to
hym the ire of his strong veniaunce, and reyne his batel
24 on hym. He schal fle yrun armuris, and he schal falle in
25 to a brasun boowe. Led out, and goynge out of his schethe,
and schynynge, *ether smytinge with leit*, in to his bittirnesse;
26 orrible *fendis* schulen go, and schulen come on hym. Alle
derknessis ben hid in hise priuytees; fier, which is not
teendid, schal deuoure hym; he schal be turmentid left in
27 his tabernacle. Heuenes schulen schewe his wickidnesse;
28 and erthe schal rise togidere aȝens hym. The seed of his
hows schal be opyn; it schal be drawun doun in the dai

20 of the strong veniaunce of the Lord. This is the part of a wickid man, *which part is ȝouun* of God, and the eritage of hise wordis of the Lord.

Cap. XXI.

1, 2 Forsothe Joob answeride, and seide, Y preye, here ȝe 3 my wordis, and do ȝe penaunce. Suffre ȝe me, that Y speke; and leiȝe ȝe aftir my wordis, if it schal seme worthi. 4 Whether my disputyng is aȝens man, that skilfuli Y owe 5 not to be sori? Perseyue ȝe me, and be ȝe astonyed; and 6 sette ȝe fyngur on ȝoure mouth. And whanne Y bithenke, 7 Y drede, and tremblyng schakith my fleisch. Whi therfor lyuen wickid men? Thei ben enhaunsid, and coumfortid 8 with richessis. Her seed dwellith bifor hem; the cumpeny of kynesmen, and of sones of sones *dwellith* in her siȝt. 9 Her housis ben sikur, and pesible; and the ȝerde of God 10 is not on hem. The cow of hem conseyuede, and caluede not a deed calf; the cow caluyde, and is not priued of hir 11 calf. Her litle children goen out as flockis; and her ȝonge 12 children maken fulli ioye with pleies. Thei holden tympan, 13 and harpe; and ioien at the soun of orgun. Thei leden in goodis her daies; and in a point thei goen doun to 14 hellis. Whiche men seiden to God, Go thou awei fro us; 15 we nylen the kunnyng of thi weies. Who is Almiȝti God, that we serue him? and what profitith it to vs, if 16 we preien him? Netheles for her goodis ben not in her hond, *that is, power*, the counsel of wickid men be fer 17 fro me. Hou ofte schal the lanterne of wickid men be quenchid, and flowing schal come on hem, and *God* schal 18 departe the sorewis of his stronge veniaunce? Thei schulen be as chaffis bifor the face of the wynd; and as a deed 19 sparcle, whiche the whirlewynd scaterith abroad. God schal kepe the sorewe of the fadir to hise sones; and whanne he

20 hath ʒoldun, thanne he schal wite. Hise iʒen schulen se
her sleyng; and he schal drynke of the stronge veniaunce
21 of Almyʒti God. For whi what perteyneth it to hym of
his hows aftir hym, thouʒ the noumbre of his monethis
22 be half takun awey? Whether ony man schal teche God
23 kunnyng, which demeth hem that ben hiʒe? This *yuel* man
dieth strong and hool, riche and blessful, *that is, myrie.*
24 Hise entrails ben ful of fatnesse; and hise boonys ben
25 moistid with merowis. Sotheli anothir *wickid* man dieth
in the bittirnesse of his soule, and with outen ony richessis.
26 And netheles thei schulen slepe togidere in dust, and wormes
27 schulen hile hem. Certis Y knowe ʒoure wickid thouʒtis,
28 and sentensis aʒens me. For ʒe seien, Where is the hows
of the prince? and where ben the tabernaclis of wickid
29 men? Axe ʒe ech of the weie-goeris; and ʒe schulen
30 knowe, that he vndurstondith these same thingis, that an
yuel man schal be kept in to the dai of perdicioun, and
31 schal be led to the dai of woodnesse. Who schal repreue
hise weies bifor hym? and who schal ʒelde to hym tho
32 thingis, whiche he hath doon? He schal be led to the
sepulcris; and he schal wake in the heep of deed men.
33 He was swete to the stoonys, *ether filthis,* of helle; and
drawith ech man aftir hym, and vnnoumbrable men bifor
34 him. Hou therfor coumforten ʒe me in veyn, sithen ʒoure
answeris ben schewid to repugne to treuthe?

Cap. XXII.

1 Forsothe Eliphat Themanytes answeride, and seide,
2 Whether a man, ʒhe, whanne he is of perfit kunnyng, mai
3 be comparisound to God? What profitith it to God, if
thou art iust? ethir what schalt thou ʒyue to hym, if thi
4 lijf is without wem? Whether he schal drede, and ˈschal

5 repreue thee, and schal come with thee in to doom, and not for thi ful myche malice, and thi wickidnessis with out
6 noumbre, *these peynes bifelden iustli to thee?* For thou hast take awei with out cause the wed of thi britheren; and
7 hast spuylid nakid men of clothis. Thou ȝauest not watir to the feynt man; and thou withdrowist breed fro the
8 hungri man. In the strengthe of thin arm thou haddist the lond in possessioun; and thou moost myȝti heldist it.
9 Thou leftist widewis voide; and al to-brakist the schuldris
10 of fadirles children. Therfor thou art cumpassid with snaris;
11 and sodeyn drede disturblith thee. And thou gessidist, that thou schuldist not se derknessis; and that thou schuldist not be oppressid with the fersnesse of watris flowyng.
12 Whether thou thenkist, that God is hiȝere than heuene,
13 and is enhaunsid aboue the coppe of sterris? And thou seist, What sotheli knowith God? and, He demeth as bi
14 derknesse. A cloude is his hidyng place, and he biholdith not oure thingis, and he goith aboute the herris of heuene.
15 Whether thou coueitist to kepe the path of worldis, which
16 wickid men han ofte go? Whiche weren takun awei bifor her tyme, and the flood distriede the foundement of hem.
17 Whiche seiden to God, Go thou awei fro vs; and as if
18 Almyȝti God may do no thing, thei gessiden hym, whanne he hadde fillid her housis with goodis; the sentence of
19 whiche men be fer fro me. Iust men schulen se, and schulen
20 be glad; and an innocent man schal scorne hem. Whether the reisyng of hem is not kit doun, and fier schal deuoure
21 the relifs of hem? Therfor assente thou to God, and haue thou pees; and bi these thingis thou schalt haue best fruytis.
22 Take thou the lawe of his mouth, and sette thou hise wordis
23 in thin herte. If thou turnest aȝen to Almyȝti God, thou schalt be bildid; and thou schalt make wickidnesse fer fro
24 thi tabernacle. He schal ȝyue a flynt for erthe, and goldun

25 strondis for a flynt. And Almyʒti God schal be aʒens thin
enemyes; and siluer schal be gaderid togidere to thee.
26 Thanne on Almyʒti God thou schalt flowe with delicis;
27 and thou schalt reise thi face to God. Thou schalt preye
hym, and he schal here thee; and thou schalt ʒelde thi
28 vowis. Thou schalt deme a thing, and it schal come to
29 thee; and lyʒt schal schyne in thi weies. For he that is
mekid, schal be in glorie; and he that bowith doun hise
30 iʒen, schal be saued. An innocent schal be saued; sotheli
he schal be saued in the clennesse of hise hondis.

CAP. XXIII.

1, 2 SOTHELI Joob answeride, and seide, Now also my word
is in bitternesse, and the hond of my wounde is agreggid
3 on my weilyng. Who ʒyueth to me, that Y knowe, and
4 fynde hym, and come til to his trone? Y schal sette doom
bifor hym, and Y schal fille my mouth with blamyngis;
5 that Y kunne the wordis, which he schal answere to me,
6 and that Y vnderstonde, what he schal speke to me. Y nyle,
that he stryue with me bi greet strengthe, nether oppresse
7 me with the heuynesse of his greetnesse. Sette he forth
equite aʒens me, and my doom come perfitli to victorie.
8 If Y go to the eest, God apperith not; if *Y go* to the west,
9 Y schal not vndurstonde hym; if *Y go* to the left side, what
schal Y do? Y schal not take hym; if Y turne me to the
10 riʒt side, Y schal not se hym. But he knowith my weie,
and he schal preue me as gold, that passith thorouʒ fier.
11 My foot suede hise steppis; Y kepte his weie, and Y bowide
12 not awey fro it. Y ʒede not awei fro the comaundementis
of hise lippis; and Y hidde in my bosum the wordis of his
13 mouth. For he is aloone, and no man may turne awei hise
thouʒtis; and what euer thing he wolde, his wille dide this

14 thing. Whanne he hath fillid his wille in me, also many
15 othere lijk thingis ben redi to hym. And therfor Y am disturblid of his face, and Y biholdynge hym am anguyschid
16 for drede. God hath maad neische myn herte, and Almy3ti
17 God hath disturblid me. For Y perischide not for derknessis nei3ynge; nethir myist hilide my face.

Cap. XXIV.

1 Tymes ben not hid fro Almy3ti God; sotheli thei that knowen
2 hym, knowen not hise daies. Othere men turneden ouer the termes *of nei3boris eritage*, thei token awei flockis, and
3 fedden tho. Thei driueden awei the asse of fadirlesse chil-
4 dren, and token awei the cow of a widewe for a wed. Thei distrieden the weie of pore men, and thei oppressiden to-
5 gidere the mylde men of erthe. Othere men as wielde assis in deseert goon out to her werk; and thei waken to prey,
6 and bifor maken redy breed to her children. Thei kitten doun a feeld not hern, and thei gaderen grapis of his
7 vyner, whom thei han oppressid bi violence. Thei leeuen men nakid, and taken awei the clothis, to whiche *men* is
8 noon hiling in coold; whiche *men* the reynes of munteyns weeten, and thei han noon hilyng, and biclippen stoonys.
9 Thei diden violence, and robbiden fadirles and modirles children; and thei spuyliden, *ether robbiden*, the comynte of
10 pore men. Thei token awey eeris of corn fro nakid men,
11 and goynge with out cloth, and fro hungry men. Thei weren hid in myddai among the heepis of tho men, that
12 thirsten, whanne the presses ben trodun. Thei maden men of citees to weile, and the soulis of woundid men schulen crye; and God suffrith it not to go awei vnpunyschid.
13 Thei weren rebel to li3t; thei knewen not the weyes therof,
14 nether thei turneden a3en bi the pathis therof. A mansleere

risith ful eerli, and sleeth a nedi man, and a pore man; 15 sotheli bi nyȝt he schal be as a nyȝt theef. The iȝe of avouter kepith derknesse, and seith, An yȝe schal not se 16 me; and he schal hile his face. Thei mynen housis in derknessis, as thei seiden togidere to hem silf in the dai; 17 and thei knewen not liȝt. If the morewtid apperith sudeynli, thei demen the schadewe of deth; and so thei goon in derk- 18 nessis as in liȝt. He is vnstablere than the face of the water; his part in erthe be cursid, and go he not bi the 19 weie of vyneris. Passe he to ful greet heete fro the watris 20 of snowis, and the synne of hym til to hellis. Merci forȝete hym; his swetnesse be a worm; be he not in mynde, but 21 be he al to-brokun as a tre vnfruytful. For he fedde the bareyn, and hir that childith not, and he dide not wel to 22 the widewe. He drow doun stronge men in his strengthe; and whanne he stondith *in greet state*, he schal not bileue 23 to his lijf. God ȝaf to hym place of penaunce, and he mysusith that in to pride; for the iȝen of God ben in the 24 weies of that man. Thei ben reisid at a litil, and thei schulen not stonde; and thei schulen be maad low as alle thingis, and thei schulen be takun awei; and as the hyȝ- 25 nessis of eeris of corn thei schulen be al to-brokun. That if it is not so, who may repreue me, that Y liede, and putte my wordis bifor God?

Cap. XXV.

1, 2 Forsothe Baldach Suytes answeride, and seide, Power and drede is anentis hym, *that is, God*, that makith acordyng in 3 hise hiȝe thingis. Whether noumbre is of hise knyȝtis? and 4 on whom schyneth not his liȝt? Whether a man comparisound to God mai be iustified, ether borun of a womman 5 mai appere cleene? Lo! also the moone schyneth not, and

6 sterris ben not cleene in his si3t; hou miche more a man rot, and the sone of a man a worm, *is vncleene and vile, if he is comparisound to God.*

Cap. XXVI.

1, 2 Forsothe Joob answeride, and seide, Whos helpere art thou? whether of the feble, and susteyneste the arm of hym, 3 which is not strong? To whom hast thou 3oue counsel? In hap to hym that hath not wisdom; and thou hast schewid 4 ful myche prudence. Ether whom woldist thou teche? 5 whether not hym, that made brething? Lo! giauntis weilen 6 vnder watris, and thei that dwellen with hem. Helle is 7 nakid bifor hym, and noon hilyng is to perdicioun. Which God stretchith forth the north on voide thing, and hangith 8 the erthe on nou3t. Which God byndith watris in her 9 cloudis, that tho breke not out togidere dounward. Whych God holdith the cheer of his secte, and spredith abrood 10 theron his cloude. He hath cumpassid a terme to watris, 11 til that li3t and derknessis be endid. The pilers of heuene 12 tremblen, and dreden at his wille. In the strengthe of hym the sees weren gaderid togidere sudeynly, and his prudence 13 smoot the proude. His spiryt ournede heuenes, and the crokid serpent was led out bi his hond, ledynge out 14 as a mydwijf ledith out a child. Lo! these thingis ben seid in partie of hise weyes; and whanne we han herd vnnethis a litil drope of his word, who may se the thundur of his greetnesse?

Cap. XXVII.

1, 2 Also Joob addide, takynge his parable, and seide, God lyueth, that hath take awey my doom, and Almy3ti God,

3 that hath brouȝt my soule to bitternesse. For as long as
4 breeth is in me, and the spirit of God is in my nose-thirlis,
my lippis schulen not speke wickidnesse, nether my tunge
5 schal thenke a leesyng. Fer be it fro me, that Y deme ȝou
iust; til Y faile, Y schal not go awei fro myn innocence.
6 Y schal not forsake my iustifiyng, which Y bigan to holde;
7 for myn herte repreueth me not in al my lijf. As my wickid
8 enemy *doth;* myn aduersarie is as wickid. For what is the
hope of an ypocrite, if he rauyschith gredili, and God de-
9 lyuerith not his soule? Whether God schal here the cry of
10 hym, whanne angwisch schal come on hym? ether whether
he may delite in Almyȝti God, and inwardli clepe God in
11 al tyme? Y schal teche ȝou bi the hond of God, what
12 thingis Almyȝti God hath; and Y schal not hide. Lo! alle
ȝe knowen, and what spoken ȝe veyn thingis with out cause?
13 This is the part of a wickid man anentis God, and the
eritage of violent men, *ether rauenours,* whiche thei schulen
14 take of Almyȝti God. If hise children ben multiplied, thei
schulen be *slayn* in swerd; and hise sones sones schulen
15 not be fillid with breed. Thei, that ben residue of hym,
schulen be biried in perischyng; and the widewis of hym
16 schulen not wepe. If he gaderith togidere siluer as erthe,
17 and makith redi clothis as cley; sotheli he made redi, but
a iust man schal be clothid in tho, and an innocent man
18 schal departe the siluer. As a mouȝte he hath bildid his
19 hous, and as a kepere he made a schadewyng place. A
riche man, whanne he schal die, schal bere no thing with
hym; he schal opene hise iȝen, and he schal fynde no thing.
20 Pouert as water schal take hym; and tempeste schal op-
21 presse hym in the nyȝt. Brennynge wynd schal take hym,
and schal do awei; and as a whirlewynd it schal rauysche
22 *hym* fro his place. He schal sende out *turmentis* on hym,
23 and schal not spare; he fleynge schal fle fro his hond. He

schal streyne hise hondis on him, and he schal hisse on hym, and schal biholde his place.

Cap. XXVIII.

1 Silver hath bigynnyngis of his veynes; and a place is to
2 gold, in which it is wellid togidere. Irun is takun fro erthe, and a stoon resolued, *ethir meltid*, bi heete, is turned in to
3 money. God hath set tyme to derknessis, and he biholdith
4 the ende of alle thingis. Also a stronde departith a stoon of derknesse, and the schadewe of deth, fro the puple goynge in pilgrymage; *it departith* tho *hillis*, whiche the foot of a
5 nedi man forȝat, and *hillis* with out weie. The erthe, wher-
6 of breed cam forth in his place, is destried bi fier. The place of saphir ben stoonys therof, and the clottis therof ben
7 gold. A brid knewe not the weie, and the iȝe of a vultur,
8 *ethir raucnouse brid*, bihelde it not. The sones of marchauntis
9 tretiden not on it, and a lyonesse passide not therbi. God stretchide forth his hond to a flynt; he distriede hillis fro
10 the rootis. He hewide doun ryuers in stoonys; and his iȝe
11 siȝ al precious thing. And he souȝte out the depthis of
12 floodis; and he brouȝte forth hid thingis in to liȝt. But where is wisdom foundun, and which is the place of vndur-
13 stondyng? A man noot the prijs therof, nether it is foundun
14 in the lond of men lyuynge swetli, *ether delicatli*. The depthe of watris seith, It is not in me; and the see spekith, It is not
15 with me. Gold ful cleene schal not be ȝouun for wisdom,
16 nether siluer schal be weied in the chaungyng therof. It schal not be comparysound to the died colours of Iynde, not to the moost preciouse stoon of sardius, nether to saphir.
17 Nether gold, nether glas schal be maad euene worth therto;
18 and hiȝe and fer-apperynge vessels of gold schulen not be chaungid for wisdom, nether schulen be had in mynde in

comparisoun therof. Forsothe wisdom is drawun of pryuy
19 thingis; topasie of Ethiope schal not be maad euene worth
to wisdom, and moost preciouse diyngis schulen not be set
20 togidere in prijs, *ether comparisound*, therto. Therfor wherof
cometh wisdom, and which is the place of vndurstondyng?
21 It is hid fro the iȝen of alle lyuynge men; also it is hid fro
22 briddis of heuene. Perdicioun and deeth seiden, With oure
23 ecris we herden the fame therof. God vndurstondith the
24 weye therof, and he knowith the place therof. For he biholdith the endis of the world, and biholdith alle thingis that ben
25 vndur heuene. Which God made weiȝte to wyndis, and
26 weiede watris in mesure. Whanne he settide lawe to reyn,
27 and weie to tempestis sownynge; thanne he siȝ wisdom, and
28 telde out, and made redi, and souȝte out. And he seide to
man, Lo! the drede of the Lord, thilke is wisdom; and to
go awei fro yuel, *is* vndurstondyng.

Cap. XXIX.

1, 2 Also Joob addide, takynge his parable, and seide, Who
ȝyueth to me, that I be bisidis the elde monethis, bi the daies
3 in whiche God kepte me? Whanne his lanterne schynede
4 on myn heed, and Y ȝede in derknessis at his liȝt. As Y
was in the daies of my ȝongthe, whanne in priuete God was
5 in my tabernacle. Whanne Almyȝti God was with me, and
6 my children *weren* in my cumpas; whanne Y waischide my
feet in botere, and the stoon schedde out to me the stremes
7 of oile; whanne Y ȝede forth to the ȝate of the citee, and in
8 the street thei maden redi a chaier to me. Ȝonge men, *that
is, wantoun*, sien me, and weren hid, and elde men risynge
9 vp stoden; princes cessiden to speke, and puttiden the
10 fyngur on her mouth; duykis refreyneden her vois, and her
11 tunge cleuyde to her throte. An eere herynge blesside me,

12 and an iȝe seynge ȝeldide witnessyng to me ; for Y hadde delyueride a pore man criynge, and a fadirles child, that
13 hadde noon helpere. The blessyng of a man to perische
14 cam on me, and Y coumfortide the herte of a widewe. Y was clothid with riȝtfulnesse ; and Y clothide me as with a
15 cloth, and with my doom a diademe. Y was iȝe to a blynde
16 man, and foot to a crokyd man. Y was a fadir of pore men ; and Y enqueride most diligentli the cause, which Y
17 knew not. Y al tobrak the grete teeth of the wickid man,
18 and Y took awei prey fro hise teeth. And Y seide, Y schal die in my nest ; and as a palm tre Y schal multiplie daies.
19 My roote is openyde bisidis watris, and deew schal dwelle in
20 my repyng. My glorie schal euere be renulid, and my
21 bouwe schal be astorid in myn hond. Thei, that herden me, abiden my sentence ; and thei weren ententif, and weren
22 stille to my counsel. Thei dursten no thing adde to my
23 wordis ; and my speche droppide on hem. Thei abididen me as reyn ; and thei openyden her mouth as to the softe
24 reyn comynge late. If ony tyme Y leiȝide to hem, thei bileueden not ; and the liȝt of my cheer felde not doun in to
25 erthe. If Y wolde go to hem, Y sat the firste ; and whanne Y sat as kyng, while the oost stood aboute, netheles Y was comfortour of hem that morenyden.

Cap. XXX.

1 But now ȝongere men in tyme scornen me, whos fadris
2 Y deynede not to sette with the doggis of my flok. Of whiche men the vertu of hondis was for nouȝt to me, and
3 thei weren gessid vnworthi to that lijf. Thei *weren* bareyn for nedynesse and hungur ; that gnawiden in wildirnesse,
4 and *weren* pale for pouert and wretchidnesse ; and eeten eerbis, and the ryndis of trees ; and the roote of iunyperis

5 was her mete. Whiche men rauyschiden these thingis fro
grete valeis; and whanne thei hadden foundun ony of alle,
6 thei runnen with cry to tho. Thei dwelliden in deseertis of
strondis, and in caues of erthe, ethir on grauel, *ethir on cley*.
7 Whiche weren glad among siche thingis, and arettiden de-
8 lices to be vndur buschis. The sones of foolis and of vn-
9 noble men, and outirli apperynge not in erthe. But now
Y am turned in to the song of hem, and Y am maad a
10 prouerbe to hem. Thei holden me abhomynable, and fleen
11 fer fro me, and dreden not to spete on my face. For God
hath openyd his arowe-caas, and hath turmentid me, and
12 hath set a bridil in to my mouth. At the riȝtside of the eest
my wretchidnessis risiden anoon; thei turneden vpsedoun
my feet, and oppressiden with her pathis as with floodis.
13 Thei destrieden my weies; thei settiden tresoun to me, and
14 hadden the maistri; and noon was that helpide. Thei felden
in on me as bi a brokun wal, and bi ȝate openyd, and weren
15 stretchid forth to my wretchidnessis. Y am dryuun in to
nouȝt; he took awei my desir as wynd, and myn helpe
16 passide awei as a cloude. But now my soule fadith in my
17 silf, and daies of turment holden me stidfastly. In nyȝt my
boon is persid with sorewis; and thei, that eten me, slepen
18 not. In the multitude of tho my cloth is wastid, and thei
19 han gird me as with coler of a coote. Y am comparisound
to cley, and Y am maad lijk to a deed sparcle and aisch.
20 Y schal cry to thee, and thou schalt not here me; Y stonde,
21 and thou biholdist not me. Thou art chaungid in to cruel
to me, and in the hardnesse of thin hond thou art aduersarie
22 to me. Thou hast reisid me, and hast set as on wynd; and
23 hast hurtlid me doun strongli. Y woot, that thow schalt
bitake me to deeth, where an hows is ordeyned to ech
24 lyuynge man. Netheles thou sendist not out thin hond to
the wastyng of hem; and if thei fallen doun, thou schalt

25 saue. Y wepte sum tyme on him, that was turmentid, and
26 my soule hadde compassioun on a pore man. Y abood
goodis, and yuelis ben comun to me; Y abood li3t, and
27 derknessis braken out. Myn ynnere thingis buyliden out
with outen my reste; daies of turment camen bifor me.
28 Y 3ede morenynge, and Y roos with out woodnesse in the
29 cumpenye, and criede. Y was the brother of dragouns, and
30 the felow of ostrigis. My skyn was maad blak on me, and
31 my boonys drieden for heete. Myn harpe is turned in to
morenyng, and myn orgun in to the vois of weperis.

Cap. XXXI.

1 I MADE couenaunt with myn i3en, that Y schulde not
2 thenke of a virgyn. For what part schulde God aboue haue
3 in me, and eritage Almy3ti God of hi3e thingis? Whether
perdicioun is not to a wickid man, and alienacioun *of God*
4 is to men worchynge wickidnesse? Whether he biholdith
5 not my weies, and noumbrith alle my goyngis? If Y 3ede
6 in vanyte, and my foot hastide in gile, God weie me in
7 a iust balaunce, and knowe my symplenesse. If my step
bowide fro the weie; if myn i3e suede myn herte, and a
8 spotte cleuede to myn hondis; sowe Y, and another ete,
9 and my generacioun be drawun out bi the root. If myn
herte was disseyued on a womman,. and if Y settide aspies
10 at the dore of my frend; my wijf be the hoore of anothir
11 man, and othir men be bowid doun on hir. For this is
12 vnleueful, and the moost wickidnesse. Fier is deourynge
til to wastyng, and drawynge vp bi the roote alle genera-
13 ciouns. If Y dispiside to take doom with my seruaunt and
14 myn hand mayde, whanne thei stryueden a3ens me. What
sotheli schal Y do, whanne God schal rise to deme? and
whanne he schal axe, what schal Y answere to hym?

15 Whether he, that wrou3te also hym, made not me in the
16 wombe, and o *God* formede me in the wombe? If Y denyede
to pore men that, that thei wolden, and if Y made the i3en
17 of a wydewe to abide: if Y aloone eet my mussel, and a
18 faderles child eet not therof; for merciful doyng encreesside
with me fro my 3ong childhed, and 3ede out of my modris
19 wombe with me; if Y dispiside a man passynge forth, for
20 he hadde not a cloth, and a pore man with out hilyng;
if hise sidis blessiden not me, and was not maad hoot
21 of the fleeces of my scheep; if Y reiside myn hond on
a fadirles child, 3he, whanne Y si3 me the hi3ere in 'the
22 3ate; my schuldre falle fro his ioynt, and myn arm with hise
23 boonys be al to-brokun. For euere Y dredde God, as
wawis wexynge gret on me; and Y my3te not bere his
24 birthun. If Y gesside gold my strengthe, and if Y seide
25 to purid gold, *Thou art* my trist; if Y was glad on my
many ritchessis, and for myn hond foond ful many thingis;
26 if Y si3 the sunne, whanne it schynede, and the moone
27 goynge clereli; and if myn herte was glad in priuyte, and
28 if Y kisside myn hond with my mouth; which is the moost
29 wickidnesse, and deniyng a3ens hi3este God; if Y hadde
ioye at the fallyng of hym, that hatide me, and if Y ioide
30 fulli, that yuel hadde founde hym; for Y 3af not my throte
to do synne, that Y schulde asaile and curse his soule;
31 if the men of my tabernacle seiden not, Who 3yueth, that
32 we be fillid of hise fleischis? a pilgryme dwellide not with
33 outforth; my dore was opyn to a weiegoere; if Y as man
hidde my synne, and helide my wickidnesse in my bosum;
34 if Y dredde at ful greet multitude, and if dispisyng of ney3-
boris made me aferd; and not more Y was stille, and 3ede
35 not out of the dore; who 3yueth an helpere to me, that
Almy3ti God here my desire? that he that demeth, write
36 a book, that Y bere it in my schuldre, and cumpasse it as

37 a coroun to me? Bi alle my degrees Y schal pronounce it,
38 and Y schal as offre it to the prynce. If my lond crieth
39 aȝens me, and hise forewis wepen with it; if Y eet fruytis
therof with out money, and Y turmentide the soule of erthe-
40 tileris of it; a brere growe to me for wheete, and a thorn
for barli.

Cap. XXXII.

1 FORSOTHE these thre men leften of to answere Joob, for
2 he semyde a iust man to hem. And Helyu, the sone of
Barachel Buzites, of the kynrede of Ram, was wrooth, and
hadde indignacioun; forsothe he was wrooth aȝens Joob,
3 for he seide hym silf to be iust bifor God. Sotheli Helyu
hadde indignacioun aȝens the thre frendis of hym, for thei
hadden not founde resonable answere, but oneli hadde con-
4 dempned Joob. Therfor Helyu abood Joob spekynge, for
5 thei, that spaken, weren eldere men. But whanne he hadde
seyn, that thre *men* myȝten not answere, he was wrooth
6 greetly. And Helyu, the sone of Barachel Buzites, answeride, and seyde, Y am ȝongere in tyme, sotheli ȝe ben
eldere; therfor with heed holdun doun Y dredde to schewe
7 to ȝou my sentence. For Y hopide that lengere age schulde
speke, and that the multitude of ȝeeris schulden teche
8 wisdom. But as Y se, spirit is in men, and the enspiryng,
ether reuelacioun, of Almyȝti God ȝyueth vndurstondyng.
9 Men of long lijf ben not wise, and elde men vndurstonden
10 not doom. Therfor Y schal seie, Here ȝe me, and Y also
11 schal schewe my kunnyng to ȝou. For Y abood ȝoure
wordis, Y herde ȝoure prudence, as long as ȝe dispuytiden
12 in ȝoure wordis. And as long as Y gesside ȝou to seie ony
thing, Y bihelde; but as Y se, noon is of ȝou, that may
13 repreue Joob, and answere to hise wordis; lest perauenture
ȝe seien, We han founde wisdom; God, and not man, hath

14 cast hym awei. Joob spak no thing to me, and Y not bi
15 ʒoure wordis schal answere hym. Thei dredden, and answeriden no more, and token awei speche from hem silf.
16 Therfor for Y abood, and thei spaken not, thei stoden, and
17 answeriden no more; also Y schal answere my part, and
18 Y schal schewe my kunnyng. For Y am ful of wordis, and the spirit of my wombe, *that is, mynde*, constreyneth
19 me. Lo! my wombe is as must with out spigot, *ether a*
20 *ventyng*, that brekith newe vessels. Y schal speke, and brethe aʒen a litil; Y schal opene my lippis, and Y schal
21 answere. Y schal not take the persoone of man, and Y
22 schal not make God euene to man. For Y woot not hou long Y schal abide, and if my Makere take me awei after a litil tyme.

Cap. XXXIII.

1 Therfor, Joob, here thou my spechis, and herkene alle
2 my wordis. Lo! Y haue openyd my mouth, my tunge
3 schal speke in my chekis. Of symple herte *ben* my wordis,
4 and my lippis schulen speke clene sentence. The spirit of God made me, and the brething of Almyʒti God quykenyde
5 me. If thou maist, answere thou to me, and stoonde thou
6 aʒens my face. Lo! God made me as and thee; and also
7 Y am formyd of the same cley. Netheles my myracle make thee not afeerd, and myn eloquence be not greuouse to thee.
8 Therfor thou seidist in myn ceris, and Y herde the vois of
9 thi wordis; Y am cleene, and with out gilt, and vnwemmed,
10 and wickidnesse is not in me. For God foond querels in
11 me, therfor he demyde me enemy to hym silf. He hath
12 set my feet in a stok; he kepte alle my pathis. Therfor this thing it is, in which thou art not maad iust; Y schal
13 answere to thee, that God is more than man. Thou stryuest

aȝenus God, that not at alle wordis he answeride to thee.
14 God spekith onys, and the secounde tyme he rehersith not
15 the same thing. *God spekith* bi a dreem in the visioun of
nyȝt, whanne sleep fallith on men, and thei slepen in the
16 bed. Thanne he openith the eeris of men, and he techith
17 hem, and techith prudence; that he turne awei a man fro
these thingis whiche he made, and delyuere hym fro pride;
18 delyerynge his soule fro corrupcioun, and his lijf, that it
19 go not in to swerd. Also *God* blameth *a synnere* bi sorewe
in the bed, and makith alle the boonys of hym to fade.
20 Breed is maad abhomynable to hym in his lijf, and mete
21 desirable bifor to his soule. His fleisch schal faile for rot,
and hise boonys, that weren hilid, schulen be maad nakid.
22 His soule schal neiȝe to corrupcioun, and his lijf to thingis
23 bryngynge deeth. If an aungel, oon of a thousynde, is
24 spekynge for hym, that he telle the equyte of man, *God*
schal haue mercy on hym, and schal seie, Delyuere thou
hym, that he go not doun in corrupcioun; Y haue founde
25 in what thing Y schal do merci to hym. His fleisch is
wastid of turmentis; turne he aȝen to the daies of his ȝonge
26 wexynge age. He schal biseche God, and he schal be
quemeful to hym; and he schal se his face in hertly ioye,
27 and he schal ȝelde to man his riȝtfulnesse. He schal biholde
men, and he schal seie, Y haue synned, and verili Y haue
trespassid; and Y haue not resseyued, as Y was worthi.
28 For he delyueride his soule, that it schulde not go in to
29 perischyng, but that he lyuynge schulde se liȝt. Lo! God
30 worchith alle these thingis in thre tymes bi alle men; that
he aȝen clepe her soulis fro corrupcioun, and liȝtne in the
31 liȝt of lyuynge men. Thou, Joob, perseyue, and here me,
32 and be thou stille, the while Y speke. Sotheli if thou hast
what thou schalt speke, answere thou to me, speke thou;
33 for Y wole, that thou appere iust. That if thou hast not,

Cap. XXXIV.

1, 2 And Helyu pronounside, and spak also these thingis, Wise men, here ȝe my wordis, and lerned men, herkne ȝe me; 3 for the eere preueth wordis, and the throte demeth metis 4 bi taast. Chese we doom to vs; and se we among vs, 5 what is the betere. For Job seide, Y am iust, and God 6 hath distried my doom. For whi lesynge is in demynge 7 me, and myn arowe is violent with out ony synne. Who 8 is a man, as Joob is, that drynkith scornyng as watir? that goith with men worchynge wickidnesse, and goith with vn-9 feithful men? For he seide, A man schal not plese God, 10 ȝhe, thouȝ he renneth with God. Therfor ȝe men hertid, *that is, vndurstonde,* here ȝe me; vnpite, *ethir cruelle,* be fer fro 11 God, and wickidnesse fro Almyȝti God. For he schal ȝelde the werk of man to hym; and bi the weies of ech man he 12 schal restore to hym. For verili God schal not condempne with out cause; nether Almyȝti God schal distrie doom. 13 What othere man hath he ordeyned on the lond? ether 14 whom hath he set on the world, which he made? If God dressith his herte to hym, he schal drawe to hym silf his 15 spirit and blast. Ech fleisch schal faile togidere; and a man 16 schal turne aȝen in to aisch. Therfor if thou hast vndur- stondyng, here thou that that is seid, and herkne the vois 17 of my speche. Whether he that loueth not doom may be maad hool? and hou condempnest thou so myche him, that 18 is iust? Which seith to the kyng, *Thou art* apostata; which 19 clepith the duykis vnpitouse, *ethir vnfeithful.* Which takith not the persoones of princes, nether knew a tyraunt, whanne he stryuede aȝens a pore man; for alle men ben the werk 20 of hise hondis. Thei schulen die sudeynli, and at mydnyȝt

puplis schulen be troblid, *ethir schulen be bowid, as othere bookis han;* and schulen passe, and schulen take awei a
21 violent man with out hond. For the iȝen of God *ben* on
22 the weies of men, and biholdith alle goyngis of hem. No derknessis ben, and no schadewe of deeth is, that thei, that
23 worchen wickidnesse, be hid there; for it is no more in
24 the power of man, that he come to God in to doom. God schal al to-breke many men and vnnoumbrable; and schal
25 make othere men to stonde for hem. For he knowith the werkis of hem; therfor he schal brynge yn niȝt, and thei
26 schulen be al to-brokun. He smoot hem, as vnpitouse
27 men, in the place of seinge men. Whiche ȝeden awei fro hym bi castyng afore, and nolden vndurstonde alle hise
28 weies. That thei schulden make the cry of a nedi man to come to hym, and that he schulde here the vois of pore
29 men. For whanne he grauntith pees, who is that condempneth? Sithen he hidith his cheer, who is that seeth hym? And on folkis and on alle men *he hath power to do*
30 *siche thingis*. Which makith a man ypocrite to regne, for
31 the synnes of the puple. Therfor for Y haue spoke to
32 God, also Y schal not forbede thee. If Y erride, teche thou me; if Y spak wickidnesse, Y schal no more adde.
33 Whether God axith that *wickidnesse* of thee, for it displeside thee? For thou hast bigunne to speke, and not Y; that
34 if thou knowist ony thing betere, speke thou. Men vndur-
35 stondynge, speke to me; and a wise man, here me. Forsothe Joob spak folili, and hise wordis sownen not techyng.
36 My fadir, be Joob preuede til to the ende; ceesse thou not
37 fro the man of wickidnesse, that addith blasfemye ouer hise synnes. Be he constreyned among vs in the meene tyme; and thanne bi hise wordis stire he God to the doom.

Cap. XXXV.

1, 2 Therfor Helyu spak eft these thingis, Whethir thi thou3t semeth euene, *ether ri3tful*, to thee, that thou schuldist scie, 3 Y am ri3tfulere than God? For thou seidist, That, that is good, plesith not thee; ethir what profitith it to thee, if Y do 4 synne? Therfor Y schal answere to thi wordis, and to thi 5 frendis with thee. Se thou, and biholde heuene, and biholde 6 thou the eir, that God is hi3ere than thou. If thou synnest *a3ens hym*, what schalt thou anoye hym? and if thi wickid- 7 nessis ben multiplied, what schalt thou do a3ens hym? Certis if thou doist iustli, what schalt thou 3yue to hym; ether 8 what schal he take of thin hond? Thi wickidnesse schal anoie a man, which is lijk thee; and thi ri3tfulnesse schal 9 helpe the sone of a man. Thei schulen cry for the mul- titude of fals chalengeris, and thei schulen weile for the 10 violence of the arm of tirauntis. And Joob seide not, Where is God, that made me, and that 3af songis in the 11 ny3t? Which God techith vs aboue the beestis of erthe, 12 and he schal teche vs aboue the briddis of heuene. There thei schulen crye, and God schal not here, for the pride 13 of yuele men. For God schal not here with out cause, 14 and Almy3ti God schal biholde the causis of ech man. 3he, whanne thou seist, He biholdith not; be thou demed bifor 15 hym, and abide thou hym. For now he bryngith not in 16 his strong veniaunce, nether vengith greetli felonye. Therfor Joob openith his mouth in veyn, and multiplieth wordis with out kunnyng.

Cap. XXXVI.

1, 2 Also Helyu addide, and spak these thingis, Suffre thou me a litil, and Y schal schewe to thee; for 3it Y haue that,

3 that Y schal speke for God. Y schal reherse my kunnyng fro the bigynnyng; and Y schal preue my worchere iust. 4 For verili my wordis ben with out leesyng, and perfit kunnyng schal be preued to thee. 5 God castith not awei my3ti 6 men, sithen he is my3ti; but he saueth not wickid men, 7 and he 3yueth dom to pore men. He takith not awei hise i3en fro a iust man; and he settith kyngis in secte with out ende, and thei ben reisid there. 8 And if thei ben in chaynes, and ben boundun with the roopis of pouert, he 9 schal shewe to hem her werkis, and her grete trespassis; 10 for thei weren violent, *ethir rauenours*. Also he schal opene her eere, that he chastise; and he schal speke, that thei 11 turne a3en fro wickidnesse. If thei heren, and kepen, thei 12 schulen fille her daies in good, and her 3eris in glorie. Sotheli if thei heren not, thei schulen passe bi swerd, and thei 13 schulen be wastid in foli. Feyneris and false men stiren the ire of God; and thei schulen not crye, whanne thei 14 ben boundun. The soule of hem schal die in tempest; and the lijf of hem among men of wymmens condiciouns. 15 He schal delyuere a pore man fro his angwisch; and he 16 schal opene the eere of hym in tribulacioun. Therfor he schal saue thee fro the streit mouth of the broddeste *tribulacioun*, and not hauynge a foundement vndur it; sotheli 17 the rest of thi table schal be ful of fatnesse. Thi cause is demed as *the cause* of a wickid man; forsothe thou schalt 18 resseyue thi cause and doom. Therfor ire ouercome thee not, that thou oppresse ony man; and the multitude of 19 3iftis bowe thee not. Putte doun thi greetnesse with out tribulacioun, and *pulle doun* alle stronge men bi strengthe. 20 Dilaie thou not ny3t, that puplis stie for hem. Be thou 21 war, that thou bowe not to wickidnesse; for thou hast 22 bigunne to sue this *wickidnesse* aftir wretchidnesse. Lo! God is hi3 in his strengthe, and noon is lijk hym among

²³ the ȝyueris of lawe. Who mai seke out the weies of God? ethir who dar seie to hym, Thou hast wrouȝt wickidnesse? ²⁴ Haue thou mynde, that thou knowist not his werk, of ²⁵ whom men sungun. Alle men seen God; ech man bi-²⁶ holdith afer. Lo! God *is* greet, ouercomynge oure kunnyng; the noumbre of hise ȝeeris is with out noumbre. ²⁷ Which takith awei the dropis of reyn; and schedith out ²⁸ reynes at the licnesse of floodȝatis, whiche comen doun of ²⁹ the cloudis, that hilen alle thingis aboue. If he wole stretche ³⁰ forthe cloudis as his tente, and leite with his liȝt fro aboue, ³¹ he schal hile, ȝhe, the herris of the see. For bi these thingis he demeth puplis, and ȝyueth mete to many deedli men.

Cap. XXXVII.

³² In hondis he hidith liȝt; and comaundith it, that it come ³³ eft. He tellith of it to his freend, that it is his possessioun; ¹ and that he may stie to it. Myn herte dredde of this thing, ² and is moued out of his place. It schal here an heryng in the feerdfulnesse of his vois, and a sown comynge forth ³ of his mouth. He biholdith ouere alle heuenes; and his ⁴ liȝt *is* ouere the termes of erthe. Sown schal rore aftir hym, he schal thundre with the vois of his greetnesse; and it ⁵ schal not be souȝt out, whanne his vois is herd. God schal thundre in his vois wondurfulli, that makith grete thingis ⁶ and that moun not be souȝt out. Which comaundith to the snow to come doun on erthe, and to the reynes of ⁷ wijntir, and to the reynes of his strengthe. Which markith in the hond of alle men, that alle men knowe her werkis. ⁸ An vnresonable beeste schal go in to his denne, and schal ⁹ dwelle in his caue, *ethir derke place.* Tempestis schulen go ¹⁰ out fro the ynnere thingis, and coold fro Arturus. Whanne God makith blowyng, frost wexith togidere; and eft ful

11 brood watris ben sched out. Whete desirith cloudis, and
12 cloudis spreeden abrood her li3t. Whiche cloudes cumpassen
alle thingis bi cumpas, whidur euere the wil of the gouernour
ledith tho, to al thing which he comaundith to tho on the
13 face of the world; whether in o lynage, ethir in his lond,
ether in what euer place of his merci he comaundith tho
14 to be foundun. Joob, herkene thou these thingis; stonde
15 thou, and biholde the meruels of God. Whethir thou woost,
whanne God comaundide to the reynes, that tho schulen
16 schewe the li3t of hise cloudis? Whether thou knowist the
17 grete weies of cloudis, and perfit kunnyngis? Whether thi
cloothis ben not hoote, whanne the erthe is blowun with
18 the south? In hap thou madist with hym heuenes, which
19 moost sad ben foundid, as of bras. Schewe thou to vs,
what we schulen seie to hym; for we ben wlappid in derk-
20 nessis. Who schal telle to hym, what thingis Y speke?
21 3he, if he spekith, a man schal be deuourid. And now men
seen not li3t; the eir schal be maad thicke sudenli in to
22 cloudis, and wynd passynge schal dryue awei tho. Gold
23 schal come fro the north, and ferdful preisyng of God. For
we moun not fynde him worthili; *he is* greet in strengthe,
and in doom, and in ri3tfulnesse, and may not be teld out.
24 Therfor men schulen drede hym; and alle men, that semen
to hem silf to be wise, schulen not be hardi to biholde.

Cap. XXXVIII.

1 Forsothe the Lord answeride fro the whirlewynd to Joob,
2 and seide, Who is this man, wlappynge sentences with vn-
3 wise wordis? Girde thou as a man thi leendis; Y schal
4 axe thee, and answere thou to me. Where were thou,
whanne Y settide the foundementis of erthe? schewe thou
5 to me, if thou hast vndurstondyng. Who settide mesures

therof, if thou knowist? ethir who stretchide forth a lyne
6 theronne? On what thing ben the foundementis therof
maad fast? ether who sente doun the corner-stoon therof,
7 whanne the morew sterris hericden me togidere, and alle
8 the sones of God sungun ioyfuli? Who closide togidere the
see with doris, whanne it brak out comynge forth as of the
9 wombe? Whanne Y settide a cloude the hilyng therof, and
Y wlappide it with derknesse, as with clothis of ȝong childhed.
10 Y cumpasside it with my termes, and Y settide a barre, and
11 doris; and Y seide, Til hidur thou schalt come, and thou
schalt not go forth ferthere; and here thou schalt breke
12 togidere thi bolnynge wawis. Whethir aftir thi birthe thou
comaundist to the bigynnyng of dai, and schewidist to the
13 morewtid his place? Whethir thou heldist schakynge togidere
the laste partis of erthe, and schakedist awei wickid men
14 therfro? A seeling schal be restorid as cley, and it schal
15 stonde as a cloth. The liȝt of wickid men schal be takun
16 awey fro hem, and an hiȝ arm schal be brokun. Whethir
thou entridist in to the depthe of the see, and walkidist in
17 the laste partis of the occian? Whether the ȝatis of deeth
18 ben openyd to thee, and siest thou the derk doris? Whethir
thou hast biholde the brede of erthe? Schewe thou to me,
19 if thou knowist alle thingis, in what weie the liȝt dwellith,
20 and which is the place of derknesse; that thou lede ech
thing to hise termes, and thou vndurstonde the weies of
21 his hows. Wistist thou thanne, that thou schuldist be borun,
22 and knew thou the noumbre of thi daies? Whethir thou
entridist in to the tresours of snow, ether biheldist thou the
23 tresours of hail? whiche thingis Y made redy in to the
tyme of an enemy, in to the dai of fiȝtyng and of batel.
24 Bi what weie is the liȝt spred abroad, heete is departid on
25 erthe? Who ȝaf cours to the strongeste reyn, and weie of
26 the thundur sownynge? That it schulde reyne on the erthe

with out man in desert, where noon of deedli men dwellith?
27 That it schulde fille a lond with out weie and desolat, and
28 schulde brynge forth greene eerbis? Who is fadir of reyn,
29 ether who gendride the dropis of deew? Of whos wombe
30 ȝede out iys, and who gendride frost fro heuene? Watris
ben maad hard in the licnesse of stoon, and the ouer part
31 of occian is streyned togidere. Whether thou schalt mowe
ioyne togidere schynynge sterris Pliades, ethir thou schalt
32 mowe distrie the cumpas of Arturis? Whether thou bryng-
ist forth Lucifer, *that is, dai-sterre*, in his tyme, and makist
33 euene-sterre to rise on the sones of erthe? Whether thou
knowist the ordre of heuene, and schalt sette the resoun
34 therof in erthe? Whethir thou schalt reise thi vois in to a
35 cloude, and the fersnesse of watris schal hile thee? Whethir
thou schalt sende leitis, and tho schulen go, and tho schulen
36 turne aȝen, and schulen seie to thee, We ben present? Who
puttide wisdoom in the entrailis of man, ethir who ȝaf vn-
37 durstondyng to the cok? Who schal telle out the resoun
of heuenes, and who schal make acordyng of heuene to
38 sleep? Whanne dust was foundid in the erthe, and clottis
39 weren ioyned togidere? Whether thou schalt take prey to
40 the lionesse, and schalt fille the soulis of hir whelpis, whanne
41 tho liggen in caues, and aspien in dennes? Who makith
redi for the crowe his mete, whanne hise briddis crien to
God, and wandren aboute, for tho han not meetis?

Cap. XXXIX.

1 Whethir thou knowist the tyme of birthe of wielde geet
in stoonys, ethir hast thou aspied hyndis bryngynge forth
2 calues? Hast thou noumbrid the monethis of her conseyuyng,
3 and hast thou knowe the tyme of her caluyng? Tho ben
4 bowid to the calf, and caluen; and senden out roryngis. Her

JOB. XXXIX.

calues ben departid, and goen to pasture; tho goen out, and
5 turnen not aȝen to tho *hyndis*. Who let go the wielde asse
6 fre, and who loside the boondis of hym? To whom Y haue
ȝoue an hows in wildirnesse, and the tabernacles of hym in
7 the lond of saltnesse. He dispisith the multitude of citee; he
8 herith not the cry of an axere. He lokith aboute the hillis of
9 his lesewe, and he sekith alle greene thingis. Whether an
vnycorn schal wilne serue thee, ethir schal dwelle at thi
10 cratche? Whether thou schalt bynde the vnicorn with thi
chayne, for to ere, ethir schal he breke the clottis of valeis
11 aftir thee? Whether thou schalt haue trist in his grete
12 strengthe, and schalt thou leeue to hym thi traueils? Whether
thou schalt bileue to hym, that he schal ȝelde seed to thee,
13 and schal gadere togidere thi cornfloor? The fethere of an
14 ostriche is lijk the fetheris of a gerfawcun, and of an hauk:
which *ostrige* forsakith hise eirun in the erthe, in hap thou schalt
15 make tho hoot in the dust. He forȝetith, that a foot tredith
16 tho, ethir that a beeste of the feeld al to-brekith *tho*. He is
maad hard to hise briddis, as if thei ben not hise; he tra-
17 ueilide in veyn, while no drede constreynede. For God hath
priued hym fro wisdom, and ȝaf not vnderstondyng to hym.
18 Whanne tyme is, he reisith the wengis an hiȝ; he scorneth
19 the hors, and his ridere. Whether thou schalt ȝyue strengthe
to an hors, ether schal ȝyue neiyng aboute his necke?
20 Whether thou schalt reyse hym as locustis? The glorie of
21 hise nosethirlis *is* drede. He diggith erthe with the foot, he
22 fulli ioieth booldli; he goith aȝens armed men. He dispisith
23 ferdfulnesse, and he ȝyueth not stide to swerd. An arowe-
caas schal sowne on hym; a spere and scheeld schal florische.
24 He is hoot, and gnastith, and swolewith the erthe: and he
25 arettith not that the crie of the trumpe sowneth. Whanne he
herith a clarioun, he seith, Joie! he smellith batel afer; the
26 excityng of duykis, and the ȝellyng of the oost. Whether an

hauk spredinge abrood hise wyngis to the south, bigynneth
27 to haue fetheris bi thi wisdom? Whether an egle schal be
reisid at thi comaundement, and schal sette his nest in hi3
28 places? He dwellith in stoonys, and he dwellith in flyntis
brokun bifor, and in rochis, to whiche me may not nei3e.
29 Fro thennus he biholdith mete, and hise i3en loken fro fer.
30 Hise briddis souken blood, and where euere a careyn is,
31 anoon he is present. And the Lord addide, and spak to
32 Joob, Whether he, that stryueth with God, schal haue rest so
li3tli? Sotheli he, that repreueth God, owith for to answere
33 to hym. Forsothe Joob answeride to the Lord, and seide,
34 What may Y answere, which haue spoke li3tli? Y schal
35 putte myn hond on my mouth. Y spak o thing, which thing
Y wold, that Y hadde not seid; and *Y spak* anothir thing, to
which Y schal no more adde.

Cap. XL.

1 FORSOTHE the Lord answeride to Joob fro the whirlewynd,
2 and seide, Girde thou as a man thi leendis, and Y schal axe
3 thee, and schewe thou to me. Whether thou schalt make
voide my doom, and schalt condempne me, that thou be
4 maad iust? And if thou hast an arm, as God *hath*, and if
thou thundrist with lijk vois, take thou fairnesse aboute thee,
5 and be thou reisid an hi3, and be thou gloriouse, and be thou
6 clothid in faire clothis. Distrie thou proude men in thi
woodnesse, and biholde thou, and make lowe ech bostere.
7 Biholde thou alle proude men, and schende thou hem; and
8 al to-breke thou wickid men in her place. Hide thou hem
in dust togidere, and drenche doun her faces in to a diche.
9 And Y schal knowleche, that thi ri3t hond may saue thee.
10 Lo! behemot, whom Y made with thee, schal as an oxe ete
11 hey. His strengthe *is* in hise leendis, and his vertu *is* in the

12 nawle of his wombe. He streyneth his tail as a cedre; the
13 senewis of his stones of gendrure ben foldid togidere. Hise
boonys *ben* as the pipis of bras; the gristil of hym *is* as platis
14 of yrun. He is the bigynnyng of the weies of God; he, that
15 made hym, schal sette his swerd *to hym*. Hillis beren eerbis
to this *behemot;* alle the beestis of the feeld pleien there.
16 He slepith vndur schadewe, in the pryuete of rehed, in moiste
17 places. Schadewis hilen his schadewe; the salewis of the
18 ryuer cumpassen hym. He schal soupe vp the flood, and he
schal not wondre; he hath trist, that Jordan schal flowe in to
19 his mouth. He schal take hem bi the iȝen of hym, as bi an
hook; and bi scharpe schaftis he schal perse hise nosethirlis.
20 Whether thou schalt mowe drawe out leuyathan with an
21 hook, and schalt bynde with a roop his tunge? Whethir
thou schalt putte a ryng in hise nosethirlis, ethir schalt perse
22 hyse cheke with an hook? Whether he schal multiplie
preieris to thee, ether schal speke softe thingis to thee?
23 Whether he schal make couenaunt with thee, and thou schalt
24 take him a seruaunt euerlastinge? Whether thou schalt
scorne hym as a brid, ethir schalt bynde hym to thin hand-
25 maidis? Schulen frendis kerue hym, schulen marchauntis
26 departe hym? Whether thou schalt fille nettis with his skyn,
27 and a leep of fischis with his heed? Schalt thou putte thin
hond on hym? haue thou mynde of the batel, and adde no
28 more to speke. Lo! his hope schal disseyue hym; and in
the siȝt of alle men he schal be cast doun.

Cap. XLI.

1 I NOT as cruel schal reise hym; for who may aȝenstonde
2 my face? And who ȝaf to me bifore, that Y ȝelde to hym?
3 Alle thingis, that ben vndur heuene, ben myne. Y schal not
4 spare hym for myȝti wordis, and m.ad faire to bisecche. Who
schal schewe the face of his clothing, and who schal entre in

5 to the myddis of his mouth? Who schal opene the ȝatis of
6 his cheer? ferdfulnesse *is* bi the cumpas of hise teeth. His
bodi *is* as ȝotun scheldys of bras, and ioyned togidere with
7 scalis ouerleiynge hem silf. Oon is ioyned to another; and
8 sotheli brething goith not thorouȝ tho. Oon schal cleue to
anothir, and tho holdynge hem silf schulen not be departid.
9 His fnesynge *is* as schynynge of fier, and hise iȝen *ben* as
10 iȝelidis of the morewtid. Laumpis comen forth of his mouth,
11 as trees of fier, that ben kyndlid. Smoke cometh forth of
12 hise nosethirlis, as of a pot set on the fier and boilynge. His
breeth makith colis to brenne, and flawme goith out of his
13 mouth. Strengthe schal dwelle in his necke, and nedynesse
14 schal go bifor his face. The membris of hise fleischis *ben*
cleuynge togidere to hem silf; God schal sende floodis aȝens
15 hym, and tho schulen not be borun to an other place. His
herte schal be maad hard as a stoon; and it schal be streyned
16 togidere as the anefeld of a smith. Whanne he schal be
takun awei, aungels schulen drede; and thei aferd schulen be
17 purgid. Whanne swerd takith hym, it may not stonde, nethir
18 spere, nether haburioun. For he schal arette irun as chaffis,
19 and bras as rotun tre. A man archere schal not dryue hym
awei; stoonys of a slynge ben turned in to stobil to hym.
20 He schal arette an hamer as stobil; and he schal scorne a
21 florischynge spere. The beemys of the sunne schulen be
vndur hym; and he schal strewe to hym silf gold as cley.
22 He schal make the depe se to buyle as a pot; and he schal
23 putte, as whanne oynementis buylen. A path schal schyne
aftir hym; he schal gesse the greet occian as wexynge eld.
24 No power is on erthe, that schal be comparisound to hym;
25 which is maad, that he schulde drede noon. He seeth al hiȝ
thing; he is kyng ouer alle the sones of pride.

Cap. XLII.

1, 2 Forsothe Joob answeride to the Lord, and seide, Y woot, that thou maist alle thingis, and no thou3t is hid fro 3 thee. Who is this, that helith counsel with out kunnyng? Therfor Y spak vnwiseli, and tho thingis that passiden ouer 4 mesure my kunnyng. Here thou, and Y schal speke; Y 5 schal axe thee, and answere thou to me. Bi heryng of eere 6 Y herde thee, but now myn i3e seeth thee. Therfor Y repreue me, and do penaunce in deed sparcle and aische. 7 Forsothe aftir that the Lord spak these wordis to Joob, he seide to Eliphat Themanytes, My stronge veniaunce is wrooth a3ens thee, and a3ens thi twey frendis; for 3e spaken not 8 bifor me ri3tful thing, as my seruaunt Joob *dide.* Therfor take 3e to 3ou seuene bolis, and seuene rammes; and go 3e to my seruaunt Joob, and offre 3e brent sacrifice for 3ou. Forsothe Joob, my seruaunt, schal preie for 3ou; Y schal resseyue his face, that foli be not arettid to 3ou ; for 3e spaken not bifor me ri3tful thing, as my seruaunt Joob *dide.* 9 Therfor Eliphat Themanytes, and Baldach Suythes, and Sophar Naamathites, 3eden, and diden, as the Lord hedde spoke to hem ; and the Lord resseyuede the face of Joob. 10 Also the Lord was conuertid to the penaunce of Joob, whanne he preiede for hise frendis. And the Lord addide 11 alle thingis double, whiche euere weren of Joob. Sotheli alle hise britheren, and alle hise sistris, and alle that knewen hym bifore, camen to hym; and thei eeten breed with hym in his hows, and moueden the heed on hym; and thei coumfortiden hym of al the yuel, which the Lord hadde brou3t in on hym ; and thei 3auen to hym ech man o scheep, 12 and o goldun eere-ring. Forsothe the Lord blesside the laste thingis of Joob, more than the bigynnyng of hym ; and fouretene thousynde of scheep weren maad to hym,

and sixe thousinde of camels, and a thousynde ȝockis of
13 oxis, and a thousynde femal assis. And he hadde seuene
sones, and thre douȝtris; and he clepide the name of o
douȝtir Dai, and the name of the secounde douȝtir Cassia,
and the name of the thridde douȝtir An horn of wymmens
14 oynement. Sotheli no wymmen weren foundun so faire in
al erthe, as the douȝtris of Joob; and her fadir ȝaf eritage
15 to hem among her britheren. Forsothe Joob lyuede aftir
these betyngis an hundrid and fourti ȝeer, and siȝ hise sones,
and the sones of hise sones, til to the fourthe generacioun;
and he was deed eld, and ful of daies.

PSALMS.

Psalm I.

The firste salm.

1 Blessid *is* the man, that ȝede not in the councel of wickid
men; and stood not in the weie of synneris, and sat not
2 in the chaier of pestilence. But his wille *is* in the lawe of
the Lord; and he schal bithenke in the lawe of hym dai
3 and nyȝt. And he schal be as a tree, which is plauntid
bisidis the rennyngis of watris; which *tre* schal ȝyue his fruyt
in his tyme. And his leef schal not falle doun; and alle
thingis which euere he schal do schulen haue prosperite.
4 Not so wickid men, not so; but *thei ben* as dust, which the
5 wynd castith awei fro the face of erthe. Therfor wickid
men risen not aȝen in doom; nethir synneres in the councel
6 of iust men. For the Lord knowith the weie of iust men;
and the weie of wickid men schal perische.

Psalm II.

The secounde salm.

1 Whi gnastiden with teeth hethene men; and puplis 2 thouȝten veyn thingis? The kyngis of erthe stoden togidere; and princes camen togidere aȝens the Lord, and aȝens his 3 Crist? Breke we the bondis of hem; and cast we awei the 4 ȝok of hem fro vs. He that dwellith in heuenes schal scorne 5 hem; and the Lord schal bimowe hem. Thanne he schal speke to hem in his ire; and he schal disturble hem in his 6 stronge veniaunce. Forsothe Y am maad of hym a kyng 7 on Syon, his hooli hil; prechynge his comaundement. The Lord seide to me, Thou art my sone; Y haue gendrid thee 8 to-dai. Axe thou of me, and Y schal ȝyue to thee hethene men thin eritage; and thi possessioun the termes of erthe. 9 Thou schalt gouerne hem in an yrun ȝerde; and thou schalt 10 breke hem as the vessel of a pottere. And now, ȝe kyngis, 11 vndurstonde; ȝe that demen the erthe, be lerud. Serue ȝe the Lord with drede; and make ȝe ful ioye to hym with 12 tremblyng. Take ȝe lore; lest the Lord be wrooth sumtyme, 13 and lest ȝe perischen fro iust waie. Whanne his ire brenneth out in schort tyme; blessed *ben* alle thei, that tristen in hym.

Psalm III.

1 *The title of the thridde salm. The salm of Dauid, whanne he fledde fro the face of Absolon, his sone.*

2, 3 Lord, whi ben thei multiplied that disturblen me? many men rysen aȝens me. Many men seien of my soule, Noon 4 helthe is to hym in his God. But thou, Lord, art myn 5 vptakere; my glorye, and enhaunsyng myn heed. With my vois Y criede to the Lord; and he herde me fro his 6 hooli hil. I slepte, and was quenchid, and Y roos vp; for

7 the Lord resseyuede me. I schal not drede thousyndis of puple cumpassynge me; Lord, rise thou vp; my God, make 8 thou me saaf. For thou hast smyte alle men beynge aduersaries to me with out cause; thou hast al to-broke the 9 teeth of synneris. Helthe is of the Lord; and thi blessyng, *Lord, is* on thi puple.

Psalm IV.

1 *The title of the fourthe salm. To the victorie in orguns; the salm of Dauid.*

2 Whanne Y inwardli clepid, God of my riȝtwisnesse herde 3 me; in tribulacioun thou hast alargid to me. Haue thou mercy on me; and here thou my preier. Sones of men, hou long *ben* ȝe of heuy herte? whi louen ȝe vanite, and 4 seken a leesyng? And wite ȝe, that the Lord hath maad merueilous his hooli man; the Lord schal here me, whanne 5 Y schal crye to hym. Be ȝe wrothe, and nyle ȝe do synne; and *for tho thingis* whiche ȝe scien in ȝoure hertis and in 6 ȝoure beddis, be ȝe compunct. Sacrifie ȝe the sacrifice of riȝtfulnesse, and hope ȝe in the Lord; many seien, Who 7 schewide goodis to vs? Lord, the liȝt of thi cheer is markid 8 on vs; thou hast ȝoue gladnesse in myn herte. Thei ben multiplied of the fruit of whete, *and* of wyn; and of her oile. 9 In pees in the same thing; Y schal slepe, and take reste. 10 For thou, Lord; hast set me syngulerli in hope.

Psalm V.

1 *The title of the fyuethe salm. To the ouercomere on the eritagis, the song of Dauid.*

2 Lord, perseyue thou my wordis with eeris; vndurstonde 3 thou my cry. Mi kyng, and my God; ȝyue thou tent to

4 the vois of my preier. For, Lord, Y schal preie to thee;
5 here thou eerly my vois. Eerli Y schal stonde ny3 thee,
and Y schal se; for thou art God not willynge wickidnesse.
6 Nethir an yuel-willid man schal dwelle bisidis thee; nethir
7 vniust men schulen dwelle bifor thin i3en. Thou hatist alle
that worchen wickidnesse; thou schalt leese alle that speken
leesyng. The Lord schal holde abhomynable a manquel-
8 lere, and gileful man. But, *Lord*, in the multitude of thi
merci Y schal entre in to thin hows; Y schal worschipe to
9 thin hooli temple in thi drede. Lord, lede thou forth me
in thi ri3tfulnesse for myn enemyes; dresse thou my weie
10 in thi si3t. For whi treuthe is not in her mouth; her herte
11 is veyn. Her throte is an opyn sepulcre, thei diden gilefuli
with her tungis; God, deme thou hem. Falle thei doun
fro her thou3tis, vp the multitude of her wickidnessis caste
thou hem doun; for, Lord, thei han terrid thee to ire. And
alle that hopen in thee, be glad; thei schulen make fulli
12 ioye with outen ende, and thou schalt dwelle in hem. And
13 alle that louen thi name schulen haue glorie in thee; for
thou schalt blesse a iust man. Lord, thou hast corouned
vs, as with the scheeld of thi good wille.

Psalm VI.

1 *The title of the sixte salm. To the ouercomere in salmes,
the salm of Dauid, on the ei3the.*

2 Lord, repreue thou not me in thi stronge veniaunce;
3 nether chastice thou me in thin ire. Lord, haue thou merci
on me, for Y am sijk; Lord, make thou me hool, for alle
4 my boonys ben troblid. And my soule is troblid greetli;
5 but thou, Lord, hou long? Lord, be thou conuertid, and
6 delyuere my soule; make thou me saaf, for thi merci. For
noon is in deeth, which is myndful of thee; but in helle

7 who schal knouleche to thee? I traueilide in my weilyng,
Y schal waische my bed bi ech ny3t; Y schal moiste, *ether*
8 *make weet*, my bedstre with my teeris. Myn i3e is disturblid
9 of woodnesse; Y waxe eld among alle myn enemyes. Alle
3e that worchen wickidnesse, departe fro me; for the Lord
10 hath herd the vois of my wepyng. The Lord hath herd
11 my bisechyng; the Lord hath resseyued my preier. Alle
my enemyes be aschamed, and be disturblid greetli; be thei
turned togidere, and be thei aschamed ful swiftli.

Psalm VII.

1 *The title of the seuenthe salm. For the ignoraunce of Dauid,
which he songe to the Lord on the wordis of Ethiopien, the
sone of Gemyny.*

2   Mi Lord God, Y haue hopid in thee; make thou me saaf
3 fro alle that pursuen me, and delyuere thou me. Lest ony
tyme he as a lioun rauysche my soule; the while noon is
4 that a3enbieth, nether that makith saaf. Mi Lord God, if Y
5 dide this thing, if wickidnesse is in myn hondis; if Y 3eldide
to men 3eldynge to me yuels, falle Y bi disseruyng voide fro
6 myn enemyes; myn enemy pursue my soule, and take, and
defoule my lijf in erthe; and brynge my glorie in to dust.
7 Lord, rise thou vp in thin ire; and be thou reysid in the
8 coostis of myn enemyes. And, my Lord God, rise thou in
the comaundement, which thou hast comaundid; and the
9 synagoge of puplis schal cumpasse thee. And for this go
thou a3en an hi3; the Lord demeth puplis. Lord, deme
thou me bi my ri3tfulnesse; and bi myn innocence on
10 me. The wickidnesse of synneris be endid; and thou,
God, sekyng the hertis and reynes, schalt dresse a iust
11 man. Mi iust help *is* of the Lord; that makith saaf ri3t-
12 ful men in herte. The Lord *is* a iust iuge, stronge and

13 pacient; whether he is wrooth bi alle daies? If ȝe ben not conuertid, he schal florische his swerd; he hath bent his
14 bouwe, and made it redi. And therynne he hath maad redi the vessels of deth; he hath fulli maad his arewis with bren-
15 nynge thingis. Lo! he conseyuede sorewe; he peynfuli
16 brouȝte forth vnriȝtfulnesse, and childide wickidnesse. He openide a lake, and diggide it out; and he felde in to the
17 dich which he made. His sorewe schal be turned in to his heed; and his wickidnesse schal come doun in to his necke.
18 I schal knouleche to the Lord bi his riȝtfulnesse; and Y schal synge to the name of the hiȝeste Lord.

Psalm VIII.

1 *The title of the ciȝthe salm. To the ouercomere, for pressours, the salm of Dauid.*

2 Lord, *thou art* oure Lord; thi name is ful wonderful in al
3 erthe. For thi greet doyng is reisid, aboue heuenes. Of the mouth of ȝonge children, not spekynge and soukynge mylk, thou madist perfitli heriyng, for thin enemyes; that thou
4 destrie the enemy and avengere. For Y schal se thin heuenes, the werkis of thi fyngris; the moone and sterris, whiche
5 thou hast foundid. What is a man, that thou art myndeful of hym; ethir the sone of a virgyn, for thou visitist hym?
6 Thou hast maad hym a litil lesse than aungels; thou hast
7 corouned hym with glorie and onour, and hast ordeyned
8 hym aboue the werkis of thin hondis. Thou hast maad suget alle thingis vndur hise feet; alle scheep and oxis,
9 ferthermore and the beestis of the feeld; the briddis of the eir, and the fischis of the see; that passen bi the pathis of
10 the see. Lord, *thou art* oure Lord; thi name is wondurful in al erthe.

Psalm IX.

1 *The title of the nynthe salm. In to the ende, for the pryuytees of the sone, the salm of Dauid.*

2 Lord, Y schal knouleche to thee in al myn herte; Y schal
3 telle alle thi merueils. Thou hiʒeste, Y schal be glad, and Y schal be fulli ioieful in thee; Y schal synge to thi name.
4 For thou turnest myn enemy abac; thei schulen be maad
5 feble, and schulen perische fro thi face. For thou hast maad my doom and my cause; thou, that demest riʒtfulnesse, hast
6 set on the trone. Thou blamedist hethene men, and the wickid perischide; thou hast do awei the name of hem in to
7 the world, and in to the world of world. The swerdis of the enemy failiden in to the ende; and thou hast distried the citees of hem. The mynde of hem perischide with sown;
8 and the Lord dwellith with outen ende. He made redi his
9 trone in doom; and he schal deme the world in equite, he
10 schal deme puplis in riʒtfulnesse. And the Lord is maad refuyt, *ether help*, to a pore man; an helpere in couenable
11 tymes in tribulacioun. And thei, that knowen thi name, haue hope in thee; for thou, Lord, hast not forsake hem that
12 seken thee. Synge ʒe to the Lord, that dwellith in Syon;
13 telle ʒe hise studyes among hethene men. God forʒetith not the cry of pore men; for he hath mynde, and sekith the
14 blood of hem. Lord, haue thou merci on me; se thou my
15 mekenesse of myn enemyes. Which enhaunsist me fro the ʒatis of deeth; that Y telle alle thi preisyngis in the ʒatis of
16 the douʒter of Syon. Y schal be fulli ioyeful in thin helthe; hethene men ben fast set in the perisching, which thei maden. In this snare, which thei hidden, the foot of hem is kauʒt.
17 The Lord makynge domes schal be knowun; the synnere is
18 takun in the werkis of hise hondis. Synneris be turned
19 togidere in to helle; alle folkis, that forʒeten God. For the

forʒetyng of a pore man schal not be in to the ende; the pacience of pore men schal not perische in to the ende.
20 Lord, rise thou vp, a man be not coumfortid; folkis be
21 demyd in thi siʒt. Lord, ordeine thou a lawe-makere on
1 hem; wite folkis, that thei ben men. (X.) Lord, whi hast thou go fer awei? thou dispisist in couenable tymes in tribu-
2 lacioun. While the wickid is proud, the pore man is brent; thei ben taken in the counsels, bi whiche thei thenken.
3 Forwhi the synnere is preisid in the desiris of his soule; and
4 the wickid is blessid. The synnere wraththide the Lord;
5 vp the multitude of his ire he schal not seke. God is not in his siʒt; hise weies ben defoulid in al tyme. God, thi domes ben takun awei fro his face; he schal be lord of alle hise
6 enemyes. For he seide in his herte, Y schal not be moued,
7 fro generacioun in to generacioun without yuel. Whos mouth is ful of cursyng, and of bitternesse, and of gyle; trauel and
8 sorewe *is* vndur his tunge. He sittith in aspies with ryche
9 men in priuytees; to sle the innocent man. Hise iʒen biholden on a pore man; he settith aspies in hid place, as a lioun in his denne. He settith aspies, for to rauysche a pore man; for to rauysche a pore man, while he drawith the
10 pore man. In his snare he schal make meke the pore man; he schal bowe hym silf, and schal falle doun, whanne he
11 hath be lord of pore men. For he seide in his herte, God hath forʒete; he hath turned awei his face, that he se not in
12 to the ende. Lord God, rise thou vp, and thin hond be
13 enhaunsid; forʒete thou not pore men. For what thing terride the wickid man God to wraththe? for he seide in his
14 herte, *God* schal not seke. Thou seest, for thou biholdist trauel and sorewe; that thou take hem in to thin hondis. The pore man is left to thee; thou schalt be an helpere to
15 the fadirles and modirles. Al to-breke thou the arme of the synnere, and yuel willid; his synne schal be souʒt, and it

16 schal not be foundun. The Lord schal regne with outen ende, and in to the world of world; folkis, ȝe schulen perische
17 fro the lond of hym. The Lord hath herd the desir of pore
18 men; thin eere hath herd the makyng redi of her herte. To deme for the modirles and meke; that a man leie to no more to magnyfie hym silf on erthe.

Psalm X (XI).

1   *The title of the tenthe salm. To the victorie of Dauid.*

2   I TRISTE in the Lord; hou seien ȝe to my soule, Passe
3 thou ouere in to an hil, as a sparowe *doith?* For lo! synneris han bent a bouwe; thei han maad redi her arowis in an arowe-caas; for to schete in derknesse riȝtful men in
4 herte. For thei han distryed, whom thou hast maad perfit;
5 but what dide the riȝtful man? The Lord *is* in his hooli temple; *he is* Lord, his seete *is* in heuene. Hise iȝen biholden on a pore man; hise iȝelidis axen the sones of men.
6 The Lord axith a iust man, and vnfeithful man; but he, that
7 loueth wickidnesse, hatith his soule. He schal reyne snaris on synful men; fier, brymston, and the spirit of tempestis
8 *ben* the part of the cuppe of hem. For the Lord *is* riȝtful, and louede riȝtfulnessis; his cheer siȝ equite, *ethir euennesse.*

Psalm XI (XII).

1   *The title of the eleuenthe salm. To the victorie on the eiȝte, the song of Dauid.*

2   LORD, make thou me saaf, for the hooli failide; for treuthis
3 ben maad litle fro the sones of men. Thei spaken veyn thingis, ech man to hys neiȝbore; *thei han* gileful lippis, thei
4 spaken in herte and herte. The Lord destrie alle gileful
5 lippis; and the greet spekynge tunge. Whiche seiden, We

schulen magnyfie oure tunge, our lippis ben of vs; who is
6 oure lord? For the wretchednesse of nedy men, and for
the weilyng of pore men; now Y schal ryse vp, seith the
Lord. I schal sette in helthe; Y schal do tristili in hym.
7 The spechis of the Lord ben chast spechis; siluer examynyd
8 bi fier, preued fro erthe, purgid seuen fold. Thou, Lord,
schalt kepe vs; and thou schalt kepe vs fro this generacioun
9 with outen ende. Wickid men goen in cumpas; bi thin hiȝnesse thou hast multiplied the sones of men.

Psalm XII (XIII).

1 *The title of the twelfthe salm. To the victorie of Dauid.*

Lord, hou long forȝetist thou me in to the ende? hou
2 long turnest thou awei thi face fro me? Hou long schal Y
sette counsels in my soule; sorewe in my herte bi dai?
3, 4 Hou long schal myn enemy be reisid on me? My Lord
God, biholde thou, and here thou me. Liȝtne thou myn
5 iȝen, lest ony tyme Y slepe in deth; lest ony tyme myn
enemye seie, Y hadde the maistri aȝens hym. Thei, that
troblen me, schulen haue ioie, if Y schal be stirid; forsothe
6 Y hopide in thi merci. Myn herte schal fulli haue ioie in
thin helthe; Y schal synge to the Lord, that ȝyueth goodis
to me, and Y schal seie salm to the name of the hiȝeste
Lord.

Psalm XIII (XIV).

1 *The title of the threttenthe salm. To the victorie of
Dauid.*

The vnwise man seide in his herte, God is not. Thei ben
corrupt, and ben maad abhomynable in her studies; noon is
2 that doith good, noon is til to oon. The Lord biheldc fro
heuene on the sones of men; that he se, if ony is vndur-

3 stondynge, ethir sekynge God. Alle bowiden awei, togidere thei ben maad vnprofitable; noon is that doth good, noon is til to oon. The throte of hem is an open sepulcre, thei diden gilefuli with her tungis; the venym of snakis *is* vndur her lippis. Whos mouth is ful of cursyng and bittirnesse; her feet *ben* swift to schede out blood. Sorewe and cursidnesse *is* in the weies of hem, and thei knewen not the weie 4 of pees; the drede of God is not bifor her iȝen. Whether alle men that worchen wickidnesse schulen not knowe; that 5 deuowren my puple, as mete of breed? Thei clepeden not the Lord; thei trembliden there for dreed, where was no 6 drede; for the Lord is in a riȝtful generacioun. Thou hast schent the counsel of a pore man; for the Lord is his hope. 7 Who schal ȝyue fro Syon helthe to Israel? Whanne the Lord hath turned awei the caitifte of his puple; Jacob schal fulli be ioiful, and Israel schal be glad.

Psalm XIV (XV).

The title of the fourtenthe salm. The salm of Dauid.

1 Lord, who schal dwelle in thi tabernacle; ether who schal 2 reste in thin hooli hil? He that entrith with out wem; and 3 worchith riȝtfulnesse. Which spekith treuthe in his herte; which dide not gile in his tunge. Nethir dide yuel to his 4 neiȝbore; and took not schenschip aȝens hise neiȝboris. A wickid man is brouȝt to nouȝt in his siȝt; but he glorifieth hem that dreden the Lord. Which swerith to his neiȝbore, 5 and disseyueth not; which ȝaf not his money to vsure; and took not ȝiftis on the innocent. He, that doith these thingis, schal not be moued with outen ende.

Psalm XV (XVI).

The title of the fiuetenthe salm. Of the meke and symple, the salm of Dauid.

1, 2 LORD, kepe thou me, for Y haue hopid in thee; Y seide to the Lord, Thou art my God, for thou hast no nede of my 3 goodis. To the seyntis that ben in the lond of hym; he 4 made wondurful alle my willis in hem. The sikenessis of hem ben multiplied; aftirward thei hastiden. I schal not gadire togidere the conuenticulis, *ethir litle couentis*, of hem of bloodis; and Y schal not be myndeful of her names bi my 5 lippis. The Lord *is* part of myn eritage, and of my passion: 6 thou art, that schalt restore myn eritage to me. Coordis felden to me in ful clere thingis; for myn eritage is ful cleer to me. 7 I schal blesse the Lord, that 3af vndurstondyng to me; fer-8 thermore and my reynes blameden me til to ny3t. I purueide euere the Lord in my si3t; for he is on the ri3thalf to me, 9 that Y be not moued. For this thing myn herte was glad, and my tunge ioyede fulli; ferthermore and my fleisch schal 10 reste in hope. For thou schalt not forsake my soule in helle: nether thou schalt 3yue thin hooli to se corrupcioun. Thou hast maad knowun to me the weies of lijf; thou schalt fille me of gladnesse with thi cheer; delityngis *ben* in thi ri3thalf til in to the ende.

Psalm XVI (XVII).

1 *The title of the sixtenthe salm. The preier of Dauid.*

LORD, here thou my ri3tfulnesse; biholde thou my preier. Perseuye thou with eeris my preier; not *maad* in gileful lippis. 2, 3 Mi doom come forth of thi cheer; thin i3en se equite. Thou hast preued myn herte, and hast visitid in ni3t; thou hast examynyd me bi fier, and wickidnesse is not foundun in me.

4 That my mouth speke not the werkis of men; for the wordis
5 of thi lippis Y haue kept harde weies. Make thou perfit my
6 goyngis in thi pathis; that my steppis be not moued. I
criede, for thou, God, herdist me; bowe doun thin eere to
7 me, and here thou my wordis. Make wondurful thi mercies;
8 that makist saaf men hopynge in thee. Kepe thou me as the
appil of the iȝe; fro men aȝenstondynge thi riȝt hond. Keuere
9 thou me vndur the schadewe of thi wyngis; fro the face of
vnpitouse men, that han turmentid me. Myn enemyes han
10 cumpassid my soule; thei han closide togidere her fatnesse;
11 the mouth of hem spak pride. Thei castiden me forth, and
han cumpassid me now; thei ordeyneden to bowe doun her
12 iȝen in to erthe. Thei, as a lioun maad redi to prey, han
take me; and as the whelp of a lioun dwellynge in hid places.
13 Lord, rise thou vp, bifor come thou hym, and disseyue thou
14 hym; delyuere thou my lijf fro the vnpitouse, *delyuere thou*
thi swerd fro the enemyes of thin hond. Lord, departe thou
hem fro a fewe men of the lond in the lijf of hem; her
wombe is fillid of thin hid thingis. Thei ben fillid with
15 sones; and thei leften her relifis to her litle children. But Y
in riȝtfulnesse schal appere to thi siȝt; Y schal be fillid,
whanne thi glorie schal appere.

Psalm XVII (XVIII).

1 *The title of the seuententhe salm. To victorie, the word of the Lord to Dauid; which spak the wordis of this song, in the dai in which the Lord delyuerede hym fro the hond of alle hise enemyes, and fro the hond of Saul; and he seide:*

2 Lord, my strengthe, Y schal loue thee; the Lord *is* my
3 stidfastnesse, and my refuyt, and mi deliuerere. Mi God *is*
myn helpere; and Y schal hope in to hym. My defendere,
4 and the horn of myn helthe; and myn vptakere. I schal

preise, and ynwardli clepe the Lord; and Y schal be saaf fro
5 myn enemyes. The sorewis of deth cumpassiden me; and
6 the strondis of wickidnesse disturbliden me. The sorewis of
helle cumpassiden me; the snaris of deeth bifor ocupieden
7 me. In my tribulacioun Y inwardli clepide the Lord; and Y
criede to my God. And he herde my vois fro his hooli
8 temple; and my cry in his siʒt entride in to hise eeris. The
erthe was mouede togidere, and tremblede togidere; the
foundementis of hillis weren troblid togidere, and weren
9 moued togidere; for he was wrooth to hem. Smoke stiede
in the ire of hym, and fier brente out fro his face; coolis
10 weren kyndlid of hym. He bowide doun heuenes, and cam
11 doun; and derknesse *was* vndur hise feet. And he stiede on
12 cherubym, and flei; he fley ouer the pennes of wyndis. And
he settide derknesses his hidyng-place, his tabernacle in his
cumpas; derk water *was* in the cloudes of the lowere eir.
13 Ful cleer cloudis passiden in his siʒt; hail and the coolis of
14 fier. And the Lord thundrid fro heuene; and the hiʒeste
15 ʒaf his vois, hail and the coolis of fier *camen doun*. And he
sente hise arowis, and distriede tho men; he multiplicde leytis,
16 and disturblide tho men. And the wellis of watris apperiden;
and the foundementis of the erthe weren schewid. Lord, of
17 thi blamyng; of the brething of the spirit of thin ire. He
sente fro the hiʒeste place, and took me; and he took me fro
18 many watris. He delyuerede me fro my strongeste enemyes;
and fro hem that hatiden me, for thei weren coumfortid on
19 me. Thei camen bifor me in the dai of my turment; and
20 the Lord was maad my defendere. And he ledde out me in
21 to breede; he maad me saaf, for he wolde me. And the
Lord schal ʒelde to me bi my riʒtfulnesse; and he schal ʒelde
22 to me bi the clennesse of myn hondis. For Y kepte the
weies of the Lord; and Y dide not vnfeithfuli fro my God.
23 For alle hise domes *ben* in my siʒt; and Y puttide not awei

24 fro me hise riȝtfulnessis. And Y schal be vnwemmed with
25 hym; and Y schal kepe me fro my wickidnesse. And the
Lord schal ȝelde to me bi my riȝtfulnesse; and bi the clen-
26 nesse of myn hondis in the siȝt of hise iȝen. With the hooli,
thou schalt be hooli; and with a man innocent, thou schalt
27 be innocent. And with a chosun man, thou schalt be chosun;
28 and with a weiward man, thou schalt be weiward. For thou
schalt make saaf a meke puple; and thou schalt make meke
29 the iȝen of proude men. For thou, Lord, liȝtnest my lanterne;
30 my God, liȝtne thou my derknessis. For bi thee Y schal be
delyuered fro temptacioun; and in my God Y schal go ouer
31 the wal. Mi God, his weie *is* vndefoulid, the speches of the
Lord *ben* examyned bi fier; he is defendere of alle men
32 hopynge in hym. For whi, who *is* God, out-takun the Lord?
33 ethir who *is* God outakun oure God? God that hath gird me
34 with vertu; and hath set my weie vnwemmed. Which made
perfit my feet as of hertis; and ordeynynge me on hiȝe
35 thingis. Which techith myn hondis to batel; and thou hast
36 set myn armys as a brasun bouwe. And thou hast ȝoue to
me the kyueryng of thin helthe; and thi riȝthond hath vptake
me. And thi chastisyng amendide me in to the ende; and
37 thilke chastisyng of thee schal teche me. Thou alargidist
my paaces vndur me; and my steppis ben not maad vnstide-
38 fast. Y schal pursue myn enemyes, and Y schal take hem;
39 and Y schal not turne til thei failen. I schal al to-breke hem,
and thei schulen not mowe stonde; thei schulen falle vndur
40 my feet. And thou hast gird me with vertu to batel; and
thou hast supplauntid, *ether disseyued*, vndur me men risynge
41 aȝens me. And thou hast ȝoue myn enemyes abac to me;
42 and thou hast distried men hatynge me. Thei crieden, and
noon was that maad hem saaf; *thei crieden* to the Lord, and
43 he herde not hem. And Y schal al to-breke hem, as dust
bifor the face of wynd; Y schal do hem awei, as the cley of

⁴⁴ stretis. Thou schalt delyuere me fro aȝenseiyngis of the
⁴⁵ puple; thou schalt sette me in to the heed of folkis. The
puple, which Y knewe not, seruede me; in the herynge of
⁴⁶ eere it obeiede to me. Alien sones lieden to me, alien sones
⁴⁷ wexiden elde; and crokiden fro thi pathis. The Lord lyueth,
and my God *be* blessid; and the God of myn helthe be
⁴⁸ enhaunsid. God, that ȝauest veniaunces to me, and makist
suget puplis vndur me; my delyuerere fro my wrathful
⁴⁹ enemyes. And thou schalt enhaunse me fro hem, that risen
⁵⁰ aȝens me; thou schalt delyuere me fro a wickid man. Therfor, Lord, Y schal knouleche to thee among naciouns; and
⁵¹ Y schal seie salm to thi name. Magnyfiynge the helthis of
his kyng; and doynge merci to his crist Dauid, and to his
seed til in to the world.

Psalm XVIII (XIX).

¹ *The title of the eiȝtenthe salm. To victorie, the salm of Dauid.*

² Heuenes tellen out the glorie of God; and the firmament
³ tellith the werkis of hise hondis. The dai tellith out to the
dai a word; and the nyȝt schewith kunnyng to the nyȝt.
⁴ No langagis ben, nether wordis; of whiche the voices of hem
⁵ ben not herd. The soun of hem ȝede out in to al erthe; and
⁶ the wordis of hem *ȝeden out* in to the endis of the world. In
the sunne he hath set his tabernacle; and he as a spouse
comynge forth of his chaumbre. He fulli ioyede, as a giaunt,
⁷ to renne his weie; his goynge out was fro hiȝeste heuene.
And his goyng aȝen was to the hiȝeste therof; and noon is
⁸ that hidith hym silf fro his heet. The lawe of the Lord is
with out wem, and conuertith soulis; the witnessyng of the
⁹ Lord is feithful, and ȝyueth wisdom to litle children. The
riȝtfulnessis of the Lord *ben* riȝtful, gladdynge hertis; the
¹⁰ comaundement of the Lord *is* cleere, liȝtnynge iȝen. The

hooli drede of the Lord dwellith in to world of world; the
11 domes of the Lord ben trewe, iustified in to hem silf. Desirable more than gold, and a stoon myche preciouse; and
12 swettere than hony and honycoomb. Forwhi thi seruaunt
13 kepith thoo; myche ʒeldyng is in tho to be kept. Who
vndurstondith trespassis? make thou me cleene fro my priuy
14 *synnes;* and of alien *synnes* spare thi seruaunt. If the *forseid
defautis* ben not, Lord, of me, than Y schal be with out wem;
15 and Y schal be clensid of the mooste synne. And the spechis
of my mouth schulen be, that tho plese; and the thenkynge
of myn herte euere in thi siʒt. Lord, myn helpere; and myn
aʒenbiere.

Psalm XIX (XX).

1 *The title of the nyntenthe salm. To victorie,
the salm of Dauid.*

2 The Lord here thee in the dai of tribulacioun; the name
3 of God of Jacob defende thee. Sende he helpe to thee fro the
4 hooli *place;* and fro Syon defende he thee. Be he myndeful of al thi sacrifice; and thi brent sacrifice be maad fat.
5 ʒyue he to thee aftir thin herte; and conferme he al thi
6 counsel. We schulen be glad in thin helthe; and we schulen
7 be magnyfied in the name of oure God. The Lord fille
alle thin axyngis; nowe Y haue knowe, that the Lord hath
maad saaf his crist. He schal here hym fro his hooly
8 heuene; the helthe of his riʒt hond *is* in poweris. Thes in
charis, and these in horsis; but we schulen inwardli clepe
9 in the name of oure Lord God. Thei ben boundun, and
10 felden doun; but we han rise, and ben reisid. Lord, make
thou saaf the kyng; and here thou vs in the dai in which
we inwardli clepen thee.

Psalm XX (XXI).

1 *The title of the twentithe salm. To victorie, the salm of Dauid.*

2 Lord, the kyng schal be glad in thi vertu; and he schal
3 ful out haue ioye greetli on thin helthe. Thou hast 3oue to
hym the desire of his herte; and thou hast not defraudid
4 hym of the wille of hise lippis. For thou hast bifor come
hym in the blessyngis of swetnesse; thou hast set on his
5 heed a coroun of preciouse stoon. He axide of thee lijf,
and thou 3auest to hym; the lengthe of daies in to the world,
6 and in to the world of world. His glorie is greet in thin
helthe; thou schalt putte glorie, and greet fayrnesse on hym.
7 For thou schalt 3yue hym in to blessing in to the world of
world; thou schalt make hym glad in ioye with thi cheer.
8 For the kyng hopith in the Lord; and in the merci of the
9 hi3este he schal not be moued. Thyn hond be foundun to
alle thin enemyes; thi ri3thond fynde alle hem that haten
10 thee. Thou schalt putte hem as a furneis of fier in the
tyme of thi cheer; the Lord schal disturble hem in his ire,
11 and fier schal deuoure hem. Thou schalt leese the fruyt of
hem fro erthe; and *thou schalt leese* the seed of hem fro the
12 sones of men. For thei bowiden yuels a3ens thee; thei
13 thou3ten counseils, whiche thei my3ten not stablische. For
thou schalt putte hem abac; in thi relifs thou schalt make
14 redi the cheer of hem. Lord, be thou enhaunsid in thi vertu;
we schulen synge, and scie opinly thi vertues.

Psalm XXI (XXII).

1 *The title of the oon and twentithe salm. To ouercome, for the morewtid hynd; the salm of Dauid.*

2 God, my God, biholde thou on me, whi hast thou forsake
me? the wordis of my trespassis *ben* fer fro myn helthe.

3 Mi God, Y schal crye bi dai, and thou schalt not here; and
4 bi nyʒt, and not to vnwisdom to me. Forsothe thou, the
5 preisyng of Israel, dwellist in holynesse; oure fadris hopiden
6 in thee, thei hopiden, and thou delyueridist hem. Thei
crieden to thee, and thei weren maad saaf; thei hopiden
7 in thee, and thei weren not schent. But Y am a worm,
and not man; the schenschip of men, and the outcastyng
8 of the puple. Alle men seynge me scorneden me; thei
9 spaken with lippis, and stiriden the heed. He hopide in
the Lord, delyuere he hym; make he hym saaf, for he wole
10 hym. For thou it art that drowist me out of the wombe,
11 *thou art* myn hope fro the tetis of my modir; in to thee Y
am cast forth fro the wombe. Fro the wombe of my modir
12 thou art my God; departe thou not fro me. For tribu-
13 lacioun is next; for noon is that helpith. Many calues
14 cumpassiden me; fatte bolis bisegiden me. Thei openyden
her mouth on me; as *doith* a lioun rauyschynge and rorynge.
15 I am sched out as watir; and alle my boonys ben scaterid.
Myn herte is maad, as wex fletynge abrood; in the myddis
16 of my wombe. Mi vertu driede as a tiyl-stoon, and my
tunge cleuede to my chekis; and thou hast brouʒt forth me
17 in to the dust of deth. For many doggis cumpassiden me;
the counsel of wickid men bisegide me. Thei delueden
18 myn hondis and my feet; thei noumbriden alle my boonys.
19 Sotheli thei lokiden, and bihelden me; thei departiden my
20 clothis to hem silf, and thei senten lot on my cloth. But
thou, Lord, delaie not thin help fro me; biholde thou to
21 my defence. God, delyuere thou my lijf fro swerd; and
delyuere thou myn oon aloone fro the hond of the dogge.
22 Make thou me saaf fro the mouth of a lioun; and my meke-
23 nesse fro the hornes of vnycornes. I schal telle thi name
to my britheren; Y schal preise thee in the myddis of the
24 chirche. ʒe that dreden the Lord, herie hym; alle the

²⁵ seed of Jacob, glorifie ȝe hym. Al the seed of Israel drede hym; for he forsook not, nethir dispiside the preier of a pore man. Nethir he turnede awei his face fro me; and whanne ²⁶ Y criede to hym, he herde me. Mi preisyng is at thee in a greet chirche; Y schal ȝelde my vowis in the siȝt of men ²⁷ dredynge hym. Pore men schulen ete, and schulen be fillid, and thei schulen herie the Lord, that seken hym; the ²⁸ hertis of hem schulen lyue in to the world of world. Alle the endis of erthe schulen bithenke; and schulen be conuertid to the Lord. And alle the meynees of hethene men; ²⁹ schulen worschipe in his siȝt. For the rewme is the Lordis; ³⁰ and he schal be Lord of hethene men. Alle the fatte men of erthe eeten and worschipiden; alle men, that goen doun ³¹ in to erthe, schulen falle doun in his siȝt. And my soule ³² schal lyue to hym; and my seed schal serue him. A generacioun to comyng schal be teld to the Lord; and heuenes schulen telle his riȝtfulnesse to the puple that schal be borun, whom the Lord made.

Psalm XXII (XXIII).

¹ *The title of the two and twentithe salm. The salm, ether the song of Dauid.*

The Lord gouerneth me, and no thing schal faile to me: ² in the place of pasture there he hath set me. He nurschide ³ me on the watir of refreischyng; he conuertide my soule. He ledde me forth on the pathis of riȝtfulnesse; for his ⁴ name. For whi thouȝ Y schal go in the myddis of schadewe of deeth; Y schal not drede yuels, for thou art with me. ⁵ Thi ȝerde and thi staf; tho han coumfortid me. Thou hast maad redi a boord in my siȝt; aȝens hem that troblen me. Thou hast maad fat myn heed with oyle; and my cuppe, ⁶ fillinge greetli, is ful cleer. And thi merci schal sue me;

in alle the daies of my lijf. And that Y dwelle in the hows of the Lord; in to the lengthe of daies.

Psalm XXIII (XXIV).

1 *The title of the thre and twentithe salm. The song of Dauid.*

The erthe and the fulnesse therof is the Lordis; the 2 world, and alle that dwellen therynne *is the Lordis*. For he 3 foundide it on the sees; and made it redi on floodis. Who schal stie in to the hil of the Lord; ethir who schal stonde 4 in the hooli place of hym? The innocent in hondis, and in cleene herte; whiche took not his soule in veyn, nether 5 swoor in gile to his neiȝbore. This man schal take blessyng 6 of the Lord; and mercy of God his helthe. This is the generacioun of men sekynge hym; of men sekynge the 7 face of God of Jacob. Ȝe princes, take vp ȝoure ȝatis, and ȝe euerelastynge ȝatis, be reisid; and the kyng of glorie 8 schal entre. Who is this kyng of glorie? the Lord strong 9 and myȝti, the Lord myȝti in batel. Ȝe princes, take vp ȝoure ȝatis, and ȝe euerlastynge ȝatis, be reisid; and the 10 kyng of glorie schal entre. Who is this kyng of glorie? the Lord of vertues, he is the kyng of glorie.

Psalm XXIV (XXV).

1 *The title of the foure and twentithe salm. To Dauid.*

2 Lord, to thee Y haue reisid my soule; my God, Y truste 3 in thee, be Y not aschamed. Nethir myn enemyes scorne me; for alle men that suffren thee schulen not be schent. 4 Alle men doynge wickyd thingis superfluli; be schent. Lord, schewe thou thi weies to me; and teche thou me 5 thi pathis. Dresse thou me in thi treuthe, and teche thou me, for thou art God my sauyour; and Y suffride thee al

6 dai. Lord, haue thou mynde of thi merciful doyngis; and
7 of thi mercies that ben fro the world. Haue thou not mynde
on the trespassis of my ӡongthe; and on myn vnkunnyngis.
Thou, Lord, haue mynde on me bi thi merci; for thi good-
8 nesse. The Lord *is* swete and riӡtful; for this he schal
9 ӡyue a lawe to men trespassynge in the weie. He schal
dresse deboner men in doom; he schal teche mylde men
10 hise weies. Alle the weies of the Lord ben mercy and
treuthe; to men sekynge his testament, and hise witness-
11 yngis. Lord, for thi name thou schalt do merci to my
12 synne; for it is myche. Who is a man, that dredith the
Lord? he ordeyneth to hym a lawe in the weie which he
13 chees. His soule schal dwelle in goodis; and his seed
14 schal enerite the lond. The Lord is a sadnesse to
men dredynge hym; and his testament is, that it be
15 schewid to hem. Myn iӡen *ben* euere to the Lord; for he
16 schal breide awey my feet fro the snare. Biholde thou on
me, and haue thou mercy on me; for Y am oon aloone
17 and pore. The tribulaciouns of myn herte ben multiplied;
18 delyuere thou me of my nedis. Se thou my mekenesse
19 and my trauel; and forӡyue thou alle my trespassis. Bihold
thou myn enemyes, for thei ben multiplied; and thei haten
20 me bi wickid hatrede. Kepe thou my soule, and delyuere
21 thou me; be Y not aschamed, for Y hopide in thee. Innocent men and riӡtful cleuyden to me; for Y suffride thee.
22 God, delyuere thou Israel; fro alle hise tribulaciouns.

PSALM XXV (XXVI).

1 *The title of the fyue and twentithe salm. To Dauid.*

Lord, deme thou me, for Y entride in myn innocens;
and Y hopynge in the Lord schal not be made vnstidfast.
2 Lord, preue thou me, and asaie me; brenne thou my reynes,

3 and myn herte. For whi thi merci is bifor myn i3en; and
4 Y pleside in thi treuthe. I sat not with the counsel of
vanyte; and Y schal not entre with men doynge wickid
5 thingis. I hatide the chirche of yuele men; and Y schal
6 not sitte with wickid men. I schal waische myn hondis
among innocentis; and, Lord, Y schal cumpasse thin auter.
7 That Y here the vois of heriyng; and that Y telle out alle
8 thi merueils. Lord, Y haue loued the fairnesse of thin hows;
9 and the place of the dwellyng of thi glorie. God, leese thou
not my soule with vnfeithful men; and my lijf with men of
10 bloodis. In whose hondis wyckidnessis ben; the ri3thond
11 of hem is fillid with 3iftis. But Y entride in myn innocens;
12 a3enbie thou me, and haue merci on me. Mi foot stood in
ri3tfulnesse; Lord, Y schal blesse thee in chirchis.

Psalm XXVI (XXVII).

1   *The title of the sixe and twentithe salm. To Dauid.*

THE Lord *is* my li3tnyng, and myn helthe; whom schal
Y drede? The Lord *is* defendere of my lijf; for whom schal
2 Y tremble? The while noiful men nei3en on me; for to ete
my fleischis. Myn enemyes, that trobliden me; thei weren
3 maad sijk and felden doun. Thou3 castels stonden togidere
a3ens me; myn herte schal not drede. Thou3 batel risith
4 a3ens me; in this thing Y schal haue hope. I axide of the
Lord o thing; Y schal seke this thing; that Y dwelle in
the hows of the Lord alle the daies of my lijf. That Y se
5 the wille of the Lord; and that Y visite his temple. For he
hidde me in his tabernacle in the dai of yuelis; he defendide
6 me in the hid place of his tabernacle. He enhaunside me
in a stoon; and now he enhaunside myn heed ouer myn
enemyes. I cumpasside, and offride in his tabernacle a
sacrifice of criyng; Y schal synge, and Y schal seie salm

7 to the Lord. Lord, here thou my vois, bi which Y criede
8 to thee; haue thou merci on me, and here me. Myn herte
seide to thee, My face souȝte thee; Lord, Y schal seke eft
9 thi face. Turne thou not awei thi face fro me; bouwe thou
not awei in ire fro thi seruaunt. Lord, be thou myn helpere,
forsake thou not me; and, God, myn helthe, dispise thou
10 not me. For my fadir and my modir han forsake me; but
11 the Lord hath take me. Lord, sette thou a lawe to me in
thi weie; and dresse thou me in thi path for myn enemyes.
12 Bitake thou not me in to the soules of hem, that troblen
me; for wickid witnessis han rise aȝens me, and wickyd-
13 nesse liede to it silf. I bileue to see the goodis of the
14 Lord; in the lond of hem that lyuen. Abide thou the
Lord, do thou manli; and thin herte be coumfortid, and
suffre thou the Lord.

Psalm XXVII (XXVIII).

1   *The title of the seuen and twentithe salm. To Dauid.*

Lord, Y schal crye to thee; my God, be thou not stille
fro me, be thou not stille ony tyme fro me; and Y schal
2 be maad lijk to hem, that goen doun in to the lake. Lord,
here thou the vois of my bisechyng, while Y preie to thee;
3 whyle Y reise myn hondis to thin hooli temple. Bitake thou
not me togidere with synneris; and leese thou not me with
hem that worchen wickidnesse. Whyche spoken pees with
4 her neiȝbore; but yuels *ben* in her hertis. Ȝyue thou to
hem vpe the werkis of hem; and vpe the wickidnesse of
her fyndyngis. Ȝyue thou to hem vpe the werkis of her
5 hondis; ȝelde thou her ȝeldyng to hem. For thei vndurstoden not the werkis of the Lord, and bi the werkis of hise
hondis thou schalt destrie hem; and thou schalt not bilde
6 hem. Blissid *be* the Lord; for he herde the vois of my

7 bisechyng. The Lord *is* myn helpere and my defendere;
and myn herte hopide in hym, and Y am helpid. And my
fleisch flouride aȝen; and of my wille Y schal knowleche
8 to hym. The Lord *is* the strengthe of his puple; and he
9 is defendere of the sauyngis of his crist. Lord, make thou
saaf thi puple, and bless thou thin eritage; and reule thou
hem, and enhaunse thou hem til in to with outen ende.

Psalm XXVIII (XXIX).

1 *The title of the eiȝt and twentithe salm. The salm,
ethir song of Dauid.*

ȜE sones of God, brynge to the Lord; brynge ȝe to the
2 Lord the sones of rammes. Brynge ȝe to the Lord glorie
and onour; brynge ȝe to the Lord glorie to his name;
3 herie ȝe the Lord in his hooli large place. The vois of
the Lord on watris, God of mageste thundride; the Lord
4 on many watris. The vois of the Lord in vertu; the vois
5 of the Lord in greet doyng. The vois of the Lord brekynge
cedris; and the Lord schal breke the cedris of the Liban.
6 And he schal al to-breke hem to dust as a calf of the Liban;
7 and the derling *was* as the sone of an vnycorn. The vois
8 of the Lord departynge the flawme of fier; the vois of the
Lord schakynge desert; and the Lord schal stire togidere
9 the desert of Cades. The vois of the Lord makynge redi
hertis, and he schal schewe thicke thingis; and in his temple
10 alle men schulen seie glorie. The Lord makith to enhabite
the greet flood; and the Lord schal sitte kyng with outen
11 ende. The Lord schal ȝyue vertu to his puple; the Lord
schal blesse his puple in pees.

Psalm XXIX (XXX).

1 *The title of the nyne and twentithe salm. The salm of song, for the halewyng of the hows of Dauid.*

2 Lord, Y schal enhaunse thee, for thou hast vp take me;
3 and thou delitidist not myn enemyes on me. Mi Lord God,
4 Y criede to thee; and thou madist me hool. Lord, thou leddist out my soule fro helle; thou sauedist me fro hem
5 that goen doun into the lake. ʒe seyntis of the Lord, synge to the Lord; and knowleche ʒe to the mynde of his hooly-
6 nesse. For ire *is* in his indignacioun; and lijf *is* in his wille. Wepyng schal dwelle at euentid; and gladnesse at
7 the morewtid. Forsothe Y seide in my plentee; Y schal
8 not be moued with outen ende. Lord, in thi wille; thou hast ʒoue vertu to my fairnesse. Thou turnedist awei thi
9 face fro me; and Y am maad disturblid. Lord, Y schal
10 crye to thee; and Y schal preye to my God. What profit *is* in my blood; while Y go doun in to corrupcioun? Whether dust schal knouleche to thee; ethir schal telle
11 thi treuthe? The Lord herde, and hadde merci on me;
12 the Lord is maad myn helpere. Thou hast turned my weilyng in to ioye to me; thou hast to-rent my sak, and
13 hast cumpassid me with gladnesse. That my glorie synge to thee, and Y be not compunct; my Lord God, Y schal knouleche to thee with outen ende.

Psalm XXX (XXXI).

1 *The title of the thrittithe salm. To victorie, the salm of Dauid.*

2 Lord, Y hopide in thee, be Y not schent with outen ende;
3 delyuere thou me in thi riʒtfulnesse. Bouwe doun thin eere

to me; haaste thou to delyuere me. Be thou to me in to
God defendere, and in to an hows of refuyt; that thou
4 make me saaf. For thou art my strengthe and my refuyt;
and for thi name thou schalt lede me forth, and schalt
5 nurische me. Thou schalt lede me out of the snare, which
6 thei hidden to me; for thou art my defendere. I bitake my
spirit in to thin hondis; Lord God of treuthe, thou hast
7 aȝen-bouȝt me. Thou hatist hem that kepen vanytees super-
8 fluli. Forsothe Y hopide in the Lord; Y schal haue fulli
ioie, and schal be glad in thi merci. For thou byheldist
9 my mekenesse; thou sauedist my lijf fro nedis. And thou
closidist not me togidere withynne the hondis of the enemy;
10 thou hast sett my feet in a large place. Lord, haue thou
merci on me, for Y am troblid; myn iȝe is troblid in ire,
11 my soule and my wombe *ben troblid*. For whi my lijf failide
in sorewe; and my ȝeeris in weilynges. Mi vertu is maad
12 feble in pouert; and my boonys ben disturblid. Ouer alle
myn enemyes Y am maad schenship greetli to my neiȝboris;
and drede to my knowun. Thei that sien me with-outforth,
13 fledden fro me; Y am ȝouun to forȝetyng, as a deed man
14 fro herte. I am maad as a lorun vessel; for Y herde dispisyng of many men dwellynge in cumpas. In that thing
the while thei camen togidere aȝens me; thei counceliden
15 to take my lijf. But, Lord, Y hopide in thee; Y seide,
16 Thou art my God; my tymes *ben* in thin hondis. Delyuer
thou me fro the hondis of mynen enemyes; and fro hem
17 that pursuen me. Make thou cleer thi face on thi seruaunt;
18 Lord, make thou me saaf in thi merci; be Y not schent,
for Y inwardli clepide thee. Unpitouse men be aschamed,
19 and be led forth in to helle; gileful lippys be maad doumbe.
That speken wickidnesse aȝens a iust man; in pride, and
20 in mysusyng. Lord, the multitude of thi swetnesse *is* ful
greet; which thou hast hid to men dredynge thee. Thou

hast maad a perfit thing to hem, that hopen in thee;_ in
21 the si3t of the sones of men. Thou schalt hide hem in
the priuyte of thi face; fro disturblyng of men. Thou
schalt defende hem in thi tabernacle; fro a3ensciyng of
22 tungis. Blessid *be* the Lord; for he hath maad wondur-
23 ful his merci to me in a strengthid citee. Forsothe Y
seide in the passyng of my soule; Y am cast out fro the
face of thin i3en. Therfor thou herdist the vois of my
24 preier; while Y criede to thee. Alle 3e hooli men of the
Lord, loue hym; for the Lord schal seke treuthe, and he
25 schal 3elde plenteuousli to hem that doen pride. Alle 3e
that hopen in the Lord, do manli; and 3oure herte be
coumfortid.

PSALM XXXI (XXXII).

The title of the oon and thrittithe salm. Lernyng to Dauid.

1 BLESSID *ben* thei, whose wickidnessis ben for3ouun; and
2 whose synnes ben hilid. Blessid *is* the man, to whom the
3 Lord arrettide not synne; nethir gile is in his spirit. For
Y was stille, my boonys wexiden elde; while Y criede al
4 dai. For bi dai and ny3t thin hond was maad greuouse
on me; Y am turned in my wretchednesse, while the thorn
5 is set in. I made my synne knowun to thee; and Y hidde
not my vnri3tfulnesse. I seide, Y schal knouleche a3ens
me myn vnri3tfulnesse to the Lord; and thou hast for3oue
6 the wickidnesse of my synne. For this thing ech hooli
man schal preye to thee; in couenable tyme. Netheles in
the greet flood of many watris; tho schulen not nei3e to
7 thee. Thou art my refuyt fro tribulacioun, that cumpasside me; thou, my fulli ioiyng, delyuere me fro hem that
8 cumpassen me. Y schal 3yue vnderstondyng to thee, and
Y schal teche thee; in this weie in which thou schalt
9 go, Y schal make stidefast myn i3en on thee. Nile 3e be

maad as an hors and mule; to whiche is noon vndurstondyng. Lord, constreyne thou the chekis of hem with a ber-
10 nacle and bridil; that nei3en not to thee. Many betyngis
ben of the synnere; but merci schal cumpasse hym that
11 hopith in the Lord. 3e iust men, be glad, and make fulli
ioie in the Lord; and alle 3e ri3tful of herte, haue glorie.

Psalm XXXII (XXXIII).

The two and threttithe salm hath no title.

1 3E iust men, haue fulli ioye in the Lord; presyng togi-
2 dere bicometh ri3tful men. Knouleche 3e to the Lord in
an harpe; synge 3e to hym in a sautre of ten strengis.
3 Synge 3e to hym a newe song; seie 3e wel salm to hym
4 in criyng. For the word of the Lord is ri3tful; and alle
5 hise werkis *ben* in feithfulnesse. He loueth merci and
6 doom; the erthe is ful of the merci of the Lord. Heuenes
ben maad stidfast bi the word of the Lord; and al the
7 vertu of tho bi the spirit of his mouth. And he gaderith
togidere the watris of the see as in a bowge; and settith
8 depe watris in tresours. Al erthe drede the Lord; sotheli
9 alle men enhabitynge the world ben mouyd of hym. For
he seide, and thingis weren maad; he comaundide, and
10 thingis weren maad of nou3t. The Lord distrieth the counsels of folkis, forsothe he repreueth the thou3tis of puplis;
11 and he repreueth the counsels of prynces. But the counsel
of the Lord dwellith with outen ende; the thou3tis of his
12 herte *dwellen* in generacioun and into generacioun. Blessid
is the folk, whose Lord is his God; the puple which he
13 chees into eritage to hym silf. The Lord bihelde fro heuene;
14 he si3 alle the sones of men. Fro his dwellyng place maad
redi bifor; he bihelde on alle men, that enhabiten the erthe.
15 Which made syngulerli the soules of hem; which vndur-

16 stondith all the werkis of hem. A kyng is not sauyd bi myche vertu; and a giaunt schal not be sauyd in the mychil-
17 nesse of his vertu. An hors *is* false to helthe; forsothe he schal not be sauyd in the habundaunce, *ether plentee,* of
18 his vertu. Lo! the iȝen of the Lord *ben* on men dredynge
19 hym; and in hem that hopen on his merci. That he de-
20 lyuere her soules fro deth; and feede hem in hungur. Oure soule suffreth the Lord; for he is oure helpere and de-
21 fendere. For oure herte schal be glad in him; and we
22 schulen haue hope in his hooli name. Lord, thi merci be maad on vs; as we hopiden in thee.

Psalm XXXIII (XXXIV).

1 *The title of the thre and thrittithe salm. To Dauid, whanne he chaungide his mouth bifor Abymalech, and he droof out Dauid, and he ȝede forth.*

2 I schal blesse the Lord in al tyme; euere his heriyng
3 *is* in my mouth. Mi soule schal be preisid in the Lord;
4 mylde men here, and be glad. Magnyfie ȝe the Lord with
5 me; and enhaunse we his name into it silf. I souȝte the Lord, and he herde me; and he delyueride me fro alle
6 my tribulaciouns. Neiȝe ȝe to him, and be ȝe liȝtned; and
7 ȝoure faces schulen not be schent. This pore man criede, and the Lord herde hym; and sauyde hym fro alle hise
8 tribulaciouns. The aungel of the Lord sendith in the cumpas of men dredynge hym; and he schal delyuere hem.
9 Taaste ȝe, and se, for the Lord is swete; blessid *is* the
10 man, that hopith in hym. Alle ȝe hooli men of the Lord, drede hym; for no nedynesse is to men dredynge hym.
11 Riche men weren nedi, and weren hungri; but men that
12 seken the Lord schulen not faile of al good. Come, ȝe sones, here ȝe me; Y schal teche ȝou the drede of the

13 Lord. Who is a man, that wole lijf; loueth to se good
14 daies? Forbede thi tunge fro yuel; and thi lippis speke
15 not gile. Turne thou awei fro yuel, and do good; seke
16 thou pees, and perfitli sue thou it. The iȝen of the Lord
17 *ben* on iust men; and hise eeren *ben* to her preiers. But
the cheer of the Lord *is* on men doynge yuels; that he
18 leese the mynde of hem fro erthe. Just men cryeden, and
the Lord herde hem; and delyueride hem fro alle her tri-
19 bulaciouns. The Lord is nyȝ hem that ben of troblid herte;
20 and he schal saue meke men in spirit. Many tribulaciouns
ben of iust men; and the Lord schal delyuere hem fro alle
21 these. The Lord kepith alle the boonys of hem; oon of
22 tho schal not be brokun. The deth of synneris *is* werst;
23 and thei that haten a iust man schulen trespasse. The
Lord schal aȝenbie the soulis of hise seruauntis; and alle,
that hopen in him, schulen not trespasse.

Psalm XXXIV (XXXV).

1 *The title of the foure and thrittithe salm. To Dauid.*

Lord, deme thou hem, that anoien me; ouercome thou
2 hem, that fiȝten aȝens me. Take thou armeris and scheeld;
3 and rise vp into help to me. Schede out the swerd, and
close togidere aȝens hem that pursuen me; seie thou to my
4 soule, Y am thin helthe. Thei that seken my lijf; be schent,
and aschamed. Thei that thenken yuels to me; be turned
5 awei bacward, and be schent. Be thei maad as dust bifor
the face of the wynd.; and the aungel of the Lord make hem
6 streit. Her weie be maad derknesse, and slydirnesse; and
7 the aungel of the Lord pursue hem. For with out cause thei
hidden to me the deth of her snare; in veyn thei dispisiden
8 my soule. The snare which he knoweth not come to hym,
and the takyng which he hidde take hym; and fall he in to

9 the snare in that thing. But my soule schal fulli haue ioye in
10 the Lord ; and schal delite on his helthe. Alle my boonys
schulen seie, Lord, who is lijk thee ? Thou delyuerist a pore
man fro the hond of his strengere ; a nedi man and pore fro
11 hem that diuersely rauischen hym. Wickid witnessis risynge
12 axiden me thingis, whiche Y knewe not. Thei ȝeldiden to
13 me yuels for goodis; bareynnesse to my soule. But whanne
thei weren diseseful to me; Y was clothid in an heire. I
mekide my soule in fastyng; and my preier schal be turned
14 with ynne my bosum. I pleside so as oure neiȝbore, as oure
brother ; Y was maad meke so as morenynge and sorewful.
15 And thei weren glad, and camen togidere aȝens me ; tur-
16 mentis weren gaderid on me, and Y knew not. Thei weren
scaterid, and not compunct, thei temptiden me, thei scorny-
den me with mowyng ; thei gnastiden on me with her teeth.
17 Lord, whanne thou schalt biholde, restore thou my soule fro
the wickidnesse of hem ; *restore thou* myn oon aloone fro
18 liouns. I schal knowleche to thee in a greet chirche ; Y
19 schal herie thee in a sad puple. Thei that ben aduersaries
wickidli to me, haue not ioye on me; that haten me with out
20 cause, and bikenen with iȝen. For sotheli thei spaken pesibli
to me ; and thei spekynge in wrathfulnesse of erthe thouȝten
21 giles. And thei maden large her mouth on me ; thei seiden,
22 Wel, wel! oure iȝen han sien. Lord, thou hast seen, be thou
23 not stille ; Lord, departe thou not fro me. Rise vp, and
ȝyue tent to my doom ; my God and my Lord, *biholde* in to
24 my cause. Mi Lord God, deme thou me bi thi riȝtfulnesse;
25 and haue thei not ioye on me. Seie thei not in her hertis,
Wel, wel, to oure soule ; nether seie thei, We schulen deuoure
26 hym. Shame thei, and drede thei togidere ; that thanken for
myn yuels. Be thei clothid with schame and drede ; that
27 speken yuele thingis on me. Haue thei ful ioie, and be thei
glad that wolen my riȝtfulnesse ; and seie thei euere, The

Lord be magnyfied, whiche wolen the pees of his seruaunt.
28 And my tunge schal bithenke thi riȝtfulnesse; al day thin heriyng.

Psalm XXXV (XXXVI).

1 *The title of the fyue and thrittithe salm. To victorie, to Dauid, the seruaunt of the Lord.*

2 The vniust man seide, that he trespasse in hym silf; the
3 drede of God is not bifor hise iȝen. For he dide gilefuli in the siȝt of God; that his wickidnesse be foundun to hatrede.
4 The wordis of his mouth *ben* wickidnesse and gile, he nolde
5 vndirstonde to do wel. He thouȝte wickidnesse in his bed, he stood nyȝ al weie not good; forsothe he hatide not malice.
6 Lord, thi merci *is* in heuene; and thi treuthe *is* til to cloudis.
7 Thi riȝtfulnesse *is* as the hillis of God; thi domes *ben* myche depthe of watris. Lord, thou schalt saue men and beestis;
8 as thou, God, hast multiplied thi merci. But the sones of
9 men; schulen hope in the hilyng of thi wyngis. Thei schulen be fillid gretli of the plentee of thin hows; and thou schalt
10 ȝyue drynke to hem with the steef streem of thi likyng. For the wel of life is at thee; and in thi liȝt we schulen se liȝt.
11 Lord, sette forth thi mercy to hem, that knowen thee; and
12 thi ryȝtfulnesse to hem that ben of riȝtful herte. The foot of pryde come not to me; and the hond of the synnere moue
13 me not. There thei felden doun, that worchen wickidnesse; thei ben cast out, and myȝten not stonde.

Psalm XXXVI (XXXVII).

1 *The title of the sixe and thrittithe salm. To Dauith.*

Nile thou sue wickid men; nether loue thou men doynge
2 wickidnesse. For thei schulen wexe drie swiftli as hey; and
3 thei schulen falle doun soone as the wortis of eerbis. Hope

thou in the Lord, and do thou goodnesse; and enhabite thou
4 the lond, and thou schalt be fed with hise richessis. Delite
thou in the Lord; and he schal ȝyue to thee the axyngis of
5 thin herte. Schewe thi weie to the Lord; and hope thou in
6 hym, and he schal do. And he schal lede out thi riȝtfulnesse
7 as liȝt, and thi doom as myddai; be thou suget to the Lord,
and preye thou hym. Nile thou sue hym, that hath prosperite
8 in his weie; a man doynge vnriȝtfulnessis. Ceese thou of
ire, and forsake woodnesse; nyle thou sue, that thou do
9 wickidli. For thei, that doen wickidli, schulen be distried;
10 but thei that suffren the Lord, schulen enerite the lond. And
ȝit a litil, and a synnere schal not be; and thou schalt seke
11 his place, and schalt not fynde. But mylde men schulen
enerite the lond; and schulen delite in the multitude of pees.
12 A synnere schal aspie a riȝtful man; and he schal gnaste
13 with hise teeth on hym. But the Lord schal scorne the
14 synnere; for he biholdith that his day cometh. Synners
drowen out swerd; thei benten her bouwe. To disseyue a
15 pore man and nedi; to strangle riȝtful men of herte. Her
swerd entre in to the herte of hem silf; and her bouwe be
16 brokun. Betere is a litil thing to a iust man; than many
17 richessis of synneris. For the armes of synneris schal be al
18 to-brokun; but the Lord confermeth iust men. The Lord
knowith the daies of vnwemmed; and her heritage schal be
19 withouten ende. Thei schulen not be schent in the yuel
20 tyme, and thei schulen be fillid in the dayes of hungur; for
synneris schulen perische. Forsothe anoon as the enemyes
of the Lord ben onourid, and enhaunsid; thei failynge schulen
21 faile as smoke. A synnere schal borewe, and schal not paie;
22 but a iust man hath merci, and schal ȝyue. For thei that
blessen the Lord schulen enerite the lond; but thei that
23 cursen hym schulen perische. The goyng of a man schal
be dressid anentis the Lord; and he schal wilne his weie.

24 Whanne he fallith, he schal not be hurtlid doun; for the
25 Lord vndursettith his hond. I was ȝongere, and sotheli Y
wexide eld, and Y siȝ not a iust man forsakun; nethir his
26 seed sekynge breed. Al dai he hath merci, and leeneth; and
27 his seed schal be in blessyng. Bouwe thou awei fro yuel,
and do good; and dwelle thou in to the world of world.
28 For the Lord loueth doom, and schal not forsake hise seyntis;
thei schulen be kept with outen ende. Vniust men schulen
be punyschid; and the seed of wickid men schal perische.
29 But iust men schulen enerite the lond; and schulen enabite
30 theronne in to the world of world. The mouth of a iust man
schal bithenke wisdom; and his tunge schal speke doom.
31 The lawe of his God *is* in his herte; and hise steppis schulen
32 not be disseyued. A synnere biholdith a iust man; and
33 sekith to sle hym. But the Lord schal not forsake hym in
hise hondis; nethir schal dampne hym, whanne it schal be
34 demed aȝens hym. Abide thou the Lord, and kepe thou his
weie, and he schal enhaunse thee, that bi eritage thou take
the lond; whanne synneris schulen perische, thou schalt se.
35 I siȝ a wickid man enhaunsid aboue; and reisid vp as the
36 cedris of Liban. And Y passide, and lo! he was not; Y
37 souȝte hym, and his place is not foundun. Kepe thou innocence, and se equite; for tho ben relikis to a pesible man.
38 Forsothe vniust men schulen perische; the relifs of wickid
39 men schulen perische togidere. But the helthe of iust men is
of the Lord; and he is her defendere in the tyme of tribula-
40 cioun. And the Lord schal helpe hem, and schal make hem
fre, and he schal delyuere hem fro synneris; and he schal
saue hem, for thei hopiden in hym.

Psalm XXXVII (XXXVIII).

1 *The title of the seuene and thrittithe salm. The salm of Dauid, to bythenke on the sabat.*

2 Lord, repreue thou not me in thi strong veniaunce; nether
3 chastice thou me in thin ire. For thin arowis ben fitchid in
4 me; and thou hast confermed thin hond on me. Noon helthe is in my fleisch fro the face of thin ire; no pees is to
5 my boonys fro the face of my synnes. For my wickidnessis ben goon ouer myn heed; as an heuy birthun, tho ben maad
6 heuy on me. Myn heelid woundis weren rotun, and ben
7 brokun; fro the face of myn vnwisdom. I am maad a wretche, and Y am bowid doun til in to the ende; al dai Y
8 entride sorewful. For my leendis ben fillid with scornyngis;
9 and helthe is not in my fleisch. I am turmentid, and maad low ful greetli; Y roride for the weilyng of myn herte.
10 Lord, al my desire *is* bifor thee; and my weilyng is not hid
11 fro thee. Myn herte is disturblid in me, my vertu forsook me; and the liȝt of myn iȝen *forsook me*, and it is not with
12 me. My frendis and my neiȝboris neiȝiden; and stoden
13 aȝens me. And thei that weren bisidis me stoden afer; and thei diden violence, that souȝten my lijf. And thei that souȝten yuels to me, spaken vanytees; and thouȝten gilis
14 al dai. But Y as a deef man herde not; and as a doumb
15 man not openynge his mouth. And Y am maad as a man not
16 herynge; and not hauynge repreuyngis in his mouth. For, Lord, Y hopide in thee; my Lord God, thou schalt here me.
17 For Y seide, Lest ony tyme myn enemyes haue ioye on me; and the while my feet ben mouyd, thei spaken grete thingis
18 on me. For Y am redi to betyngis; and my sorewe *is* euere
19 in my siȝt. For Y schal telle my wickidnesse; and Y schal
20 thenke for my synne. But myn enemyes lyuen, and ben

confermed on me; and thei ben multiplyed, that haten me
21 wickidli. Thei that ȝelden yuels for goodis, backbitiden me;
22 for Y suede goodnesse. My Lord God, forsake thou not
23 me; go thou not awei fro me. Lord God of myn helthe;
biholde thou in to myn help.

Psalm XXXVIII (XXXIX).

1   *The title of the eiȝte and threttithe salm. For victorie, to Iditum, the song of Dauid.*

2   I seide, Y schal kepe my weies; that Y trespasse not in my tunge. I settide kepyng to my mouth; whanne a syn-
3 nere stood aȝens me. I was doumb, and was mekid ful gretli, and was stille fro goodis; and my sorewe was renulid.
4 Myn herte was hoot with ynne me; and fier schal brenne
5 out in my thenkyng. I spak in my tunge; Lord, make thou myn eende knowun to me. And the noumbre of my daies
6 what it is; that Y wite, what failith to me. Lo! thou hast set my daies mesurable; and my substaunce is as nouȝt
7 bifor thee. Netheles al vanytee; ech man lyuynge. Netheles a man passith in ymage; but also he is disturblid veynli. He tresorith; and he noot, to whom he schal gadere tho
8 thingis. And now which is myn abiding? whether not the
9 Lord? and my substaunce is at thee. Delyuere thou me fro alle my wickidnessis; thou hast ȝoue me schenschip to the
10 vnkunnynge. I was doumbe, and openyde not my mouth;
11 for thou hast maad, remoue thou thi woundis fro me.
12 Fro the strengthe of thin hond Y failide in blamyngis; for wickidnesse thou hast chastisid man. And thou madist his lijf to faile as an yreyne; netheles ech man is disturblid in
13 veyn. Lord, here thou my preier and my bisechyng; per-
14 seyue thou with eeris my teeris. Be thou not stille, for Y am
15 a comelyng at thee; and a pilgrime, as alle my fadris. For-

ȝyue thou to me, that Y be refreischid, bifor that Y go; and Y schal no more be.

Psalm XXXIX (XL).

1 *The title of the nyne and threttithe salm. For victorie, the song of Dauid.*

2 Y ABIDYNGE abood the Lord; and he ȝaf tent to me.
3 And he herde my preieris; and he ledde out me fro the lake of wretchidnesse, and fro the filthe of draft. And he ordeynede my feet on a stoon; and he dresside my goyngis.
4 And he sente in to my mouth a newe song; a song to oure God. Many men schulen se, and schulen drede; and schulen
5 haue hope in the Lord. Blessid *is* the man, of whom the name of the Lord is his hope; and he bihelde not in to
6 vanitees, and in to false woodnesses. Mi Lord God, thou hast maad thi merueils manye; and in thi thouȝtis noon is, that is lijk thee. I teld, and Y spak; and thei ben multiplied
7 aboue noumbre. Thou noldist sacrifice and offryng; but thou madist perfitli eeris to me. Thou axidist not brent sacri-
8 fice, and sacrifice for synne; thanne Y seide, Lo! Y come. In
9 the heed of the book it is writun of me, that Y schulde do thi wille; my God, Y wolde; and thi lawe in the myddis of myn
10 herte. I telde thi riȝtfulnesse in a greet chirche; lo! Y
11 schal not refreine my lippis, Lord, thou wistist. I hidde not thi riȝtfulnesse in myn herte; Y seide thi treuthe and thin helthe. I hidde not thi mercy and thi treuthe: fro a myche
12 counsel. But thou, Lord, make not fer thi merciful doyngis
13 fro me; thi mercy and treuthe euere token me vp. For whi yuels, of whiche is no noumbre, cumpassiden me; my wick-idnessis token me, and Y myȝte not, that Y schulde se. Tho ben multiplied aboue the heeris of myn heed; and myn herte
14 forsook me. Lord, plese it to thee, that thou delyuere me;

15 Lord, biholde thou to helpe me. Be thei schent, and aschamed togidere; that seken my lijf, to take awei it. Be thei turned 16 abac, and be thei schamed; that wolen yuels to me. Bere thei her confusioun anoon; that seien to me, Wel! wel! 17 *that is, in scorn.* Alle men that seken thee, be fulli ioyful, and be glad on thee; and seie thei, that louen thin helthe, 18 The Lord be magnyfied euere. Forsothe Y am a beggere and pore; the Lord is bisi of me. Thou arte myn helpere and my defendere; my God, tarie thou not.

PSALM XL (XLI).

1 *The title of the fourtithe salm. For victorie, the song of Dauid.*

2 BLESSID *is* he that vndurstondith on a nedi man and pore; 3 the Lord schal delyuere hym in the yuel dai. The Lord kepe hym, and quykene hym, and make hym blesful in the lond; and bitake not hym in to the wille of his enemyes. 4 The Lord bere help to hym on the bed of his sorewe; thou 5 hast ofte turned al his bed-stre in his sijknesse. I seide, Lord, haue thou mercy on me; heele thou my soule, for Y 6 synnede aȝens thee. Myn enemyes seiden yuels to me; 7 Whanne schal he die, and his name schal perische? And if he entride for to se, he spak veyn thingis; his herte gaderide 8 wickidnesse to hym silf. He ȝede with-out-forth; and spak to the same thing. Alle myn enemyes bacbitiden 9 pryuyli aȝens me; aȝens me thei thouȝten yuels to me. Thei ordeineden an yuel word aȝens me; Whether he that slepith, 10 schal not leie to, that he rise aȝen? For whi the man of my pees, in whom Y hopide, he that eet my looues; made greet 11 disseit on me. But thou, Lord, haue merci on me, and reise 12 me aȝen; and Y schal ȝelde to hem. In this thing Y knew, that thou woldist me; for myn enemye schal not haue ioye on

13 me. Forsothe thou hast take me vp for ynnocence; and hast
14 confermed me in thi si3t with-outen ende. Blessid *be* the Lord God of Israel, fro the world and in to the world; be it doon, be it doon.

Psalm XLI (XLII).

1 *The title of the oon and fourtithe salm. To victorie, to the sones of Chore.*

2 As an hert desirith to the wellis of watris; so thou, God,
3 my soule desirith to thee. Mi soule thirstide to God, *that is* a quik welle; whanne schal Y come, and appere bifor
4 the face of God? Mi teeris weren looues to me bi dai and ny3t; while it is seid to me ech dai, Where is thi God?
5 I bithou3te of these thingis, and Y schedde out in me my soule; for Y schal passe in to the place of the wonderful tabernacle, til to the hows of God. In the vois of ful out
6 ioiyng and knoulechyng; *is* the sown of the etere. Mi soule, whi art thou sory; and whi disturblist thou me? Hope thou
7 in God, for 3it Y schal knouleche to hym; *he is* the helthe of my cheer, and my God. My soule is disturblid at my silf; therfor, *God*, Y schal be myndeful of thee fro the lond of
8 Jordan, and fro the litil hil Hermonyim. Depthe clepith depthe; in the vois of thi wyndows. Alle thin hi3e thingis
9 and thi wawis; passiden ouer me. The Lord sente his merci
10 in the dai; and his song in the ny3t. At me *is* a preier to the God of my lijf; Y schal seie to God, Thou art my takere vp. Whi for3etist thou me; and whi go Y sorewful, while
11 the enemy turmentith me? While my boonys ben brokun togidere; myn enemyes, that troblen me, dispiseden me. While thei seien to me, bi alle daies; Where is thi God?
12 Mi soule, whi art thou sori; and whi disturblist thou me? Hope thou in God, for 3it Y schal knouleche to hym; *he is* the helthe of my cheer, and my God.

Psalm XLII (XLIII).
The two and fourtithe salm.

1 God, deme thou me, and departe thou my cause fro a folc not hooli; delyuere thou me fro a wickid man, and gileful. 2 For thou art God, my strengthe; whi hast thou put me abac, and whi go Y soreuful, while the enemy turmentith 3 me? Sende out thi liȝt, and thi treuthe; tho ledden me forth, and brouȝten in to thin hooli hil, and in to thi taber- 4 naclis. And Y schal entre to the auter of God; to God, that gladith my ȝongthe. God, my God, Y schal know- 5 leche to thee in an harpe; my soule, whi art thou sory, and whi troblist thou me? Hope thou in God, for ȝit Y schal knouleche to hym; *he is* the helthe of my cheer, and my God.

Psalm XLIII (XLIV).

1 *The title of the thre and fourtithe salm. To victorie, lernyng to the sones of Chore.*

2 God, we herden with oure eeris; our fadris telden to vs. The werk, which thou wrouȝtist in the daies of hem; and 3 in elde daies. Thin hond lost hethene men, and thou plauntidist hem; thou turmentidist puplis, and castidist hem 4 out. For the *children of Israel* weldiden the lond not bi her swerd; and the arm of hem sauyde not hem. But thi riȝt hond, and thin arm, and the liȝtnyng of thi cheer; 5 for thou were plesid in hem. Thou art thi silf, my kyng 6 and my God; that sendist helthis to Jacob. Bi thee we schulen wyndewe oure enemyes with horn; and in thi name 7 we schulen dispise hem, that risen aȝen vs. For Y schal not hope in my bouwe; and my swerd schal not saue me. 8 For thou hast sauedst vs fro men turmentinge vs; and thou

9 hast schent men hatinge vs. We schulen be preisid in God al dai; and in thi name we schulen knoulcche to thee in
10 to the world. ·But now thou hast put vs abac, and hast schent vs; and thou, God, schalt not go out in oure ver-
11 tues. Thou hast turned vs awei bihynde aftir oure ene- myes; and thei, that hatiden vs, rauyschiden dyuerseli to
12 hem silf. Thou hast 30ue vs as scheep of meetis; and
13 among hethene men thou hast· scaterid vs. Thou hast seeld thi puple with out prijs; and multitude was not in the
14 chaungyngis of hem. Thou hast set vs schenschip to oure nei3boris; mouwyng and scorn to hem that ben in oure
15 cumpas. Thou hast set vs into licnesse to hethene men;
16 stiryng of heed among puplis. Al dai my schame is a3ens
17 me; and the schenschipe of my face hilide me. Fro the vois of dispisere, and yuele-spekere; fro the face of enemy,
18 and pursuere. Alle these thingis camen on vs, and we han not for3ete thee; and we diden not wickidli in thi
19 testament. And oure· herte 3ede not awei bihynde; and
20 thou hast bowid awei oure pathis fro thi weie. For thou hast maad vs lowe in the place of turment; and the scha-
21 dewe of deth hilide vs. If we for3aten the name of oure God; and if we helden forth oure hondis to an alien God.
22 Whether God schal not seke these thingis? for he knowith the hid thingis of herte. For whi we ben slayn al dai for
23 thee; we ben demed as scheep of sleyng. Lord, rise vp, whi slepist thou? rise vp, and putte not awei in to the
24 ende. Whi turnest thou awei thi face? thou for3etist oure
25 pouert, and oure tribulacioun. For oure lijf is maad low
26 in dust; oure wombe is glued togidere in the erthe. Lord, rise vp thou, and helpe vs; and a3enbie vs for thi name.

Psalm XLIV (XLV).

1 *The title of the foure and fourtithe salm. To the ouercomere for the lilies, the most loued song of lernyng of the sones of Chore.*

2 Myn herte hath teld out a good word; Y seie my workis to the kyng. Mi tunge *is* a penne of a writere; writynge 3 swiftli. *Crist, thou art* fairer in schap than the sones of men; grace is spred abroad in thi lippis; therfor God bles- 4 sid thee withouten ende. Be thou gird with thi swerd; on 5 thi hipe most myȝtili. Biholde thou in thi schaplynesse and thi fairnesse; come thou forth with prosperite, and regne thou. For treuthe, and myldenesse, and riȝtfulnesse; 6 and thi riȝt hond schal lede forth thee wondurfuli. Thi scharpe arowis schulen falle in to the hertis of the enemyes 7 of the kyng; puplis *schulen be* vndur thee. God, thi seete is in to the world of world; the ȝerde of thi rewme *is* a 8 ȝerde of riȝt reulyng, *ethir of equite*. Thou louedist riȝtful- nesse, and hatidist wickidnesse; therfor thou, God, thi God, anoyntide thee with the oile of gladnesse, more than thi 9 felowis. Mirre, and gumme, and cassia, of thi clothis, of 10 the housis yuer; of whiche the douȝtris of kyngis delitiden thee. A queen stood nyȝ on thi riȝt side in clothing ouer- 11 gildid; cumpassid with dyuersitee. Douȝter, here thou, and se, and bowe doun thin cere; and forȝete thi puple, and 12 the hows of thi fadir. And the kyng schal coueyte thi fair- nesse; for he is thi Lord God, and thei schulen worschipe 13 hym. And the douȝtris of Tire in ȝiftis; alle the riche 14 men of the puple schulen bisèche thi cheer. Al the glorye of that douȝter of the kyng *is* with ynne in goldun hemmes; 15 sche *is* clothid aboute with dyuersitees. Virgyns schulen be brouȝt to the kyng aftir hir; hir neiȝboressis schulen be 16 brouȝt to thee. Thei schulen be brouȝt in gladnesse, and

ful out ioiyng; thei schulen be brou3t in to the temple of
17 the kyng. Sones ben borun to thee, for thi fadris; thou
18 schalt ordeyne hem princes on al erthe. Lord, thei schulen
be myndeful of thi name; in ech generacioun, and in to
generacioun. Therfor puplis schulen knouleche to thee
withouten ende; and in to the world of world.

Psalm XLV (XLVI).

1 *The title of the fiue and fourtithe salm. To the ouercomere,
the song of the sones of Chore, for 3ongthis.*

2 Oure God, *thou art* refuyt, and vertu; helpere in tribu-
3 lacions, that han founde vs greetly. Therfor we schulen
not drede, while the erthe schal be troblid; and the hillis
4 schulen be borun ouer in to the herte of the see. The
watris of hem sowneden, and weren troblid; hillis weren
5 troblid togidere in the strengthe of hym. The feersnesse
of flood makith glad the citee of God; the hi3este God
6 hath halewid his tabernacle. God in the myddis therof
schal not be moued; God schal helpe it eerli in the grey
7 morewtid. Hethene men weren disturblid togidere, and
rewmes weren bowid doun; *God* 3af his vois, the erthe
8 was moued. The Lord of vertues *is* with vs; God of
9 Jacob *is* oure vptakere. Come 3e, and se the werkis of
10 the Lord; whiche wondris he hath set on the erthe. He
doynge awei batels til to the ende of the lond; schal al
to-brese bouwe, and schal breke togidere armuris, and schal
11 brenne scheldis bi fier. 3yue 3e tent, and se 3e, that Y am
God; Y schal be enhaunsid among hethene men; and Y
12 schal be enhaunsid in erthe. The Lord of vertues *is* with
vs; God of Jacob *is* oure vptakere.

Psalm XLVI (XLVII).

1 *The title of the sixte and fourtithe salm. To victorie, a salm to the sones of Chore.*

2 Alle ʒe folkis, make ioie with hondis; synge ʒe hertli to
3 God in the vois of ful out ioiyng. For the Lord *is* hiʒ and
4 ferdful; a greet kyng on al erthe. He made puplis suget
5 to vs; and hethene men vndur oure feet. He chees his
6 eritage to vs; the fairnesse of Jacob, whom he louyde. God stiede in hertli song; and the Lord in the vois of a trumpe.
7 Synge ʒe to oure God, synge ʒe; synge ʒe to oure kyng,
8 synge ʒe. For God *is* kyng of al erthe; synge ʒe wiseli.
9 God schal regne on hethene men; God sittith on his hooli
10 seete. The princes of puplis ben gaderid togidere with God of Abraham; for the stronge goddis of erthe ben reisid greetli.

Psalm XLVII (XLVIII).

1 *The title of the seuene and fourtithe salm. The song of salm, of the sones of Chore.*

2 The Lord *is* greet, and worthi to be preisid ful myche;
3 in the citee of oure God, in the hooli hil of hym. It is foundid in the ful out ioiyng of al erthe; the hil of Syon;
4 the sidis of the north, the citee of the greet kyng. God schal be knowun in the housis therof; whanne he schal
5 take it. For lo! the kyngis of erthe weren gaderid togidere;
6 thei camen into o place. Thei seynge so wondriden; thei weren disturblid, thei weren mouyd togidere, tremblyng took
7 hem. There sorewis as of a womman trauelynge of child;
8 in a greet spirit thou schalt al to-breke the schippis of
9 Tharsis. As we herden, so we sien, in the citee of the Lord of vertues, in the citee of oure God; God hath foundid that

10 citee with-outen ende. God, we han resseyued thi mercy;
11 in the myddis of thi temple. Aftir thi name, God, so thin
heriyng *is spred abrood* in to the endis of erthe; thi riʒt hond
12 is ful of riʒtfulnesse. The hil of Sion be glad, and the
13 douʒtris of Judee be fulli ioiful; for thi domes, Lord. Cumpasse ʒe Syon, and biclippe ʒe it; telle ʒe in the touris
14 therof. Sette ʒe ʒoure hertis in the vertu of him; and departe ʒe the housis of hym, that ʒe telle out in an other
15 generacioun. For this is God, oure God, in to withouten
ende, and in to the world of world; he schal gouerne vs
in to worldis.

Psalm XLVIII (XLIX).

1 *The title of the ciʒte and fourtithe salm. To victorie,
a salm to the sones of Chore.*

2 Alle ʒe folkis, here these thingis; alle ʒe that dwellen in
3 the world, perseyue with eeris. Alle the sones of erthe and
the sones of men; togidere the riche man and the pore in
4 to oon. Mi mouth schal speke wisdom; and the thenkyng
5 of myn herte *schal speke* prudence. I schal bouwe doun
myn eere in to a parable; Y schal opene my resoun set
6 forth in a sautree. Whi schal Y drede in the yuel dai? the
7 wickidnesse of myn heele schal cumpasse me. Whiche
tristen in her owne vertu; and han glorie in the mu'titude
8 of her richessis. A brother aʒenbieth not, schal a man
9 aʒenbie? and he schal not ʒyue to God his plesyng. And
he schal not ʒyue the prijs of raunsum of his soule; and
10 he schal trauele with outen ende, and he schal lyue ʒit in
11 to the ende. He schal not se perischyng, whanne he schal
se wise men diynge; the vnwise man and fool schulen
perische togidere. And thei schulen leeue her richessis to
12 aliens; and the sepulcris of hem *ben* the housis of hem with-
outen ende. The tabernaclis of hem *ben* in generacioun

and generacioun; thei clepiden her names in her londis.
13 A man, whanne he was in honour, vndurstood not; he is comparisound to vnwise beestis, and he is maad lijk to tho.
14 This weie of hem *is* sclaundir to hem; and aftirward thei
15 schulen plese togidere in her mouth. As scheep thei ben set in helle; deth schal gnawe hem. And iust men schulen be lordis of hem in the morewtid; and the helpe of hem
16 schal waxe eld in helle, for the glorie of hem. Netheles God schal aȝenbie my soule from the power of helle; whanne
17 he schal take me. Drede thou not, whanne a man is maad
18 riche; and the glorie of his hows is multiplied. For whanne he schal die, he schal not take alle thingis; and his glorie
19 schal not go doun with him. For his soule schal be blessid in his lijf; he schal knouleche to thee, whanne thou hast do
20 wel to hym. He schal entre til in to the generaciouns of hise fadris; and til in-to with-outen ende he schal not se
21 liȝt. A man, whanne he was in honour, vndurstood not; he is comparisound to vnwise beestis, and is maad lijk to tho.

Psalm XLIX (L).

1 *The title of the nyne and fourtithe salm. The salm of Asaph.*

God, the Lord of goddis, spak; and clepide the erthe,
2 fro the risynge of the sunne til to the goyng doun. The
3 schap of his fairnesse fro Syon, God schal come opynli; oure God, and he schal not be stille. Fier schal brenne an
4 hiȝe in his siȝt; and a strong tempest in his cumpas. He clepide heuene aboue; and the erthe, to deme his puple.
5 Gadere ȝe to hym hise seyntis; that ordeynen his testament
6 aboue sacrifices. And heuenes schulen schewe his riȝtful-
7 nesse; for God is the iuge. Mi puple, here thou, and Y schal speke to Israel; and Y schal witnesse to thee, Y am
8 God, thi God. I schal not repreue thee in thi sacrifices;

9 and thi brent sacrifices ben euere bifor me. I schal not take calues of thin hows; nethir geet buckis of thi flockis. 10 For alle the wyelde beestis of wodis ben myne; werk 11 beestis, and oxis in hillis. I haue knowe alle the volatils 12 of heuene; and the fairnesse of the feeld is with me. If Y schal be hungry, Y schal not seie to thee; for the world 13 and the fulnesse therof is myn. Whether Y schal eete the fleischis of boolis? ethir schal Y drynke the blood of geet 14 buckis? Offre thou to God the sacrifice of heriyng: 15 and ʒelde thin avowis to the hiʒeste *God*. And inwardli clepe thou me in the dai of tribulacioun; and Y schal de-16 lyuere thee, and thou schalt onoure me. But God seide to the synnere, Whi tellist thou out my riʒtfulnessis; and 17 takist my testament bi thi mouth? Sotheli thou hatidist 18 lore; and hast cast awey my wordis bihynde. If thou siʒest a theef, thou hast runne with hym; and thou settidist thi 19 part with avowtreris. Thi mouth was plenteuouse of malice; 20 and thi tunge medlide togidere giles. Thou sittynge spakist aʒens thi brother, and thou settidist sclaundir aʒens the sone 21 of thi modir; thou didist these thingis, and Y was stille. Thou gessidist wickidli, that Y schal be lijk thee; Y schal 22 repreue thee, and Y schal sette aʒens thi face. Ʒe that for-ʒeten God, vndurstonde these thingis; lest sum tyme he 23 rauysche, and noon be that schal delyuere. The sacrifice of heriyng schal onoure me; and there *is* the weie, where ynne Y schal schewe to hym the helthe of God.

Psalm L (LI).

1 *The title of the fiftithe salm. To victorie, the salm of Dauid;*
2 *whanne Nathan the prophete cam to hym, whanne he entride to Bersabee.*

3 God, haue thou merci on me; bi thi greet merci. And bi the mychilnesse of thi merciful doyngis; do thou awei my

4 wickidnesse. More waische thou me fro my wickidnesse;
5 and clense thou me fro my synne. For Y knouleche my
6 wickidnesse; and my synne is euere aȝens me. I haue
synned to thee aloone, and Y haue do ȝuel bifor thee; that
thou be iustified in thi wordis, and ouercome whanne thou
7 art demed. For lo! Y was conseyued in wickednessis; and
8 my modir conceyuede me in synnes. For lo! thou louedist
treuthe; thou hast schewid to me the vncerteyn thingis, and
9 pryuy thingis of thi wisdom. Lord, sprenge thou me with
ysope, and Y schal be clensid; waische thou me, and Y
10 schal be maad whijt more than snow. Ȝyue thou ioie, and
gladnesse to myn heryng; and boonys maad meke schulen
11 ful out make ioye. Turne awei thi face fro my synnes; and
12 do awei alle my wickidnesses. God, make thou a clene
herte in me; and make thou newe a riȝtful spirit in my
13 entrailis. Caste thou me not awei fro thi face; and take
14 thou not awei fro me thin hooli spirit. Ȝiue thou to me
the gladnesse of thyn helthe; and conferme thou me with
15 the principal spirit. I schal teche wickid men thi weies;
16 and vnfeithful men schulen be conuertid to thee. God, the
God of myn helthe, delyuere thou me fro bloodis; and my
17 tunge schal ioyfuli synge thi riȝtfulnesse. Lord, opene thou
18 my lippis; and my mouth schal telle thi preysyng. For if
thou haddist wold sacrifice, Y hadde ȝoue; treuli thou schalt
19 not delite in brent sacrifices. A sacrifice to God is a spirit
troblid; God, thou schalt not dispise a contrit herte and
20 maad meke. Lord, do thou benygneli in thi good wille
21 to Syon; that the wallis of Jerusalem be bildid. Thanne
thou schalt take plesauntli the sacrifice of riȝtfulnesse, offryngis, and brent sacrifices; thanne thei schulen putte calues
on thin auter.

Psalm LI (LII).

1, 2 *The title of the oon and fiftithe salm. To victorie, the salm of Dauid, whanne Doech Idumei cam, and telde to Saul, and seide to him, Dauid cam in to the hows of Abymelech.*

3 What hast thou glorie in malice; which art miʒti in
4 wickidnesse? Al dai thi tunge thouʒte vnriʒtfulnesse; as
5 a scharp rasour thou hast do gile. Thou louedist malice more than benygnite; *thou louedist* wickidnesse more than
6 to speke equite. Thou louedist alle wordis of casting doun;
7 with a gileful tunge. Therfor God schal distrie thee in to the ende, he schal drawe thee out bi the roote, and he schal make thee to passe awei fro thi tabernacle; and thi roote fro
8 the lond of lyuynge men. Iust men schulen se, and schulen drede; and thei schulen leiʒe on hym, and thei schulen seie,
9 Lo! the man that settide not God his helpere. But he hopide in the multitude of his richessis; and hadde maistrie
10 in his vanite. Forsothe Y, as a fruytful olyue tre in the hous of God; hopide in the merci of God with-outen ende,
11 and in to the world of world. Y schal knowleche to thee in to the world, for thou hast do *mercy to me;* and Y schal abide thi name, for it is good in the siʒt of thi seyntis.

Psalm LII (LIII).

1 *The title of the two and fiftithe salm. To the ouercomer bi the quere, the lernyng of Dauid.*

2 The vnwise man seide in his herte; God is not. Thei ben corrupt, and maad abhomynable in her wickidnessis;
3 noon is that doith good. God bihelde fro heuene on the sones of men; that he se, if ony is vndurstondynge, ether
4 sekynge God. Alle boweden awei, thei ben maad vnprofit-

able togidre; noon is that doith good, ther is not til to oon.
5 Whether alle men, that worchen wickidnesse, schulen not
wite; whiche deuouren my puple as the mete of breed?
6 Thei clepiden not God; there thei trembliden for drede,
where no drede was. For God hath scaterid the boones of
hem, that plesen men; thei ben schent, for God hath forsake
7 hem. Who schal ʒyue fro Syon helthe to Israel? whanne
the Lord hath turned the caitifte of his puple, Jacob schal
ful out make ioie, and Israel schal be glad.

Psalm LIII (LIV).

1 *The title of the thre and fiftithe salm. To victorie in orguns,*
2 *ether in salmes, the lernyng of Dauid, whanne Zyfeys camen,
and seiden to Saul, Whethir Dauid is not hid at vs?*

3 God, in thi name make thou me saaf; and in thi vertu
4 deme thou me. God, here thou my preier; with eeris per-
5 seyue thou the wordis of my mouth. For aliens han rise
aʒens me, and stronge men souʒten my lijf; and thei settiden
6 not God bifor her siʒt. For, lo! God helpith me; and the
7 Lord is vptaker of my soule. Turne thou awei yuelis to
8 myn enemyes; and leese thou hem in thi treuthe. Wilfuli
Y schal make sacrifice to thee; and, Lord, Y schal knou-
9 leche to thi name, for it is good. For thou delyueridist me
fro al tribulacioun; and myn iʒe dispiside on myn enemyes.

Psalm LIV (LV).

1 *The title of the foure and fiftithe salm. In Ebreu thus, To
victorie in orguns, the lernyng of Dauid. In Jeroms translacioun thus, To the ouercomer in salmes of Dauid lernid.*

2 God, here thou my preier, and dispise thou not my
3 bisechyng; ʒyue thou tent to me, and here thou me.

I am sorewful in myn exercising; and Y am disturblid
4 of the face of the enemye, and of the tribulacioun of the
synner. For thei bowiden wickidnessis in to me; and in
5 ire thei weren diseseful to me. Myn herte was disturblid
6 in me; and the drede of deth felde on me. Drede and
7 trembling camen on me; and derknessis hiliden me. And
Y seide, Who schal ʒyue to me fetheris, as of a culuer; and
8 Y schal fle, and schal take rest? Lo! Y ʒede fer awei, and
9 fledde; and Y dwellide in wildirnesse. I abood hym, that
made me saaf fro the litilnesse, *ether drede*, of spirit; and fro
10 tempest. Lord, caste thou doun, departe thou the tungis of
11 hem; for Y siʒ wickidnesse and aʒenseiyng in the citee. Bi
dai and nyʒt wickidnesse schal cumpasse it on the wallis
12 therof; and trauel and vnriʒtfulnesse *ben* in the myddis therof.
13 And vsure and gile failide not; fro the stretis therof. For if
myn enemye hadde cursid me; sotheli Y hadde suffride.
And if he, that hatide me, hadde spoke greet thingis on me;
14 in hap Y hadde hid me fro hym. But thou art a man of o
15 wille; my leeder, and my knowun. Which tokist togidere
swete meetis with me; we ʒeden with consent in the hous
16 of God. Deth come on hem; and go thei doun quyk in to
helle. For weiwardnessis ben in the dwelling places of hem;
17 in the myddis of hem. But Y criede to thee, Lord; and the
18 Lord sauede me. In the euentid and morewtid and in myddai Y schal telle, and schewe; and he schal here my vois.
19 He schal aʒenbie my soule in pees fro hem, that neiʒen to
20 me; for among manye thei weren with me. God schal
here; and he that is bifore the worldis schal make hem low.
21 For chaungyng is not to hem, and thei dredden not God; he
holdith forth his hoond in ʒelding. Thei defouliden his
22 testament, the cheris therof weren departid fro ire; and his
herte neiʒede. The wordis therof weren softer than oyle; and
23 tho ben dartis. Caste thi cure on the Lord, and he schal

fulli nurische thee; and he schal not ȝyue with-outen ende
24 flotering to a iust man. But thou, God, schalt lede hem
forth; in to the pit of deth. Menquelleris and gilours schulen
not haue half her daies; but, Lord, Y schal hope in thee.

Psalm LV (LVI).

1 *The title of the fyue and fiftithe salm. In Ebreu thus, To the
ouercomyng on the doumb culuer of fer drawing awei, the
comely song of Dauid, whanne Filisteis helden hym in Geth.
In Jeroms translacioun thus, To the ouercomer for the doumb
culuer, for it ȝede awei fer. Dauid meke and symple made
this salm, whanne Palesteyns helden hym in Geth.*

2 God, haue thou merci on me, for a man hath defoulid me;
3 al dai he impugnyde, and troublide me. Myn enemyes de-
4 fouliden me al dai; for manye fiȝteris *weren* aȝens me. Of
the hiȝnesse of dai Y schal drede; but God Y schal hope in
5 thee. In God Y schal preise my wordis; Y hopide in God,
6 Y schal not drede what thing fleisch schal do to me. Al dai
thei cursiden my wordis; aȝens me alle her thouȝtis *weren* in
7 to yuel. Thei schulen dwelle, and schulen hide; thei schulen
8 aspie myn heele. As thei abiden my lijf, for nouȝt schalt
thou make hem saaf; in ire thou schalt breke togidere puplis.
9 God, Y schewide my lijf to thee; thou hast set my teeris in
10 thi siȝt. As and in thi biheest, Lord; thanne myn enemyes
schulen be turned abak. In what euere dai Y schal inwardli
11 clepe thee; lo! Y haue knowe, that thou art my God. In
God Y schal preyse a word; in the Lord Y schal preyse a
word. Y schal hope in God; Y schal not drede what thing
12 a man schal do to me. God, thin auowis ben in me; whiche
13 Y schal ȝelde heriyngis to thee. For thou hast delyuerid my
lijf fro deth, and my feet fro slidyng; that Y pleese bifore
God in the liȝt of hem that lyuen.

Psalm LVI (LVII).

1 *The title of the sixte and fiftithe salm. In Ebreu thus, To the victorie, lese thou not the semeli song, ether the swete song of Dauid, whanne he fledde fro the face of Saul in to the denne. In Jeroms translacioun thus, For victorie, that thou lese not Dauid, meke and simple, whanne he fledde fro the face of Saul in to the denne.*

2 God, haue thou merci on me, haue thou merci on me; for my soule tristith in thee. And Y schal hope in the 3 schadewe of thi wyngis; til wickidnesse passe. I shall crye 4 to God altherhi3este; to God that dide wel to me. He sente fro heuene, and delyuerede me; he 3af in to schenschip hem 5 that defoulen me. God sente his merci and his treuthe, and delyuerede my soule fro the myddis of whelpis of liouns; Y slepte disturblid. The sones of men, the teeth of hem *ben* 6 armuris and arowis; and her tunge *is* a scharp swerd. God, be thou enhaunsid aboue heuenes; and thi glorie aboue al 7 erthe. Thei maden redi a snare to my feet; and thei greetly boweden my lijf. Thei delueden a diche bifore my face; and 8 thei felden doun in to it. God, myn herte *is* redi, myn herte 9 *is* redi; Y schal singe, and Y schal seie salm. Mi glorie, rise thou vp; sautrie and harpe, rise thou vp; Y schal rise vp 10 eerli. Lord, Y schal knouleche to thee among puplis; and 11 Y schal seie salm among hethene men. For thi merci is 12 magnified til to heuenes; and thi treuthe til to cloudis. God, be thou enhaunsid aboue heuenes; and thi glorie ouer al erthe.

Psalm LVII (LVIII).

1 *The title of the seuene and fiftithe salm. In Ebreu thus, To victorie; lese thou not the swete song, ether the semely salm, of Dauid. In Jeroms translacioun thus, To the ouercomere, that thou lese not Dauid, meke and simple.*

2 Forsothe if ȝe speken riȝtfulnesse verili; ȝe sones of men,
3 deme riȝtfuli. For in herte ȝe worchen wickidnesse in erthe;
4 ȝoure hondis maken redi vnriȝtfulnessis. Synneris weren maad aliens fro the wombe; thei erriden fro the wombe, thei
5 spaken false thingis. Woodnesse *is* to hem, bi the licnesse of a serpent; as of a deef snake, and stoppynge hise eeris.
6 Which schal not here the vois of charmeris; and of a venym-
7 makere charmynge wiseli. God schal al to-breke the teeth of hem in her mouth; the Lord schal breke togidere the greet
8 teeth of liouns. Thei schulen come to nouȝt, as water rennynge
9 awei; he bente his bouwe, til thei ben maad sijk. As wexe that fletith awei, thei schulen be takun awei; fier felle aboue,
10 and thei siȝen not the sunne. Bifore that ȝoure thornes vndurstoden the ramne; he swolewith hem so in ire, as lyuynge
11 men. The iust man schal be glad, whanne he schal se veniaunce; he schal waische hise hondis in the blood of a
12 synner. And a man schal scie treuli, For fruyt is to a iust man; treuli God is demynge hem in erthe.

Psalm LVIII (LIX).

1 *The title of the eiȝte and fiftithe salm. In Jeroms translacioun thus, To the ouercomer, that thou lese not Dauid, meke and simple, whanne Saul sente and kepte the hous, to slee hym. In Ebreu thus, To the ouercomyng, leese thou not the semeli song of Dauid, and so forth.*

2 Mi God, delyuer thou me fro myn enemyes; and delyuer
3 thou me fro hem that risen aȝens me. Delyuer thou me fro

hem that worchen wickidnesse; and saue thou me fro men-
4 quelleris. For lo! thei han take my soule; stronge men
5 fellen in on me. Nethir my wickidnesse, nether my synne;
Lord, Y ran with out wickidnesse, and dresside *my werkis*.
6 Rise vp thou in to my meetyng, and se; and thou, Lord God
of vertues, *art* God of Israel. ȝyue thou tent to visite alle
folkis; do thou not merci to alle that worchen wickidnesse.
7 Thei schulen be turned at euentid, and thei as doggis schulen
8 suffre hungir; and thei schulen cumpas the citee. Lo! thei
schulen speke in her mouth, and a swerd in her lippis; for
9 who herde? And thou, Lord, schalt scorne hem; thou schalt
10 bringe alle folkis to nouȝt. I schal kepe my strengthe to
11 thee; for God *is* myn vptaker, my God, his mercy schal come
12 byfore me. God schewide to me on myn enemyes, slee thou
not hem; lest ony tyme my puples forȝete. Scatere thou
hem in thi vertu; and, Lord, my defender, putte thou hem
13 doun. *Putte thou doun* the trespas of her mouth, and the
word of her lippis; and be thei takun in her pride. And of
cursyng and of leesyng; thei schulen be schewid in the.
14 endyng. In the ire of ending, and thei schulen not be; and
thei schulen wite, that the Lord schal be Lord of Jacob, and
15 of the endis of erthe. Thei schulen be turned at euentid,
and thei as doggis schulen suffre hungur; and thei schulen
16 cumpas the citee. Thei schulen be scaterid abrood, for to
eete; sotheli if thei ben not fillid, and thei schulen grutche.
17 But Y schal synge thi strengthe; and eerli Y schal enhaunse
thi merci. For thou art maad myn vptaker; and my refuyt,
18 in the dai of my tribulacioun. Myn helper, Y schal synge to
thee; for *thou art* God. myn vptaker, my God, my mercy.

Psalm LIX (LX).

1 *The title of the nyne and fiftithe salm. In Ebreu thus, To victorie, on the witnessyng of roose, the swete song of Dauid,*
2 *to teche, whanne he fauʒte aʒens Aram of floodis, and Sirie of Soba; and Joab turnede aʒen, and smoot Edom in the valei of salt pittis, twelue thousynde. In Jeroms translacioun thus, To the ouercomer for lilies, the witnessing of meke and parfit Dauid, to teche, whanne he fauʒte aʒens Sirie of Mesopotamye, and Soba, and so forth.*

3 God, thou hast put awei vs, and thou hast distried vs; 4 thou were wrooth, and thou hast do merci to vs. Thou mouedist the erthe, and thou disturblidist it; make thou hool 5 the sorewis therof, for it is moued. Thou schewidist harde thingis to thi puple; thou ʒauest drynk to vs with the wyn of 6 compunccioun. Thou hast ʒoue a signefiyng to hem that dreden thee; that thei fle fro the face of the bouwe. That 7 thi derlyngis be delyuered; make thou saaf with thi riʒt hond 8 *the puple of Israel*, and here thou me. God spak bi his hooli; Y schal be glad, and Y schal departe Siccimam, and Y schal 9 meete the greet valei of tabernaclis. Galaad is myn, and Manasses is myn; and Effraym *is* the strengthe of myn heed. 10 Juda *is* my king; Moab *is* the pot of myn hope. In to Idumee Y schal stretche forth my scho; aliens ben maad 11 suget to me. Who schal lede me in to a citee maad strong; 12 who schal leede me til in to Ydumee? Whether not thou, God, that hast put awei vs; and schalt thou not, God, go out 13 in oure vertues? Lord, ʒyue thou to vs help of tribulacioun; 14 for the heelthe of man is veyn. In God we schulen make vertu; and he schal bringe to nouʒt hem that disturblen vs.

Psalm LX (LXI).

1 *The titil of the sixtithe salm. To the victorie on orgun, to Dauid hym silf.*

2 God, here thou my biseching; ȝyue thou tent to my preyer.
3 Fro the endis of the lond Y criede to thee; the while myn herte was angwischid, thou enhaunsidist me in a stoon.
4 Thou laddest me forth, for thou art maad myn hope; a tour
5 of strengthe fro the face of the enemye. I schal dwelle in thi tabernacle in to worldis; Y schal be keuered in the hilyng of
6 thi wengis. For thou, my God, hast herd my preier; thou
7 hast ȝoue eritage to hem that dreden thi name. Thou schalt adde daies on the daies of the king; hise ȝeeris til in to the
8 dai of generacioun and of generacioun. He dwellith withouten ende in the siȝt of God; who schal seke the merci and
9 treuthe of hym? So Y schal seie salm to thi name in to the world of world; that Y ȝelde my vowis fro dai in to dai.

Psalm LXI (LXII).

1 *The titil of the oon and sixtithe salm. To the victorie on Iditum, the salm of Dauid.*

2 Whether my soule schal not be suget to God; for myn
3 heelthe *is* of hym. For whi he *is* bothe my God, and myn
4 heelthe; my taker vp, Y schal no more be moued. Hou longe fallen ȝe on a man? alle ȝe sleen; as to a wal bowid,
5 and a wal of stoon with out morter cast doun. Netheles thei thouȝten to putte awei my prijs, Y ran in thirst; with her
6 mouth thei blessiden, and in her herte thei cursiden. Netheles, my soule, be thou suget to God; for my pacience *is* of hym.
7 For *he is* my God, and my saueour; myn helpere, Y schal
8 not passe out. Myn helthe, and my glorie *is* in God; God *is*

9 *the ȝyuer* of myn help, and myn hope is in God. Al the gaderyng togidere of the puple, hope ȝe in God, schede ȝe out ȝoure hertis bifore hym; God *is* oure helpere with outen 10 ende. Netheles the sones of men *ben* veyne; the sones of men *ben* liers in balauncis, that thei disseyue of vanytee in to 11 the same thing. Nile ȝe haue hope in wickidnesse, and nyle ȝe coueyte raueyns; if ritchessis be plenteuouse, nyle ȝe sette 12 the herte therto. God spak onys, Y herde these twei thingis, 13 that power is of God, and, thou Lord, mercy *is* to thee; for thou schalt ȝelde to ech man bi hise werkis.

Psalm LXII (LXIII).

1 *The titil of the two and sixtithe salm. The salm of Dauid, whanne he was in the desert of Judee.*

2 God, my God, Y wake to thee ful eerli. Mi soule thirstide 3 to thee; my fleisch *thirstide* to thee ful many foold. In a lond forsakun with out wei, and with out water, so Y apperide to thee in hooli; that Y schulde se thi vertu, and thi glorie. 4 For thi merci is betere than lyues; my lippis schulen herie 5 thee. So Y schal blesse thee in my lijf; and in thi name Y 6 schal reise myn hondis. Mi soule be fillid as with inner fatnesse and vttermere fatnesse; and my mouth schal herie with 7 lippis of ful out ioiyng. So Y hadde mynde on thee on my 8 bed, in morewtidis Y shal thenke of thee; for thou were myn helpere. And in the keueryng of thi wyngis Y schal make 9 ful out ioye, my soule cleuede after thee; thi riȝthond took 10 me vp. Forsothe thei souȝten in veyn my lijf, thei schulen 11 entre in to the lower thingis of erthe; thei schulen be bitakun in to the hondis of swerd, thei schulen be maad the partis of 12 foxis. But the king schal be glad in God; and alle men schulen be preysid that sweren in hym, for the mouth of hem, that speken wickid thingis, is stoppid.

PSALM LXIII (LXIV).

1 *The titil of the thre and sixtithe salm. In Ebrewe thus, To the victorie, the salm of Dauid. In Jerom thus, To the ouercomer, the song of Dauid.*

2 GOD, here thou my preier, whanne Y bisechе; delyuere
3 thou my soule fro the drede of the enemy. Thou hast defendid me fro the couent of yuele-doers; fro the multitude of
4 hem that worchen wickidnesse. For thei scharpiden her
5 tungis as a swerd, thei benten a bowe, a bittir thing; for to
6 schete in priuetees hym that is vnwemmed. Sodeynli thei schulen schete hym, and thei schulen not drede; thei maden stidefast to hem silf a wickid word. Thei telden, that thei
7 schulden hide snaris; thei seiden, Who schal se hem? Thei souȝten wickidnessis; thei souȝten, and failiden in sekinge.
8 A man neiȝhe to deep herte; and God schal be enhaunsid.
9 The arowis of litle men ben maad the woundis of hem; and the tungis of hem ben maad sijk aȝens hem. Alle men ben
10 disturblid, that sien hem; and ech man dredde. And thei telden the werkis of God; and vndurstoden the dedis of God.
11 The iust man schal be glad in the Lord, and schal hope in hym; and alle men of riȝtful herte schulen be preisid.

PSALM LXIV (LXV).

1 *The titil of the foure and sixtithe salm. To victorie, the salm of the song of Dauid.*

2 GOD, heriyng bicometh thee in Syon; and a vow schal be
3 ȝolden to thee in Jerusalem. Here thou my preier; ech man
4 schal come to thee. The wordis of wickid men hadden the maistrye ouer vs; and thou schalt do merci to oure wickid-
5 nessis. Blessid *is* he, whom thou hast chose, and hast take;

he schal dwelle in thin hallis. We schulen be fillid with the
6 goodis of thin hous; thi temple is hooli, wondurful in equite.
God, oure heelthe, here thou vs; *thou art* hope of alle coostis
7 of erthe, and in the see afer. And thou makest redi hillis in
8 thi vertu, and art gird with power; which disturblist the
9 depthe of the see, the soun of the wawis therof. Folkis
schulen be disturblid, and thei that dwellen in the endis
schulen drede of thi signes; thou schalt delite the outgoingis
10 of the morewtid and euentid. Thou hast visitid the lond,
and hast greetli fillid it; thou hast multiplied to make it
riche. The flood of God was fillid with watris; thou madist
11 redi the mete of hem, for the makyng redi therof is so. Thou
fillynge greetli the stremes therof, multiplie the fruytis therof;
the lond bringinge forth fruytis schal be glad in goteris of it.
12 Thou schalt blesse the coroun of the ȝeer of thi good wille;
13 and thi feeldis schulen be fillid with plentee of fruytis. The
feire thingis of desert schulen wexe fatte; and litle hillis
14 schulen be cumpassid with ful out ioiyng. The wetheris of
scheep ben clothid, and valeis schulen be plenteuouse of
wheete; thei schulen crye, and sotheli thei schulen seye
salm.

Psalm LXV (LXVI).

1 *The titil of the fyue and sixtithe salm. To the victorie, the song
of salm.*

2   Al the erthe, make ȝe ioie hertli to God, seie ȝe salm to
3 his name; ȝyue ȝe glorie to his heriyng. Seie ȝe to God,
Lord, thi werkis ben dredeful; in the multitude of thi vertu
4 thin enemyes schulen lie to thee. God, al the erthe worschipe
5 thee, and synge to thee; seie it salm to thi name. Come ȝe
and se ȝe the werkis of God; ferdful in counseils on the
6 sones of men. Which turnede the see in to drie lond; in
the flood thei schulen passe with foot, there we schulen be

7 glad in hym. Which is Lord in his vertu withouten ende,
hise iȝen biholden on folkis; thei that maken scharp be not
8 enhaunsid in hem silf. Ȝe hethen men, blesse oure God;
9 and make ȝe herd the vois of his preising. That hath set my
10 soule to lijf, and ȝaf not my feet in to stiryng. For thou,
God, hast preued vs; thou hast examyned vs bi fier, as siluer
11 is examyned. Thou leddist vs in to a snare, thou puttidist
12 tribulaciouns in oure bak; thou settidist men on oure heedis.
We passiden bi fier and water; and thou leddist vs out in to
13 refreschyng. I schal entre in to thin hous in brent sacrifices;
14 Y schal ȝelde to thee my vowis, which my lippis spaken dis-
15 tinctly. And my mouth spake in my tribulacioun; Y shal
offre to thee brent sacrificis ful of merowȝ, with the brennyng
of rammes; Y schal offre to thee oxis with buckis of geet.
16 Alle ȝe that dreden God, come and here, and Y schal telle;
17 hou grete thingis he hath do to my soule. I criede to hym
18 with my mouth; and Y ioyede fulli vndir my tunge. If Y
bihelde wickidnesse in myn herte; the Lord schal not here.
19 Therfor God herde; and perseyuede the vois of my bisech-
20 yng. Blessid *be* God; that remeued not my preyer, and *took
not awei* his merci fro me.

PSALM LXVI (LXVII).

1 *The titil of the sixe and sixtithe salm. In Ebreu thus, To the
victorie in orguns, the salm of the song. In Jerom thus, To
the ouercomer in salmes, the song of writing of a delitable
thing with metre.*

2 God haue merci on vs, and blesse vs; liȝtne he his cheer
3 on vs, and haue merci on vs. That we knowe thi weie on
4 erthe; thin heelthe in alle folkis. God, puplis knowleche to
5 thee; alle puplis knouleche to thee. Hethen men be glad,
and make fulli ioye, for thou demest puplis in equite; and

6 dressist hethene men in erthe. God, puplis knouleche to
7 thee, alle puplis knouleche to thee; the erthe 3af his fruyt.
God, oure God blesse vs, God blesse vs; and alle the coostis
of erthe drede hym.

Psalm LXVII (LXVIII).

1 *The titil of the seuene and sixtithe salm. To the victorie, the salm of the song of Dauid.*

2 God rise vp, and hise enemyes be scaterid; and thei that
3 haten hym fle fro his face. As smoke failith, faile thei; as
wax fletith fro the face of fier, so perische synneris fro the
4 face of God. And iust men eete, and make fulli ioye in the
5 si3t of God; and delite thei in gladnesse. Synge 3e to God,
seie 3e salm to his name; make 3e weie to hym, that stieth
on the goyng doun, the Lord *is* name to hym. Make 3e fulli
ioye in his si3t, *enemyes* schulen be disturblid fro the face of
6 hym, *which is* the fadir of fadirles and modirles children;
7 and the iuge of widewis. God *is* in his hooli place; God
that makith men of o wille to dwelle in the hous. Which
leedith out bi strengthe hem that ben boundun; in lijk maner
8 hem that maken scharp, that dwellen in sepulcris. God,
whanne thou 3edist out in the si3t of thi puple; whanne thou
9 passidist forth in the desert. The erthe was moued, for
heuenes droppiden doun fro the face of God of Synay; fro
10 the face of God of Israel. God, thou schalt departe wilful
reyn to thin eritage, and it was sijk; but thou madist it par-
11 fit. Thi beestis schulen dwelle therynne; God, thou hast
12 maad redi in thi swetnesse to the pore man. The Lord
schal 3yue a word; to hem that prechen the gospel with
13 myche vertu. The kyngis of vertues *ben maad* loued of the
derlyng; and to the fairnesse of the hous to departe spuylis.
14 If 3e slepen among the myddil of *eritagis*, the fetheris of the

culuer ben, of siluer; and the hyndrere thingis of the bak
15 therof *ben* in the shynyng of gold. While *the king of* heuene
demeth kyngis theronne, thei schulen be maad whitter then
16 snow in Selmon ; the hille of God *is* a fat hille. The crud-
17 did hil *is* a fat hil; wherto bileuen ȝe falsli, cruddid hillis?
The hil in which it plesith wel God to dwelle ther ynne ; for
18 the Lord schal dwelle in to the ende. The chare of God is
manyfoold with ten thousynde, a thousynde of hem that ben
19 glad; the Lord was in hem, in Syna, in the hooli. Thou
stiedist an hiȝ, thou tokist caitiftee ; thou resseyuedist ȝiftis
among men. For whi *thou tokist* hem that bileueden not;
20 for to dwelle in the Lord God. Blessid *be* the Lord ech dai ;
21 the God of oure heelthis schal make an eesie wei to vs. Oure
God *is* God to make men saaf; and outgoyng fro deeth *is*
22 of the Lord God. Netheles God schal breke the heedis of
hise enemyes ; the cop of the heere of hem that goen in her
23 trespassis. The Lord seide, Y schal turne fro Basan ; Y
24 schal turne in to the depthe of the see. That thi foot be
deppid in blood ; the tunge of thi doggis *be dippid in blood* of
25 the enemyes of hym. God, thei sien thi goyngis yn ; the
goyngis yn of my God, of my king, which is in the hooli.
26 Prynces ioyned with syngeris camen bifore ; in the myddil of
27 ȝonge dameselis syngynge in tympans. In chirchis blesse ȝe
28 God ; *blesse ȝe* the Lord fro the wellis of Israel. There
Beniamyn, a ȝonge man ; in the rauyschyng of mynde. The
princis of Juda *weren* the duykis of hem ; the princis of
29 Zabulon, the princis of Neptalym. God, comaunde thou to
thi vertu ; God, conferme thou this thing, which thou hast
30 wrouȝt in vs. Fro thi temple, which is in Jerusalem ; kyngis
31 schulen offre ȝiftis to thee. Blame thou the wielde beestis of
the reheed, the gaderyng togidere of bolis is among the kien
of puplis ; that thei exclude hem that ben preuyd bi siluer.
32 Distrie thou folkis that wolen batels, legatis schulen come fro

Egipt; Ethiopie schal come bifore the hondis therof to God.
33 Rewmes of the erthe, synge ȝe to God; seie ȝe salm to
34 the Lord. Singe ȝe to God; that stiede on the heuene
of heuene at the eest. Lo! he schal ȝyue to his vois the
35 vois of vertu, ȝyue ȝe glorie to God on Israel; his greet
36 doyng and his vertu *is* in the cloudis. God *is* wondirful in
hise scyntis; God of Israel, he schal ȝyue vertu, and strengthe
to his puple; blessid be God.

Psalm LXVIII (LXIX).

1 *The titil of the eiȝte and sixtithe salm. In Ebreu thus, To the victorie, on the roosis of Dauid. In Jerom thus, To the ouercomer, for the sones of Dauid.*

2 God, make thou me saaf; for watris entriden til to my
3 soule. I am set in the sliym of the depthe; and substaunce
is not. I cam in to the depthe of the see; and the tempest
4 drenchide me. I traueilide criynge, my cheekis weren maad
hoose; myn iȝen failiden, the while Y hope in to my God.
5 Thei that hatiden me with out cause; weren multiplied aboue
the heeris of myn heed. Myn enemyes that pursueden me
vniustli weren coumfortid; Y paiede thanne tho thingis,
6 whiche Y rauischide not. God, thou knowist myn vnkun-
7 nyng; and my trespassis ben not hid fro thee. Lord, Lord
of vertues; thei, that abiden thee, be not aschamed in me.
God of Israel; thei, that seken thee, be not schent on me.
8 For Y suffride schenschipe for thee; schame hilide my face.
9 I am maad a straunger to my britheren; and a pilgryme to
10 the sones of my modir. For the feruent loue of thin hous eet
me; and the schenschipis of men sciynge schenschipis to
11 thee fellen on me. And Y hilide my soule with fastyng;
12 and it was maad in to schenschip to me. And Y puttide my
cloth an heire; and Y am maad to hem in to a parable.

13 Thei, that saten in the ȝate, spaken aȝens me; and thei, that
14 drunken wien, sungen of me. But Lord, *Y dresse* my preier
to thee; God, *Y abide* the tyme of good plesaunce. Here
thou me in the multitude of thi mercy; in the treuthe of thin
15 heelthe. Delyuer thou me fro the cley, that Y be not faste
set in; delyuere thou me fro hem that haten me, and fro
16 depthe of watris. The tempest of watir drenche not me,
nethir the depthe swolowe me; nethir the pit make streit his
17 mouth on me. Lord, here thou me, for thi merci is benygne;
vp the multitude of thi merciful doyngis biholde thou in to
18 me. And turne not awei thi face fro thi child; for Y am in
19 tribulacioun, here thou me swiftli. Ȝyue thou tente to my
soule, and delyuer thou it; for myn enemyes delyuere thou
20 me. Thou knowist my schenschip, and my dispysyng; and
21 my schame. Alle that troblen me ben in thi siȝt; myn herte
abood schendschipe, and wretchidnesse. And Y abood hym,
that was sory togidere, and noon was; and that schulde
22 coumforte, and Y foond not. And thei ȝauen galle in to my
meete; and in my thirst thei ȝauen to me drinke with
23 vynegre. The boord of hem be maad bifore hem in to a
24 snare; and in to ȝeldyngis, and in to sclaundir. Her iȝen
be maad derk, that thei se not; and euere bouwe doun the
25 bak of hem. Schede out thin ire on hem; and the strong
26 veniaunce of thin ire take hem. The habitacioun of hem be
maad forsakun; and noon be that dwelle in the tabernaclis
27 of hem. For thei pursueden hym, whom thou hast smyte;
28 and thei addiden on the sorewe of my woundis. Adde thou
wickidnesse on the wickidnesse of hem; and entre thei not
29 in to thi riȝtwisnesse. Be thei don awei fro the book of
30 lyuynge men; and be thei not writun with iust men. I am
31 pore and sorewful; God, thin heelthe took me vp. I schal
herye the name of God with song; and Y schal magnefye
32 hym in heriyng. And it schal plese God more than a newe

33 calf; bryngynge forth hornes and clees. Pore men se, and
34 be glad; seke ʒe God, and ʒoure soule schal lyue. For the
Lord herde pore men; and dispiside not hise boundun men.
35 Heuenes and erthe, herye hym; the se, and alle crepynge
36 bestis in tho, *herye hym*. For God schal make saaf Syon;
and the citees of Juda schulen be bildid. And thei schulen
37 dwelle there; and thei schulen gete it bi eritage. And the
seed of hise seruauntis schal haue it in possessioun; and thei
that louen his name, schulen dwelle ther-ynne.

Psalm LXIX (LXX).

1 *The titil of the nyne and sixtithe salm. To the victorie of Dauid, to haue mynde.*

2   God, biholde thou in to myn heelp; Lord, hast thou to
3 helpe me. Be thei schent, and aschamed; that seken my
lijf. Be thei turned a-bak; and schame thei, that wolen
4 yuels to me. Be thei turned awei anoon, and schame thei;
5 that seien to me, Wel! wel! Alle men that seken thee,
make fulli ioie, and be glad in thee; and thei that louen thin
6 heelthe, seie euere, The Lord be magnyfied. Forsothe Y am
a nedi man, and pore; God, helpe thou me. Thou art myn
helper and my delyuerere; Lord, tarye thou not.

Psalm LXX (LXXI).

1   *The seuentithe salm hath no title.*

Lord, Y hopide in thee, be Y not schent with-outen ende;
2 in thi riʒtwisnesse delyuere thou me, and rauysche me out.
3 Bowe doun thin eere to me; and make me saaf. Be thou to
me in to God a defendere; and in to a strengthid place, that
thou make me saaf. For thou art my stidefastnesse; and
4 my refuit. My God, delyuere thou me fro the hoond of the

synner; and fro the hoond of a man doynge a3ens the lawe,
5 and of the wickid man. For thou, Lord, art my pacience;
6 Lord, *thou art* myn hope fro my 3ongthe. In thee Y am
confermyd fro the wombe; thou art my defendere fro the
7 wombe of my modir. My syngyng *is* euere in thee; Y am
maad as a greet wonder to many men; and thou *art* a strong
8 helpere. My mouth be fillid with heriyng; that Y synge thi
9 glorie, al dai thi greetnesse. Caste thou not awei me in the
tyme of eldnesse; whanne my vertu failith, forsake thou not
10 me. For myn enemyes seiden of me; and thei that kepten
11 my lijf maden counsel togidere. Seiynge, God hath forsake
hym; pursue 3e, and take hym; for noon is that schal
12 delyuere. God, be thou not maad afer fro me; my God,
13 biholde thou in to myn help. Men that bacbiten my soule,
be schent, and faile thei; and be thei hilid with schenschip
14 and schame, that seken yuels to me. But Y schal hope
15 euere; and Y schal adde euere ouer al thi preising. Mi
mouth schal telle thi ri3tfulnesse; al dai thin helthe. For Y
knewe not lettrure, Y schal entre in to the poweres of the
16 Lord; Lord, Y schal bithenke on thi ri3tfulnesse aloone.
17 God, thou hast tau3t me fro my 3ongthe, and til to now; Y
18 schal telle out thi merueilis. And til in to the eldnesse and
the laste age; God, forsake thou not me. Til Y telle thin
arm; to eche generacioun, that schal come. *Til Y telle* thi
19 my3t, and thi ri3tfulnesse, God, til in to the hi3este grete dedis
20 which thou hast do; God, who is lijk thee? Hou grete
tribulaciouns many and yuele hast thou schewid to me; and
thou conuertid hast quykenyd me, and hast eft brou3t me
21 a3en fro the depthis of erthe. Thou hast multiplied thi greet
22 doyng; and thou conuertid hast coumfortid me. For whi
and Y schal knowleche to thee, thou God, thi treuthe in the
instrumentis of salm; Y schal synge in an harpe to thee, *that*
23 *art* the hooli of Israel. Mi lippis schulen make fulli ioye,

whanne Y schal synge to thee; and my soule, which thou
24 aȝen-bouȝtist. But and my tunge schal thenke al dai on thi
riȝtfulnesse; whanne thei schulen be schent and aschamed,
that seken yuelis to me.

Psalm LXXI (LXXII).

1   *The tille of the oon and seuentithe salm.   To Salomon.*

2   God, ȝyue thi doom to the king; and thi riȝtfulnesse to the
sone of a king.   To deme thi puple in riȝtfulnesse; and thi
3 pore men in doom.   Mounteyns resseyue pees to the puple;
4 and litle hillis *resseyue* riȝtfulnesse.   He schal deme the pore
men of the puple, and he schal make saaf the sones of pore
5 men; and he schal make low the false chalengere.   And he
schal dwelle with the sunne, and bifore the moone; in genera-
6 cioun and in to generacioun.   He schal come doun as reyn
7 in to a flees; and as goteris droppinge on the erthe.   Riȝtfulnesse schal come forth in hise dayes, and the aboundaunce
8 of pees; til the moone be takun awei.   And he schal be lord
fro the see til to the see; and fro the flood til to the endis of
9 the world.   Ethiopiens schulen falle doun bifore hym; and
10 hise enemyes schulen licke the erthe.   The kyngis of Tarsis
and ilis schulen offre ȝiftis; the kyngis of Arabie and of Saba
11 schulen brynge ȝiftis.   And alle kyngis schulen worschipe
12 hym; alle folkis schulen serue hym.   For he schal delyuer a
pore man fro the miȝti; and a pore man to whom was noon
13 helpere.   He schal spare a pore man and nedi; and he schal
14 make saaf the soulis of pore men.   He schal aȝen-bie the
soulis of hem fro vsuris, and wickidnesse; and the name of
15 hem *is* onourable bifor hym.   And he schal lyue, and me
schal ȝyue to hym of the gold of Arabie; and thei schulen
euere worschipe of hym, al dai thei schulen blesse hym.
16 Stidefastnesse schal be in the erthe, in the hiȝeste places of

mounteyns; the fruyt therof schal be enhaunsid aboue the
Liban; and thei schulen blosme fro the citee, as the hey of
17 erthe doith. His name be blessid in to worldis; his name
dwelle bifore the sunne. And all the lynagis of erthe schulen
18 be blessid in hym; alle folkis schulen magnyfie hym. Blessid
be the Lord God of Israel; which aloone makith merueiylis.
19 Blessid be the name of his maieste with-outen ende; and
al erthe schal be fillid with his maieste; be it doon, be it
doon.
20 *The preieris of Dauid, the sone of Ysay, ben endid.*

Psalm LXXII (LXXIII).

1 *The title of the two and seuentithe salm. The salm of Asaph.*

God of Israel *is* ful good; to hem that ben of ri3tful herte.
2 But my feet weren moued almeest; my steppis weren sched
3 out almeest. For Y louede feruentli on wickid men; seynge
4 the pees of synneris. For biholdyng is not to the deth of
5 hem; and stidefastnesse in the sikenesse of hem. Thei ben
not in the trauel of men; and thei schulen not be betun with
6 men. Therfore pride helde hem; thei weren hilid with her
7 wickidnesse and vnfeithfulnesse. The wickidnesse of hem
cam forth as of fatnesse; thei 3eden in to desire of herte.
8 Thei thou3ten and spaken weiwardnesse; thei spaken wickid-
9 nesse an hi3. Thei puttiden her mouth in to heuene; and
10 her tunge passide in erthe. Therfor my puple schal be conuertid here; and fulle daies schulen be foundun in hem.
11 And thei sciden, How woot God; and whether kunnyng is
12 an hei3e, *that is, in heuene?* Lo! thilke synneris and hauynge
13 aboundance in the world; helden richessis. And Y seide,
Therfor without cause Y iustifiede myn herte; and waischide
14 myn hoondis among innocentis. And Y was betun al dai;
15 and my chastisyng *was* in morutidis. If Y seide, Y schal telle

16 thus; lo! Y repreuede the nacioun of thi sones. I gesside,
17 that Y schulde knowe this; trauel is bifore me. Til Y entre
in to the seyntuarie of God; and vndurstonde in the last
18 thingis of hem. Netheles for gilis thou hast put to hem;
19 thou castidist hem doun; while thei weren reisid. Hou ben
thei maad into desolacioun; thei failiden sodeynli, thei peri-
20 schiden for her wickidnesse. As the dreem of men that
risen; Lord, thou schalt dryue her ymage to nou3t in thi
21 citee. For myn herte is enflaumed, and my reynes ben
22 chaungid; and Y am dryuun to nou3t, and Y wiste not.
23 As a werk-beeste Y am maad at thee; and Y am euere
24 with thee. Thou heldist my ri3thond, and in thi wille thou
25 leddist me forth; and with glorie thou tokist me vp. For
whi what is to me in heuene; and what wolde Y of thee on
26 erthe? Mi fleische and myn herte failide; God of myn herte,
27 and my part *is* God withouten ende. For lo! thei that
drawen awei fer hem silf fro thee, *bi deedli synne*, schulen
perische; thou hast lost alle men that doen fornycacioun fro
28 thee. But it is good to me to cleue to God; and to sette
myn hope in the Lord God. That Y telle alle thi prechyngis;
in the 3atis of the dou3ter of Syon.

Psalm LXXIII (LXXIV).

1 *The title of the thre and seuentithe salm. The lernyng of Asaph.*

God, whi hast thou put awei in to the ende; thi strong
2 veniaunce is wrooth on the scheep of thi leesewe? Be thou
myndeful of thi gaderyng togidere; which thou haddist in
possessioun fro the bigynnyng. Thou a3enbou3tist the 3erde
of thin eritage; the hille of Syon in which thou dwellidist
3 ther ynne. Reise thin hondis in to the prides of hem; hou
4 grete thingis the enemy dide wickidli in the hooli. And

thei that hatiden thee; hadden glorie in the myddis of thi
5 solempnete. Thei settiden her signes, *ethir baneris*, signes
on the hi3este, as in the outgoing; and thei knewen not.
6 As in a wode of trees thei heweden doun with axis the 3atis
therof in to it silf; thei castiden doun it with an ax, and
7 a brood fallinge ax. Thei brenten with fier thi seyntuarie;
8 thei defouliden the tabernacle of thi name in erthe. The
kynrede of hem seiden togidere in her herte; Make we alle
9 the feest-daies of God to ceesse fro the erthe. We han not
seyn oure signes, now no profete is; and he schal no more
10 knowe vs. God, hou long schal the enemye seie dispit? the
11 aduersarie territh to ire thi name in to the ende. Whi turnest
thou awei thin hoond, and *to drawe out* thi ri3thond fro the
12 myddis of thi bosum, til in to the ende? Forsothe God
oure kyng bifore worldis; wrou3te heelthe in the mydis of
13 erthe. Thou madist sad the see bi thi vertu; thou hast
14 troblid the heedis of dragouns in watris. Thou hast broke
the heedis of the dragoun; thou hast 3oue hym to mete to
15 the puplis of Ethiopiens. Thou hast broke wellis, and
16 strondis; thou madist drie the flodis of Ethan. The dai is
thin, and the ni3t is thin; thou madist the moreutid and the
17 sunne. Thou madist alle the endis of erthe; somer and
18 veer-tyme, thou fourmedist tho. Be thou myndeful of this
thing, the enemye hath seid schenschip to the Lord; and
19 the vnwijs puple hath excitid to ire thi name. Bitake thou
not to beestis men knoulechenge to thee; and for3ete thou
20 not in to the ende the soulis of thi pore men. Biholde
in to thi testament; for thei that ben maad derk of erthe,
21 ben fillid with the housis of wickidnessis. A meke man
be not turned awei maad aschamed; a pore man and nedi
22 schulen herie thi name. God, rise vp, deme thou thi cause;
be thou myndeful of thin vpbreidyngis, of tho that ben
23 al dai of the vnwise man. For3ete thou not the voices

of thin enemyes; the pride of hem that haten thee, stieth cuere.

Psalm LXXIV (LXXV).

1 *The title of the foure and seuentithe salm. To the ouercomere; leese thou not the salm of the song of Asaph.*

2 God, we schulen knouleche to thee, we schulen knou-
3 leche; and we schulen inwardli clepe thi name. We schulen telle thi merueilis; whanne Y schal take tyme, Y schal deme
4 riȝtfulnesses. The erthe is meltid, and alle that duellen ther-
5 ynne; Y confermede the pileris therof. I seide to wickid men, Nyle ȝe do wickidli; and to trespassouris, Nyle ȝe
6 enhaunce the horn. Nyle ȝe reise an hiȝ ȝoure horn; nyle
7 ȝe speke wickidnesse aȝens God. For nether fro the eest,
8 nethir fro the west, nethir fro desert hillis; for God is the
9 iuge. He mekith this *man*, and enhaunsith hym; for a cuppe of cleene wyn ful of meddling *is* in the hoond of the Lord. And he bowide of this in to that; netheles the drast therof is not anyntischid; alle synneris of erthe schulen
10 drinke therof. Forsothe Y schal telle in to the world;
11 Y schal synge to God of Jacob. And Y schal breke alle the hornes of synneris; and the hornes of the iust man schulen be enhaunsid.

Psalm LXXV (LXXVI).

1 *The title of the fyue and seuentithe salm. To the victorie in orguns, the salm of the song of Asaph.*

2 God is knowun in Judee; his name is greet in Israel.
3 And his place is maad in pees; and his dwellyng *is* in Syon.
4 Ther he brak poweris; bowe, scheeld, swerd, and batel.
5 And thou, God, liȝtnest wondirfuli fro euerlastynge hillis;

6 alle vnwise men of herte weren troblid. Thei slepten her
sleep; and alle men founden no thing of richessis in her
7 hondis. Thei that stieden on horsis; slepten for thi blam-
8 yng, thou God of Jacob. Thou art feerful, and who schal
9 aȝenstonde thee? fro that tyme thin ire. Fro heuene thou
10 madist doom herd; the erthe tremblide, and restide. Whanne
God roos vp in to doom; to make saaf al the mylde men of
11 erthe. For the thouȝt of man schal knouleche to thee; and
12 the relifs of thouȝt schulen make a feeste-dai to thee. Make
ȝe a vow, and ȝelde ȝe to ȝoure Lord God; alle that bringen
13 ȝiftis in the cumpas of it. To God ferdful, and to him that
takith awei the spirit of prynces; to the ferdful at the kyngis
of erthe.

Psalm LXXVI (LXXVII).

1 *The title of the sixte and seuentithe salm. To the ouercomere
on Yditum, the salm of Asaph.*

2 With my vois Y criede to the Lord; with my vois to
3 God, and he ȝaf tent to me. In the dai of my tribulacioun
Y souȝte God with myn hondis; in the nyȝt to-fore hym, and
4 Y am not disseyued. Mi soule forsook to be coumfortid; Y
was myndeful of God, and Y delitide, and Y was exercisid;
5 and my spirit failide. Myn iȝen bifore took wakyngis; Y
6 was disturblid, and Y spak not. I thouȝte elde daies; and
7 Y hadde in mynde euerlastinge ȝeeris. And Y thouȝte in
the nyȝt with myn herte; and Y was exercisid, and Y clensid
8 my spirit. Whether God schal caste awei with-outen ende;
9 ether schal he not lei to, that he be more plesid ȝit? Ethir
schal he kitte awei his merci into the ende; fro generacioun
10 in to generacioun? Ethir schal God forȝete to do mercy;
11 ethir schal he withholde his mercies in his ire? And Y
seide, Now Y bigan; this *is* the chaunging of the riȝthond of
12 the hiȝe *God.* I hadde mynde on the werkis of the Lord;

K 2

for Y schal haue mynde fro the bigynnyng of thi merueilis.
13 And Y schal thenke in alle thi werkis; and Y schal be
14 occupied in thi fyndyngis. God, thi weie *was* in the hooli;
15 what God *is* greet as oure God? thou art God, that doist
merueilis. Thou madist thi vertu knowun among puplis;
16 thou aʒenbouʒtist in thi arm thi puple, the sones of Jacob and
17 of Joseph. God, watris sien thee, watris sien thee, and
18 dredden; and depthis of watris weren disturblid. The mul-
19 titude of the soun of watris; cloudis ʒauen vois. For whi
thin arewis passen; the vois of thi thundir *was* in a wheel.
Thi liʒtnyngis schyneden to the world; the erthe was moued,
20 and tremblid. Thi weie in the see, and thi pathis in many
21 watris; and thi steppis schulen not be knowun. Thou
leddist forth thi puple as scheep; in the hond of Moyses
and of Aaron.

Psalm LXXVII (LXXVIII).

1 *The title of the seuene and scuentithe salm. The lernyng of Asaph.*

Mɪ puple, perseyue ʒe my lawe; bowe ʒoure eere in to
2 the wordis of my mouth. I schal opene my mouth in para-
3 blis; Y schal speke perfite resouns fro the bigynnyng. Hou
grete thingis han we herd, and we han knowe tho; and oure
4 fadris telden to vs. Tho ben not hid fro the sones of hem;
in anothir generacioun. And thei telden the heriyngis of
the Lord, and the vertues of hym; and hise merueilis,
5 whyche he dide. And he reiside witnessyng in Jacob; and
he settide lawe in Israel. Hou grete thingis comaundide he
6 to oure fadris, to make tho knowun to her sones; that
another generacioun knowe. Sones, that schulen be born,
7 and schulen rise vp; schulen telle out to her sones. That
thei sette her hope in God, and forʒete not the werkis of
8 God; and that thei seke hise comaundementis. Lest thei

be maad a schrewid generacioun; and terrynge to wraththe, as the fadris of hem. A generacioun that dresside not his herte; and his spirit was not bileued with God. The sones of Effraym, bendinge a bouwe and sendynge arowis; weren turned in the dai of batel. Thei kepten not the testament of God; and thei nolden go in his lawe. And thei forʒaten hise benefices; and hise merueils, whiche he schewide to hem. He dide merueils bifore the fadris of hem in the loond of Egipt; in the feeld of Taphneos. He brak the see, and ledde hem thorou; and he ordeynede the watris as in a bouge. And he ledde hem forth in a cloude of the dai; and al niʒt in the liʒtnyng of fier. He brak a stoon in deseert; and he ʒaf watir to hem as in a myche depthe. And he ledde watir out of the stoon; and he ledde forth watris as floodis. And thei leiden to ʒit to do synne aʒens hym; thei excitiden hiʒe *God* in to ire, in a place with out water. And thei temptiden God in her hertis; that thei axiden meetis to her lyues. And thei spaken yuel of God; thei seiden, Whether God may make redi a bord in desert? For he smoot a stoon, and watris flowiden; and streemys ʒeden out in aboundaunce. Whether also he may ʒyue breed; ether make redi a bord to his puple? Therfor the Lord herde, and delaiede; and fier was kindelid in Jacob, and the ire of God stiede on Israel. For thei bileueden not in God; nether hopiden in his heelthe. And he comaundide to the cloudis aboue; and he openyde the ʒatis of heuene. And he reynede to hem manna for to eete; and he ʒaf to hem breed of heuene. Man eet the breed of aungels; he sent to hem meetis in aboundance. He turnede ouere the south wynde fro heuene; and he brouʒte in bi his vertu the weste wynde. And he reynede fleischis as dust on hem; and *he reinede* volatils fethered, as the grauel of the see. And tho felden doun in the myddis of her castels; aboute

29 the tabernaclis of hem. And thei eeten, and weren fillid
30 greetli, and he brouȝte her desire to hem; thei weren not
defraudid of her desier. ȝit her metis weren in her mouth;
31 and the ire of God stiede on hem. And he killide the fatte
32 men of hem; and he lettide the chosene men of Israel. In
alle these thingis thei synneden ȝit; and bileuede not in the
33 merueils of God. And the daies of hem failiden in vanytee;
34 and the ȝeeris of hem *faileden* with haste. Whanne he
killide hem, thei souȝten hym; and turneden aȝen, and eerli
35 thei camen to hym. And thei bithouȝten, that God is the
helper of hem; and the hiȝ God is the aȝenbier of hem.
36 And thei loueden hym in her mouth; and with her tunge thei
37 lieden to hym. Forsothe the herte of hem was not riȝtful
with hym; nethir thei weren had feithful in his testament.
38 But he is merciful, and he schal be maad merciful to the
synnes of hem; and he schal not destrie hem. And he dide
greetli, to turne awei his yre; and he kyndelide not al his ire.
39 And he bithouȝte, that thei ben fleische; a spirit goynge, and
40 not turnynge aȝen. Hou oft maden thei hym wrooth in
desert; thei stireden hym in to ire in a place with out watir.
41 And thei weren turned, and temptiden God; and thei
42 wraththiden the hooli of Israel. Thei bithouȝten not on
his hond; in the dai in the which he aȝen-bouȝte hem fro
43 the hond of the trobler. As he settide hise signes in
Egipt; and hise grete wondris in the feeld of Taphneos.
44 And he turnede the flodis of hem and the reynes of hem
45 in to blood; that thei schulden not drynke. He sente a
fleisch flie in to hem, and it eet hem; and *he sente* a paddok,
46 and it loste hem. And he ȝaf the fruytis of hem to rust; and
47 *he ȝaf* the trauels of hem to locustis. And he killide the
vynes of hem bi hail; and the moore trees of hem bi a frost.
48 And he bitook the beestis of hem to hail; and the posses-
49 sioun of hem to fier. He sente in to hem the ire of his

indignacioun; indignacioun, and ire, and tribulacioun, send-
50 ingis in bi iuel aungels. He made weie to the path of his
ire, and he sparide not fro the deth of her lyues; and he
51 closide togidere in deth the beestis of hem. And he smoot
al the first gendrid thing in the lond of Egipt; the first
fruytis of alle the trauel of hem in the tabernaclis of Cham.
52 And he took awei his puple as scheep; and he ledde hem
53 forth as a flok in desert. And he ledde hem forth in hope,
and thei dredden not; and the see hilide the enemyes of
54 hem. And he brouȝte hem in to the hil of his halewyng; in
to the hil which his riȝthond gat. And he castide out hethene
men fro the face of hem; and bi lot he departide to hem the
55 lond in a cord of delyng. And he made the lynagis of Israel
56 to dwelle in the tabernaclis of hem. And thei temptiden, and
wraththiden heiȝ God; and thei kepten not hise witnessyngis.
57 And thei turneden awei hem silf, and thei kepten not couenaunt; as her fadris weren turned in to a schrewid bouwe.
58 Thei stiriden him in to ire in her litle hillis; and thei
59 terriden hym to indignacioun of her grauen ymagis. God
herde, and forsook; and brouȝte to nouȝt Israel greetli.
60 And he puttide awei the tabernacle of Sylo; his tabernacle
61 where he dwellide among men. And he bitook the vertu
of hem in to caitiftee; and the fairnesse of hem in to the
62 hondis of the enemye. And he closide togidere his puple in
63 swerd; and he dispiside his erytage. Fier eet the ȝonge
men of hem; and the virgyns of hem weren not biweilid.
64 The prestis of hem fellen doun bi swerd; and the widewis of
65 hem weren not biwept. And the Lord was reisid, as slep-
66 ynge; as miȝti greetli fillid of wiyn. And he smoot hise
enemyes on the hynderere partis; he ȝaf to hem euerlastyng
67 schenschipe. And he puttide awei the tabernacle of Joseph;
68 and he chees not the lynage of Effraym. But he chees the
lynage of Juda; *he chees* the hil of Syon, which he louede.

69 And he as an vnicorn bildide his hooli place ; in the lond.
70 which he foundide in to worldis. And he chees Dauid his
seruaunt, and took hym vp fro the flockis of scheep; he took
71 hym fro bihyndc scheep with lambren. To feed Jacob his
72 seruaunt ; and Israel his eritage. And he fedde hem in the
innocens of his herte ; and he ledde hem forth in the vndur-
stondyngis of his hondis.

Psalm LXXVIII (LXXIX).

1   *The title of the eiȝte and seuentithe salm. Of Asaph.*

God, hethene men cam in to thin eritage; thei defouliden
thin hooli temple, thei settiden Jerusalem in to the keping
2 of applis. Thei settiden the slayn bodies of thi seruauntis,
meetis to the volatilis of heuenes ; the fleischis of thi seyntis
3 to the beestis of the erthe. Thei schedden out the blood
of hem, as watir in the cumpas of Jerusalem ; and noon
4 was that biriede. We ben maad schenschipe to oure neiȝboris ; mowynge and scornynge to hem, that ben in oure
5 cumpas. Lord, hou longe schalt thou be wrooth in to
6 the ende ? schal thi veniaunce be kyndelid as fier ? Schede
out thin ire in to hethene men, that knowen not thee ; and
7 in to rewmes, that clepiden not thi name. For thei eeten
8 Jacob ; and maden desolat his place. Haue thou not mynde
on oure elde wickidnesses ; thi mercies biforc take vs soone,
9 for we ben maad pore greetli. God, oure heelthe, helpe
thou vs, and, Lord, for the glorie of thi name delyuer thou
10 vs ; and be thou merciful to oure synnes for thi name. Lest
perauenture thei seie among hethene men, Where is the
God of hem ? and be he knowun among naciouns bifore
oure iȝen. The veniaunce of the blood of thi seruauntis,
which is sched out ; the weilyng of feterid men entre in
11 thi siȝt. Vpe the greetnesse of thin arm ; welde thou the

12 sones of slayn men. And ȝelde thou to oure neiȝboris seuenfoold in the bosum of hem; the schenschip of hem, 13 which thei diden schenschipfuli to thee, thou Lord. But we *that ben* thi puple, and the scheep of thi leesewe; schulen knouleche to thee in to the world. In generacioun and in to generacioun; we schulen telle thin heriyng.

Psalm LXXIX (LXXX).

1 *The title of the nyne and seuentithe salm. To victorie; this salm is witnessing of Asaph for lilies.*

2 Thou that gouernest Israel, ȝyue tent; that leedist forth Joseph as a scheep. Thou that sittist on cherubym; be 3 schewid bifore Effraym, Beniamyn, and Manasses. Stire 4 thi power, and come thou; that thou make vs saaf. God of vertues, turne thou vs; and schewe thi face, and we 5 schulen be saaf. Lord God of vertues; hou longe schalt 6 thou be wrooth on the preier of thi seruaunt? *Hou longe* schalt thou feede vs with the breed of teeris; and schalt 7 ȝyue drynke to vs with teeris in mesure? Thou hast set vs in to aȝenseiyng to oure neiȝboris; and oure enemyes 8 han scornyde vs. God of vertues, turne thou vs; and 9 schewe thi face, and we schulen be saaf. Thou translatidist a vyne fro Egipt; thou castidist out hethene men, 10 and plauntidist it. Thou were leeder of the weie in the siȝt therof; and thou plauntidist the rootis therof, and it 11 fillide the lond. The schadewe therof hilide hillis; and 12 the braunchis therof *filliden* the cedris of God. It streiȝte forth hise siouns til to the see, and the generacioun ther-13 of til to the flood. Whi hast thou destried the wal therof; and alle men that goen forth bi the weie gaderiden awei 14 the grapis therof? A boor of the wode distriede it; and 15 a singuler wielde beeste deuouride it. God of vertues, be

thou turned; biholde thou fro heuene, and se, and visite
16 this vyne. And make thou it perfit, which thi riȝthond
plauntide; and *biholde thou* on the sone of man, which
17 thou hast confermyd to thee. Thingis brent with fier, and
vndurmyned; schulen perische for the blamyng of thi cheer.
18 Thin hond be maad on the man of thi riȝthond; and on
the sone of man, whom thou hast confermed to thee.
19 And we departiden not fro thee; thou schalt quykene vs,
20 and we schulen inwardli clepe thi name. Lord God of
vertues, turne thou vs; and schewe thi face, and we schulen
be saaf.

Psalm LXXX (LXXXI).

1 *The title of the ciȝtetithe salm. To the ouercomer*
in the pressours of Asaph.

2 Make ȝe fulli ioye to God, oure helpere; synge ȝe hertli
3 to God of Jacob. Take ȝe a salm, and ȝyue ȝe a tympan;
4 a myrie sautere with an harpe. Blowe ȝe with a trumpe
5 in Neomenye; in the noble dai of ȝoure solempnite. For
whi comaundement is in Israel; and doom *is* to God of
6 Jacob. He settide that witnessing in Joseph; whanne he
ȝede out of the lond of Egipt, he herde a langage, which
7 he knew not. He turnede a-wei his bak fro birthens; hise
8 hondis serueden in a coffyn. In tribulacioun thou inwardli
clepidist me, and Y delyuerede thee; Y herde thee in the
hid place of tempest, Y preuede thee at the water of aȝen-
9 seiyng. My puple, here thou, and Y schal be witnesse
10 aȝens thee; Israel, if thou herist me, a fresche God schal
not be in thee, and thou schalt not worschipe an alien
11 god. For Y am thi Lord God, that ladde thee out of
the lond of Egipt; make large thi mouth, and Y schal
12 fille it. And my puple herde not my vois; and Israel
13 ȝaue not tente to me. And Y lefte hem aftir the desiris

14 of her herte; thei schulen go in her fyndyngis. If my puple hadde herde me; if Israel hadde go in my weies. 15 For nou3t in hap Y hadde maad low her enemyes; and Y hadde send myn hond on men doynge tribulacioun to 16 hem. The enemyes of the Lord lieden to hym; and her 17 tyme schal be in to worldis. And he fedde hem of the fatnesse of whete; and he fillide hem with hony of the stoon.

Psalm LXXXI (LXXXII).

1 *The title of the oon and ei3tetithe salm. Of Asaph.*

God stood in the synagoge of goddis; forsothe he demeth 2 goddis in the myddil. Hou longe demen 3e wickidnesse; 3 and taken the faces of synneris? Deme 3e to the nedi man, and to the modirles child; iustifie 3e the meke man 4 and pore. Raueische 3e out a pore man; and delyuere 3e 5 the nedi man fro the hond of the synner. Thei knewen not, nether vndirstoden, thei goen in derknessis; alle the 6 foundementis of erthe schulen be moued. I seide, 3e ben 7 goddis; and alle 3e ben the sones of hi3 *God*. But 3e schulen die as men; and 3e schulen falle doun as oon of 8 the princis. Ryse, thou God, deme thou the erthe; for thou schalt haue eritage in alle folkis.

Psalm LXXXII (LXXXIII).

1 *The title of the two and ei3tetithe salm. The song of the salm of Asaph.*

2 God, who schal be lijk thee? God, be thou not stille, 3 nether be thou peesid. For lo! thin enemyes sowneden; 4 and thei that haten thee reisiden the heed. Thei maden a wickid counsel on thi puple; and thei thou3ten a3ens 5 thi seyntis. Thei seiden, Come 3e, and leese we hem fro

the folk; and the name of Israel be no more hadde in
6, 7 mynde. For thei thou3ten with oon acord; the tabernaclis
of Ydumeys, and men of Ismael disposiden a testament
8 togidere a3ens thee. Moab, and Agarenus, Jebal, and Amon,
9 and Amalech; alienys with hem that dwellen in Tyre. For
Assur cometh with hem; thei ben maad in to help to the
10 sones of Loth. Make thou to hem as to Madian, and
11 Sisara; as to Jabyn in the stronde of Sison. Thei perischiden in Endor; thei weren maad as a toord of erthe.
12 Putte thou the prynces of hem as Oreb and Zeb; and
Zebee and Salmana. Alle the princis of hem, that seiden:
13, 14 Holde we bi eritage the seyntuarie of God. My God,
putte thou hem as a wheele; and as stobil bifor the face
15 of the wynde. As fier that brenneth a wode; and as
16 flawme brynnynge hillis. So thou schalt pursue hem in
thi tempeste; and thou schalt disturble hem in thin ire.
17 Lord, fille thou the faces of hem with schenschipe; and
18 thei schulen seke thi name. Be thei aschamed, and be
thei disturblid in to world of world; and be thei schent
19 and perische thei. And knowe thei, that the Lord is name
to thee; thou aloone *art* the hi3este in ech lond.

Psalm LXXXIII (LXXXIV).

1 *The title of the thre and ci3tetithe salm. The salm
of the sones of Chore.*

2, 3 Lord of vertues, thi tabernaclis ben greetli loued; my
soule coueitith, and failith in to the porchis of the Lord.
Myn herte and my fleische; ful out ioyeden in to quyk
4 God. For whi a sparewe fyndith an hous to it silf; and
a turtle *fyndith* a neste to it silf, where it schal kepe hise
bryddis. Lord of vertues, thin auteris; my king, and my
5 God. Lord, blessid *ben* thei that dwellen in thin hous;

6 thei schulen preise thee in to the worldis of worldis. Blessid *is* the man, whos help is of thee; he hath disposid stiyngis 7 in his herte, in the valei of teeris, in the place which he 8 hath set. For the ȝyuer of the lawe schal ȝyue blessyng, thei schulen go fro vertu in to vertu; God of goddis schal 9 be seyn in Sion. Lord God of vertues, here thou my preier; 10 God of Jacob, perseyue thou with eeris. God, oure defender, biholde thou; and biholde in to the face of thi 11 crist. For whi o dai in thin hallis is bettere; than a thousynde. I chees to be an out-cast in the hous of my God; 12 more than to dwelle in the tabernaclis of synneris. For God loueth merci and treuthe; the Lord schal ȝyue grace 13 and glorie. He schal not depriue hem fro goodis, that gon in innocence; Lord of vertues, blessid *is* the man, that hopith in thee.

Psalm LXXXIV (LXXXV).

1 *The title of the foure and eiȝtetithe salm. Of the sones of Chore.*

2 Lord, thou hast blessid thi lond; thou hast turned awei 3 the caitifte of Jacob. Thou hast forȝoue the wickidnesse 4 of thi puple; thou hast hilid alle the synnes of hem. Thou hast aswagid al thin ire; thou hast turned awei fro the ire 5 of thin indignacioun. God, oure helthe, conuerte thou vs; 6 and turne awei thin ire fro vs. Whether thou schalt be wrooth to vs withouten ende; ether schalt thou holde forth 7 thin ire fro generacioun in to generacioun? God, thou conuertid schalt quykene vs; and thi puple schal be glad 8 in thee. Lord, schewe thi merci to vs; and ȝyue thin 9 helthe to vs. I schal here what the Lord God schal speke in me; for he schal speke pees on his puple. And on hise hooli men; and on hem that ben turned to herte.

10 Netheles his helthe *is* niȝ men dredynge him; that glorie
11 dwelle in oure lond. Merci and treuthe metten hem silf;
12 riȝtwisnesse and pees weren kissid. Treuthe cam forth of
13 erthe; and riȝtfulnesse bihelde fro heuene. For the Lord
schal ȝyue benignyte; and oure erthe schal ȝyue his fruyt.
14 Riȝtfulnesse schal go bifore him; and schal sette hise steppis
in the weie.

Psalm LXXXV (LXXXVI).

The title of the fyue and ciȝtetithe salm. The preier of Dauid.

1 LORD, bowe doun thin eere, and here me; for Y am
2 nedi and pore. Kepe thou my lijf, for Y am holi; my
3 God, make thou saaf thi seruaunt hopynge in thee. Lord,
4 haue thou merci on me, for Y criede al day to thee; make
thou glad the soule of thi seruaunt, for whi, Lord, Y haue
5 reisid my soule to thee. For thou, Lord, *art* swete and
mylde; and of myche merci to alle men inwardli clepynge
6 thee. Lord, perseyue thou my preier with eeris; and ȝyue
7 thou tente to the vois of my bisechyng. In the dai of my
8 tribulacioun Y criede to thee; for thou herdist me. Lord,
noon among goddis is lijk thee; and noon is euene to thi
9 werkis. Lord, alle folkis, whiche euere thou madist, schulen
come, and worschipe bifore thee; and thei schulen glorifie
10 thi name. For thou art ful greet, and makinge merueils;
11 thou art God aloone. Lord, lede thou me forth in thi weie,
and Y schal entre in thi treuthe; myn herte be glad, that
12 it drede thi name. Mi Lord God, Y schal knouleche to
thee in al myn herte; and Y schal glorifie thi name with-
13 outen ende. For thi merci is greet on me; and thou de-
14 liueridist my soule fro the lower helle. God, wickid men
han rise vp on me; and the synagoge of myȝti men han
souȝt my lijf; and thei han not set forth thee in her siȝt.
15 And thou, Lord God, doynge merci, and merciful; pacient,

16 and of myche merci, and sothefast. Biholde on me, and haue mercy on me, ȝyue thou the empire to thi child; and 17 make thou saaf the sone of thin handmayden. Make thou with me a signe in good, that thei se, that haten me, and be aschamed; for thou, Lord, hast helpid me, and hast coumfortid me.

Psalm LXXXVI (LXXXVII).

1 *The title of the sixte and eiȝtetithe salm. The salm of the song of the sones of Chore.*

2 THE foundementis therof *ben* in hooli hillis; the Lord loueth the ȝatis of Sion, more than alle the tabernaclis of 3 Jacob. Thou citee of God, with-outen ende; gloriouse 4 thingis ben seide of thee. I schal be myndeful of Raab, and Babiloyne; knowynge me. Lo! aliens, and Tyre, and 5 the puple of Ethiopiens; thei weren there. Whether a man schal seie to Sion, And a man is born ther-ynne; and that 6 man altherhiȝeste foundide it? The Lord schal telle in the scripturis of puplis; and of these princis, that weren ther 7 ynne. As the dwellyng of alle that ben glad; is in thee.

Psalm LXXXVII (LXXXVIII).

1 *The title of the seuene and eiȝtetithe salm. The song of salm, to the sones of Chore, to victorie on Mahalat, for to answere, the lernyng of Heman Ezraite.*

2 LORD God of myn helthe; Y criede in dai and nyȝt 3 bifore thee. Mi preier entre bifore thi siȝt; bowe doun thin 4 eere to my preier. For my soule is fillid with yuels; and my 5 lijf neiȝede to helle. I am gessid with hem that goon doun 6 in to the lake; Y am maad as a man with-outen help, and fre among deed men. As men woundid slepinge in sepulcris, of whiche men noon is myndeful aftir; and thei ben put awei

7 fro thin hond. Thei han put me in the lower lake; in derke
8 places, and in the schadewe of deth. Thi strong veniaunce
is confermed on me; and thou hast brou3t in alle thi wawis
9 on me. Thou hast maad fer fro me my knowun; thei han
set me abhomynacioun to hem silf. I am takun, and Y 3ede
10 not out; myn i3en weren sijk for pouert. Lord, Y criede to
11 thee; al dai Y spredde abrood myn hondis to thee. Whethir
thou schalt do merueils to deed men; ether leechis schulen
12 reise, and thei schulen knouleche to thee? Whether ony
man in sepulcre schal telle thi merci; and thi treuthe in per-
13 dicioun? Whether thi merueilis schulen be knowun in derk-
14 nessis; and thi ri3tfulnesse in the lond of for3etyng? And,
Lord, Y criede to thee; and erli my preier schal bifor come
15 to thee. Lord, whi puttist thou awei my preier; turnest
16 awei thi face fro me? I am pore, and in traueils fro my
3ongthe; sotheli Y am enhaunsid, and Y am maad low, and
17 disturblid. Thi wraththis passiden on me; and thei dredis
18 disturbliden me. Thei cumpassiden me as watir al dai;
19 thei cumpassiden me togidere. Thou madist fer fro me a
frend and nei3bore; and my knowun fro wretchidnesse.

Psalm LXXXVIII (LXXXIX).

1 *The title of the ci3te and ci3ketithe salm. The lernyng of Ethan, Ezraite.*

2 I schal synge with-outen ende; the mercies of the Lord. In generacioun and in to generacioun; Y schal telle thi
3 treuthe with my mouth. For thou seidist, With-outen ende merci schal be bildid in heuenes; thi treuthe schal be maad
4 redi in tho. I disposide a testament to my chosun men; Y
5 swoor to Dauid, my seruaunt, Til in to with-outen ende I schal make redi thi seed. And Y schal bilde thi seete;
6 in generacioun, and in to generacioun. Lord, heuenes

schulen knoulcche thi merueilis; and thi treuthe in the
7 chirche of seyntis. For who in the cloudis schal be maad
euene to the Lord; schal be lijk God among the sones of
8 God? God, which is glorified in the counsel of seyntis;
is greet, and dreedful ouere alle that ben in his cumpas.
9 Lord God of vertues, who *is* lijk thee? Lord, thou art
10 miȝti, and thi treuthe *is* in thi cumpas. Thou art Lord
of the power of the see; forsothe thou aswagist the stiryng
11 of the wawis therof. Thou madist lowe the proude, as
woundid; in the arm of thi vertu thou hast scaterid thin
12 enemyes. Heuenes ben thin, and erthe is thin; thou hast
13 foundid the world, and the fulnesse therof; thou madist of
nouȝt the north and the see. Thabor and Hermon schulen
14 make ful out ioye in thi name; thin arm with power. Thin
15 hond be maad stidefast, and thi riȝthond be enhaunsid; riȝtfulnesse and doom *is* the makyng redy of thi seete. Merci
16 and treuthe schulen go bifore thi face; blessid *is* the puple
that kan hertli song. Lord, thei schulen go in the liȝt of
17 thi cheer; and in thi name thei schulen make ful out ioye al
18 dai; and thei schulen be enhaunsid in thi riȝtfulnesse. For
thou art the glorie of the vertu of hem; and in thi good
19 plesaunce oure horn schal be enhaunsid. For oure takyng
vp is of the Lord; and of the hooli of Israel oure kyng.
20 Thanne thou spakist in reuelacioun to thi seyntis, and seidist,
Y haue set help in the myȝti; and Y haue enhaunsid the
21 chosun man of my puple. I foond Dauid, my seruaunt; Y
22 anoyntide hym with myn hooli oile. For myn hond schal
23 helpe him; and myn arm schal conferme hym. The enemye schal no thing profite in him; and the sone of wickid-
24 nesse schal not ley to, for to anoye him. And Y schal sle
hise enemyes fro his face; and Y schal turne in to fliȝt hem
25 that haten hym. And my treuthe and mercy *schal be* with
26 him: and his horn schal be enhaunsid in my name. And Y

schal sette his hond in the see; and his riȝt hoond in flodis.
27 He schal inwardli clepe me, Thou art my fadir; my God, and
28 the vptaker of myn heelthe. And Y schal sette him the
29 firste gendrid sone; hiȝer than the kyngis of erthe. With-
outen ende Y schal kepe my merci to hym; and my tes-
30 tament feithful to him. And Y schal sette his seed in to the
31 world of world; and his trone as the daies of heuene. Forsothe if hise sones forsaken my lawe; and goen not in my
32 domes. If thei maken vnhooli my riȝtfulnessis; and kepen
33 not my comaundementis. I schal visite in a ȝerde the
wickidnessis of hem; and in betyngis the synnes of hem.
34 But Y schal not scatere my mercy fro hym; and in my
35 treuthe Y schal not anoye hym. Nethir Y schal make
vnhooli my testament; and Y schal not make voide tho
36 thingis that comen forth of my lippis. Onys Y swoor in myn
37 hooli; Y schal not lie to Dauid, his seed schal dwelle with-
38 outen ende. And his trone as sunne in my siȝt, and as
a perfit mone with-outen ende; and a feithful witnesse in
39 heuene. But thou hast put awei, and hast dispisid; and
40 hast dilaied thi crist. Thou hast turned awei the testament
of thi seruaunt; thou madist vnhooli his seyntuarie in erthe.
41 Thou distriedist alle the heggis therof; thou hast set the
42 stidefastnesse therof drede. Alle men passynge bi the weie
rauyschiden him; he is maad schenschipe to hise neiȝboris.
43 Thou hast enhaunsid the riȝthond of men oppressinge him;
44 thou hast gladid alle hise enemyes. Thou hast turned awei
the help of his swerd; and thou helpidist not hym in batel.
45 Thou destriedist him fro clensing; and thou hast hurtlid
46 doun his seete in erthe. Thou hast maad lesse the daies of
47 his time; thou hast bisched him with schenschip. Lord, hou
longe turnest thou awei in to the ende; schal thin ire brenne
48 out as fier? Bithenke thou what *is* my substaunce; for
whether thou hast ordeyned veynli alle the sones of men?

49 Who is a man, that schal lyue, and schal not se deth; schal
50 delyuere his soule fro the hond of helle? Lord, where ben
thin elde mercies; as thou hast swore to Dauid in thi
51 treuthe? Lord, be thou myndeful of the schenschipe of thi
seruauntis, of many hethene men; whiche Y helde togidere
52 in my bosum. Whiche thin enemyes, Lord, diden schenschipfuli; for thei dispisiden the chaungyng of thi crist.
53 Blessid *be* the Lord with outen ende; be it don, be it
don.

Psalm LXXXIX (XC).

1 *The title of the nyne and cistetithe salm. The preier of Moises, the man of God.*

Lord, thou art maad help to vs; fro generacioun in to
2 generacioun. Bifore that hillis weren maad, ether the erthe
and the world was formed; fro the world and in to the world
3 thou art God. Turne thou not awei a man in to lownesse;
4 and thou seidist, 3e sones of men, be conuertid. For a
thousynde 3eer *ben* bifore thin i3en; as 3istirdai, which is
5 passid, and as keping in the ni3t. The 3eeris of hem schulen
6 be; that ben had for nou3t. Eerli passe he, as an eerbe,
eerli florische he, and passe; in the euentid falle he doun, be
7 he hard, and wexe drie. For we han failid in thin ire; and
8 we ben disturblid in thi strong veniaunce. Thou hast set
oure wickidnessis in thi si3t; oure world in the li3tning of thi
9 cheer. For alle oure daies han failid; and we han failid
10 in thin ire. Oure 3eris schulen bithenke, as an yreyn; the
daies of oure 3eeris *ben* in tho seuenti 3eeris. Forsothe, if
fourescoor 3eer *ben* in my3ti men; and the more tyme of
hem is trauel and sorewe. For myldenesse cam aboue;
11 and we schulen be chastisid. Who knew the power of thin
12 ire; and *durste* noumbre thin ire for thi drede? Make thi
ri3thond so knowun; and *make* men lerned in herte bi wis-

13 dom. Lord, be thou conuertid sumdeel; and be thou able
14 to be preied on thi seruauntis. We weren fillid eerli with thi
merci; we maden ful out ioye, and we delitiden in alle oure
15 daies. We weren glad for the daies in whiche thou madist
16 vs meke; for the ʒeeris in whiche we siʒen yuels. Lord,
biholde thou into thi seruauntis, and in to thi werkis; and
17 dresse thou the sones of hem. And the schynyng of oure
Lord God be on vs; and dresse thou the werkis of oure
hondis on vs, and dresse thou the werk of oure hondis.

Psalm XC (XCI).

The nyntithe salm.

1 He that dwellith in the help of the hiʒeste *God;* schal
2 dwelle in the proteccioun of God of heuene. He schal
seie to the Lord, Thou art myn vptaker, and my refuit; my
3 God, Y schal hope in him. For he delyuered me fro the
4 snare of hunteris; and fro a scharp word. With hise schuldris he schal make schadowe to thee; and thou schalt haue
5 hope vnder hise fetheris. His treuthe schal cumpasse thee
6 with a scheld; thou schalt not drede of nyʒtis drede. Of an
arowe fliynge in the dai, of a gobelyn goynge in derknessis;
7 of asailing, and a myddai feend. A thousynde schulen falle
doun fro thi side, and ten thousynde fro thi riʒtside; forsothe
8 it schal not neiʒe to thee. Netheles thou schalt biholde with
9 thin iʒen; and thou schalt se the ʒelding of synneris. For
thou, Lord, art myn hope; thou hast set thin help alther-
10 hiʒeste. Yuel schal not come to thee; and a scourge schal
11 not neiʒe to thi tabernacle. For *God* hath comaundid to
hise aungels of thee; that thei kepe thee in alle thi weies.
12 Thei schulen beere thee in the hondis; leste perauenture
13 thou hirte thi foot at a stoon. Thou schalt go on a snake,
and a cocatrice; and thou schalt defoule a lioun and a dra-

14 goun. For he hopide in me, Y schal delyuere hym; Y
15 schal defende him, for he knew my name. He criede to me,
and Y schal here him, Y am with him in tribulacioun; Y
16 schal delyuere him, and Y schal glorifie hym. I schal fille
hym with the lengthe of daies; and Y schal schewe myn
helthe to hym.

Psalm XCI (XCII).

1   *The title of the oon and nyntithe salm. The salm of
song, in the dai of sabath.*

2 It is good to knouleche to the Lord; and to synge to thi
3 name, thou hi3este. To schewe eerli thi merci; and thi
4 treuthe bi ny3t. In a sautrie of ten cordis; with song
5 in harpe. For thou, Lord, hast delitid me in thi makyng;
and Y schal make ful out ioye in the werkis of thin hondis.
6 Lord, thi werkis ben magnefied greetli; thi thou3tis ben
7 maad ful depe. An vnwise man schal not knowe; and a
8 fool schal not vndirstonde these thingis. Whanne synneris
comen forth, as hey; and alle thei apperen, that worchen
9 wickidnesse. That thei perische in to the world of world;
10 forsothe thou, Lord, *art* the hi3est, with-outen ende. For
lo! Lord, thin enemyes, for lo! thin enemyes schulen
perische; and alle schulen be scaterid that worchen wickid-
11 nesse. And myn horn schal be reisid as an vnicorn; and
12 myn eelde in plenteuouse merci. And myn i3e dispiside myn
enemyes; and whanne wickid men rysen a3ens me, myn eere
13 schal here. A iust man schal floure as a palm tree: he
14 schal be multiplied as a cedre of Liban. Men plauntid in
the hous of the Lord; schulen floure in the porchis of the
15 hous of oure God. 3it thei schulen be multiplied in plenteuouse elde; and thei schulen be suffryng wel. That thei
telle, that oure Lord God is ri3tful; and no wickidnesse is in
hym.

Psalm XCII (XCIII).

The two and nyntithe salm.

1 The Lord hath regned, he is clothid with fairnesse; the
2 Lord is clothid with strengthe, and hath gird hym silf. For
3 he made stidefast the world; that schal not be moued. God, thi seete was maad redi fro that tyme; thou art fro the world. Lord, the flodis han reisid; the flodis han reisid her vois. Flodis reisiden her wawis; of the voicis of many
4 watris. The reisyngis of the see *ben* wondurful; the Lord
5 *is* wondurful in hi3e thingis. Thi witnessingis ben maad able to be bileued greetli; Lord, holynesse bicometh thin house, in to the lengthe of daies.

Psalm XCIII (XCIV).

The thre and nyntithe salm.

1 God *is* Lord of veniauncis; God of veniauncis dide freli.
2 Be thou enhaunsid that demest the erthe; 3elde thou 3eld-
3 inge to proude men. Lord, hou longe synneris; hou longe
4 schulen synneris haue glorie? Thei schulen telle out, and schulen speke wickidnesse; alle men schulen speke that
5 worchen vnri3tfulnesse. Lord, thei han maad lowe thi puple;
6 and thei han disesid thin eritage. Thei killiden a widowe and a comelyng; and thei han slayn fadirles children and modir-
7 les. And thei seiden, The Lord schal not se; and God of
8 Jacob schal not vndurstonde. 3e vnwise men in the puple,
9 vndirstonde; and, 3e foolis, lerne sum tyme. Schal not he here, that plauntide the eere; ethere biholdith not he, that
10 made the i3e? Schal not he repreue, that chastisith folkis;
11 which techith man kunnyng? The Lord knowith the
12 thou3tis of men; that tho ben veyne. Blessid *is* the man, whom thou, Lord, hast lerned; and hast tau3t him of thi

13 lawe. That thou aswage hym fro yuele daies; til a diche be
14 diggid to the synner. For the Lord schal not putte awei his
15 puple; and he schal not forsake his eritage. Til riȝtfulnesse
be turned in to dom; and who ben niȝ it, alle that ben
16 of riȝtful herte. Who schal rise with me aȝens mysdoeris;
ether who schal stonde with me aȝens hem that worchen
17 wickidnesse? No but for the Lord helpide me; almest my
18 soule hadde dwellid in helle. If Y seide, My foot was stirid;
19 Lord, thi merci helpide me. Aftir the multitude of my
sorewis in myn herte; thi coumfortis maden glad my soule.
20 Whether the seete of wickidnesse cleueth to thee; that
21 makist trauel in comaundement? Thei schulen take aȝens
the soule of a iust man; and thei schulen condempne inno-
22 cent blood. And the Lord was maad to me in to refuyt; and
23 my God *was maad* in to the help of myn hope. And he
schal ȝelde to hem the wickidnesse of hem; and in the malice
of hem he schal lese hem, oure Lord God schal lese hem.

Psalm XCIV (XCV).

The foure and nyntithe salm.

1 Come ȝe, make we ful out ioie to the Lord; hertli synge
2 we to God, oure heelthe. Bifore ocupie we his face in
3 knowleching; and hertli synge we to him in salmes. For
God *is* a greet Lord, and a greet king aboue alle goddis;
4 for the Lord schal not putte awei his puple. For alle the
endis of erthe ben in his hond; and the hiȝnesses of hillis
5 ben hise. For the see is his, and he made it; and hise
6 hondis formeden the drie lond. Come ȝe, herie we, and
falle we doun bifore God, wepe we bifore the Lord that
7 made vs; for he is oure Lord God. And we *ben* the puple
8 of his lesewe; and the scheep of his hond. If ȝe han herd
9 his vois to dai; nyle ȝe make hard ȝoure hertis. As in the

terryng to wraththe; bi the dai of temptacioun in desert.
Where ȝoure fadris temptiden me; thei preueden and sien
10 my werkis. Fourti ȝeer I was offendid to this generacioun;
11 and Y seide, Euere thei erren in herte. And these men
knewen not my weies; to whiche Y swoor in myn ire, thei
schulen not entre in to my reste.

Psalm XCV (XCVI).
The fyue and nyntithe salm hath no title.

1 SINGE ȝe a newe song to the Lord; al erthe, synge ȝe
2 to the Lord. Synge ȝe to the Lord, and blesse ȝe his
3 name; telle ȝe his heelthe fro dai in to dai. Telle ȝe his
glorie among hethene men; hise merueilis among alle
4 puplis. For the Lord *is* greet, and worthi to be preisid
5 ful myche; he is ferdful aboue alle goddis. For alle the
goddis of hethene men *ben* feendis; but the Lord made
6 heuenes. Knouleching and fairnesse *is* in his siȝt; hooly-
7 nesse and worthi doyng *is* in his halewing. Ȝe cuntrees of
hethene men, brynge to the Lord, bringe ȝe glorye and
8 onour to the Lord; bringe ȝe to the Lord glorie to hys
name. Take ȝe sacrificis, and entre ȝe in to the hallis of
9 hym; herie ȝe the Lord in his hooli halle. Al erthe be
10 moued of his face; seie ȝe among hethene men, that the
Lord hath regned. And he hath amendid the world, that
schal not be moued; he schal deme puplis in equite.
11 Heuenes be glad, and the erthe make ful out ioye, the
12 see and the fulnesse therof be moued togidere; feeldis
schulen make ioye, and alle thingis that ben in tho. Thanne
alle the trees of wodis schulen make ful out ioye, for the
13 face of the Lord, for he cometh; for he cometh to deme
the erthe. He schal deme the world in equite; and puplis
in his treuthe.

Psalm XCVI (XCVII).

The sixe and nyntithe salm.

1 THE Lord hath regned, the erthe make ful out ioye;
2 many ilis be glad. Cloude and derknesse in his cumpas;
3 riʒtfulnesse and doom *is* amending of his seete. Fier schal go bifore him; and schal enflawme hise enemyes in cumpas.
4 Hise leitis schyneden to the world; the erthe siʒ, and was
5 moued. Hillis as wax fletiden doun fro the face of the
6 Lord; al erthe fro the face of the Lord. Heuenes telden
7 his riʒtfulnesse; and alle puplis sien his glorie. Alle that worschipen sculptilis be schent, and thei that han glorie in her symelacris; alle ʒe aungels of the Lord, worschipe
8 him. Sion herde, and was glad, and the douʒtris of Juda
9 maden ful out ioye; for thi domes, Lord. For thou, Lord, *art* the hiʒeste on al erthe; thou art greetli enhaunsid ouere
10 alle goddis. Ʒe that louen the Lord, hate yuel; the Lord kepith the soulis of hise seyntis; he schal delyuer hem fro
11 the hond of the synner. Liʒt is risun to the riʒtful man;
12 and gladnesse to riʒtful men of herte. Juste men, be ʒe glad in the Lord; and knouleche ʒe to the mynde of his halewyng.

Psalm XCVII (XCVIII).

The seuen and nyntithe salm hath no title.

1 SINGE ʒe a newe song to the Lord; for he hath do merucils. His riʒt hond and his hooli arm; hath maad
2 heelthe to hym. The Lord hath maad knowun his heelthe: in the siʒt of hethene men he hath schewid his riʒtfulnesse.
3 He bithouʒte on his merci; and on his treuthe, to the hous of Israel. Alle the endis of erthe; sien the heelthe of oure
4 God. Al erthe, make ʒe hertli ioye to God; synge ʒe, and

5 make ȝe ful out ioye, and seie ȝe salm. Singe ȝe to the
6 Lord in an harpe, in harpe and vois of salm; in trumpis
betun out with hamer, and in vois of a trumpe of horn.
7 Hertli synge ȝe in the siȝt of the Lord, the king; the see
and the fulnesse therof be moued; the world, and thei
8 that dwellen therynne. Flodis schulen make ioie with hond,
toȝidere hillis schulen make ful out ioye, for siȝt of the
9 Lord; for he cometh to deme the erthe. He schal deme
the world in riȝtfulnesse; and puplis in equite.

Psalm XCVIII (XCIX).

The eiȝte and nyntithe salm.

1 The Lord hath regned, puplis ben wrooth; thou that
2 sittist on cherubyn, the erthe be moued. The Lord *is*
3 greet in Sion; and hiȝ aboue alle puplis. Knouleche thei
4 to thi greet name, for it is ferdful and hooli; and the
onour of the king loueth doom. Thou hast maad redi
dressyngis; thou hast maad doom and riȝtfulnesse in Jacob.
5 Enhaunse ȝe oure Lord God; and worschipe ȝe the stool of
6 hise feet, for it is hooli. Moises and Aaron *weren* among
hise preestis; and Samuel *was* among hem that inwardli
clepen his name. Thei inwardli clepiden the Lord, and
7 he herde hem; in a piler of cloude he spak to hem. Thei
kepten hise witnessyngis; and the comaundement which
8 he ȝaf to hem. Oure Lord God, thou herdist hem; God,
thou were merciful to hem, and thou tokist veniaunce on
9 al her fyndyngis. Enhaunse ȝe oure Lord God, and worschipe ȝe in his hooli hil; for oure Lord God *is* hooli.

Psalm XCIX (C).

1 *The titil of the nyne and nyntithe salm. A salm to knouleche; in Ebrew thus, A salm for knouleching.*

2 Al erthe, singe ȝe hertli to God; serue ȝe the Lord in 3 gladnesse. Entre ȝe in his siȝt; in ful out ioiyng. Wite ȝe, that the Lord hym silf is God; he made vs, and not we maden vs. His puple, and the scheep of his lesewe, 4 entre ȝe in to hise ȝatis in knoulechyng; *entre ȝe in to hise* 5 *porchis*, knouleche ȝe to him in ympnes. Herye ȝe his name, for the Lord is swete, his merci *is* with-outen ende; and his treuthe *is* in generacioun and in to generacioun.

Psalm C (CI).

1 *The titil of the hundrid salm. The salm of Dauid.*

2 Lord, Y schal synge to thee; merci and doom. I schal synge, and Y schal vndurstonde in a weie with out wem; whanne thou schalt come to me. I ȝede perfitli in the innocence of myn herte; in the myddil of myn hous. 3 I settide not forth bifore myn iȝen an vniust thing; Y 4 hatide hem that maden trespassyngis. A schrewide herte cleuede not to me; Y knewe not a wickid man bowynge 5 awei fro me. I pursuede hym; that bacbitide priueli his neiȝbore. With the proude iȝe and an herte vnable to be 6 fillid; Y eet not with this. Myn iȝen *weren* to the feithful men of erthe, that thei sitte with me; he that ȝede in a weie 7 with out wem, mynystride to me. He that doith pride, schal not dwelle in the myddil of myn hous; he that spekith 8 wickid thingis, seruede not in the siȝt of myn iȝen. In the morutid Y killide alle the synners of erthe; that Y schulde leese fro the citee of the Lord alle men worchynge wickidnesse.

Psalm CI (CII).

1 The title of the hundrid and o salm. The preier of a pore man, whanne he was angwishid, and schedde out his speche bifore the Lord.

2 Lord, here thou my preier; and my crie come to thee.
3 Turne not awei thi face fro me; in what euere dai Y am troblid, bowe doun thin eere to me. In what euere day
4 Y schal inwardli clepe thee; here thou me swiftli. For my daies han failid as smoke; and my boonus han dried vp as
5 critouns. I am smytun as hei, and myn herte dried vp; for
6 Y haue forʒete to eete my breed. Of the vois of my weilyng;
7 my boon cleuede to my fleische. I am maad lijk a pellican
8 of wildirnesse; Y am maad as a niʒt-crowe in an hous. I wakide; and Y am maad as a solitarie sparowe in the roof.
9 Al dai myn enemyes dispisiden me; and thei that preisiden
10 me sworen aʒens me. For Y eet aschis as breed; and Y
11 meddlide my drinke with weping. Fro the face of the ire of thin indignacioun; for thou reisinge me hast hurtlid me
12 doun. Mi daies boweden awei as a schadewe; and Y
13 wexede drie as hei. But, Lord, thou dwellist with-outen ende; and thi memorial in generacioun and in to genera-
14 cioun. Lord, thou risinge vp schalt haue merci on Sion; for the tyme to haue merci therof cometh, for the tyme
15 cometh. For the stones therof plesiden thi seruauntis; and
16 thei schulen haue merci on the lond therof. And, Lord, hethen men schulen drede thi name; and alle kingis of
17 erthe *schulen drede* thi glori. For the Lord hath bildid Sion;
18 and he schal be seen in his glorie. He bihelde on the preier of meke men; and he dispiside not the preier of hem.
19 Be these thingis writun in an othere generacioun; and the
20 puple that schal be maad schal preise the Lord. For he

bihelde fro his hi3e hooli place ; the Lord lokide fro heuene
21 in to erthe. For to here the weilingis of feterid men ; and
22 for to vnbynde the sones of slayn men. That thei telle in
Sion the name of the Lord ; and his preising in Jerusalem.
23 In gaderinge togidere puplis in to oon ; and kingis, that thei
24 serue the Lord. It answeride to hym in the weie of his
25 vertu ; Telle thou to me the fewnesse of my daies. A3enclepe
thou not me in the myddil of my daies ; thi 3eris *ben* in
26 generacioun and in to generacioun. Lord, thou foundidist
the erthe in the bigynnyng ; and heuenes ben the werkis
27 of thin hondis. Tho schulen perische, but thou dwellist
perfitli ; and alle schulen wexe eelde as a clooth. And thou
schalt chaunge hem as an hiling, and tho schulen be chaungid ;
28 but thou art the same thi silf, and thi 3eeris schulen not faile.
29 The sones of thi seruauntis schulen dwelle ; and the seed
of hem schal be dressid in to the world.

Psalm CII (CIII).

1   *The title of the hundred and secounde salm.   Of Dauid.*

Mi soule, blesse thou the Lord ; and alle thingis that ben
2 with-ynne me, *blesse* his hooli name. Mi soule, blesse thou
the Lord ; and nyle thou for3ete alle the 3eldyngis of him.
3 Which doith merci to alle thi wickidnessis ; which heelith
4 alle thi sijknessis. Which a3enbieth thi lijf fro deth ; which
5 corowneth thee in merci and merciful doyngis. Which fillith
thi desijr in goodis ; thi 3ongthe schal be renulid as *the*
6 *3ongthe* of an egle. The Lord doynge mercies ; and doom
7 to alle men suffringe wrong. He made hise weies knowun
8 to Moises ; hise willis to the sones of Israel. The Lord *is*
a merciful doer, and merciful in wille ; longe abidinge, and
9 myche merciful. He schal not be wrooth with-outen ende ;
10 and he schal not thretne with-outen ende. He dide not to

vs aftir oure synnes; nether he ȝeldide to vs aftir oure wickidnessis. For bi the hiȝnesse of heuene fro erthe; he made strong his merci on men dredynge hym. As myche as the eest is fer fro the west; he made fer oure wickidnessis fro vs. As a fadir hath merci on sones, the Lord hadde merci on men dredynge him; for he knewe oure makyng. He bithouȝte that we ben dust, a man is as hey; his dai schal flowre out so as a flour of the feeld. For the spirit schal passe in hym, and schal not abide; and schal no more knowe his place. But the merci of the Lord is fro with out bigynnyng, and til in to with outen ende; on men dredinge hym. And his riȝtfulnesse is in to the sones of sones; to hem that kepen his testament. And ben myndeful of hise comaundementis; to do tho. The Lord hath maad redi his seete in heuene; and his rewme schal be lord of alle. Aungels of the Lord, blesse ȝe the Lord; ȝe myȝti in vertu, doynge his word, to here the vois of hise wordis. Alle vertues of the Lord, blesse ȝe the Lord; ȝe mynystris of hym that doen his wille. Alle werkis of the Lord, blesse ȝe the Lord, in ech place of his lordschipe; my soule, blesse thou the Lord.

Psalm CIII (CIV).

The hundrid and thridde salm.

Mi soule, blesse thou the Lord; my Lord God, thou art magnyfied greetli. Thou hast clothid knouleching and fairnesse; and thou art clothid with liȝt, as with a cloth. And thou stretchist forth heuene as a skyn; and thou hilist with watris the hiȝer partis therof. Which settist a cloude thi stiyng; which goest on the fetheris of wyndis. Which makist spiritis thin aungels; and thi mynystris brennynge fier. Which hast foundid the erthe on his stablenesse; it schal not be bowid in to the world of world. The depthe

of watris as a cloth is the clothing therof; watris schulen
7 stonde on hillis. Tho schulen fle fro thi blamyng; men
8 schulen be aferd of the vois of thi thundur. Hillis stien vp,
and feeldis goen doun; in to the place which thou hast
9 foundid to tho. Thou hast set a terme, which tho schulen
not passe; nether tho schulen be turned, for to hile the erthe.
10 And thou sendist out wellis in grete valeis; watris schulen
11 passe bitwix the myddil of hillis. Alle the beestis of the feeld
schulen drynke; wielde assis schulen abide in her thirst.
12 Briddis of the eir schulen dwelle on tho; fro the myddis
13 of stoonys thei schulen 3yue voices. And thou moistist hillis
of her hi3er thingis; the erthe schal be fillid of the fruyt of
14 thi werkis. And thou bringist forth hei to beestis; and
eerbe to the seruyce of men. That thou bringe forth breed
15 of the erthe; and that wiyn make glad the herte of men.
That he make glad the face with oile; and that breed make
16 stidefast the herte of man. The trees of the feeld schulen be
fillid, and the cedris of the Liban, whiche he plauntide;
17 sparewis schulen make nest there. The hous of the ger-
18 faukun is the leeder of tho; hi3e hillis *ben refute* to hertis;
19 a stoon *is* refutt to irchouns. He made the moone in to
20 tymes; the sunne knewe his goyng doun. Thou hast set
derknessis, and ny3t is maad; alle beestis of the wode
21 schulen go ther ynne. Liouns whelpis rorynge for to
22 rauysche; and to seke of God meete to hem silf. The
sunne is risun, and tho ben gaderid togidere; and tho
23 schulen be set in her couchis. A man schal go out to his
24 werk; and to his worching, til to the euentid. Lord, thi
werkis ben magnefiede ful myche, thou hast maad alle thingis
25 in wisdom; the erthe is fillid with thi possessioun. This see
is greet and large to hondis; there *ben* crepinge beestis, of
26 which is noon noumbre. Litil beestis with grete; schippis
schulen passe there. This dragoun which thou hast formyd;

27 for to scorne hym. Alle thingis abiden of thee; that thou
28 ȝyue to hem meete in tyme. Whanne thou schalt ȝyue to
hem, thei schulen gadere; whanne thou schalt opene thin
29 hond, alle thingis schulen be fillid with goodnesse. But
whanne thou schalt turne awey the face, thei schulen be
disturblid; thou schalt take awei the spirit of them, and thei
schulen faile; and thei schulen turne aȝen in to her dust.
30 Sende out thi spirit, and thei schulen be formed of the newe;
31 and thou schalt renule the face of the erthe. The glorie
of the Lord be in to the world; the Lord schal be glad in
32 hise werkis. Which biholdith the erthe, and makith it to
33 tremble; which touchith hillis, and tho smoken. I schal
singe to the Lord in my lijf; Y schal seie salm to my God,
34 as longe as Y am. Mi speche be myrie to him; forsothe
35 Y schal delite in the Lord. Synneris faile fro the erthe, and
wickid men *faile*, so that thei be not; my soule, blesse thou
the Lord.

Psalm CIV (CV).

The title of the hundrid and fourthe salm. Alleluya.

1 Knouleche ȝe to the Lord, and inwardli clepe ȝe his
2 name; telle ȝe hise werkis among hethen men. Synge ȝe
to hym, and seie ȝe salm to him, and telle ȝe alle hise
3 merueylis: be ȝe preisid in his hooli name. The herte of
4 men sekynge the Lord be glad; seke ȝe the Lord, and be
5 ȝe confermed; seke ȝe euere his face. Haue ȝe mynde
on hise merueilis, whiche he dide; on his grete wondris,
6 and domes of his mouth. The seed of Abraham, his ser-
7 uaunt; the sones of Jacob, his chosun man. He *is* oure
8 Lord God; hise domes *ben* in al the erthe. He was
myndeful of his testament in to the world; of the word
which he comaundide in to a thousynde generaciouns.
9 Which he disposide to Abraham; and of his ooth to

10 Isaac. And he ordeynede it to Jacob in to a comaunde-
11 ment ; and to Israel in to euerlastinge testament. And he
seide, I shal ȝiue to thee the lond of Canaan ; the cord
12 of ȝoure eritage. Whanne thei weren in a litil noumbre ;
13 and the comelingis of hem weren ful fewe. And thei
passiden fro folk in to folk ; and fro a rewme in to ano-
14 ther puple. He lefte not a man to anoye hem ; and he
15 chastiside kyngis for hem. Nile ȝe touche my cristis ; and
16 nyle ȝe do wickidli among my prophetis. And *God* clepide
hungir on erthe ; and he wastide al the stidefastnesse of
17 breed. He sente a man bifore hem ; Joseph was seeld in
18 to a seruaunt. Thei maden lowe hise feet in stockis, irun
19 passide by his soule ; til the word of him cam. The speche
20 of the Lord enflawmede him ; the king sente and vnbond
21 hym ; the prince of puplis *sente* and delyuerede him. He
ordeynede him the lord of his hous ; and the prince of al
22 his possessioun. That he schulde lerne hise princis as him
silf ; and that he schulde teche hise elde men prudence.
23 And Israel entride in to Egipt ; and Jacob was a comeling
24 in the lond of Cham. And *God* encreeside his puple
25 greetli ; and made hym stidefast on hise enemyes. He
turnede the herte of hem, that thei hatiden his puple ; and
26 diden gile aȝens hise seruauntis. He sent Moises, his ser-
27 uaunt ; thilke Aaron, whom he chees. He puttide in hem
the wordis of hise myraclis ; and of hise grete wondris in
28 the lond of Cham. He sente derknessis, and made derk ;
29 and he made not bitter hise wordis. He turnede the watris
of hem in to blood ; and he killide the fischis of hem.
30 And the lond of hem ȝaf paddoks ; in the priue places of
31 the kyngis of hem. *God* seide, and a fleische flie cam ; and
32 gnattis in alle the coostis of hem. He settide her reynes
33 hail ; fier brennynge in the lond of hem. And he smoot
the vynes of hem, and the fige-trees of hem ; and al to-

34 brak the tree of the coostis of hem. He seide, and a locuste cam; and a bruk of which was noon noumbre.
35 And it eet al the hey in the lond of hem; and it eet al
36 the fruyt of the lond of hem. And he killide ech the firste gendrid thing in the lond of hem; the firste fruitis
37 of alle the trauel of hem. And he ledde out hem with siluer and gold; and noon was sijk in the lynagis of hem.
38 Egipt was glad in the goyng forth of hem; for the drede
39 of hem lai on Egipcians. He spredde abroad a cloude, in to the hiling of hem; and fier, that it schynede to hem
40 bi ny3t. Thei axiden, and a curlew cam; and he fillide
41 hem with the breed of heuene. He brak a stoon, and
42 watris flowiden; floodis 3eden forth in the drye place. For he was myndeful of his hooli word; which he hadde to
43 Abraham, his child. And he ledde out his puple in ful
44 out ioiyng; and hise chosun men in gladnesse. And he 3af to hem the cuntreis of hethen men; and thei hadden
45 in possessioun the trauels of puplis. That thei kepe hise iustifiyngis; and seke his lawe.

Psalm CV (CVI).

The title of the hundrid and fifthe salm. Alleluya.

1 Knouleche 3e to the Lord, for *he is* good; for his mercy
2 *is* with-outen ende. Who schal speke the powers of the
3 Lord; schal make knowun alle hise preisyngis? Blessid *ben* thei that kepen dom; and doon ri3tfulnesse in al tyme.
4 Lord, haue thou mynde on vs in the good plesaunce of
5 thi puple; visite thou vs in thin heelthe. To se in the goodnesse of thi chosun men, to be glad in the gladnes
6 of thi folk; that thou be heried with thin eritage. We han synned with oure fadris; we han do vniustli, we han do

7 wickidnesse. Oure fadris in Egipt vndirstoden not thi merueils; thei weren not myndeful of the multitude of thi merci.
And thei stiynge in to the see, in to the reed see, terreden
8 to wraththe; and he sauede hem for his name, that he
9 schulde make knowun his power. And he departide the
reed see, and it was dried; and he lede forth hem in the
10 depthis of watris as in deseert. And he sauede hem fro
the hond of hateris; and he aȝen-bouȝte hem fro the hond
11 of the enemye. And the watir hilide men troublynge hem;
12 oon of hem abood not. And thei bileueden to hise wordis;
13 and thei preisiden the heriynge of hym. Thei hadden soone
do, thei forȝaten hise werkis; and thei abididen not his
14 councel. And thei coueitiden coueitise in deseert; and
15 temptiden God in a place with-out watir. And he ȝaf to
hem the axyng of hem; and he sente fulnesse in to the
16 soulis of hem. And thei wraththiden Moyses in the cas-
17 tels; Aaron, the hooli of the Lord. The erthe was opened,
and swolewid Datan; and hilide on the congregacioun of
18 Abiron. And fier brente an hiȝe in the synagoge of hem;
19 flawme brente synneris. And thei maden a calf in Oreb;
20 and worschipiden a ȝotun ymage. And thei chaungiden
21 her glorie; in to the liknesse of a calf etynge hei. Thei
22 forȝaten God, that sauede hem, that dide grete werkis in
Egipt, merueils in the lond of Cham; feerdful thingis in
23 the reed see. And *God* seide, that he wolde leese hem;
if Moises, his chosun man, hadde not stonde in the brekyng
of his siȝt. That he schulde turne awei his ire; lest he
24 loste hem. And thei hadden the desirable lond for nouȝt,
25 thei bileueden not to his word, and thei grutchiden in her
26 tabernaclis; thei herden not the vois of the Lord. And
he reiside his hond on hem; to caste doun hem in desert.
27 And to caste awei her seed in naciouns; and to leese hem
28 in cuntreis. And thei maden sacrifice to Belfagor; and

29 thei eeten the sacrificis of deed beestis. And thei wraththiden *God* in her fyndyngis; and fallyng was multiplied
30 in hem. And Fynees stood, and pleeside *God;* and the
31 veniaunce cecsside. And it was arrettid to hym to riȝtfulnesse; in generacioun and in to generacioun, til in to
32 with-outen ende. And thei wraththiden *God* at the watris
of aȝenseiyng; and Moises was trauelid for hem, for thei
33 maden bittere his spirit, and he departide in his lippis.
34 Thei losten not hethen men; whiche the Lord seide to
35 hem. And thei weren meddlid among hethene men, and
36 lerneden the werkis of hem, and serueden the grauen ymagis
of hem; and it was maad to hem in to sclaundre. And
37 thei offriden her sones; and her douȝtris to feendis. And
38 thei schedden out innocent blood, the blood of her sones
and of her douȝtris; whiche thei sacrificiden to the grauun
39 ymagis of Chanaan. And the erthe was slayn in bloodis,
and was defoulid in the werkis of hem; and thei diden
40 fornicacioun in her fyndyngis. And the Lord was wrooth
bi strong veniaunce aȝens his puple; and hadde abhomin-
41 acioun of his eritage. And he bitook hem in to the
hondis of hethene men; and thei that hatiden hem, weren
42 lordis of hem. And her enemyes diden tribulacioun to
hem, and thei weren mekid vndir the hondis of enemyes;
43 ofte he delyuerede hem. But thei wraththiden hym in her
counsel; and thei weren maad low in her wickidnessis.
44 And he siȝe, whanne thei weren set in tribulacioun; and
45 he herde the preyer of hem. And he was myndeful of
his testament; and it repentide hym bi the multitude of
46 his merci. And he ȝaf hem in to mercies; in the siȝt of
47 alle men, that hadden take hem. Oure Lord God, make
thou vs saaf; and gadere togidere vs fro naciouns. That
we knouleche to thin hooli name; and haue glorie in thi
48 preisyng. Blessid be the Lord God of Israel fro the world

and til in to the world; and al the puple schal seye, Be it don, be it don.

Psalm CVI (CVII).

The tille of the hundrid and sixte salm. Alleluya.

1 Knouleche ȝe to the Lord, for *he is* good; for his merci
2 *is* in to the world. Sei thei, that ben aȝen-bouȝt of the Lord; whiche he aȝen-bouȝte fro the hond of the enemye, fro
3 cuntreis he gaderide hem togidere. Fro the risyng of the sunne, and fro the goyng doun; fro the north, and fro the
4 see. Thei erriden in wildirnesse, in a place with-out watir;
5 thei founden not weie of the citee of dwellyng place. Thei
6 *weren* hungri and thirsti; her soule failide in hem. And thei crieden to the Lord, whanne thei weren set in tribula-
7 cioun; and he delyuerede hem fro her nedynesses. And he ledde forth hem in to the riȝt weie; that thei schulden go in
8 to the citee of dwelling. The mercies of the Lord knouleche to hym; and hise merueilis *knouleche* to the sones of men.
9 For he fillide a voide man; and he fillide with goodis an
10 hungry man. *God delyuerede* men sittynge in derknessis, and in the schadowe of deth; and men prisoned in beggerye
11 and in yrun. For thei maden bitter the spechis of God;
12 and wraththiden the councel of the hiȝeste. And the herte of hem was maad meke in trauelis; and thei weren sijk, and
13 noon was that helpide. And thei crieden to the Lord, whanne thei weren set in tribulacioun; and he delyuerede
14 hem from her nedynessis. And he ledde hem out of derk- nessis, and schadowe of deth; and brak the boondis
15 of hem. The mercies of the Lord knouleche to hym; and
16 hise merueils *knouleche* to the sones of men. For he al
17 to-brak brasun ȝatis; and he brak yrun barris. He vp-took hem fro the weie of her wickidnesse; for thei weren maad

18 lowe for her vnriʒtfulnesses. The soule of hem wlatide al
19 mete; and thei neiʒeden til to the ʒatis of deth. And thei
crieden to the Lord, whanne thei weren set in tribulacioun;
20 and he delyuerede hem fro her nedynessis. He sente his
word, and heelide hem; and delyuerede hem fro the per-
21 ischingis of hem. The mercies of the Lord knouleche to
22 hym; and hise merucils to the sones of men. And offre
thei the sacrifice of heriyng; and telle thei hise werkis in ful
23 out ioiyng. Thei that gon doun in to the see in schippis;
24 and maken worching in many watris. Thei sien the werkis
25 of the Lord; and hise merueilis in the depthe. He seide,
and the spirit of tempest stood; and the wawis therof weren
26 arerid. Thei stien til to heuenes, and goen doun til to the
27 depthis; the soule of hem failide in yuelis. Thei weren
troblid, and thei weren moued as a drunkun man; and al
28 the wisdom of hem was deuourid. And thei crieden to the
Lord, whanne thei weren set in tribulacioun; and he ledde
29 hem out of her nedynessis. And he ordeynede the tempest
therof in to a soft wynde; and the wawis therof weren
30 stille. And thei weren glad, for tho weren stille; and he
31 ladde hem forth in to the hauene of her wille. The mercies
of the Lord knouleche to hym; and hise merueilis to the
32 sones of men. And enhaunse thei him in the chirche of the
33 puple; and preise thei him in the chaier of eldre men. He
hath set floodis in to deseert; and the out-goingis of watris
34 in to thirst. *He hath set* fruytful lond in to saltnesse; for the
35 malice of men dwellyng ther-ynne. He hath set deseert in
to pondis of watris; and erthe with-out watir in to out-
36 goyngis of watris. And he settide there hungri men; and
37 thei maden a citee of dwelling. And thei sowiden feeldis,
38 and plauntiden vynes; and maden fruyt of birthe. And
he blesside hem, and thei weren multiplied greetli; and he
39 made not lesse her werk-beestis. And thei weren maad

fewe; and thei weren trauelid of tribulacioun of yuelis and
40 of sorewis. Strijf was sched out on princes; and he
made hem for to erre without the weie, and not in the weie.
41 And he helpide the pore man fro pouert; and settide
42 meynees as a scheep *bringynge forth lambren*. Riȝtful men
schulen se, and schulen be glad; and al wickidnesse schal
43 stoppe his mouth. Who *is* wijs, and schal kepe these
thingis; and schal vndirstonde the mercies of the Lord?

Psalm CVII (CVIII).

1 *The title of the hundrid and seuenthe salm. The song of
the salm of Dauid.*

2 Myn herte is redi, God, myn herte is redi; Y schal singe,
3 and Y schal seie salm in my glorie. My glorie, ryse thou vp,
4 sautrie and harp, rise thou vp; Y schal rise vp eerli. Lord,
Y schal knouleche to thee among puplis; and Y schal
5 seie salm to thee among naciouns. For whi, God, thi
merci *is* greet on heuenes; and thi treuthe *is* til to the
6 cloudis. God, be thou enhaunsid aboue heuenes; and thi
7 glorie ouer al erthe. That thi derlingis be delyuerid, make
thou saaf with thi riȝthond, and here me; God spak in his
8 hooli. I schal make ful out ioye, and Y schal departe
Siccimam; and Y schal mete the grete valei of tabernaclis.
9 Galaad is myn, and Manasses is myn; and Effraym *is* the
vptaking of myn heed. Juda *is* my king; Moab *is* the
10 caudron of myn hope. In to Ydume Y schal stretche forth
11 my scho; aliens ben maad frendis to me. Who schal lede
me forth in to a stronge citee; who schal lede me forth til in
12 to Idume? Whether not thou, God, that hast put vs awei;
13 and, God, schalt thou not go out in oure vertues? Ȝyue
thou help to vs of tribulacioun; for the heelthe of man is

14 veyn. We schulen make vertu in God; and he schal bringe oure enemyes to nouȝt.

Psalm CVIII (CIX).

1 *The title of the hundrid and eiȝtthe salm. To victorye, the salm of Dauid.*

2 God, holde thou not stille my preisyng; for the mouth of the synner, and the mouth of the gileful man is openyd on 3 me. Thei spaken aȝens me with a gileful tunge, and thei cumpassiden me with wordis of hatrede; and fouȝten aȝens 4 me with-out cause. For that thing that thei schulden loue 5 me, thei bacbitiden me; but Y preiede. And thei settiden aȝens me yuelis for goodis; and hatrede for my loue. 6 Ordeyne thou a synner on him; and the deuel stonde on 7 his riȝt half. Whanne he is demed, go he out condempned; 8 and his preier be maad in to synne. Hise daies be maad 9 fewe; and another take his bischopriche. Hise sones be 10 maad faderles; and his wijf a widewe. Hise sones tremblinge be born ouer, and begge; and be cast out of her 11 habitaciouns. An vsurere seke al his catel; and aliens 12 rauysche hise trauelis. Noon helpere be to him; nether 13 ony be that haue mercy on hise modirles children. Hise sones be maad in to persching; the name of him be don 14 awei in oon generacioun. The wickidnesse of hise fadris come aȝen in to mynde in the siȝt of the Lord; and the 15 synne of his modir be not don awei. Be thei maad euere aȝens the Lord; and the mynde of hem perische fro erthe. 16, 17 For that thing that he thouȝte not to do merci, and he pursuede a pore man and beggere; and to slee a man com-18 punct in herte. And he louede cursing, and it schal come to hym; and he nolde blessing, and it schal be maad fer fro him. And he clothide cursing as a cloth, and it entride as

water in to hise ynnere thingis; and as oile in hise boonus.
19 Be it maad to him as a cloth, with which he is hilyd; and as
20 a girdil, with which he is euere gird. This is the werk of
hem that bacbiten me anentis the Lord; and that speke
21 yuels aȝens my lijf. And thou, Lord, Lord, do with me for
22 thi name; for thi merci is swete. Delyuere thou me, for Y
am nedi and pore; and myn herte is disturblid with ynne me.
23 I am takun awei as a schadowe, whanne it bowith awei; and
24 Y am schakun awei as locustis. Mi knees ben maad feble
25 of fasting; and my fleische was chaungid for oile. And
Y am maad schenschipe to hem; thei sien me, and moueden
26 her heedis. Mi Lord God, helpe thou me; make thou me
27 saaf bi thi merci. And thei schulen wite, that this is thin
28 hond; and thou, Lord, hast do it. Thei schulen curse, and
thou schalt blesse, thei that risen aȝens me, be schent; but
29 thi seruaunt schal be glad. Thei that bacbiten me, be
clothid with schame; and be thei hilid with her schenschipe
30 as with a double cloth. I schal knouleche to the Lord greetli
with my mouth; and Y schal herie hym in the myddil of
31 many men. Which stood nyȝ on the riȝt half of a pore man;
to make saaf my soule fro pursueris.

PSALM CIX (CX).

1 *The title of the hundrid and nynthe salm. The salm
of Dauith.*

THE Lord seide to my Lord; Sitte thou on my riȝt side.
2 Til Y putte thin enemyes; a stool of thi feet. The Lord
schal sende out fro Syon the ȝerde of thi vertu; be thou
3 lord in the myddis of thin enemyes. The bigynnyng *is* with
thee in the dai of thi vertu, in the briȝtnessis of seyntis;
4 Y gendride thee of the wombe before the dai-sterre. The
Lord swoor, and it schal not repente him; Thou art a preest·

5 with-outen ende, bi the ordre of Melchisedech. The Lord on thi ri3t side; hath broke kyngis in the dai of his ven- 6 iaunce. He schal deme among naciouns, he schal fille fallyngis; he schal schake heedis in the lond of many men. 7 He dranke of the stronde in the weie; therfor he enhaunside the heed.

Psalm CX (CXI).

The title of the hundrid and tenthe salm. Alleluya.

1 LORD, Y schal knouleche to thee in al myn herte; in the 2 counsel and congregacioun of iust men. The werkis of the 3 Lord *ben* greete; sou3t out in to alle hise willis. His werk *is* knoulechyng and grete doyng; and his ri3tfulnesse dwellith 4 in to the world of world. The Lord merciful in wille, and 5 a merciful doere, hath maad a mynde of hise merueilis; he hath 3oue meete to men dredynge hym. He schal be 6 myndeful of his testament in to the world; he schal telle to 7 his puple the vertu of hise werkis. That he 3yue to hem the eritage of folkis; the werkis of hise hondis *ben* treuthe and 8 doom. Alle hise comaundementis *ben* feithful, confermed in 9 to the world of world; maad in treuthe and equite. The Lord sente redempcioun to hys puple; he comaundide his testament with outen ende. His name *is* hooli and dreedful; 10 the bigynnyng of wisdom *is* the drede of the Lord. Good vndirstondyng *is* to alle that doen it; his preising dwellith in to the world of world.

Psalm CXI (CXII).

The title of the hundrid and enleuenthe salm. Alleluya.

1 BLISSID *is* the man that dredith the Lord; he schal wilne 2 ful myche in hise comaundementis. His seed schal be my3ti in erthe; the generacioun of ri3tful men schal be blessid. 3 Glorie and richessis *ben* in his hous; and his ri3tfulnesse

4 dwellith in to the world of world. Li3t is risun vp in derknessis to ri3tful men; *the Lord* is merciful in wille, and
5 a merciful doere, and ri3tful. The man *is* merye, that doith
6 merci, and leeneth; he disposith hise wordis in dom; for he
7 schal not be moued with-outen ende. A iust man schal be in euerlastinge mynde; he schal not drede of an yuel heryng.
8 His herte *is* redi for to hope in the Lord; his herte is confermed, he schal not be moued, til he dispise hise enemyes.
9 He spredde abrood, he 3af to pore men; his ri3twisnesse dwellith in to the world of world; his horn schal be reisid in
10 glorie. A synner schal se, and schal be wrooth; he schal gnaste with hise teeth, and schal faile; the desijr of synneris schal perische.

PSALM CXII (CXIII).

The title of the hundrid and twelfthe salm. Alleluya.

1 CHILDREN, preise 3e the Lord; preise 3e the name of the
2 Lord. The name of the Lord be blessid; fro this tyme now
3 and til in to the world. Fro the risyng of the sunne til to the goyng doun; the name of the Lord *is* worthi to be
4 preisid. The Lord *is* hi3 aboue alle folkis; and his glorie *is*
5 aboue heuenes. Who *is* as oure Lord God, that dwellith in
6 hi3e thingis; and biholdith meke thingis in heuene and in
7 erthe? Reisynge a nedi man fro the erthe; and enhaunsinge
8 a pore man fro drit. That he sette hym with princes; with
9 the princes of his puple. Which makith a bareyn womman dwelle in the hous; a glad modir of sones.

PSALM CXIII (CXIV).

The titil of the hundrid and thrittenthe salm. Alleluya.

1 IN the goyng out of Israel fro Egipt; of the hous of Jacob
2 fro the hethene puple. Judee was maad the halewyng of

3 hym; Israel the power of hym. The see siȝ, and fledde;
4 Jordan was turned abac. Munteyns ful out ioyeden as
5 rammes; and litle hillis as the lambren of scheep. Thou
see, what was to thee, for thou fleddist; and thou, Jordan,
6 for thou were turned abak? Munteyns, ȝe maden ful out
ioye as rammes; and litle hillis, as the lambren of scheep.
7 The erthe was moued fro the face of the Lord; fro the face of
8 God of Jacob. Which turnede a stoon in to pondis of watris;
1 and an hard rooch in to wellis of watris. (CXV.) Lord, not
2 to vs, not to vs; but ȝyue thou glorie to thi name. On thi
merci and thi treuthe; lest ony tyme hethene men seien,
3 Where is the God of hem? Forsothe oure God in heuene;
4 dide alle thingis, whiche euere he wolde. The symulacris
of hethene men *ben* siluer and gold; the werkis of mennus
5 hondis. Tho han mouth, and schulen not speke; tho han
6 iȝen, and schulen not se. Tho han eeris, and schulen not
7 here; tho han nose-thurls, and schulen not smelle. Tho
han hondis, and schulen not grope; tho han feet, and
8 schulen not go; tho schulen not crye in her throte. Thei
that maken tho ben maad lijk tho; and alle that triste in
9 tho. The hous of Israel hopide in the Lord; he is the
10 helpere of hem, and the defendere of hem. The hous of
Aaron hopide in the Lord; he is the helpere of hem, and the
11 defendere of hem. Thei that dreden the Lord, hopiden in
the Lord; he is the helpere of hem, and the defendere of
12 hem. The Lord was myndeful of vs; and blesside vs. He
blesside the hous of Israel; he blesside the hous of Aaron.
13 He blesside alle men that dreden the Lord; *he blesside* litle
14 men with the grettere. The Lord´encreesse on ȝou; on ȝou
15 and on ȝoure sones. Blessid be ȝe of the Lord; that made
16 heuene and erthe. Heuene of heuene *is* to the Lord; but
17 he ȝaf erthe to the sones of men. Lord, not deed men
schulen herie thee; nether alle men that goen doun in to

18 helle. But we that lyuen, blessen the Lord; fro this tyme now and til in to the world.

Psalm CXIV (CXVI).

The titil of the hundrid and fourtenthe salm. Alleluia.

1 I LOUEDE *the Lord;* for the Lord schal here the vois of 2 my preier. For he bowide doun his eere to me; and Y 3 schal inwardli clepe in my daies. The sorewis of deth 4 cumpassiden me; and the perelis of helle founden me. I foond tribulacioun and sorewe; and Y clepide inwardli the 5 name of the Lord. Thou, Lord, delyuere my soule; the 6 Lord *is* merciful, and iust; and oure God doith merci. And the Lord kepith litle children; Y was mekid, and he de- 7 lyuerede me. Mi soule, turne thou in to thi reste; for the 8 Lord hath do wel to thee. For he hath delyuered my soule fro deth; myn i3en fro wepingis, my feet fro fallyng doun. 9 I schal plese the Lord; in the cuntrei of hem that lyuen.

Psalm CXV (CXVI, *continued*).

The titil of the hundrid and fiftenthe salm. Alleluya.

10 I BILEUEDE, for which thing Y spak; forsoth Y was maad 11 low ful myche. I seide in my passing; Ech man *is* a lier. 12 What schal Y 3elde to the Lord; for alle thingis which he 13 3eldide to me? I schal take the cuppe of heelthe; and 14 Y schal inwardli clepe the name of the Lord. I schal 3elde 15 my vowis to the Lord bifor al his puple; the deth of seyntis 16 of the Lord *is* precious in his si3t. O! Lord, for Y *am* thi seruant; Y *am* thi seruaunt, and the sone of thi handmaide. 17 Thou hast broke my bondys, to thee Y schal offre a sacrifice of heriyng; and Y schal inwardli clepe the name of the 18 Lord. I schal 3elde my vowis to the Lord, in the si3t of al

19 his puple; in the porchis of the hous of the Lord, in the myddil of thee, Jerusalem.

Psalm CXVI (CXVII).

The title of the hundrid and sixtenthe salm. Alleluya.

1 ALLE hethen men, herie 3e the Lord; alle puplis, herie 3e
2 hym. For his merci is confermyd on vs; and the treuthe of the Lord dwellith with-outen ende.

Psalm CXVII (CXVIII).

The titil of the hundrid and seuententhe salm. Alleluia.

1 KNOULECHE 3e to the Lord, for he is good; for his merci
2 is with-outen ende. Israel seie now, for he is good; for his
3 merci is with-outen ende. The hous of Aaron seie now;
4 for his merci is with-outen ende. Thei that dreden the
5 Lord, seie now; for his merci is with-outen ende. Of tribulacioun Y inwardli clepide the Lord; and the Lord
6 herde me in largenesse. The Lord is an helpere to me;
7 Y schal not drede what a man schal do to me. The Lord
8 is an helpere to me; and Y schal dispise myn enemyes. It is betere for to trist in the Lord; than for to triste in man.
9 It is betere for to hope in the Lord; than for to hope in
10 princes. Alle folkis cumpassiden me; and in the name of
11 the Lord it *bifelde*, for Y am auengide on hem. Thei cumpassinge cumpassiden me; and in the name of the Lord,
12 for Y am auengid on hem. Thei cumpassiden me as been, and thei brenten out as fier *doith* among thornes; and in the
13 name of the Lord, for Y am avengid on hem. I was hurlid, and turnede vpsedoun, that Y schulde falle doun; and the
14 Lord took me vp. The Lord is my strengthe, and my
15 heryyng; and he is maad to me in to heelthe. The vois

of ful out ioiyng and of heelthe; *be* in the tabernaclis of iust
16 men. The riȝt hond of the Lord hath do vertu, the riȝt
hond of the Lord enhaunside me; the riȝt hond of the Lord
17 hath do vertu. I schal not die, but Y schal lyue; and Y
18 schal telle the werkis of the Lord. The Lord chastisinge
19 hath chastisid me; and he ȝaf not me to deth. Opene ȝe
to me the ȝatis of riȝtfulnesse, and Y schal entre bi tho, and
20 Y schal knouleche to the Lord; this ȝate *is* of the Lord, and
21 iust men schulen entre bi it. I schal knouleche to thee, for
22 thou herdist me; and art maad to me in to heelthe. The
stoon which the bilderis repreueden; this is maad in to the
23 heed of the corner. This thing is maad of the Lord; and it
24 is wonderful bifore oure iȝen. This is the dai which the
Lord made; make we ful out ioye, and be we glad ther
25 ynne. O! Lord, make thou me saaf, O! Lord, make thou
26 wel prosperite; blessid *is he* that cometh in the name of the
27 Lord. We blesseden ȝou of the hous of the Lord; God *is*
Lord, and hath ȝoue liȝt to vs. Ordeyne ȝe a solempne dai
28 in thicke *puplis;* til to the horn of the auter. Thou art my
God, and Y schal knouleche to thee; thou art my God, and
Y schal enhaunse thee. I schal knouleche to thee, for thou
29 herdist me; and thou art maad to me in to heelthe. Knouleche ȝe to the Lord, for he is good; for his merci *is* with
outen ende.

Psalm CXVIII (CXIX).

The titil of the hundrid and eiȝtenthe salm. Alleluia.

Aleph.

1 Blessid *ben* men with-out wem in the weie; that gon
2 in the lawe of the Lord. Blessid *ben thei,* that seken hise
3 witnessingis; seken him in al the herte. For thei that
4 worchen wickidnesse; ȝeden not in hise weies. Thou hast

5 comaundid; that thin heestis be kept greetly. I wolde that
6 my weies be dressid; to kepe thi iustifiyngis. Thanne Y
schal not be schent; whanne Y schal biholde perfitli in alle
7 thin heestis. I schal knouleche to thee in the dressing of
herte; in that that Y lernyde the domes of thi riȝtfulnesse.
8 I schal kepe thi iustifiyngis; forsake thou not me on ech
side.

Beth.

9 In what thing amendith a ȝong waxinge man his weie?
10 in keping thi wordis. In al myn herte Y souȝte thee; putte
11 thou me not awei fro thin heestis. In myn herte Y hidde thi
12 spechis; that Y do not synne aȝens thee. Lord, thou art
13 blessid; teche thou me thi iustifiyngis. In my lippis Y haue
14 pronounsid; alle the domes of thi mouth. I delitide in the
15 weie of thi witnessingis; as in alle richessis. I schal be
16 ocupied in thin heestis; and Y schal biholde thi weies. I
schal bithenke in thi iustifiyngis; Y schal not forȝete thi
wordis.

Gimel.

17 Ȝelde to thi seruaunt; quiken thou me, and Y schal
18 kepe thi wordis. Liȝtne thou myn iȝen; and Y schal
19 biholde the merueils of thi lawe. I am a comeling in
20 erthe; hide thou not thin heestis fro me. Mi soule coueitide
21 to desire thi iustifiyngis; in al tyme. Thou blamedist the
proude; thei ben cursid, that bowen awei fro thin heestis.
22 Do thou awei fro me schenschipe and dispising; for Y
23 souȝte thi witnessingis. For whi princis saten, and spaken
aȝens me; but thi seruaunt was exercisid in thi iustifiyngis.
24 For whi and thi witnessyngis is my thenkyng; and my
counsel is thi iustifiyngis.

Deleth.

25 Mi soule cleuede to the pawment; quykine thou me bi

26 thi word. I telde out my weies, and thou herdist me;
27 teche thou me thi iustifiyngis. Lerne thou me the weie
of thi iustifiyngis; and Y schal be exercisid in thi merueils.
28 Mi soule nappide for anoye; conferme thou me in thi
29 wordis. Remoue thou fro me the weie of wickidnesse; and
30 in thi lawe haue thou merci on me. I chees the weie of
31 treuthe; Y forʒat not thi domes. Lord, Y cleuede to thi
32 witnessyngis; nyle thou schende me. I ran the weie of
thi comaundementis; whanne thou alargidist myn herte.

He.

33 Lord, sette thou to me a lawe, the weie of thi iustifiyngis;
34 and Y schal seke it euere. Ʒyue thou vndurstonding to me,
and Y schal seke thi lawe; and Y schal kepe it in al myn
35 herte. Lede me forth in the path of thin heestis; for Y
36 wolde it. Bowe thou myn herte in to thi witnessingus;
37 and not in to aueryce. Turne thou awei myn iʒen, that
38 tho seen not vanyte; quykene thou me in thi weie. Or-
39 deyne thi speche to thi seruaunt; in thi drede. Kitte awey
my schenschip, which Y supposide; for thi domes *ben* myrie.
40 Lo! Y coueitide thi comaundementis; quikene thou me in
thin equite.

Vau.

41 And, Lord, thi merci come on me; thin heelthe *come*
42 bi thi speche. And Y schal answere a word to men seiynge
43 schenschipe to me; for Y hopide in thi wordis. And take
thou not awei fro my mouth the word of treuthe outerli; for
44 Y hopide aboue in thi domes. And Y schal kepe thi lawe
45 euere; in to the world, and in to the world of world. And Y
46 ʒede in largenesse; for Y souʒte thi comaundementis. And
Y spak of thi witnessyngis in the siʒt of kingis; and Y was
47 not schent. And Y bithouʒte in thin heestis; whiche Y
48 louede. And Y reiside myn hondis to thi comaundementis,

whiche Y louede; and Y schal be excercisid in thi iustifiyngis.

Zai.

49 Lord, haue thou mynde on thi word to thi seruaunt; in 50 which *word* thou hast ʒoue hope to me. This coumfortide 51 me in my lownesse; for thi word quikenede me. Proude men diden wickidli bi alle thingis; but Y bowide not awei 52 fro thi lawe. Lord, Y was myndeful on thi domes fro the 53 world; and Y was coumfortid. Failing helde me; for 54 synneris forsakinge thi lawe. Thi iustifiyngis weren delitable to me to be sungun; in the place of my pilgrimage. 55 Lord, Y hadde mynde of thi name bi niʒt; and Y kepte thi 56 lawe. This thing was maad to me; for Y souʒte thi iustifiyngis.

Heth.

57, 58 Lord, my part; Y seide to kepe thi lawe. I bisouʒte thi face in al myn herte; haue thou merci on me bi thi 59 speche. I bithouʒte my weies; and Y turnede my feet in to 60 thi witnessyngis. I am redi, and Y am not disturblid; to 61 kepe thi comaundementis. The coordis of synneris han 62 biclippid me; and Y haue not forʒete thi lawe. At mydnyʒt Y roos to knouleche to thee; on the domes of thi iusti- 63 fiyngis. I am parcener of alle that dreden thee; and kepen 64 thin heestis. Lord, the erthe is ful of thi merci; teche thou me thi iustifiyngis.

Teth.

65 Lord, thou hast do goodnesse with thi seruaunt; bi thi 66 word. Teche thou me goodnesse, and loore, and kunnyng; 67 for Y bileuede to thin heestis. Bifor that Y was maad meke, 68 Y trespasside; therfor Y kepte thi speche. Thou art good; 69 and in thi goodnesse teche thou me thi iustifiyngis. The wickidnesse of hem that ben proude, is multiplied on me; 70 but in al myn herte Y schal seke thin heestis. The herte of

71 hem is cruddid as mylk; but Y bithouȝte thi lawe. It is good to me, that thou hast maad me meke ; that Y lerne thi
72 iustifiyngis. The lawe of thi mouth is betere to me; than thousyndis of gold and of siluer.

Joth.

73 Thin hondis maden me, and fourmeden me ; ȝyue thou
74 vndurstondyng to me, that Y lerne thin heestis. Thei that dreden thee schulen se me, and schulen be glad; for Y
75 hopide more on thi wordis. Lord, Y knewe, that thi domes
76 *ben* equite ; and in thi treuth thou hast maad me meke. Thi merci be maad, that it coumforte me; bi thi speche to thi
77 seruaunt. Thi merciful doyngis come to me, and Y schal
78 lyue ; for thi lawe is my thenkyng. Thei that ben proude be schent, for vniustli thei diden wickidnesse aȝens me ; but Y
79 schal be exercisid in thin heestis. Thei that dreden thee be
80 turned to me ; and thei that knowen thi witnessyngis. Myn herte be maad vnwemmed in thi iustifiyngis ; that Y be not schent.

Caf.

81 Mi soule failide in to thin helthe ; and Y hopide more on
82 thi word. Myn iȝen failiden in to thi speche ; seiynge,
83 Whanne schalt thou coumforte me ? For Y am maad as
84 a bowge in frost ; Y haue not forȝete thi iustifiyngis. Hou many ben the daies of thi seruaunt ; whanne thou schalt
85 make doom of hem that pursuen me ? Wickid men telden
86 to me ianglyngis ; but not as thi lawe. Alle thi comaundementis *ben* treuthe ; wickid men han pursued me, helpe thou
87 me. Almeest thei endiden me in erthe ; but 1 forsook not
88 thi comaundementis. Bi thi mersi quikene thou me ; and Y schal kepe the witnessingis of thi mouth.

Lameth.

89 Lord, thi word dwellith in heuene; with-outen ende.
90 Thi treuthe *dwellith* in generacioun, and in to generacioun;
91 thou hast foundid the erthe, and it dwellith. The dai lastith contynueli bi thi ordynaunce; for alle thingis seruen to thee.
92 No but that thi lawe was my thenking; thanne perauenture
93 Y hadde perischid in my lownesse. With-outen ende Y schal not forȝete thi iustifiyngis; for in tho thou hast
94 quikened me. I am thin, make thou me saaf; for Y haue
95 souȝt thi iustifiyngis. Synneris aboden me, for to leese me;
96 Y vndurstood thi witnessingis. I siȝ the ende of al ende; thi comaundement *is* ful large.

Men.

97 Lord, hou louede Y thi lawe; al dai it is my thenking.
98 Aboue myn enemyes thou madist me prudent bi thi co-
99 maundement; for it is to me with-outen ende. I vndurstood aboue alle men techinge me; for thi witnessingis is
100 my thenking. I vndirstood aboue eelde men; for Y souȝte
101 thi comaundementis. I forbeed my feet fro al euel weie;
102 that Y kepe thi wordis. I bowide not fro thi domes; for
103 thou hast set lawe to me. Thi spechis ben ful swete to
104 my cheekis; aboue hony to my mouth. I vnderstood of thin heestis; therfor Y hatide al the weie of wickidnesse.

Nun.

105 Thi word *is* a lanterne to my feet; and liȝt to my pathis.
106 I swoor, and purposide stidefastli; to kepe the domes of
107 thi riȝtfulnesse. I am maad low bi alle thingis; Lord,
108 quykene thou me bi thi word. Lord, make thou wel plesinge the wilful thingis of my mouth; and teche thou
109 me thi domes. Mi soule *is* euere in myn hondis; and
110 Y forȝat not thi lawe. Synneris settiden a snare to me;

111 And Y erride not fro thi comaundementis. I purchasside
thi witnessyngis bi eritage with-outen ende; for tho ben
112 the ful ioiyng of myn herte. I bowide myn herte to do
thi iustifiyngis with-outen ende; for reward.

Sameth.

113, 114 I hatide wickid men; and Y louede thi lawe. Thou
art myn helpere, and my taker vp; and Y hopide more
115 on thi word. Ʒe wickide men, bowe awei fro me; and
116 Y schal seke the comaundementis of my God. Vp-take
thou me bi thi word, and Y schal lyue; and schende thou
117 not me fro myn abydyng. Helpe thou me, and Y schal
be saaf; and Y schal bithenke euere in thi iustifiyngis.
118 Thou hast forsake alle men goynge awey fro thi domes;
119 for the thouʒt of hem *is* vniust. I arettide alle the synneris of erthe brekeris of the lawe; therfor Y louede thi
120 witnessyngis. Naile thou my fleischis with thi drede; for
Y dredde of thi domes.

Ayn.

121 I dide doom and riʒtwisnesse; bitake thou not me to
122 hem that falsli chalengen me. Take vp thi seruaunt in
123 to goodnesse; thei that ben proude chalenge not me. Myn
iʒen failiden in to thin helthe; and in to the speche of thi
124 riʒtfulnesse. Do thou with thi seruaunt bi thi merci; and
125 teche thou me thi iustifiyngis. I am thi seruaunt, ʒyue
thou vndurstondyng to me; that Y kunne thi witnessingis.
126, 127 Lord, *it is* tyme to do; thei han distried thi lawe. Therfor Y louede thi comaundementis; more than gold and
128 topazion. Therfor Y was dressid to alle thin heestis; Y
hatide al wickid weie.

Phee.

129 Lord, thi witnessingis *ben* wondirful; therfor my soule

130 souȝte tho. Declaring of thi wordis liȝtneth; and ȝyueth
131 vnderstonding to meke men. I openede my mouth, and
132 drouȝ the spirit; for Y desiride thi comaundementis. Biholde thou on me, and haue merci on me; bi the dom
133 of hem that louen thi name. Dresse thou my goyingis
bi thi speche; that al vnriȝtfulnesse haue not lordschip on
134 me. Aȝeyn-bie thou me fro the false chalengis of men;
135 that Y kepe thin heestis. Liȝtne thi face on thi seruaunt;
136 and teche thou me thi iustifiyngis. Myn iȝen ledden forth
the outgoynges of watris; for thei kepten not thi lawe.

Sade.

137, 138 Lord, thou art iust; and thi dom is riȝtful. Thou hast
comaundid riȝtfulnesse, thi witnessingis; and thi treuthe
139 greetli *to be kept*. Mi feruent loue made me to be meltid;
140 for myn enemys forȝaten thi wordis. Thi speche is greetli
141 enflawmed; and thi seruaunt louede it. I am ȝong, and
142 dispisid; Y forȝat not thi iustifiyngis. Lord, thi riȝtfulnesse
is riȝtfulnesse with-outen ende; and thi lawe *is* treuthe.
143 Tribulacioun and angwische founden me; thin heestis is
144 my thenking. Thi witnessyngis *is* equite with-outen ende;
ȝyue thou vndirstondyng to me, and Y schal lyue.

Cof.

145   I criede in al myn herte, Lord, here thou me; and Y
146 schal seke thi iustifiyngis. I criede to thee, make thou
147 me saaf; that Y kepe thi comaundementis. I bifor cam
in ripenesse, and Y criede; Y hopide aboue on thi wordis.
148 Myn iȝen bifor camen to thee ful eerli; that Y schulde
149 bithenke thi speches. Lord, here thou my vois bi thi
150 merci; and quykene thou me bi thi doom. Thei that
pursuen me neiȝden to wickidnesse; forsothe thei ben maad
151 fer fro thi lawe. Lord, thou art nyȝ; and alle thi weies

152 *ben* treuthe. In the bigynnyng Y knewe of thi witnessingis; for thou hast foundid tho with-outen ende.

Res.

153 Se thou my mekenesse, and delyuere thou me; for Y
154 forȝat not thi lawe. Deme thou my dom, and aȝenbie thou
155 me; quikene thou me for thi speche. Heelthe *is* fer fro
156 synners; for thei souȝten not thi iustifiyngis. Lord, thi
157 mercies *ben* manye; quykene thou me bi thi dom. *Thei ben* manye that pursuen me, and doen tribulacioun to me;
158 Y bowide not awei fro thi witnessingis. I siȝ brekers of the lawe, and Y was meltid; for thei kepten not thi spechis.
159 Lord, se thou, for Y louede thi comaundementis; quikene
160 thou me in thi merci. The bigynnyng of thi wordis *is* treuthe; alle the domes of thi riȝtwisnesse *ben* with-outen ende.

Sin.

161 Princes pursueden me with-outen cause; and my herte
162 dredde of thi wordis. I schal be glad on thi spechis; as
163 he that fyndith many spuylis. I hatide and wlatide wickid-
164 nesse; forsothe Y louede thi lawe. I seide heriyngis to thee seuene sithis in the dai; on the domes of thi riȝtful-
165 nesse. Miche pees *is* to hem that louen thi lawe; and
166 no sclaundir is to hem. Lord, Y abood thin heelthe; and
167 Y louede thin heestis. Mi soule kepte thi witnessyngis;
168 and louede tho greetli. I kepte thi comaundementis, and thi witnessingis; for alle my weies *ben* in thi siȝt.

Tau.

169 Lord, my biseching come niȝ in thi siȝt; bi thi speche
170 ȝyue thou vndurstonding to me. Myn axing entre in thi
171 siȝt; bi thi speche delyuere thou me. Mi lippis schulen telle out an ympne; whanne thou hast tauȝte me thi iusti-

172 fiyngis. Mi tunge schal pronounce thi speche; for whi
173 alle thi comaundementis *ben* equite. Thin hond be maad,
174 that it saue me; for Y haue chose thin heestis. Lord, Y
175 coueitide thin heelthe; and thi lawe is my thenking. Mi
soule schal lyue, and schal herie thee; and thi domes
176 schulen helpe me. I erride as a scheep that perischide;
Lord, seke thi seruaunt, for Y forʒat not thi comaundementis.

Psalm CXIX (CXX.)

1 *The title of the hundrid and nyntenthe salm.*
The song of greces.

Whanne Y was set in tribulacioun, Y criede to the Lord;
2 and he herde me. Lord, delyuere thou my soule fro wickid
3 lippis; and fro a gileful tunge. What schal be ʒouun to
thee, ether what schal be leid to thee; to a gileful tunge?
4 Scharpe arowis of the myʒti; with colis that maken de-
5 solat. Allas to me! for my dwelling in an alien lond is
6 maad long, Y dwellide with men dwellinge in Cedar; my
7 soule was myche a comelyng. I was pesible with hem
that hatiden pees; whanne Y spak to hem, thei aʒenseiden
me with-outen cause.

Psalm CXX (CXXI).

1 *The title of the hundrid and twentithe salm.*
The song of greces.

I reiside myn iʒen to the hillis; fro whannus help schal
2 come to me. Myn help *is* of the Lord; that made heuene
3 and erthe. *The Lord* ʒyue not thi foot in to mouyng;
4 nether he nappe, that kepith thee. Lo! he schal not nappe,
5 nether slepe; that kepith Israel. The Lord kepith thee;

6 the Lord is thi proteccioun aboue thi ri3thond. The sunne schal not brenne thee bi dai; nether the moone bi ny3t. 7 The Lord kepe thee fro al yuel; the Lord kepe thi soule. 8 The Lord kepe thi goyng in and thi goyng out; fro this tyme now and in to the world.

Psalm CXXI (CXXII).

1   *The title of the hundrid and oon and twentithe salm.*
    The song of the grecis of Dauid.

I AM glad in these thingis, that ben seid to me; We 2 schulen go in to the hous of the Lord. Oure feet weren 3 stondynge; in thi hallis, thou Jerusalem. Jerusalem, which is bildid as a citee; whos part taking therof is in to the 4 same thing. For the lynagis, the lynagis of the Lord stieden thidir, the witnessing of Israel; to knouleche to the name 5 of the Lord. For thei saten there on seetis in doom; sectis 6 on the hous of Dauid. Preie 3e tho thingis, that ben to the pees of Jerusalem; and abundaunce be to hem that 7 louen thee. Pees be maad in thi vertu; and abundaunce 8 in thi touris. For my britheren and my nei3boris; Y spak 9 pees of thee. For the hous of oure Lord God; Y sou3te goodis to thee.

Psalm CXXII (CXXIII).

1   *The title of the hundrid and two and twentithe salm.   The*
    song of grecis.

To thee Y haue reisid myn i3en; that dwellist in heuenes. 2 Lo! as the i3en of scruauntis; *ben* in the hondis of her lordis. As the i3en of the handmaide *ben* in the hondis of her ladi; so oure i3en *ben* to oure Lord God, til he haue mercy on vs. 3 Lord, haue thou merci on vs, haue thou merci on vs; for we

4 ben myche fillid with dispisyng. For oure soule is myche fillid; *we ben* schenschipe to hem that ben abundaunte *with richessis*, and dispising to proude men.

Psalm CXXIII (CXXIV).

1 *The title of the hundrid and thre and twentithe salm. The song of grecis of Dauith.*

2 Israel seie now, No but for the Lord was in vs; no but for the Lord was in vs. Whanne men risiden vp a3ens vs; 3 in hap thei hadden swalewid vs quike. Whanne the wood-4 nesse of hem was wrooth a3ens vs; in hap watir hadde sope 5 vs vp. Oure soule passide thoru3 a stronde; in hap oure 6 soule hadde passide thoru3 a watir vnsuffrable. Blessid be 7 the Lord; that 3af not vs in taking to the teeth of hem. Oure soule, as a sparowe, is delyuered; fro the snare of hunters. 8 The snare is al to-brokun; and we ben delyuered. Oure helpe *is* in the name of the Lord; that made heuene and erthe.

Psalm CXXIV (CXXV).

1 *The title of the hundrid and foure and twentithe salm. The song of greces.*

Thei that tristen in the Lord *ben* as the hil of Syon; 2 he schal not be moued with-outen ende, that dwellith in Jerusalem. Hillis *ben* in the cumpas of it, and the Lord *is* in the cumpas of his puple; fro this tyme now and in 3 to the world. For the Lord schal not leeue the 3erde of synneris on the part of iust men; that iust men holde not 4 forth her hondis to wickidnesse. Lord, do thou wel; to 5 good men, and of ri3tful herte. But the Lord schal lede them that bowen in to obligaciouns, with hem that worchen wickidnesse; pees *be* on Israel.

Psalm CXXV (CXXVI).

1 *The title of the hundrid and fyue and twentithe salm.*
The song of grecis.

Whanne the Lord turnede the caitifte of Sion; we weren 2 maad as coumfortid. Thanne oure mouth was fillid with ioye; and oure tunge with ful out ioiyng. Thanne thei schulen seie among hethene men; The Lord magnefiede 3 to do with hem. The Lord magnefiede to do with vs; we 4 ben maad glad. Lord, turne thou oure caitifte; as a stronde 5 in the south. Thei that sowen in teeris; schulen repe in ful 6 out ioiyng. Thei goynge ȝeden, and wepten; sendynge her seedis. But thei comynge schulen come with ful out ioiyng; berynge her handfullis.

Psalm CXXVI (CXXVII).

1 *The title of the hundrid and sixe and twentithe salm.*
The song of greces of Salomon.

No but the Lord bilde the hous; thei that bilden it han trauelid in veyn. No but the Lord kepith the citee; he 2 wakith in veyn that kepith it. It is veyn to ȝou to rise bifore the liȝt; rise ȝe after that ȝe han sete, that eten the breed of sorewe. Whanne he schal ȝyue sleep to his loued; 3 lo! the eritage of the Lord *is* sones, the mede *is* the fruyt of 4 wombe. As arowis *ben* in the hond of the miȝti; so the 5 sones of hem that ben schakun out. Blessid *is* the man, that hath fillid his desier of tho; he schal not be schent, whanne he schal speke to hise enemyes in the ȝate.

Psalm CXXVII (CXXVIII).

1 *The title of the hundrid and seuene and twentithe salm.
The song of greces.*

Blessid *ben* alle men, that dreden the Lord; that gon in
2 hise weies. For thou schalt ete the trauels of thin hondis;
3 thou art blessid, and it schal be wel to thee. Thi wijf as a
plenteous vyne; in the sidis of thin hous. Thi sones as the
newe sprenges of olyue-trees; in the cumpas of thi bord.
4 Lo! so a man schal be blessid; that dredith the Lord.
5 The Lord blesse thee fro Syon; and se thou the goodis of
6 Jerusalem in alle the daies of thi lijf. And se thou the sones
of thi sones; *se thou* pees on Israel.

Psalm CXXVIII (CXXIX).

1 *The title of the hundrid and ei3te and twentithe salm.
The song of greces.*

Israel seie now; Ofte thei fou3ten a3ens me fro my
2 3ongth. Ofte thei fou3ten a3ens me fro my 3ongthe; and
3 sotheli thei mi3ten not to me. Synneris forgeden on my
4 bak; thei maden long her wickidnesse. The iust Lord
5 schal beete the nollis of synneris; alle that haten Sion be
6 schent, and turned abak. Be thei maad as the hey of hous-
7 coppis; that driede vp, bifore that it be drawun vp. Of
which hei he that schal repe, schal not fille his hond; and he
8 that schal gadere hondfullis, *schal not fille* his bosum. And
thei that passiden forth seiden not, The blessing of the Lord
be on 3ou; we blessiden 3ou in the name of the Lord.

Psalm CXXIX (CXXX).

1 *The title of the hundrid and nyne and twentithe salm.*
The song of greces.

Lord, Y criede to thee fro depthes; Lord, here thou mi 2 vois. Thin eeris be maad ententif; in to the vois of my 3 biseching. Lord, if thou kepist wickidnessis; Lord, who 4 schal susteyne? For merci is at thee; and, Lord, for thi 5 lawe Y abood thee. Mi soule susteynede in his word; my 6 soule hopide in the Lord. Fro the morewtid keping til to 7 ni3t; Israel hope in the Lord. For whi merci *is* at the Lord; 8 and plenteous redempcioun *is* at hym. And he schal a3en- bie Israel; fro alle the wickidnessis therof.

Psalm CXXX (CXXXI).

1 *The title of the hundrid and thrittithe salm. The song of greces, to Dauith himself.*

Lord, myn herte is not enhaunsid; nether myn i3en ben reisid. Nether Y 3ede in the grete thingis; nether in mer- 2 ueilis aboue me. If Y feelide not mekely; but enhaunside my soule. As a childe wenyde on his modir; so 3elding *be* 3 in my soule. Israel hope in the Lord; fro this tyme now and in to the world.

Psalm CXXXI (CXXXII).

1 *The title of the hundrid and oon and thrittithe salm.*
The song of greces.

Lord, haue thou mynde on Dauid; and of al his mylde- 2 nesse. As he swoor to the Lord; he made a vowe to God 3 of Jacob. I schal not entre in to the tabernacle of myn hous;

4 Y schal not stie in to the bed of mi restyng. I schal not
5 yue sleep to myn iȝen; and napping to myn iȝe-liddis.
5 And rest to my templis, til Y fynde a place to the Lord;
6 a tabernacle to God of Jacob. Lo! we herden that *arke of
testament* in Effrata, *that is, in Silo;* we founden it in the
7 feeldis of the wode. We schulen entre in to the tabernacle
of hym; we schulen worschipe in the place, where hise feet
8 stoden. Lord, rise thou in to thi reste; thou and the ark of
9 thin halewing. Thi prestis be clothid with riȝtfulnesse; and
10 thi seyntis make ful out ioye. For Dauid, thi seruaunt;
11 turne thou not awei the face of thi crist. The Lord swoor
treuthe to Dauid, and he schal not make hym veyn; of the
12 fruyt of thi wombe Y schal sette on thi seete. If thi sones
schulen kepe my testament; and my witnessingis, these
whiche Y schal teche hem. And the sones of hem til in to
13 the world; thei schulen sette on thi seete. For the Lord
14 chees Sion; he chees it in to dwelling to hym silf. This *is*
my reste in to the world of world; Y schal dwelle here, for Y
15 chees it. I blessynge schal blesse the widewe of it; Y schal
16 fille with looues the pore men of it. I schal clothe with
heelthe the preestis therof; and the hooli men therof schulen
17 make ful out ioye in ful reioisinge. Thidir Y schal bringe
forth the horn of Dauid; Y made redi a lanterne to my crist.
18 I schal clothe hise enemyes with schame; but myn halewing
schal floure out on hym.

Psalm CXXXII (CXXXIII).

1 *The title of the hundrid and two and thrittithe salm.
The song of grecis.*

Lo! hou good and hou myrie *it is;* that britheren dwelle
2 togidere. As oynement in the heed; that goith doun in to
the beerd, in to the beerd of Aaron. That goith doun in to

₃ the coler of his cloth; as the dew of Ermon, that goith doun in to the hil of Sion. For there the Lord sente blessing; and lijf til in to the world.

Psalm CXXXIII (CXXXIV).

1 *The title of the hundrid and thre and thrittithe salm.*
The song of greces.

Lo! now blesse ȝe the Lord; alle the seruauntis of the Lord. Ȝe that stonden in the hous of the Lord; in the 2 hallis of the hous of oure God. In nyȝtis reise ȝoure hondis 3 in to hooli thingis; and blesse ȝe the Lord. The Lord blesse thee fro Syon; which *Lord* made heuene and erthe.

Psalm CXXXIV (CXXXV).

1 *The title of the hundrid and foure and thrittithe salm.*
Alleluya.

Herie ȝe the name of the Lord; ȝe seruauntis of the 2 Lord, herie ȝe. Ȝe that stonden in the hous of the Lord; 3 in the hallis of the hous of oure God. Herie ȝe the Lord, for 4 the Lord is good; singe ȝe to his name, for it is swete. For the Lord chees Jacob to him silf; Israel in to possessioun to 5 him silf. For Y haue knowe, that the Lord is greet; and 6 oure God bifore alle goddis. The Lord made alle thingis, what euere thingis he wolde, in heuene and in erthe; in the 7 see, and in alle depthis of watris. He ledde out cloudis fro the ferthest part of erthe; and made leitis in to reyn. Which 8 bringith forth wyndis fro hise tresours; which killide the 9 firste gendrid thingis of Egipt, fro man til to beeste. He sente out signes and greete wondris, in the myddil of thee, 10 thou Egipt; in to Farao and in to alle hise seruauntis. Which 11 smoot many folkis; and killide stronge kingis. Seon, the

king of Ammorreis, and Og, the king of Basan; and alle
12 the rewmes of Chanaan. And he ȝaf the lond of hem
13 eritage; eritage to Israel, his puple. Lord, thi name *is* with
outen ende; Lord, thi memorial *be* in generacioun and in to
14 generacioun. For the Lord schal deme his puple; and he
15 schal be preied in hise seruauntis. The symulacris of hethene
men *ben* siluer and gold; the werkis of the hondis of men.
16 Tho han a mouth, and schulen not speke; tho han iȝen, and
17 schulen not se. Tho han eeris, and schulen not here; for
18 nether spirit is in the mouth of tho. Thei that maken tho,
19 be maad lijk tho; and alle that tristen in tho. The hous of
Israel, blesse ȝe the Lord; the house of Aaron, blesse ȝe the
20 Lord. The hous of Leuy, blesse ȝe the Lord; ȝe that dreden
21 the Lord, blesse ȝe the Lord. Blessid be the Lord of Syon;
that dwellith in Jerusalem.

Psalm CXXXV (CXXXVI).

*The title of the hundrid and fyue and thrittithe salm.
Alleluya.*

1 Knouleche ȝe to the Lord, for he is good, for his merci
2 *is* withouten ende. Knouleche ȝe to the God of goddis.
3, 4 Knouleche ȝe to the Lord of lordis. Which aloone makith
5 grete merueils. Which made heuenes bi vndurstondyng.
6, 7 Which made stidefast erthe on watris. Which made grete
8, 9 liȝtis. The sunne in to the power of the dai. The moone
10 and sterris in to the power of the niȝt. Which smoot Egipt
11 with the firste gendrid thingis of hem. Which ledde out
12 Israel fro the myddil of hem. In a miȝti hond and in an
13 hiȝ arm. Whiche departide the reed see in to departyngis.
14, 15 And ledde out Israel thoruȝ the myddil therof. And
he caste a-down Farao and his pouer in the reed see.
16, 17 Which ledde ouer his puple thoruȝ desert. Which

18, 19 smoot grete kingis. And killide strong kingis. Seon, 20 the king of Amorreis. And Og, the king of Baasan. 21, 22 And he ȝaf the lond of hem eritage. Eritage to Israel, 23 his seruaunt. For in oure lownesse he hadde mynde on 24, 25 vs. And he aȝenbouȝte vs fro oure enemyes. Which 26 ȝyueth mete to ech fleisch. Knouleche ȝe to God of heuene. Knouleche ȝe to the Lord of lordis; for his merci *is* withouten ende.

PSALM CXXXVI (CXXXVII).

The hundrid and sixe and thrittithe salm.

1 ON the floodis of Babiloyne there we saten, and wepten;
2 while we bithouȝten on Syon. In salewis in the myddil
3 therof; we hangiden vp oure orguns. For thei that ledden vs prisoners; axiden vs there the wordis of songis. And thei that ledden awei vs *seiden;* Synge ȝe to vs an ympne
4 of the songis of Syon. Hou schulen we singe a songe
5 of the Lord; in an alien lond? If Y forȝete thee, Jeru-
6 salem; my riȝt hond be ȝouun to forȝeting. Mi tunge cleue to my chekis; if Y bithenke not on thee. If Y purposide not of thee, Jerusalem; in the bigynnyng of my
7 gladnesse. Lord, haue thou mynde on the sones of Edom; for the dai of Jerusalem. Whiche seien, Anyntische ȝe,
8 anyntische ȝe; til to the foundement ther-ynne. Thou wretchid douȝter of Babiloyne; he *is* blessid, that schal
9 ȝelde to thee thi ȝelding, which thou ȝeldidist to vs. He *is* blessid, that schal holde; and hurtle doun hise litle children at a stoon.

Psalm CXXXVII (CXXXVIII).

*The title of the hundrid and scuene and thrittithe salm.
To Dauith him silf.*

1 LORD, Y schal knouleche to thee in al myn herte; for thou herdist the wordis of my mouth. Mi God, Y schal 2 singe to thee in the siʒt of aungels; Y schal worschipe to thin hooli temple, and Y schal knoulechc to thi name. On thi merci and thi treuthe; for thou hast magnefied thin 3 hooli name aboue al thing. In what euere dai Y schal inwardli clepe thee, here thou me; thou schalt multipli 4 vertu in my soule. Lord, alle the kingis of erthe knou- lechc to thee; for thei herden alle the wordis of thi mouth. 5 And singe thei in the weies of the Lord; for the glorie 6 of the Lord is greet. For the Lord *is* hiʒ, and biholdith 7 meke thingis; and knowith afer hiʒ thingis. If Y schal go in the myddil of tribulacioun, thou schalt quikene me; and thou stretchidist forth thin hond on the ire of myn 8 enemyes, and thi riʒt hond made me saaf. The Lord schal ʒelde for me, Lord, thi merci *is* with-outen ende; dispise thou not the werkis of thin hondis.

Psalm CXXXVIII (CXXXIX).

*The title of the hundrid and eiʒte and thrittithe salm.
To victorie, the salm of Dauith.*

1, 2 LORD, thou hast preued me, and hast knowe me; thou 3 hast knowe my sitting, and my rising aʒen. Thou hast vndirstonde my thouʒtis fro fer; thou hast enquerid my 4 path and my corde. And thou hast bifor seien alle my 5 weies; for no word is in my tunge. Lo! Lord, thou hast knowe alle thingis, the laste thingis and elde; thou hast

6 formed me, and hast set thin hond on me. Thi kunnyng
is maad wondirful of me; it is coumfortid, and Y schal
7 not mowe to it. Whidir schal Y go fro thi spirit; and
8 whider schal Y fle fro thi face? If Y schal stie in to
heuene, thou art there; if Y schal go doun to helle, thou
9 art present. If Y schal take my fetheris ful eerli; and
10 schal dwelle in the last partis of the see. And sotheli thider
thin hond schal leede me forth; and thi ri3t hond schal
11 holde me. And Y seide, In hap derknessis schulen defoule
12 me; and the ny3t *is* my li3tnyng in my delicis. For whi
derknessis schulen not be maad derk fro thee, and the ni3t
schal be li3tned as the dai; as the derknessis therof, so
13 and the li3t therof. For thou haddist in possessioun my
reines; thou tokist me vp fro the wombe of my modir.
14 I schal knouleche to thee, for thou art magnefied dreedfuli;
thi werkis *ben* wondirful, and my soule schal knouleche ful
15 miche. Mi boon, which thou madist in priuete, is not hyd
fro thee; and my substaunce in the lower partis of erthe.
16 Thin i3en sien myn vnperfit thing, and alle men schulen
be writun in thi book; daies schulen be formed, and no
17 man *is* in tho. Forsothe, God, thi frendis ben maad onourable ful myche to me; the princehed of hem is coumfortid
18 ful myche. I schal noumbre hem, and thei schulen be multiplied aboue grauel; Y roos vp, and 3it Y am with thee
19 For thou, God, schalt slee synneris; 3e menquelleris, bowe
20 awei fro me. For 3e seien in thou3t; Take thei her citees
21 in vanite. Lord, whether Y hatide not hem that hatiden
22 thee; and Y failide on thin enemyes? Bi perfite haterede
23 Y hatide hem; thei weren maad enemyes to me. God,
preue thou me, and knowe thou myn herte; axe thou me,
24 and knowe thou my pathis. And se thou, if weie of wickidnesse is in me; and lede thou me forth in euerlastinge wei.

Psalm CXXXIX (CXL).

1 *The title of the hundrid and nyne and thrittithe salm.*
To victorie, the salm of Dauith.

2 Lord, delyuere thou me fro an yuel man; delyuere thou
3 me fro a wickid man. Whiche thou3ten wickidnesses in
4 the herte; al dai thei ordeyneden batels. Thei scharpiden
her tungis as serpentis; the venym of snakis vndir the lippis
5 of hem. Lord, kepe thou me fro the hond of the synnere;
and delyuere thou me fro wickid men. Which thou3ten
to disseyue my goyngis; proude men hidden a snare to
6 me. And thei leiden forth cordis in to a snare; thei set-
7 tiden sclaundir to me bisidis the weie. I seide to the Lord,
Thou art mi God; Lord, here thou the vois of my bisech-
8 ing. Lord, Lord, the vertu of myn heelthe; thou madist
9 schadowe on myn heed in the dai of batel. Lord, bitake
thou not me fro my desire to the synnere; thei thou3ten
a3ens me, forsake thou not me, lest perauenture thei ben
10 enhaunsid. The heed of the cumpas of hem; the trauel
11 of her lippis schal hile hem. Colis schulen falle on hem,
thou schalt caste hem doun in to fier; in wretchidnessis
12 thei schulen not stonde. A man a greet ianglere schal not
be dressid in erthe; yuels schulen take an vniust man in
13 perisching. I haue knowe, that the Lord schal make dom
14 of a nedi man; and the veniaunce of pore men. Netheles
iust men schulen knouleche to thi name; and ri3tful men
schulen dwelle with thi cheer.

Psalm CXL (CXLI).

1 *The title of the hundrid and fourtithe salm.*
The salm of Dauith.

Lord, Y criede to thee, here thou me; 3yue thou tent
2 to my vois, whanne Y schal crye to thee. Mi preier be

dressid as encense in thi si3t; the reisyng of myn hondis 3 *be as* the euentid sacrifice. Lord, sette thou a keping to my mouth; and a dore of stonding aboute to my lippis. 4 Bowe thou not myn herte in to wordis of malice; to excuse excusingis in synne. With men worchinge wickidnesse; and 5 Y schal not comyne with the chosun men of hem. A iust man schal repreue me in mersi, and schal blame me; but the oile of a synner make not fat myn heed. For whi and 6 3it my preier *is* in the wel plesaunt thingis of hem; for the domesmen of hem ioyned to the stoon weren sopun vp. 7 Here thei my wordis, for tho weren my3ti. As fatnesse is brokun out on the erthe; oure bonys ben scatered ni3 helle. 8 Lord, Lord, for myn i3en ben to thee, Y hopide in thee; 9 take thou not awei my soule. Kepe thou me fro the snare which thei ordeyneden to me; and fro the sclaundris of hem that worchen wickidnesse. Synneris schulen falle in 10 the nett therof; Y am aloone til Y passe.

PSALM CXLI (CXLII).

1 *The title of the hundrid and oon and fourtithe salm. The lernyng of Dauid; his preier, whanne he was in the denne.*

2 WITH my vois Y criede to the Lord; with my vois Y 3 preiede hertli to the Lord. I schede out my preier in his 4 si3t; and Y pronounce my tribulacioun bifor him. While my spirit failith of me; and thou hast knowe my pathis. In this weie in which Y 3ede; proude men hidden a snare 5 to me. I bihelde to the ri3t side, and Y si3; and noon was that knew me. Fli3t perischide fro me; and noon is 6 that sekith my soule. Lord, Y criede to thee, Y seide. 7 Thou art myn hope; my part in the lond of lyueris. 3yue thou tent to my bisechyng; for Y am maad low ful greetli. Delyuere thou me fro hem that pursuen me; for thei ben

8 coumfortid on me. Lede my soule out of keping to knou-leche to thi name; iust men abiden me, til thou ȝelde to me.

Psalm CXLII (CXLIII).

1 *The title of the hundrid and two and fourtithe salm.*
The salm of Dauid.

Lord, here thou my preier, with eeris perseyue thou my biseching; in thi treuthe here thou me, in thi riȝtwisnesse. 2 And entre thou not in to dom with thi seruaunt; for ech 3 man lyuynge schal not be maad iust in thi siȝt. For the enemy pursuede my soule; he made lowe my lijf in erthe. 4 He hath set me in derk placis, as the deed men of the world, and my spirit was angwischid on me; myn herte was disturblid 5 in me. I was myndeful of elde daies, Y bithouȝte in alle thi 6 werkis; Y bithouȝte in the dedis of thin hondis. I helde forth myn hondis to thee; my soule as erthe with-out water 7 to thee. Lord, here thou me swiftli; my spirit failide. Turne thou not a-wei thi face fro me; and Y schal be lijk 8 to hem that gon doun in to the lake. Make thou erli thi merci herd to me; for Y hopide in thee. Make thou knowun to me the weie in which Y schal go; for Y reiside my 9 soule to thee. Delyuere thou me fro myn enemyes, Lord, 10 Y fledde to thee; teche thou me to do thi wille, for thou art my God. Thi good spirit schal lede me forth in to a riȝtful 11 lond; Lord, for thi name thou schalt quikene me in thin 12 equite. Thou schalt lede my soule out of tribulacioun; and in thi merci thou schalt scatere alle myn enemyes. And thou schalt leese alle them, that troublen my soule; for Y am thi seruaunt.

Psalm CXLIII (CXLIV).

1 *The title of the hundrid and thre and fourtithe salm. A salm.*

Blessid *be* my Lord God, that techith myn hondis to 2 werre; and my fyngris to batel. Mi merci, and my refuyt; my takere vp, and my delyuerer. Mi defender, and Y hopide in him; and thou makist suget my puple vnder me. 3 Lord, what is a man, for thou hast maad knowun to him; ether the sone of man, for thou arettist him of sum valu? 4 A man is maad lijk vanyte; hise daies passen as schadow. 5 Lord, bowe doun thin heuenes, and come thou doun; touche 6 thou hillis, and thei schulen make smoke. Leite thou schynyng, and thou schalt scatere hem; sende thou out thin 7 arowis, and thou schalt disturble hem. Sende out thin hond fro an hi3, rauysche thou me out, and delyuere thou me fro 8 many watris; and fro the hond of alien sones. The mouth of which spak vanite; and the ri3thond of hem *is* the ri3t 9 hond of wickidnesse. God, Y schal synge to thee a new song; I schal seie salm to thee in a sautre of ten stringis. 10 Which 3yuest heelthe to kingis; which a3en-bou3tist Dauid, thi seruaunt, fro the wickid swerd rauische thou out me. 11 And delyuere thou me fro the hond of alien sones; the mouth of whiche spak vanyte, and the ri3thond of hem *is* the 12 ri3t hond of wickidnesse. Whose sones *ben*; as new plauntingis in her 3ongthe. The dou3tris of hem *ben* arayed; 13 ourned about as the licnesse of the temple. The selers of hem *ben* fulle; bringinge out fro this *vessel* in to that. The scheep of hem *ben* with lambre, plenteuouse in her goingis 14 out; her kien *ben* fatte. No falling of wal is, nether passing 15 ouere; nether cry *is* in the stretis of hem. Thei seiden, The puple *is* blessid, that hath these thingis; blessid *is* the puple, whos Lord is the God of it.

Psalm CXLIV (CXLV).

1 *The title of the hundrid and foure and fourtithe salm. The ympne of Dauith.*

1 Mi God king, Y schal enhaunse thee; and Y schal blesse
2 thi name in to the world, and in to the world of world. Bi alle daies Y schal blesse thee; and Y schal herie thi name
3 in to the world, and in to the world of the world. The Lord *is* greet, and worthi to be preisid ful myche; and noon ende
4 is of his greetnesse. Generacioun and generacioun schal preise thi werkis; and thei schulen pronounse thi power.
5 Thei schulen speke the greet doyng of the glorie of thin
6 holynesse; and thei schulen telle thi merueils. And thei schulen seye the vertu of thi ferdful thingis; and thei schulen
7 telle thi greetnesse. Thei schulen bringe forth the mynde of the abundaunce of thi swetnesse; and thei schulen telle
8 with ful out ioiyng thi riȝtfulnesse. The Lord *is* a merciful doere, and merciful in wille; paciente, and myche merciful.
9 The Lord *is* swete in alle thingis; and hise merciful doyngis
10 ben on alle hise werkis. Lord, alle thi werkis knouleche to
11 thee; and thi seyntis blesse thee. Thei schulen seie the
12 glorie of thi rewme; and thei schulen speke thi power. That thei make thi power knowun to the sones of men; and
13 the glorie of the greetnesse of thi rewme. Thi rewme *is* the rewme of alle worldis; and thi lordschipe *is* in al generacioun and in to generacioun. The Lord *is* feithful in alle hise
14 wordis; and hooli in alle hise werkis. The Lord liftith vp alle that fallen doun; and reisith alle men hurtlid doun.
15 Lord, the iȝen of alle *beestis* hopen in thee; and thou ȝyuest
16 the mete of hem in couenable tyme. Thou openest thin
17 hond; and thou fillist ech beeste with blessing. The Lord
18 *is* iust in alle hise weies; and hooli in alle hise werkis. The

Lord is ni3 to alle that inwardli clepen him; to alle that
inwardli clepen him in treuthe. He schal do the wille of
hem, that dreden him, and he schal here the bisechyng of
hem; and he schal make hem saaf. The Lord kepith alle
men louynge him; and he schal leese alle synners. Mi
mouth schal speke the heriyng of the Lord; and ech man
blesse his hooli name in to the world, and in to the world
of world.

Psalm CXLV (CXLVI).

1 *The title of the hundred and fyue and fourtithe salm.
Alleluya.*

2 Mi soule, herie thou the Lord; Y schal herie the Lord in
my lijf, Y schal synge to my God as longe as Y schal be.
3 Nile 3e triste in princis; nether in the sones of men, in
4 whiche is noon helthe. The spirit of hym schal go out, and
he schal turne a3en in to his erthe; in that dai alle the
5 thou3tis of hem schulen perische. He *is* blessid, of whom
the God of Jacob is his helpere, his hope *is* in his Lord God,
6 that made heuene and erthe; the see, and alle thingis that
7 ben in tho. Which kepith treuthe in to the world, makith
dom to hem that suffren wrong; 3yueth mete to hem that
8 ben hungri. The Lord vnbyndith feterid men; the Lord
li3tneth blynde men. The Lord reisith men hurtlid doun:
9 the Lord loueth iust men. The Lord kepith comelyngis, he
schal take vp a modirles child, and widewe; and he schal
10 distrie the weies of synners. The Lord schal regne in to the
worldis; Syon, thi God schal regne in generacioun and in to
generacioun.

Psalm CXLVI (CXLVII).

1 *The title of the hundrid and sixe and fourtithe salm. Alleluya.*

Herie 3e the Lord, for the salm is good; heriyng be 2 myrie, and fair to oure God. The Lord schal bilde Jerusalem; and schal gadere togidere the scateryngis of Israel. 3 Which *Lord* makith hool men contrit in herte; and byndith 4 togidere the sorewes of hem. Which noumbrith the multi-5 tude of sterris; and clepith names to alle tho. Oure Lord *is* greet, and his vertu *is* greet; and of his wisdom is no 6 noumbre. The Lord takith vp mylde men; forsothe he 7 makith low synneris til to the erthe. Bifore synge 3e to the Lord in knoulechyng; seye 3e salm to oure God in an 8 harpe. Which hilith heuene with cloudis; and makith redi reyn to the erthe. Which bryngith forth hei in hillis; and 9 eerbe to the seruice of men. Which 3yueth mete to her werk beestis; and to the briddys of crowis clepinge hym. 10 He schal not haue wille in the strengthe of an hors; nether it schal be wel plesaunt to hym in the leggis of a man. It is 11 wel plesaunt to the Lord on men that dreden hym; and in hem that hopen on his mercy.

Psalm CXLVII (CXLVII, *continued*).

The hundrid and seuene and fourtithe salm.

12 Jerusalem, herie thou the Lord; Syon, herie thou thi 13 God. For he hath coumfortid the lockis of thi 3atis; he 14 hath blessid thi sones in thee. Which hath set thi coostis 15 pees; and fillith thee with the fatnesse of wheete. Which sendith out his speche to the erthe; his word renneth swiftli. 16 Which 3yueth snow as wolle; spredith abrood a cloude as

17 aische. He sendith his cristal as mussels; who schal suffre
18 bifore the face of his cooldnesse? He schal sende out his
word, and schal melte tho; his spirit schal blowe, and watris
19 schulen flowe. Which tellith his word to Jacob; and hise
20 riȝtfulnessis and domes to Israel. He dide not so to ech
nacioun; and he schewide not hise domes to hem.

Psalm CXLVIII.

1   *The title of the hundrid and eiȝte and fourtithe salm.*
    Alleluya.

ȜE of heuenes, herie the Lord; herie ȝe hym in hiȝe
2 thingis. Alle hise aungels, herie ȝe hym; alle hise vertues,
3 herye ȝe hym. Sunne and moone, herie ȝe hym; alle sterris
4 and liȝt, herie ȝe hym. Heuenes of heuenes, herie ȝe hym;
5 and the watris that ben aboue heuenes, herie ȝe the name
6 of the Lord. For he seide, and thingis weren maad; he
comaundide, and thingis weren maad of nouȝt. He ordeynede tho thingis in to the world, and in to the world of
world; he settide a comaundement, and it schal not passe.
7 Ȝe of erthe, herie ȝe the Lord; dragouns, and alle depthis
8 of watris. Fier, hail, snow, iys, spiritis of tempestis; that
9 don his word. Mounteyns, and alle litle hillis; trees berynge
10 fruyt, and alle cedris. Wielde beestis, and alle tame beestis;
11 serpentis, and fetherid briddis. The kingis of erthe, and alle
12 puplis; the princis, and alle iugis of erthe. Ȝonge men, and
virgyns, elde men with ȝongere, herie ȝe the name of the
13, 14 Lord; for the name of hym aloone is enhaunsid. His
knouleching *be* on heuene and erthe; and he hath enhaunsid
the horn of his puple. An ympne *be* to alle hise seyntis; to
the children of Israel, to a puple neiȝynge to hym.

Psalm CXLIX.

1 *The title of the hundrid and nyne and fourtithe salm. Alleluya.*

Synge ʒe to the Lord a newe song; hise heriyng *be* in the 2 chirche of seyntis. Israel be glad in hym that made hym; and the douʒtris of Syon make ful out ioye in her king. 3 Herie thei his name in a queer; seie thei salm to hym in 4 a tympan, and sautre. For the Lord is wel plesid in his 5 puple; and he hath reisid mylde men in to heelthe. Seyntis schulen make ful out ioye in glorie; thei schulen be glad in 6 her beddis. The ful out ioiyngis of God in the throte of hem; and swerdis scharp on ech side in the hondis of hem. 7, 8 To do veniaunce in naciouns; blamyngis in puplis. To bynde the kyngis of hem in stockis; and the noble men 9 of hem in yrun manaclis. That thei make in hem doom writun; this is glorye to alle hise seyntis.

Psalm CL.

1 *The title of the hundrid and fiftithe salm. Alleluya.*

Herie ʒe the Lord in hise seyntis; herie ʒe hym in the 2 firmament of his vertu. Herie ʒe hym in hise vertues; herie 3 ʒe hym bi the multitude of his greetnesse. Herie ʒe hym in the soun of trumpe; herie ʒe hym in a sautre and harpe. 4 Herie ʒe hym in a tympane and queer; herie ʒe hym in 5 strengis and orgun. Herie ʒe hym in cymbalis sownynge 6 wel, herye ʒe hym in cymbalis of iubilacioun; ech spirit, herye the Lord.

PROVERBS.

Cap. I.

1 THE parablis of Salomon, the sone of Dauid, king of
2, 3 Israel; to kunne wisdom and kunnyng; to vndurstonde
the wordis of prudence; and to take the lernyng of teching;
4 *to take* riʒtfulnesse, and dom, and equyte; that felnesse be
ʒouun to litle children, and kunnyng, and vndurstonding to
5 a ʒong wexynge man. A wise man heringe schal be wisere;
6 and a man vndurstondinge schal holde gouernails. He schal
perseyue a parable, and expownyng; the wordis of wise
7 men, and the derk figuratif spechis of hem. The drede of
the Lord *is* the bigynning of wisdom; foolis dispisen wisdom
8 and teching. My sone, here thou the teching of thi fadir,
9 and forsake thou not the lawe of thi modir; that grace be
addid, *ethir encreessid*, to thin heed, and a bie to thi necke.
10 Mi sone, if synneris flateren thee, assente thou not to hem.
11 If thei seien, Come thou with vs, sette we aspies to blood,
hide we snaris of disseitis aʒens an innocent without cause;
12 swolowe we him, as helle *swolowith* a man lyuynge; and
13 al hool, as goynge doun in to a lake; we schulen fynde al
preciouse catel, we schulen fille oure housis with spuylis;
14, 15 sende thou lot with vs, o purs be of vs alle; my sone, go
thou not with hem; forbede thi foot fro the pathis of hem.
16 For the feet of hem rennen to yuel; and thei hasten to
17 schede out blood. But a net is leid in veyn bifore the iʒen
18 of briddis, that han wengis. Also thilke *wickid disseyueris*
setten aspies aʒens her owne blood; and maken redi fraudis
19 aʒens her soulis. So the pathis of ech auerouse man
20 rauyschen the soulis of hem that welden. Wisdom prechith

²¹ with-outforth; in stretis it ȝyueth his vois. It crieth ofte in the heed of cumpenyes; in the leeues of ȝatis of the citee it ²² bringith forth hise wordis, and seith, Hou long, ȝe litle men *in wit*, louen ȝong childhod, and foolis schulen coueyte tho thingis, that ben harmful to hem silf, and vnprudent men ²³ schulen hate kunnyng? Be ȝe conuertid at my repreuyng; lo, Y schal profre forth to ȝou my spirit, and Y schal schewe ²⁴ my wordis. For Y clepide, and ȝe forsoken; Y helde forth ²⁵ myn hond, and noon was that bihelde. Ȝe dispisiden al my ²⁶ councel; and chargiden not my blamyngis. And Y schal leiȝe in ȝoure perisching; and Y schal scorne ȝou, whanne ²⁷ that, that ȝe dreden, cometh to ȝou. Whanne sodeyne wretchidnesse fallith in, and perisching bifallith as tempest; ²⁸ whanne tribulacioun and angwisch cometh on ȝou. Thanne thei schulen clepe me, and Y schal not here; thei schulen ²⁹ rise eerli, and thei schulen not fynde me. For thei hatiden ³⁰ teching, and thei token not the drede of the Lord, nether assentiden to my councel, and deprauden al myn amendyng. ³¹ Therfor thei schulen ete the fruytis of her weie; and thei ³² schulen be fillid with her counseils. The turnyng awei of litle men *in wit* schal sle hem; and the prosperite of foolis ³³ schal leese hem. But he that herith me, schal reste withouten drede; and he schal vse abundaunce, whanne the drede of yuels is takun awei.

Cap. II.

¹ Mi sone, if thou resseyuest my wordis, and hidist myn ² heestis anentis thee; that thin eere here wisdom, bowe thin ³ herte to knowe prudence. For if thou inwardli clepist wis- ⁴ dom, and bowist thin herte to prudence; if thou sekist it as ⁵ money, and diggist it out as tresours; thanne thou schalt vndirstonde the drede of the Lord, and schalt fynde the

6 kunnyng of God. For the Lord ȝyueth wisdom; and pru-
7 dence and kunnyng *is* of his mouth. He schal kepe the
heelthe of riȝtful men, and he schal defende hem that goen
8 sympli. And he schal kepe the pathis of riȝtfulnesse, and he
9 schal kepe the weies of hooli men. Thanne thou schalt
vndirstonde riȝtfulnesse, and dom, and equytee, and ech good
10 path. If wysdom entrith in to thin herte, and kunnyng
11 plesith thi soule, good councel schal kepe thee, and pru-
12 dence schal kepe thee; that thou be delyuered fro an yuel
13 weie, and fro a man that spekith weiward thingis. Whiche
14 forsaken a riȝtful weie, and goen bi derk weies; whiche ben
glad, whanne thei han do yuel, and maken ful out ioye in
15 worste thingis; whose weies *ben* weywerd, and her goyingis
16 *ben* of yuel fame. That thou be delyuered fro an alien
womman, and fro a straunge *womman*, that makith soft hir
17 wordis; and forsakith the duyk of hir tyme of mariage, and
18 hath forȝete the couenaunt of hir God. For the hous of hir
19 is bowid to deeth, and hir pathis to helle. Alle that entren
to hir, schulen not turne aȝen, nether schulen catche the
20 pathis of lijf. That thou go in a good weie, and kepe the
21 pathis of iust men. Forsothe thei that ben riȝtful, schulen
dwelle in the lond; and symple men schulen perfitli dwelle
22 ther-ynne. But vnfeithful men schulen be lost fro the
loond; and thei that doen wickidli, schulen be takun awey
fro it.

CAP. III.

1 Mi sone, forȝete thou not my lawe; and thyn herte kepe
2 my comaundementis. For tho schulen sette to thee the
3 lengthe of daies, and the ȝeeris of lijf, and pees. Merci and
treuthe forsake thee not; bynde thou tho to thi throte, and
4 write in the tablis of thin herte. And thou schalt fynde
5 grace, and good teching bifore God and men. Haue thou

trist in the Lord, of al thin herte; and triste thou not to thi
6 prudence. In alle thi weies thenke thou on hym, and he
7 schal dresse thi goyngis. Be thou not wijs anentis thi silf;
8 drede thou God, and go awei fro yuel. For-whi helthe
9 schal be in thi nawle, and moisting of thi boonys. Onoure
thou the Lord of thi catel, and of the beste of alle thi fruytis
10 ȝyue thou to pore men; and thi bernes schulen be fillid with
11 abundaunce, and pressours schulen flowe with wiyn. My
sone, caste thou not awei the teching of the Lord, and faile
12 thou not, whanne thou art chastisid of him. For the Lord
chastisith hym, whom he loueth; and as a fadir in the sone he
13 plesith hym. Blessid *is* the man that fyndith wisdom, and
14 which flowith with prudence. The geting therof is betere
than the marchaundie of gold and of siluer; the fruytis
15 therof *ben* the firste and clenneste. It is preciousere than
alle richessis; and alle thingis that ben desirid, moun not be
16 comparisound to this. Lengthe of daies *is* in the riȝthalf therof,
17 and richessis and glorie *ben* in the lifthalf therof. The weies
therof *ben* feire weies, and alle the pathis therof *ben* pesible.
18 It is a tre of lijf to hem that taken it; and he that holdith it,
19 is blessid. The Lord foundide the erthe bi wisdom; he
20 stablischide heuenes bi prudence. The depthis of watris
braken out bi his wisdom; and cloudis wexen togidere bi
21 dewe. My sone, these thingis flete not awey fro thin iȝen;
22 kepe thou my lawe, and my counsel; and lijf schal be to thi
23 soule, and grace *schal be* to thi chekis. Thanne thou schalt
24 go tristili in thi weie; and thi foot schal not snapere. If
thou schalt slepe, thou schalt not drede; thou schalt reste,
25 and thi sleep schal be soft. Drede thou not bi sudeyne feer,
26 and the powers of wickid men fallynge in on thee. For the
Lord schal be at thi side; and he schal kepe thi foot, that
27 thou be not takun. Nil thou forbede to do wel him that mai;
28 if thou maist, and do thou wel. Seie thou not to thi frend, Go,

and turne thou aȝen, and to morewe Y schal ȝyue to thee;
29 whanne thou maist ȝyue anoon. Ymagyne thou not yuel to
30 thi freend, whanne he hath trist in thee. Stryue thou not
aȝens a man with-out cause, whanne he doith noon yuel to
31 thee. Sue thou not an vniust man, sue thou not hise weies.
32 For ech disseyuer is abhomynacioun of the Lord; and his
33 speking *is* with simple men. Nedinesse *is sent* of the Lord in
the hous of a wickid man; but the dwelling places of iust
34 men schulen be blessid. He schal scorne scorneris; and he
35 schal ȝyue grace to mylde men. Wise men schulen haue
glorie; enhaunsing of foolis *is* schenschipe.

CAP. IV.

1 SONES, here ȝe the teching of the fadir; and perseiue ȝe,
2 that ȝe kunne prudence. Y schal ȝyue to ȝou a good ȝifte;
3 forsake ȝe not my lawe. For-whi and Y was the sone of my
fadir, a tendir sone, and oon gendride bifore my modir.
4 And *my fadir* tauȝte me, and seide, Thin herte resseyue my
wordis; kepe thou myn heestis, and thou schalt lyue.
5 Welde thou wisdom, welde thou prudence; forȝete thou not,
6 nethir bowe thou awey fro the wordis of my mouth. Forsake
thou not it, and it schal kepe thee; loue thou it, and it schal
7 kepe thee. The bigynnyng of wisdom, welde thou wisdom;
8 and in al thi possessioun gete thou prudence. Take thou it,
and it schal enhaunse thee; thou schalt be glorified of it,
9 whanne thou hast biclippid it. It schal ȝyue encresyngis of
graces to thin heed; and a noble coroun schal defende thee.
10 Mi sone, here thou, and take my wordis; that the ȝeris of lijf
11 be multiplied to thee. Y schal schewe to thee the weie of
12 wisdom; and Y schal lede thee bi the pathis of equyte. In
to whiche whanne thou hast entrid, thi goyngis schulen not
be maad streit; and thou schalt rennen, and schalt not haue

13 hirtyng. Holde thou teching, and forsake it not; kepe thou
14 it, for it is thi lijf. Delite thou not in the pathis of wyckid
15 men; and the weie of yuele men plese not thee. Fle thou
fro it, and passe thou not therbi; bowe thou awei, and for-
16 sake it. For thei slepen not, no-but thei han do yuele; and
17 sleep is rauyschid fro hem, no-but thei han disseyued. Thei
eten the breed of vnpite, and drinken the wyn of wickidnesse.
18 But the path of iust men goith forth as li3t schynynge, and
19 encreessith til to perfit dai. The weie of wickid men *is* derk;
20 thei witen not where thei schulen falle. Mi sone, herkene thou
21 my wordis; and bowe doun thin eeris to my spechis. Go
not tho awei fro thyn i3en; kepe thou hem in the myddil of
22 thin herte. For tho ben lijf to men fyndynge thoo, and
23 heelthe of al fleisch. With al keping kepe thin herte, for lijf
24 cometh forth of it. Remoue thou a schrewid mouth fro
25 thee; and backbitynge lippis be fer fro thee. Thin i3en
se ri3tful thingis; and thin i3eliddis go bifore thi steppis.
26 Dresse thou pathis to thi feet, and alle thi weies schulen be
27 stablischid. Bowe thou not to the ri3tside, nether to the
leftside; turne awei thi foot fro yuel. For the Lord knowith
the weies that ben at the ri3tside; but the weies ben weiward,
that ben at the leftside. Forsothe he schal make thi goyngis
ri3tful; and thi weies schulen be brou3t forth in pees.

Cap. V.

1 Mi sone, perseyue thou my wisdom, and bowe doun thin
2 eere to my prudence; that thou kepe thi thou3tis, and thi
lippis kepe teching. 3yue thou not tent to the falsnesse
3 of a womman; for the lippis of an hoore *ben* an hony-
4 coomb droppinge, and hir throte *is* clerere than oile; but
the last thingis *ben* bittir as wormod, and hir tunge *is* scharp
5 as a swerd keruynge on ech side. Hir feet gon doun in

6 to deeth; and hir steppis persen to hellis. Tho goon not
bi the path of lijf; hir steppis ben vncerteyn, and moun
7 not be souȝt out. Now therfor, my sone, here thou me,
8 and go not awei fro the wordis of my mouth. Make fer
thi weie fro hir, and neiȝe thou not to the doris of hir
9 hous. Ȝyue thou not thin onour to aliens, and thi ȝeeris
10 to the cruel; lest perauenture straungeris be fillid with thi
11 strengthis, and lest thi trauels be in an alien hous; and
thou biweile in the laste daies, whanne thou hast wastid
12 thi fleschis, and thi bodi; and thou seie, Whi wlatide Y
13 teching, and myn herte assentide not to blamyngis; nether
Y herde the voys of men techinge me, and Y bowide not
14 doun myn ecre to maistris? Almest Y was in al yuel, in
15 the myddis of the chirche, and of the synagoge. Drinke
16 thou watir of thi cisterne, and the floodis of thi pit. Thi
wellis be stremed forth; and departe thi watris in stretis.
17 Haue thou aloone tho *watris;* and aliens be not thi par-
18 ceneris. Thi veyne be blessid; and be thou glad with the
19 womman of thi ȝong wexynge age. An hynde moost dereworthe; and an hert calf moost acceptable. Hir teetis fille
thee in al tyme; and delite thou contynueli in the loue of hir.
20 Mi sone, whi art thou disseyued of an alien womman; and
21 art fostrid in the bosum of an othere? The Lord seeth
22 the weie of a man; and biholdith alle hise steppis. The
wickidnessis of a wyckid man taken hym; and he is boundun
23 with the roopis of hise synnes. He schal die, for he hadde
not lernyng; and he schal be disseyued in the mychilnesse
of his fooli.

Cap. VI.

1 Mi sone, if thou hast bihiȝt for thi freend; thou hast
2 fastned thin hoond at a straunger. Thou art boundun bi
the wordis of thi mouth; and *thou art* takun with thin owne

3 wordis. Therfor, my sone, do thou that that Y seie, and delyuere thi silf; for thou hast fallun in to the hond of thi neiȝbore. Renne thou aboute, haste thou, reise thi 4 freend; ȝyue thou not sleep to thin iȝen, nether thin iȝeliddis 5 nappe. Be thou rauyschid as a doo fro the hond; and as 6 a bridde fro aspiyngis of the foulere. O! thou slowe man, go to the amte, *ether pissemyre;* and biholde thou hise weies, 7 and lerne thou wisdom. Which whanne he hath no duyk, 8 nethir comaundour, nether prince; makith redi in somer mete to hym silf, and gaderith togidere in heruest that, that he 9 schal ete. Hou long schalt thou, slow man, slepe? whanne 10 schalt thou rise fro thi sleep? A litil thou schalt slepe, a litil thou schalt nappe; a litil thou schalt ioyne togidere 11 thin hondis, that thou slepe. And nedynesse, as a weigoere, schal come to thee; and pouert, as an armed man. Forsothe if thou art not slow, thi ripe corn schal come as a 12 welle; and nedynesse schal fle fer fro thee. A man apostata, a man vnprofitable, he goith with a weiward mouth; 13 he bekeneth with iȝen, he trampith with the foot, he spekith 14 with the fyngur, bi schrewid herte he ymagyneth yuel, and 15 in al tyme he sowith dissenciouns. His perdicioun schal come to hym anoon, and he schal be brokun sodeynli; and 16 he schal no more haue medecyn. Sixe thingis ben, whyche the Lord hatith; and hise soule cursith the seuenthe thing. 17 Hiȝe iȝen, a tunge liere, hondis schedinge out innocent 18 blood, an herte ymagynynge worste thouȝtis, feet swifte to 19 renne in to yuel, a man bringynge forth lesingis, a fals witnesse; and him that sowith discordis among britheren. 20 Mi sone, kepe the comaundementis of thi fadir; and for-21 sake not the lawe of thi modir. Bynde thou tho continueli 22 in thin herte; and cumpasse to thi throte. Whanne thou goist, go tho with thee; whanne thou slepist, kepe tho 23 thee; and thou wakynge speke with tho. For the comaunde-

ment *of God* is a lanterne, and the lawe *is* liȝt, and the
24 blamyng of techyng *is* the weie of lijf; that *the comaundementis* kepe thee fro an yuel womman, and fro a flaterynge
25 tunge of a straunge womman. Thin herte coueite not the
fairnesse of hir; nether be thou takun bi the signes of hir.
26 For the prijs of an hoore is vnnethe of o loof; but a
27 womman takith the preciouse soule of a man. Whether
a man mai hide fier in his bosum, that hise clothis brenne
28 not; ethir go on colis, and hise feet be not brent? So
29 he that entrith to the wijf of his neiȝbore; schal not be
30 cleene, whanne he hath touchid hir. It is not greet synne,
whanne a man stelith; for he stelith to fille an hungri soule.
31 And he takun schal ȝelde the seuenthe fold; and he schal
ȝyue al the catel of his hous, and schal delyuere hym silf.
32 But he that is avouter; schal leese his soule, for the pouert
33 of herte. He gaderith filthe, and sclaundrith to hym silf;
34 and his schenschip schal not be don awei. For the feruent
loue and strong veniaunce of the man schal not spare in
35 the dai of veniaunce, nether schal assente to the preieris
of ony; nether schal take ful many ȝiftis for raunsum.

Cap. VII.

1 Mi sone, kepe thou my wordis; and kepe myn heestis to
thee. Sone, onoure thou the Lord, and thou schalt be
2 myȝti; but outakun hym drede thou not an alien. Kepe
thou myn heestis, and thou schalt lyue; and my lawe as the
3 appil of thin iȝen. Bynde thou it in thi fyngris; write thou
4 it in the tablis of thin herte. Seie thou to wisdom, Thou art
5 my sistir; and clepe thou prudence thi frendesse. That it
kepe thee fro a straunge womman; and fro an alien wom-
6 man, that makith hir wordis swete. For-whi fro the wyndow
of myn hous bi the latijs Y bihelde; and Y se litle children.

7, 8 I biholde a ȝong man coward, that passith bi the stretis, 9 bisidis the corner; and he goith niȝ the weie of hir hous in derk tyme, whanne the dai drawith to niȝt, in the derknessis 10 and myst of the nyȝt. And lo! a womman, maad redi with ournement of an hoore to disseyue soulis, meetith hym, and 11 *sche is* a ianglere, and goynge about, and vnpacient of reste, 12 and mai not stonde in the hous with hir feet; and now without-forth, now in stretis, now bisidis corneris sche 13 aspieth. And sche takith, and kissith the ȝong man; and 14 flaterith with wowynge cheer, and seith, Y ouȝte sacrifices for 15 heelthe; to-dai Y haue ȝolde my vowis. Therfor Y ȝede out in to thi meetyng, and Y desiride to se thee; and Y 16 haue founde *thee*. Y haue maad my bed with coordis, Y haue 17 arayed with tapetis peyntid of Egipt; Y haue bispreynt my 18 bed with myrre, and aloes, and canel. Come thou, be we fillid with tetis, and vse we collyngis *that ben* coueitid; til the 19 dai bigynne to be cleer. For *myn* hosebonde is not in his 20 hows; he is goon a ful long weie. He took with hym a bagge of money; he schal turne aȝen in to his hous in 21 the dai of ful moone. Sche boonde hym with many wordis; 22 and sche drow forth hym with flateryngis of lippis. Anoon he as an oxe led to slayn sacrifice sueth hir, and as a ioli lomb and vnkunnynge; and the fool woot not, that he is drawun 23 to bondys, til an arowe perse his mawe. As if a brid hastith to the snare; and woot not, that it is don of the perel of his 24 lijf. Now therfor, my sone, here thou me; and perseyue 25 the wordis of my mouth. Lest thi soule be drawun awei in the weies of hir; nether be thou disseyued in the pathis of 26 hir. For sche castide doun many woundid men; and alle 27 strongeste men weren slayn of hir. The weies of helle *is* hir hous; and persen in to ynnere thingis of deeth.

Cap. VIII.

1 Whether wisdom crieth not ofte; and prudence ʒyueth
2 his vois? In souereyneste and hiʒ coppis, aboue the weie, in
3 the myddis of pathis, and it stondith bisidis the ʒate of the
4 citee, in thilke closyngis, and spekith, and seith, A! ʒe men,
Y crie ofte to ʒou; and my vois *is* to the sones of men.
5 Litle children, vndirstonde ʒe wisdom; and ʒe vnwise men,
6 perseyue *wisdom.* Here ʒe, for Y schal speke of grete
thingis; and my lippis schulen be openyd, to preche riʒtful
7 thingis. My throte schal bithenke treuthe; and my lippis
8 schulen curse a wickid man. My wordis ben iust; no
9 schrewid thing, nether weiward is in tho. *My wordis* ben
riʒtful to hem that vndurstonden; and *ben* euene to hem that
10 fynden kunnyng. Take ʒe my chastisyng, and not money;
11 chese ʒe teching more than tresour. For wisdom is betere
than alle richessis moost preciouse; and al desirable thing
12 mai not be comparisound therto. Y, wisdom, dwelle in
13 counsel; and Y am among lernyd thouʒtis. The drede of
the Lord hatith yuel; Y curse boost, and pride, and a
14 schrewid weie, and a double tungid mouth. Counseil is
myn, and equyte *is myn;* prudence is myn, and strengthe
15 *is myn.* Kyngis regnen bi me; and the makeris of lawis
16 demen iust thingis *bi me.* Princis comaunden bi me; and
17 myʒti men demen riʒtfulnesse *bi me.* I loue hem that louen
me; and thei that waken eerli to me, schulen fynde me.
18 With me ben rychessis, and glorie; souereyn richessis, and
19 riʒtfulnesse. My fruyt is betere than gold, and precyouse
20 stoon; and my seedis *ben betere* than chosun siluer. Y go in
the weies of riʒtfulnesse, in the myddis of pathis of doom;
21 that Y make riche hem that louen me, and that Y fille her
22 tresouris. The Lord weldide me in the bigynnyng of hise
weies; bifore that he made ony thing, at the bigynnyng.

23 Fro with-out bigynnyng Y was ordeined; and fro elde tymes,
24 bifor that the erthe was maad. Depthis of watris weren not
ȝit; and Y was conseyued thanne. The wellis of watris
25 hadden not brokun out ȝit, and hillis stoden not togidere
26 ȝit bi sad heuynesse; bifor litil hillis Y was born. Ȝit he
hadde not maad erthe; and floodis, and the herris of the
27 world. Whanne he made redi heuenes, Y was present;
whanne he cumpasside the depthis of watris bi certeyn
28 lawe and cumpas. Whanne he made stidfast the eir aboue;
29 and weiede the wellis of watris. Whanne he cumpasside to
the see his marke; and settide lawe to watris, that tho
schulden not passe her coostis. Whanne he peiside the
30 foundementis of erthe; Y was making alle thingis with
him. And Y delitide bi alle daies, and pleiede bifore hym
31 in al tyme, and Y pleiede in the world; and my delices *ben*
32 to be with the sones of men. Now therfor, sones, here ȝe
33 me; blessid *ben thei* that kepen my weies. Here ȝe teching,
34 and be ȝe wise men; and nile ȝe caste it awei. Blessid
is the man that herith me, and that wakith at my ȝatis al
35 dai; and kepith at the postis of my dore. He that fyndith
me, schal fynde lijf; and schal drawe helthe of the Lord.
36 But he that synneth aȝens me, schal hurte his soule; alle
that haten me, louen deeth.

Cap. IX.

1 Wisdom bildide an hous to him silf; he hewide out seuene
2 pileris, he offride his slayn sacrifices, he medlide wijn, and
3 settide forth his table. He sente hise handmaides, that thei
4 schulden clepe to the tour; and to the wallis of the citee. If
ony man is litil; come he to me. And *wisdom* spak to
5 vnwise men, Come ȝe, ete ȝe my breed; and drynke ȝe the
6 wiyn, which Y haue medlid to ȝou. Forsake ȝe ȝong

childhed, and lyue ȝe; and go ȝe bi the weyes of prudence.
7 He that techith a scornere, doith wrong to him silf; and he
that vndirnymmeth a wickid man, gendrith a wem to him
8 silf. Nile thou vndirnyme a scornere; lest he hate thee.
9 Vndirnyme thou a wise man; and he schal loue thee. Ȝyue
thou occasioun to a wise man; and wisdom schal be encreessid to hym. Teche thou a iust man; and he schal
10 haste to take. The bigynnyng of wisdom *is* the dreed of
11 the Lord; and prudence *is* the kunnyng of seyntis. For
thi daies schulen be multiplied bi me; and ȝeeris of lijf
12 schulen be encreessid to thee. If thou art wijs; thou schalt
be to thi silf, and to thi neiȝboris. Forsothe if *thou art*
13 a scornere; thou aloone schalt bere yuel. A fonned womman, and ful of cry, and ful of vnleueful lustis, and that kan
14 no thing outirli, sittith in the doris of hir hous, on a seete, in
15 an hiȝ place of the cite; to clepe men passinge bi the weie,
16 and men goynge in her iournei. Who is a litil man *of wit;*
17 bowe he to me. And sche spak to a coward, Watris of
18 thefte ben swettere, and breed hid is swettere. And wiste
not that giauntis ben there; and the gestis of hir *ben* in the
depthis of helle. Sotheli he that schal be applied, *ether
fastned*, to hir; schal go doun to hellis. For-whi he that
goith awei fro hir; schal be saued.

Cap. X.

1 *The parablis of Salomon.* A wijs sone makith glad the
2 fadir; but a fonned sone is the sorewe of his modir. Tresouris of wickidnesse schulen not profite; but riȝtfulnesse
3 schal delyuere fro deth. The Lord schal not turmente
the soule of a iust man with hungur; and he schal distrie
4 the tresouns of vnpitouse men. A slow hond hath wrouȝt
nedynesse; but the hond of stronge men makith redi rich-

essis. Forsothe he that enforsith *to gete ony thing* bi leesyngis, fedith the wyndis; sotheli the same man sueth
5 briddis fleynge. He that gaderith togidere in heruest, is a wijs sone; *but* he that slepith in sommer, is a sone of
6 confusioun. The blessing of God *is* ouer the heed of a iust man; but wickidnesse hilith the mouth of wickid men.
7 The mynde of a iust man *schal be* with preisingis; and the
8 name of wickid men schal wexe rotun. A wijs man schal resseyue comaundementis with herte; a fool is betun
9 with lippis. He that goith simpli, goith tristili; *but* he that
10 makith schrewid hise weies, schal be opyn. He that bekeneth with the iȝe, schal ȝyue sorewe; a fool schal be
11 betun with lippis. The veyne of lijf *is* the mouth of a iust man; but the mouth of wickid men hilith wickidnesse.
12 Hatrede reisith chidingis; and charite hilith alle synnes.
13 Wisdom is foundun in the lippis of a wise man; and a ȝerd
14 in the bak of him that is nedi of herte. Wise men hiden kunnyng; but the mouth of a fool is nexte to confusioun.
15 The catel of a riche man *is* the citee of his strengthe; the
16 drede of pore men *is* the nedynesse of hem. The werk of a iust man *is* to lijf; but the fruyt of a wickid man *is*
17 to synne. The weie of lijf *is* to him that kepith chastising;
18 but he that forsakith blamyngis, errith. False lippis hiden
19 hatrede; he that bringith forth dispisinge is vnwijs. Synne schal not faile in myche spekyng; but he that mesurith hise
20 lippis, is moost prudent. Chosun siluer *is* the tunge of a
21 iust man; the herte of wickid men *is* for nouȝt. The lippis of a iust man techen ful manye men; but thei that ben
22 vnlerned, schulen die in nedinesse of herte. The blessing of the Lord makith riche men; and turment schal not be
23 felowschipid to hem. A fool worchith wickidnesse as bi leiȝ-
24 yng; but wisdom is prudence to a man. That that a wickid man dredith, schal come on hym; the desire of iust men

25 schalbe ȝouun to hem. As a tempeste passynge, a wickid
man schal not be; but a iust man *schal be* as an euerlastynge
26 foundement. As vynegre *noieth* the teeth, and smoke *noieth* the
iȝen; so a slow man *noieth* hem that senten hym in the weie.
27 The drede of the Lord encreesith daies; and the ȝeeris of
28 wickid men schulen be maad schort. Abiding of iust men *is*
29 gladnesse; but the hope of wickid men schal perische. The
strengthe of a symple man *is* the weie of the Lord; and
30 drede to hem that worchen yuel. A iust man schal not
be moued with-outen ende; but wickid men schulen not
31 dwelle on the erthe. The mouth of a iust man schal bringe
32 forth wisdom; the tunge of schrewis schal perische. The
lippis of a iust man biholden pleasaunt thingis; and the
mouth of wickid men *byholdith* weiward thingis.

Cap. XI.

1 A GILEFUL balaunce is abhominacioun anentis God; and
2 an euene weiȝte *is* his wille. Where pride is, there also
dispising schal be; but where meeknesse is, there also *is*
3 wisdom. The simplenesse of iust men schal dresse hem;
and the disseyuyng of weiward men schal destrie hem.
4 Richessis schulen not profite in the dai of veniaunce; but
5 riȝtfulnesse schal delyuere fro deth. The riȝtfulnesse of a
simple man schal dresse his weie; and a wickid man schal
6 falle in his wickidnesse. The riȝtfulnesse of riȝtful men
schal delyuere hem; and wickid men schulen be takun in
7 her aspiyngis. Whanne a wickid man is deed, noon hope
schal be ferther; and abidyng of bisy men schal perische.
8 A iust man is delyuered from angwisch; and a wickid man
9 schal be ȝouun for hym. A feynere bi mouth disseyueth his
10 freend; but iust men schulen be deliuered bi kunnyng. A
citee schal be enhaunsid in the goodis of iust men; and

11 preysyng schal be in the perdicioun of wickid men. A citee schal be enhaunsid bi blessing of iust men; and it schal be 12 distried bi the mouth of wickid men. He that dispisith his freend, is nedi in herte; but a prudent man schal be stille. 13 He that goith gilefuli, schewith priuetees; but he that is 14 feithful, helith the priuetee of a freend. Where a gouernour is not, the puple schal falle; but helthe *of the puple is*, where 15 ben many counsels. He that makith feith for a straunger, schal be turmentid with yuel; but he that eschewith snaris, 16 schal be sikur. A graciouse womman schal fynde glorie; 17 and stronge men schulen haue richessis. A merciful man doith wel to his soule; but he that is cruel, castith awei, ȝhe, 18 kynnesmen. A wickid man makith vnstable werk; but 19 feithful mede *is* to hym, that sowith riȝtfulnesse. Merci schal make redi lijf; and the suyng of yuels *schal make redi* 20 deth. A schrewid herte *is* abhomynable to the Lord; and 21 his wille *is* in hem, that goen symply. Thouȝ hond *be* in the hond, an yuel man schal not be innocent; but the seed of 22 iust men schal be sauyd. A goldun sercle, *ether ryng*, in the 23 nose-thrillis of a sowe, a womman fair and fool. The desir of iust men is al good; abiding of wickid men *is* woodnesse. 24 Sum men departen her owne thingis, and ben maad richere; other men rauyschen *thingis, that ben* not hern, and ben 25 euere in nedynesse. A soule that blessith, schal be maad 26 fat; and he that fillith, schal be fillid also. He that hidith wheete in tyme, schal be cursid among the puplis; but 27 blessyng *schal come* on the heed of silleris. Wel he risith eerli, that sekith good thingis; but he that is a serchere 28 of yuels, schal be oppressid of tho. He that tristith in hise richessis, schal falle; but iust men schulen buriowne as a 29 greene leef. He that disturblith his hows, schal haue wyndis *in possessioun;* and he that is a fool, schal serue a wijs man. 30 The fruyt of a riȝtful man *is* the tre of lijf; and he that

31 takith soulis, is a wijs man. If a iust man receyueth in erthe, how miche more an vnfeithful man, and synnere.

Cap. XII.

1 He that loueth chastisyng, loueth kunnyng; but he that
2 hatith blamyngis, is vnwijs. He that is good, schal drawe to hym silf grace of the Lord; but he that tristith in hise
3 thou3tis, doith wickidli. A man schal not be maad strong by wyckidnesse; and the root of iust men schal not be moued.
4 A diligent womman is a coroun to hir hosebond; and rot is in the boonys of that *womman*, that doith thingis worthi of
5 confusioun. The thou3tis of iust men *ben* domes; and the
6 counselis of wickid men *ben* gileful. The wordis of wickid men setten tresoun to blood; the mouth of iust men schal
7 delyuere hem. Turne thou wickid men, and thei schulen not be; but the housis of iust men schulen dwelle perfitli.
8 A man schal be knowun bi his teching; but he that is veyn
9 and hertles, schal be open to dispising. Betere is a pore man, and sufficient to him silf, than a gloriouse man, and nedi
10 of breed. A iust man knowith the soulis of hise werk
11 beestis; but the entrailis of wickid men *ben* cruel. He that worchith his lond, schal be fillid with looues; but he that sueth idilnesse, is moost fool. He that is swete, lyueth in temperaunces; and in hise monestyngis he forsakith dis-
12 pisyngis. The desir of a wickid man is the memorial of worste thingis; but the roote of iust men schal encreesse.
13 For the synnes of lippis falling doun nei3eth to an yuel
14 man; but a iust man schal scape fro angwisch. Of the fruyt of his mouth ech man schal be fillid with goodis; and bi the werkis of hise hondis it schal be 3oldun to him.
15 The weie of a fool *is* ri3tful in hise i3en; but he that is wijs,
16 herith counsels. A fool schewith anoon his ire; but he that

17 dissymelith wrongis, is wijs. He that spekith that, that he knowith, is a iuge of riʒtfulnesse; but he that lieth, is a
18 gileful witnesse. A man is that bihetith, and he is prickid as with the swerd of conscience; but the tunge of wise men is
19 helthe. The lippe of treuthe schal be stidfast with-outen ende; but he that is a sudeyn witnesse, makith redi the
20 tunge of leesyng. Gile *is* in the herte of hem that thenken yuels; but ioye sueth hem, that maken counsels of pees.
21 What euere bifallith to a iust man, it schal not make hym
22 sori; but wickid men schulen be fillid with yuel. False lippis is abhominacioun to the Lord; but thei that don
23 feithfuli, plesen him. A fel man hilith kunnyng; and the
24 herte of vnwise men stirith foli. The hond of stronge men schal haue lordschip; but the hond that is slow, schal serue
25 to tributis. Morenynge in the herte of a iust man schal make hym meke; and he schal be maad glad bi a good
26 word. He that dispisith harm for a frend, is a iust man;
27 but the weie of wickid men schal disseyue hem. A gileful man schal not fynde wynnyng; and the substaunce of man
28 schal be the prijs of gold. Lijf *is* in the path of riʒtfulnesse: but the wrong weie leedith to deeth.

Cap. XIII.

1 A wijs sone *is* the teching of the fadir; but he that is
2 a scornere, herith not, whanne he is repreuyd. A man schal be fillid with goodis of the fruit of his mouth; but the soule
3 of vnpitouse men *is* wickid. He that kepith his mouth, kepith his soule; but he that is vnwar to speke, schal feel
4 yuels. A slow man wole, and wole not; but the soule of
5 hem that worchen schal be maad fat. A iust man schal wlate a fals word; but a wickid man schendith, and schal be
6 schent. Riʒtfulnesse kepith the weie of an innocent man;

7 but wickidnesse disseyueth a synnere. A man is as riche, whanne he hath no thing; and a man is as pore, whanne he
8 is in many richessis. Redempcioun of the soule of man *is* hise richessis; but he that is pore, suffrith not blamyng.
9 The liȝt of iust men makith glad; but the lanterne of wickid
10 men schal be quenchid. Stryues ben euere a-mong proude men; but thei that don alle thingis with counsel, ben
11 gouerned bi wisdom. Hastid catel schal be maad lesse; but that that is gaderid litil and litil with hond, schal be
12 multiplied. Hope which is dilaied, turmentith the soule;
13 a tre of lijf *is* desir comyng. He that bacbitith ony thing, byndith hym silf in to tyme to comynge; but he that dredith
14 the comaundement, schal lyue in pees. The lawe of a wise man *is* a welle of lijf; that he bowe awei fro the falling of
15 deth. Good teching schal ȝyue grace; a swolowe *is* in the
16 weie of dispiseris. A fel man doith alle thingis with counsel;
17 but he that is a fool, schal opene foli. The messanger of a wickid man schal falle in to yuel; a feithful messanger is
18 helthe. Nedynesse and schenschip *is* to him that forsakith techyng; but he that assentith to a blamere, schal be
19 glorified. Desir, if it is fillid, delitith the soule; foolis
20 wlaten hem that fleen yuels. He that goith with wijs men, schal be wijs; the freend of foolis schal be maad lijk hem.
21 Yuel pursueth synneris; and goodis schulen be ȝoldun to
22 iust men. A good man schal leeue *aftir him* eiris, sones, and the sones of sones; and the catel of a synnere is kept to
23 a iust man. Many meetis *ben* in the new tilid feeldis of
24 fadris; and ben gaderid to othere men with-out doom. He that sparith the ȝerde, hatith his sone; but he that loueth
25 him, techith bisili. A iust man etith, and fillith his soule; but the wombe of wickid men *is* vnable to be fillid.

Cap. XIV.

1 A wijs womman bildith hir hous; and an unwijs womman
2 schal distrie with hondis an hous bildid. A man goynge in
rijtful weie, and dredinge God, is dispisid of hym, that goith
3 in a weie of yuel fame. The ʒerde of pride *is* in the mouth
4 of a fool; the lippis of wijs men kepen hem. Where oxis
ben not, the cratche is void; but where ful many cornes
5 apperen, there the strengthe of oxe is opyn. A feithful
witnesse schal not lie; a gileful witnesse bringith forth a
6 leesing. A scornere sekith wisdom, and he fyndith not; the
7 teching of prudent men *is* esy. Go thou aʒens a man a
8 fool; and he schal not knowe the lippis of prudence. The
wisdom of a fel man is to vndirstonde his weie; and the
9 vnwarnesse of foolis errith. A fool scorneth synne; grace
10 schal dwelle among iust men. The herte that knowith the
bittirnesse of his soule; a straunger schal not be meddlid in
11 the ioie therof. The hous of wickid men schal be don
12 awei; the tabernaclis of iust men schulen buriowne. Sotheli
a weie is, that semeth iust to a man; but the laste thingis
13 therof leden forth to deth. Leiʒyng schal be medlid with
sorewe; and morenyng ocupieth the laste thingis of ioye.
14 A fool schal be fillid with hise weies; and a good man schal
15 be aboue hym. An innocent man bileueth to eche word;
16 a felle man biholdith hise goyngis. A wijs man dredith, and
bowith awei fro yuel; a fool skippith ouer, and tristith.
17 A man vnpacient schal worche foli; and a gileful man is
18 odiouse. Litle men *of wit* schulen holde foli; and felle men
19 schulen abide kunnyng. Yuel men schulen ligge bifor
goode men; and vnpitouse men bifor the ʒatis of iust men.
20 A pore man schal be hateful, ʒhe, to his neiʒbore; but many
21 men *ben* frendis of riche men. He that dispisith his neiʒbore,
doith synne; but he that doith merci to a pore man, schal

22 be blessid. He that bileueth in the Lord, loueth merci; thei
   erren that worchen yuel. Merci and treuthe maken redi
23 goodis; abundaunce schal be in ech good werk. Sotheli
24 where ful many wordis ben, there nedynesse is ofte. The
   coroun of wise men *is* the richessis of hem; the fooli of
25 foolis *is* vnwarnesse. A feithful witnesse delyuereth soulis;
26 and a fals man bringith forth leesyngis. In the drede of the
   Lord *is* triste of strengthe; and hope schal be to the sones
27 of it. The drede of the Lord *is* a welle of lijf; that it bowe
28 awei fro the fallyng of deth. The dignite of the king *is* in
   the multitude of puple; and the schenschipe of a prince *is* in
29 the fewnesse of puple. He that is pacient, is gouerned bi
   myche wisdom; but he that is vnpacient, enhaunsith his foli.
30 Helthe of herte *is* the lijf of fleischis; enuye *is* rot of
31 boonys. He that falsli chalengith a nedi man, dispisith his
   maker; but he that hath merci on a pore man, onourith that
32 makere. A wickid man is put out for his malice; but a iust
33 man hopith in his deth. Wisdom restith in the herte of a
34 wijs man; and he schal teche alle vnlerned men. Riȝtful-
35 nesse reisith a folc; synne makith puplis wretchis. A
   mynystre vndurstondynge is acceptable to a kyng; a *mynystre*
   vnprofitable schal suffre the wrathfulnesse of him.

Cap. XV.

1 A SOFT answere brekith ire; an hard word reisith wood-
2 nesse. The tunge of wise men ourneth kunnyng; the
3 mouth of foolis buylith out foli. In ech place the iȝen of
4 the Lord biholden good men, and yuel men. A plesaunt
   tunge *is* the tre of lijf; but the tunge which is vnmesurable,
5 schal defoule the spirit. A fool scorneth the techyng of
   his fadir; but he that kepith blamyngis, schal be maad
   wisere. Moost vertu schal be in plenteuouse riȝtfulnesse;

but the thou3tis of wickid men schulen be drawun vp bi
6 the roote. The hous of a iust man *is* moost strengthe;
7 and disturbling *is* in the fruitis of a wickid man. The
lippis of wise men schulen sowe abrood kunnyng; the
8 herte of foolis schal be vnlijc. The sacrifices of wickyd
men *ben* abhomynable to the Lord; avowis of iust men
9 *ben* plesaunt. The lijf of the vnpitouse man is abhomynacioun to the Lord; he that sueth ri3tfulnesse, schal be
10 loued of the Lord. Yuel teching is of men forsakinge the
11 weie of lijf; he that hatith blamyngis, schal die. Helle
and perdicioun *ben open* bifor the Lord; hou myche more
12 the hertis of sones of men. A man ful of pestilence loueth
not hym that repreueth him; and he goith not to wyse
13 men. A ioiful herte makith glad the face; the spirit is
14 cast doun in the morenyng of soule. The herte of a wijs
man sekith techyng; and the mouth of foolis is fed with
15 vnkunnyng. Alle the daies of a pore man *ben* yuele; a sikir
16 soule *is* a contynuel feeste. Betere is a litil with the drede
17 of the Lord, than many tresouris and vnfillable. It is betere
to be clepid to wortis with charite, than with hatrede to
18 a calf maad fat. A wrathful man reisith chidyngis; he that
19 is pacient, swagith *chidyngis* reisid. The weie of slow men
is an hegge of thornes; the weie of iust men *is* with-out
20 hirtyng. A wise sone makith glad the fadir; and a fonned
21 man dispiseth his modir. Foli is ioye to a fool; and a
22 prudent man schal dresse hise steppis. Thou3tis ben distried, where no counsel is; but where many counseleris ben,
23 tho ben confermyd. A man is glad in the sentence of his
24 mouth; and a couenable word is best. The path of lijf
is on a lernyd man; that he bowe awei fro the laste helle.
25 The Lord schal distrie the hows of proude men; and he
26 schal make stidefast the coostis of a widewe. Iuele thou3tis
is abhomynacioun of the Lord; and a cleene word moost

27 fair schal be maad stidfast of hym. He that sueth aueryce, disturblith his hous; but he that hatith ʒiftis schal lyue. Synnes ben purgid bi merci and feith; ech man bowith 28 awei fro yuel bi the drede of the Lord. The soule of a iust man bithenkith obedience; the mouth of wickid men is ful 29 of yuelis. The Lord is fer fro wickid men; and he schal 30 here the preyers of iust men. The liʒt of iʒen makith glad 31 the soule; good fame makith fat the boonys. The eere that herith the blamyngis of lijf, schal dwelle in the myddis 32 of wise men. He that castith awei chastisyng, dispisith his soule; but he that assentith to blamyngis, is pesible holdere 33 of the herte. The drede of the Lord *is* teching of wisdom; and mekenesse goith bifore glorie.

Cap. XVI.

1 It perteyneth to man to make redi the soule; and *it per-* 2 *teyneth* to the Lord to gouerne the tunge. Alle the weies of men ben opyn to the iʒen of God; the Lord is a weiere 3 of spiritis. Schewe thi werkys to the Lord; and thi thouʒtis 4 schulen be dressid. The Lord wrouʒte alle thingis for hym 5 silf; and he *made redi* a wickid man to the yuel dai. Abhomynacioun of the Lord is ech proude man; ʒhe, thouʒ the hond is to the hond, he schal not be innocent. The bigynnyng of good weie *is* to do riʒtwisnesse: forsothe it is more 6 acceptable at God, than to offre sacrifices. Wickidnesse is aʒen-bouʒt bi merci and treuthe; and me bowith awei fro 7 yuel bi the drede of the Lord. Whanne the weyes of man plesen the Lord, he schal conuerte, ʒhe, hise enemyes to 8 pees. Betere is a litil with riʒtfulnesse, than many fruytis 9 with wickidnesse. The herte of a man schal dispose his weie; but it perteyneth to the Lord to dresse hise steppis. 10 Dyuynyng *is* in the lippis of a king; his mouth schal not

11 erre in doom. The domes of the Lord ben wei3te and a balaunce; and hise werkis *ben* alle the stoonys of the world.
12 Thei that don wickidli *ben* abhomynable to the king; for
13 the trone *of the rewme* is maad stidfast bi ri3tfulnesse. The wille of kyngis *is* iust lippis; he that spekith ri3tful thingis,
14 schal be dressid. Indignacioun of the kyng *is* messangeris
15 of deth; and a wijs man schal plese him. Lijf *is* in the gladnesse of the cheer of the king; and his merci *is* as
16 a reyn comynge late. Welde thou wisdom, for it is betere than gold; and gete thou prudence, for it is precyousere
17 than siluer. The path of iust men bowith awei yuelis; the
18 kepere of his soule kepith his weie. Pride goith bifore sorewe; and the spirit schal be enhaunsid byfor fallyng.
19 It is betere to be maad meke with mylde men, than to
20 departe spuylis with proude men. A lerned man in word schal fynde goodis; and he that hopith in the Lord is
21 blessid. He that is wijs in herte, schal be clepid prudent; and he that is swete in speche, schal fynde grettere thingis.
22 The welle of lijf *is* the lernyng of him that weldith; the
23 techyng of foolis *is* foli. The herte of a wijs man schal teche his mouth; and schal encreesse grace to hise lippis.
24 Wordis wel set togidere *is* a coomb of hony; helthe of
25 boonys is the swetnesse of soule. A weye is that semeth ri3tful to a man; and the laste thingis therof leden to deth.
26 The soule of a man trauelinge trauelith to hym silf; for
27 his mouth compellide hym. An vnwijs man diggith yuel;
28 and fier brenneth in hise lippis. A weiward man reisith
29 stryues; and a man ful of wordis departith princis. A wickid man flaterith his friend; and ledith hym bi a weie
30 not good. He that thenkith schrewid thingis with i3en
31 astonyed, bitith hise lippis, and parformeth yuel. A coroun of dignyte *is* eelde, that schal be foundun in the weies of
32 ri3tfulnesse. A pacient man is betere than a stronge man;

and he that is lord of his soule, *is betere* than an ouer-
33 comere of citees. Lottis ben sent into the bosum; but tho
ben temperid of the Lord.

Cap. XVII.

1 Betere is a drie mussel with ioye, than an hous ful of
2 sacrifices with chidyng. A wijs seruaunt schal be lord of
fonned sones; and he schal departe critage among bri-
3 theren. As siluer is preued bi fier, and gold *is preued* bi
4 a chymnei, so the Lord preueth hertis. An yuel man
obeieth to a wickid tunge; and a fals man obeieth to false
5 lippis. He that dispisith a pore man, repreueth his maker;
and he that is glad in the fallyng of another man, schal
6 not be vnpunyschid. The coroun of elde men *is* the sones
of sones; and the glorie of sones *is* the fadris of hem.
7 Wordis wel set togidere bisemen not a fool; and a liynge
8 lippe *bicometh* not a prince. A preciouse stoon moost acceptable *is* the abiding of hym that sekith; whidur euere
9 he turneth hym silf, he vndurstondith prudentli. He that
helith trespas, sekith frenschipis; he that rehersith bi an
hiʒ word, departith hem, that ben knyt togidere in pees.
10 A blamyng profitith more at a prudent man, than an
11 hundryd woundis at a fool. Euere an yuel man sekith
12 stryues; forsothe a cruel aungel schal be sent aʒens hym. It
spedith more to meete a femal bere, whanne the whelpis ben
13 rauyschid, than a fool tristynge to hym silf in his foli. Yuel
schal not go a-wei fro the hous of hym, that ʒeldith yuels
14 for goodis. He that leueth watir, is heed of stryues; and
15 bifor that he suffrith wrong, he forsakith dom. Bothe he
that iustifieth a wickid man, and he that condempneth a iust
16 man, euer ethir is abhomynable at God. What profitith
it to a fool to haue richessis, sithen he mai not bie wisdom?

He that makith his hous hiȝ, sekith falling; and he that
17 eschewith to lerne, schal falle in to yuels. He that is a
frend, loueth in al tyme; and a brother is preuyd in ang-
18 wischis. A fonned man schal make ioie with hondis, whanne
19 he hath bihiȝt for his frend. He that bithenkith discordis,
loueth chidingis; and he that enhaunsith his mouth, sekith
20 fallyng. He that is of weiward herte, schal not fynde good;
21 and he that turneth the tunge, schal falle in to yuel. A fool
is borun in his schenschipe; but nether the fadir schal be
22 glad in a fool. A ioiful soule makith likinge age; a sorew-
23 ful spirit makith drie boonys. A wickid man takith ȝiftis
24 fro the bosum, to mys turne the pathis of doom. Wisdom
schyneth in the face of a prudent man; the iȝen of foolis
25 ben in the endis of erthe. A fonned sone *is* the ire of the
26 fadir, and the sorewe of the modir that gendride hym. It
is not good to brynge in harm to a iust man; nether to
27 smyte the prince that demeth riȝtfuli. He that mesurith
his wordis, is wijs and prudent; and a lerud man is of
28 preciouse spirit. Also a foole, if he is stille, schal be gessid
a wijs man; and, if he pressith togidre hise lippis, *he schal
be gessid* an vndurstondynge man.

Cap. XVIII.

1 He that wole go a-wei fro a frend, sekith occasiouns;
2 in al tyme he schal be dispisable. A fool resseyueth not
the wordis of prudence; no-but thou seie tho thingis, that
3 ben turned in his herte. A wickid man, whanne he cometh
in to depthe of synnes, dispisith; but sclaundre and schen-
4 schipe sueth hym. Deep watir *is* the wordis of the mouth
of a man; and a stronde fletinge ouer *is* the welle of wis-
5 dom. It is not good to take the persoone of a wickid man
6 in doom, that thou bowe awei fro the treuthe of dom. The

lippis of a fool medlen hem silf with chidyngis; and his
7 mouth excitith stryues. The mouth of a fool *is* defoulyng
8 of hym; and hise lippis *ben* the fallynge of his soule. The
wordis of a double tungid man *ben* as symple; and tho
comen til to the ynnere thingis of the wombe. Drede
castith doun a slowe man; forsothe the soulis of men turned
9 in to wymmens condicioun schulen haue hungur. He that
is neisch, and vnstidfast in his werk, is the brother of a man
10 distriynge hise werkis. A strongeste tour *is* the name of
the Lord; a iust man renneth to hym, and schal be en-
11 haunsid. The catel of a riche man *is* the citee of his
12 strengthe; and as a stronge wal cumpassinge hym. The
herte of man is enhaunsid, bifor that it be brokun; and
13 it is maad meke, bifore that it be glorified. He that answerith bifore that he herith, shewith hym silf to be a fool;
14 and worthi of schenschipe. The spirit of a man susteyneth
his feblenesse; but who may susteyne a spirit liʒt to be
15 wrooth? The herte of a prudent man schal holde stidfastli kunnyng; and the eere of wise men sekith techyng.
16 The ʒift of a man alargith his weie; and makith space to
17 hym bifore princes. A iust man is the first accusere of
18 hym silf; his frend cometh, and schal serche hym. Lot
ceessith aʒenseiyngis; and demeth also among miʒti men.
19 A brother that is helpid of a brothir, *is* as a stidfast citee;
20 and domes *ben* as the barris of citees. A mannus wombe
schal be fillid of the fruit of his mouth; and the seedis of
21 hise lippis schulen fille hym. Deth and lijf *ben* in the werkis
of tunge; thei that louen it, schulen ete the fruytis therof.
22 He that fyndith a good womman, fyndith a good thing;
and of the Lord he schal drawe vp myrthe. He that puttith
a wey a good womman, puttith awei a good thing; but he
23 that holdith auowtresse, is a fool and vnwijs. A pore man
schal speke with bisechingis; and a riche man schal speke

24 sterneli. A man freendli to felouschipe schal more be a frend, than a brothir.

Cap. XIX.

1 Betere is a pore man, that goith in his simplenesse, than
2 a riche man bitynge hise lippis, and vnwijs. Where is not kunnyng of the soule, is not good; and he that is hasti,
3 in feet hirtith. The foli of a man disseyueth hise steppis;
4 and he brenneth in his soule a3ens God. Richessis encreessen ful many freendis; forsothe also thei ben departid
5 fro a pore man, whiche he hadde. A fals witnesse schal not be vnpunyschid; and he that spekith leesingis, schal
6 not ascape. Many men onouren the persoone of a my3ti
7 man; and ben frendis of hym that deelith 3iftis. The britheren of a pore man haten hym; ferthermore and the freendis 3eden awei fer fro hym. He that sueth wordis
8 oonli, schal haue no thing; but he that holdith stabli the mynde, loueth his soule, and the kepere of prudence schal
9 fynde goodis. A fals witnesse schal not be vnpunyschid;
10 and he that spekith leesyngis, schal perische. Delices bicomen not a fool; nether *it bicometh* a seruaunt to be lord
11 of princes. The teching of a man is knowun bi pacience;
12 and his glorie is to passe ouere wickid thingis. As the gnasting of a lioun, so and the ire of the king; and as
13 deewe on eerbe, so and the gladnesse of the kyng. The sorewe of the fadir *is* a fonned sone; and roofes droppynge
14 contynueli *is* a womman ful of chiding. Housis and richessis ben 3ouun of fadir and modir; but a prudent wijf *is*
15 3*ouun* propirli of the Lord. Slouth bringith in sleep; and
16 a negligent soule schal haue hungur. He that kepith the comaundement *of God*, kepith his soule; but he that chargith
17 not his weie, schal be slayn. He that hath mercy on a pore man, leeneth to the Lord; and he schal 3elde his while to

18 hym. Teche thi sone, and dispeire thou not; but sette thou
19 not thi soule to the sleyng of hym. Forsothe he that is
vnpacient, schal suffre harm; and whanne he hath rauyschid,
20 he schal leie to anothir thing. Here thou counsel, and take
21 thou doctryn; that thou be wijs in thi laste thingis. Many
thouȝtis *ben* in the herte of a man; but the wille of the
22 Lord schal dwelle. A nedi man is merciful; and betere
23 *is* a pore iust man, than a man liere. The drede of the
Lord *ledith* to lijf of blis; and he *that dredith God* schal
24 dwelle in plentee, with-outen visityng of the worste. A slow
man hidith his hond vndur the armpit; and putteth it not
25 to his mouth. Whanne a man ful of pestilence is betun,
a fool schal be wisere. If thou blamist a wijs man, he schal
26 vndurstonde techyng. He that turmentith the fadir, and
fleeth fro the modir, schal be ful of yuel fame, and *schal*
27 *be* cursid. Sone, ceesse thou not to here techyng; and
28 knowe thou the wordis of kunnyng. A wickid witnesse
scorneth doom; and the mouth of vnpitouse men deuourith
29 wickidnesse. Domes ben maad redi to scorneris; and
hameris smytynge *ben maad redi* to the bodies of foolis.

Cap. XX.

1 Wiyn *is* a letcherouse thing, and drunkenesse *is* ful of
2 noise; who euere delitith in these, schal not be wijs. As
the roryng of a lioun, so and the drede of the kyng; he that
3 territh hym to ire, synneth aȝens his owne lijf. It is onour
to a man that departith hym silf fro stryuyngis; but fonned
4 men ben medlid with dispisyngis. A slow man nolde ere for
coold; therfor he schal begge in somer, and me schal not
5 ȝyue to hym. As deep watir, so counsel *is* in the herte of
6 a man; but a wijs man schal drawe it out. Many men ben
7 clepid merciful; but who schal fynde a feithful man? For-

sothe a iust man that goith in his simplenesse, schal leeue
8 blessid sones aftir hym. A king that sittith in the seete of
9 doom, distrieth al yuel bi his lokyng. Who may seie, Myn
10 herte is clene; Y am clene of synne? A wei3te and a
wei3te, a mesure and a mesure, euer eithir is abhomynable at
11 God. A child is vndurstondun bi hise studies, yf his werkis
12 ben ri3tful and cleene. An eere heringe, and an i3e seynge,
13 God made cuere eithir. Nyle thou loue sleep, lest nedynesse
oppresse thee; opene thin i3en, and be thou fillid with
14 looues. Ech biere seith, It is yuel, it is yuel; and whanne
15 he hath go awey, thanne he schal haue glorie. Gold, and
the multitude of iemmes, and a preciouse vessel, *ben* the
16 lippis of kunnyng. Take thou awei the cloth of hym, that
was borewe of an othere man; and for straungeris take
17 thou awei a wed fro hym. The breed of a leesing is sweet
to a man; and aftirward his mouth schal be fillid with
18 rikenyng. Thou3tis ben maad strong bi counselis; and
19 bateils schulen be tretid bi gouernals. Be thou not medlid
with him that schewith pryuetees, and goith gylefulli, and
20 alargith hise lippis. The li3t of hym that cursith his fadir
and modir, schal be quenchid in the myddis of derknessis.
21 Eritage to which me haastith in the bigynnyng, schal wante
22 blessing in the laste *tyme.* Seie thou not, I schal 3elde yuel
for yuel; abide thou the Lord, and he schal delyuere thee.
23 Abhomynacioun at God is wei3te and wei3te; a gileful
24 balaunce is not good. The steppis of man ben dressid of
the Lord; who forsothe of men mai vndurstonde his weie?
25 Falling of man is to make auow to seyntis, and aftirward to
26 withdrawe the vowis. A wijs kyng scaterith wickid men;
27 and bowith a bouwe of victorie ouer hem. The lanterne
of the Lord *is* the spirit of man, that sekith out alle the
28 priuetees of the wombe. Merci and treuthe kepen a kyng;
29 and his trone is maad strong bi mekenesse. The ful out

ioiyng of ȝonge men *is* the strengthe of hem; and the
30 dignyte of elde men *is* hoornesse. The wannesse of wounde
schal wipe aweie yuels, and woundis in the priuyere thingis
of the wombe.

Cap. XXI.

1 As departyngis of watris, so the herte of the kyng *is* in the
power of the Lord; whidur euer he wole, he schal bowe it.
2 Ech weye of a man semeth riȝtful to hym silf; but the Lord
3 peisith the hertis. To do merci and doom, plesith more the
4 Lord, than sacrifices *doen*. Enhaunsyng of iȝen is alargyng
5 of the herte; the lanterne of wickid men *is* synne. The
thouȝtis of a stronge man *ben* euere in abundaunce; but ech
6 slow man is euere in nedynesse. He that gaderith tresours
bi the tunge of a leesing, is veyne, and with-outen herte;
7 and he schal be hurtlid to the snaris of deth. The raueyns
of vnpitouse men schulen drawe hem doun; for thei nolden
8 do doom. The weiward weie of a man is alien fro God;
9 but the werk of hym that is cleene, is riȝtful. It is betere to
sitte in the corner of an hous with-oute roof, than with a
10 womman ful of chydyng, and in a comyn hous. The soule
of an vnpitouse man desirith yuel; he schal not haue merci
11 on his neiȝbore. Whanne a man ful of pestilence is
punyschid, a litil man *of wit* schal be the wisere; and if he
12 sueth a wijs man, he schal take kunnyng. A iust man of
the hous of a wickid man thenkith, to withdrawe wickid men
13 fro yuel. He that stoppith his eere at the cry of a pore
14 man, schal crye also, and schal not be herd. A ȝift hid
quenchith chidyngis; and a ȝift in bosum *quenchith* the
15 moost indignacioun. It is ioye to a iust man to make
doom; and *it is* drede to hem that worchen wickidnesse.
16 A man that errith fro the weie of doctryn, schal dwelle in the
17 cumpany of giauntis. He that loueth metis, schal be in

nedynesse; he that loueth wiyn and fatte thingis, schal not
18 be maad riche. An vnpitouse man schal be ȝouun for a iust
19 man; and a wickid man *schal be ȝouun* for a riȝtful man. It
is betere to dwelle in a desert lond, than with a womman ful
20 of chidyng, and wrathful. Desirable tresoure and oile *is* in
the dwelling places of a iust man; and an vnprudent man
21 schal distrie it. He that sueth riȝtfulnesse and mercy, schal
22 fynde lijf and glorie. A wijs man stiede in to the citee of
23 stronge men, and distriede the strengthe of trist therof. He
that kepith his mouth and his tunge, kepith his soule from
24 angwischis. A proude man and boosteere is clepid a fool,
25 that worchith pride in ire. Desiris sleen a slow man; for
26 hise hondis nolden worche ony thing. Al dai he coueitith
and desirith; but he that is a iust man, schal ȝyue, and schal
27 not ceesse. The offringis of wickid men, that ben offrid of
28 greet trespas, *ben* abhomynable. A fals witnesse schal
29 perische; a man obedient schal speke victorie. A wickid
man makith sad his cheer vnschamefastli; but he that is
30 riȝtful, amendith his weie. No wisdom is, no prudence is,
31 no counsel is aȝens the Lord. An hors is maad redi to the
dai of batel; but the Lord schal ȝyue helthe.

Cap. XXII.

1 BETERE is a good name, than many richessis; for good
2 grace *is* aboue siluer and gold. A riche man and a
pore man metten hem silf; the Lord is worchere of euer
3 eithir. A felle man seeth yuel, and hidith him silf; and an
4 innocent man passid, and he was turmentid bi harm. The
ende of temperaunce *is* the drede of the Lord; richessis, and
5 glorye, and lijf. Armuris and swerdis *ben* in the weie of
a weiward man; but the kepere of his soule goith awei fer
6 fro tho. It is a prouerbe, A ȝong wexynge man bisidis his

weie, and whanne he hath wexe elde, he schal not go awei
7 fro it. A riche man comaundith to pore men; and he that
8 takith borewyng, is the seruaunt of the leenere. He that
sowith wickidnes, schal repe yuels; and the ʒerde of his yre
9 schal be endid. He that is redi to merci, schal be blessid;
for of his looues he ʒaf to a pore man. He that ʒyueth
ʒiftis, schal gete victorie and onour; forsothe he takith awei
10 the soule of the takeris. Caste thou out a scornere, and
strijf schal go out with hym; and causis and dispisyngis
11 schulen ceesse. He that loueth the clennesse of herte, schal
12 haue the kyng a freend, for the grace of hise lippis. The
iʒen of the Lord kepen kunnyng; and the wordis of a
13 wickid man ben disseyued. A slow man schal seie, A lioun
is withoutforth; Y schal be slayn in the myddis of the
14 stretis. The mouth of an alien womman *is* a deep diche; he
15 to whom the Lord is wrooth, schal falle in to it. Foli is
boundun togidere in the herte of a child; and a ʒerde of
16 chastisyng schal dryue it awey. He that falsli chalengith
a pore man, to encreesse hise owne richessis, schal ʒyue to
17 a richere man, and schal be nedi. My sone, bowe doun thin
eere, and here thou the wordis of wise men; but sette thou
18 the herte to my techyng. That schal be fair to thee, whanne
thou hast kept it in thin herte, and it schal flowe aʒen in thi
19 lippis. That thi trist be in the Lord; wherfor and Y haue
20 schewid it to thee to-dai. Lo! Y haue discryued it in thre
21 maneres, in thouʒtis and kunnyng, that Y schulde schewe to
thee the sadnesse and spechis of trewthe; to answere of
22 these thingis to hem, that senten thee. Do thou not violence
to a pore man, for he is pore; nethir defoule thou a nedi
23 man in the ʒate. For the Lord schal deme his cause, and
24 he schal turmente hem, that turmentiden his soule. Nyle
thou be freend to a wrathful man, nether go thou with a
25 wood man; lest perauenture thou lerne hise weies, and take

26 sclaundir to thi soule. Nyle thou be with hem that oblischen
27 her hondis, and that proferen hem silf borewis for dettis; for
if he hath not wherof he schal restore, what of cause is, that
28 thou take awei hilyng fro thi bed? Go thou not ouer the
29 elde markis, whiche thi faders han set. Thou hast seyn a
man smert in his werk; he schal stonde bifore kyngis, and
he schal not be bifor vnnoble men.

Cap. XXIII.

1 Whanne thou sittist, to ete with the prince, perseyue thou
2 diligentli what thingis ben set bifore thi face, and sette thou
a withholding in thi throte. If netheles thou hast power on,
3 thi soule, desire thou not of his metis, in whom is the breed
4 of a leesing. Nyle thou trauele to be maad riche, but sette
5 thou mesure to thi prudence. Reise not thin iȝen to richessis,
whiche thou maist not haue; for tho schulen make to hem
silf pennes, as of an egle, and tho schulen flee in to heuene.
6 Ete thou not with an enuyouse man, and desire thou not hise
7 metis; for at the licnesse of a fals dyuynour and of a
coniectere, he gessith that, that he knowith not. He schal
seie to thee, Ete thou and drinke; and his soule is not with
8 thee. Thou schalt brake out the metis, whiche thou hast
9 ete; and thou schalt leese thi faire wordis. Speke thou not
in the eeris of vnwise men; for thei schulen dispise the
10 teching of thi speche. Touche thou not the termes of litle
children; and entre thou not in to the feeld of fadirles and
11 modirles children. For the neiȝbore of hem is strong, and
12 he schal deme her cause aȝens thee. Thin herte entre to
techyng, and thin eeris *be redi* to the wordis of kunnyng.
13 Nile thou withdrawe chastisyng fro a child; for thouȝ thou
14 smyte hym with a ȝerde, he schal not die. Thou schalt
smyte hym with a ȝerde, and thou schalt delyuere his soule

15 fro helle. Mi sone, if thi soule is wijs, myn herte schal haue
16 ioye with thee; and my reynes schulen make ful out ioye,
17 whanne thi lippis speken riȝtful thing. Thin herte sue not
18 synneris; but be thou in the drede of the Lord al dai. For
thou schalt haue hope at the laste, and thin abidyng schal
19 not be don awei. Mi sone, here thou, and be thou wijs, and
20 dresse thi soule in the weie. Nyle thou be in the feestis of
drinkeris, nether in the ofte etyngis of hem, that bryngen
21 togidere fleischis to ete. For men ȝyuynge tent to drinkis,
and ȝyuyng mussels togidere, schulen be waastid, and napp-
22 ing schal be clothid with clothis. Here thi fadir, that
gendride thee; and dispise not thi modir, whanne sche is
23 eld. Bie thou treuthe, and nyle thou sille wisdom, and
24 doctryn, and vndurstonding. The fadir of a iust man ioieth
ful out with ioie; he that gendride a wijs man, schal be glad
25 in hym. Thi fadir and thi modir haue ioye, and he that
26 gendride thee, make ful out ioye. My sone, ȝyue thin herte
27 to me, and thin iȝen kepe my weyes. For an hoore is a
28 deep diche, and an alien *womman* is a streit pit. Sche settith
aspie in the weie, as a theef; and sche schal sle hem, whiche
29 sche schal se vnwar. To whom *is* wo? to whos fadir *is*
wo? to whom *ben* chidingis? to whom *ben* dichis? to
whom *ben* woundis with-out cause? to whom *is* puttyng out
30 of iȝen? Whether not to hem, that dwellen in wyn, and
31 studien to drynke al of cuppis? Biholde thou not wyn,
whanne it sparclith, whanne the colour therof schyneth in
32 a ver. It entrith swetli, but at the laste it schal bite as an
eddre *doith*, and as a cocatrice it schal schede abrood venyms.
33 Thin iȝen schulen se straunge wymmen, and thi herte schal
34 speke weiwerd thingis. And thou schalt be as a man
slepinge in the myddis of the see, and as a gouernour aslepid,
35 whanne the steere is lost. And thou schalt seie, Thei beeten
me, but Y hadde not sorewe; thei drowen me, and Y feelide

not; whanne schal Y wake out, and Y schal fynde wynes eft?

Cap. XXIV.

1 Sue thou not yuele men, desire thou not to be with hem.
2 For the soule of hem bithenkith raueyns, and her lippis speken
3 fraudis. An hous schal be bildid bi wisdom, and schal be
4 maad strong bi prudence. Celeris schulen be fillid in teching,
5 al riches preciouse and ful fair. A wijs man is strong, and a
6 lerned man is stalworth and miȝti. For-whi batel is bigunnun with ordenaunce, and helthe schal be, where many counsels
7 ben. Wisdom *is* hiȝ to a fool; in the ȝate he schal not opene
8 his mouth. He that thenkith to do yuels, schal be clepid a
9 fool. The thouȝte of a fool is synne; and a bacbitere *is*
10 abhomynacioun of men. If thou that hast slide, dispeirist in
11 the dai of angwisch, thi strengthe schal be maad lesse. Delyuere thou hem, that ben led to deth; and ceesse thou not
12 to delyuere hem, that ben drawun to deth. If thou seist, Strengthis suffisen not; he that is biholdere of the herte, vndirstondith, and no thing disseyueth the kepere of thi soule,
13 and he schal ȝelde to a man bi hise werkis. Mi sone, ete thou hony, for *it is* good; and an honycomb ful swete to thi throte.
14 So and the techyng of wisdom *is good* to thi soule; and whanne thou hast founde it, thou schalt haue hope in the
15 laste thingis, and thin hope schal not perische. Aspie thou not, and seke not wickidnesse in the hous of a iust man,
16 nether waste thou his reste. For a iust man schal falle seuene sithis *in the dai*, and schal rise aȝen; but wickid men schulen
17 falle in to yuele. Whanne thin enemye fallith, haue thou not
18 ioye; and thin herte haue not ful out ioiyng in his fal; lest perauenture the Lord se, and it displese hym, and he take
19 awei his ire fro hym. Stryue thou not with the worste men,
20 nether sue thou wickid men. For whi yuele men han not

hope of thingis to comynge, and the lanterne of wickid men
²¹ schal be quenchid. My sone, drede thou God, and the kyng;
²² and be thou not medlid with bacbiteris. For her perdicioun
schal rise togidere sudenli, and who knowith the fal of euer
²³ either? Also these thingis *that suen* ben to wise men. It is
²⁴ not good to knowe a persoone in doom. Puplis schulen curse
hem, that seien to a wickid man, Thou art iust; and lynagis
²⁵ schulen holde hem abhomynable. Thei that repreuen *iustli*
synners, schulen be preisid; and blessing schal come on hem.
²⁶,²⁷ He that answerith riȝtful wordis, schal kisse lippis. Make
redi thi werk with-outforth, and worche thi feelde dilygentli,
²⁸ that thou bilde thin hous aftirward. Be thou not a witnesse
with-out resonable cause aȝens thi neiȝbore; nether flatere
²⁹ thou ony man with thi lippis. Seie thou not, As he dide to
me, so Y schal do to him, and Y schal ȝelde to ech man aftir
³⁰ his werk. I passide bi the feeld of a slow man, and bi the
³¹ vyner of a fonned man; and, lo! nettlis hadden fillid al,
thornes hadden hilid the hiȝere part therof, and the wal of
³² stoonys with-out morter was distried. And whanne Y hadde
seyn this thing, Y settide in myn herte, and bi ensaumple Y
³³ lernyde techyng. Hou longe slepist thou, slow man? whanne
schalt thou ryse fro sleep? Sotheli thou schalt slepe a litil,
thou schalt nappe a litil, thou schalt ioyne togidere the hondis
³⁴ a litil, to take reste; and thi nedynesse as a currour schal come
to thee, and thi beggerie as an armed man.

CAP. XXV.

¹ ALSO these *ben* the Parablis of Salomon, whiche the men of
² Ezechie, kyng of Juda, translatiden. The glorie of God is to
hele a word; and the glorie of kyngis *is* to seke out a word.
³ Heuene aboue, and the erthe bynethe, and the herte of kyngis
⁴ *is* vnserchable. Do thou a-wei rust fro siluer, and a ful cleene

5 vessel schal go out. Do thou awei vnpite fro the cheer of the kyng, and his trone schal be maad stidfast bi riȝtfulnesse. 6 Appere thou not gloriouse bifore the kyng, and stonde thou 7 not in the place of grete men. For it is betere, that it be seid to thee, Stie thou hidur, than that thou be maad low bifore 8 the prince. Brynge thou not forth soone tho thingis in strijf, whiche thin iȝen sien; lest aftirward thou maist not amende, 9 whanne thou hast maad thi frend vnhonest. Trete thi cause with thi frend, and schewe thou not priuyte to a straunge 10 man; lest perauenture he haue ioye of thi fal, whanne he hath herde, and ceesse not to do schenschipe to thee. Grace and frenschip delyueren, whiche kepe thou to thee, that thou be 11 not maad repreuable. A goldun pomel in beddis of siluer *is* 12 *he*, that spekith a word in his time. A goldun cere-ryng, and a schinynge peerle *is he*, that repreueth a wijs man, and an 13 eere obeiynge. As the coold of snow in the dai of heruest, so a feithful messanger to hym that sente thilke *messanger*, makith 14 his soule to haue reste. A cloude and wind, and reyn not· 15 suynge, *is* a gloriouse man, and not fillynge biheestis. A prince schal be maad soft bi pacience; and a soft tunge schal 16 breke hardnesse. Thou hast founde hony, ete thou that that suffisith to thee; lest perauenture thou be fillid, and brake it 17 out. Withdrawe thi foot fro the hous of thi neiȝbore; lest 18 sum tyme he be fillid, and hate thee. A dart, and a swerd, and a scharp arowe, a man that spekith fals witnessing aȝens 19 his neiȝbore. A rotun tooth, and a feynt foot *is* he, that hopith 20 on an vnfeithful man in the dai of angwisch, and leesith his mentil in the dai of coold. Vynegre in a vessel of salt *is* he, that singith songis to the worste herte. As a mouȝte *noieth* a cloth, and a worm *noieth* a tree, so the sorewe of a man noieth 21 the herte. If thin enemy hungrith, feede thou him; if he 22 thirstith, ȝyue thou watir to hym to drinke; for thou schalt gadere togidere coolis on his heed; and the Lord schal ȝelde

23 to thee. The north wind scatereth reynes; and a sorewful
24 face distrieth a tunge bacbitinge. It is betere to sitte in the
corner of an hous without roof, than with a womman ful of
25 chidyng, and in a comyn hous. Coold watir to a thirsti man;
26 and a good messanger fro a fer lond. A welle disturblid with
foot, and a veyne brokun, a iust man fallinge bifore a wickid
27 man. As it is not good to hym that etith myche hony; so
he that is a serchere of maieste, schal be put doun fro glorie.
28 As a citee opyn, and with-out cumpas of wallis; so *is* a man
that mai not refreyne his spirit in speking.

Cap. XXVI.

1 As snow in somer, and reyn in heruest; so glorie is vn-
2 semeli to a fool. For-whi as a brid fliynge ouer to hiȝ thingis,
and a sparowe goynge in to vncerteyn; so cursing brouȝt
forth with-out resonable cause schal come aboue in to sum
3 man. Beting to an hors, and a bernacle to an asse; and a
4 ȝerde in the bak of vnprudent men. Answere thou not to a
5 fool bi his foli, lest thou be maad lijk hym. Answere thou
6 a fool bi his fooli, lest he seme to him silf to be wijs. An
haltinge man in feet, and drinkinge wickidnesse, he that sendith
7 wordis by a fonned messanger. As an haltinge man hath faire
leggis in veyn; so a parable is vnsemeli in the mouth of foolis.
8 As he that casteth a stoon in to an heep of mercurie; so he
9 that ȝyueth onour to an vnwijs man. As if a thorn growith in
the hond of a drunkun man; so a parable in the mouth of
10 foolis. Doom determyneth causis; and he that settith silence
11 to a fool, swagith iris. As a dogge that turneth aȝen to his
spuyng; so *is* an vnprudent man, that rehersith his fooli.
12 Thou hast seyn a man seme wijs to hym silf; an vnkunnyng
13 man schal haue hope more than he. A slow man seith, A
14 lioun is in the weie, a liounnesse is in the foot-pathis. As a

15 dore is turned in his hengis; so a slow man in his bed. A
slow man hidith hise hondis vndur his armpit; and he trauel-
16 ith, if he turneth tho to his mouth. A slow man semeth wysere
17 to hym silf, than seuene men spekynge sentensis. As he that
takith a dogge bi the eeris; so he that passith, and *is* vn-
18 pacient, and is meddlid with the chiding of anothir man.
19 As he is gilti, that sendith speris and arowis in to deth; so a
man that anoieth gilefuli his frend, and whanne he is takun,
20 he schal seie, Y dide pleiynge. Whanne trees failen, the fier
schal be quenchid; and whanne a priuy bacbitere is with-
21 drawun, stryues resten. As deed coolis at quic coolis, and
22 trees at the fier; so a wrathful man reisith chidyngis. The
wordis of a pryuei bacbitere *ben* as symple; and tho comen
23 til to the ynneste thingis of the herte. As if thou wolt ourne
a vessel of erthe with foul siluer; so *ben* bolnynge lippis felous-
24 chipid with the werste herte. An enemy is vndirstondun bi
25 hise lippis, whanne he tretith giles in the herte. Whanne he
makith low his vois, bileue thou not to hym; for seuene
26 wickidnessis ben in his herte. The malice of hym that hilith
27 hatrede gilefuli, schal be schewid in a counsel. He that
delueth a diche, schal falle in to it; and if a man walewith a
28 stoon, it schal turne aȝen to hym. A fals tunge loueth not
treuth; and a slidir mouth worchith fallyngis.

Cap. XXVII.

1 Haue thou not glorie on the morewe, not knowynge what
2 thing the dai to comynge schal bringe forth. Another man,
and not thi mouth preise thee; a straunger, and not thi
3 lippis *preise thee*. A stoon is heuy, and grauel is chariouse;
4 but the ire of a fool is heuyere than euer eithir. Ire hath no
merci, and woodnesse brekynge out *hath no merci;* and who
5 mai suffre the fersnesse of a spirit stirid? Betere is opyn

6 repreuyng, than loue hid. Betere ben the woundis of hym
7 that loueth, than the gileful cossis of hym that hatith. A
man fillid schal dispise an hony-coomb; but an hungri man
8 schal take, ȝhe, bittir thing for swete. As a brid passinge
9 ouer fro his nest, so is a man that forsakith his place. The
herte delitith in oynement, and dyuerse odours; and a soule
10 is maad swete bi the good counsels of a frend. Forsake
thou not thi frend, and the frend of thi fadir; and entre thou
not in to the hous of thi brothir, in the dai of thi turment.
11 Betere is a neiȝbore nyȝ, than a brothir afer. Mi sone, studie
thou a-boute wisdom, and make thou glad myn herte; that
12 thou maist answere a word to a dispisere. A fel man seynge
yuel was hid; litle men of wit passinge forth suffriden
13 harmes. Take thou awei his clooth, that bihiȝte for a
straunger; and take thou awei a wed fro hym for an alien
14 man. He that blessith his neiȝbore with greet vois; and
15 risith bi niȝt, schal be lijk hym that cursith. Roouys droppynge in the dai of coold, and a womman ful of chidyng ben
16 comparisond. He that withholdith hir, as if he holdith
17 wynd; and auoidith the oile of his riȝt hond. Yrun is
whettid bi irun; and a man whettith the face of his frend.
18 He that kepith a fige-tre, schal ete the fruyts therof; and he
19 that is a kepere of his lord, schal be glorified. As the cheris
of men biholdinge schynen in watris; so the hertis of men
20 ben opyn to prudent men. Helle and perdicioun schulen
21 not be fillid; so and the iȝen of men moun not be fillid. As
siluer is preuyd in a wellyng place, and gold *is preued* in
a furneys; so a man is preued bi the mouth of preyseris.
The herte of a wickid man sekith out yuels; but a riȝtful
22 herte sekith out kunnyng. Thouȝ thou beetist a fool in a
morter, as with a pestel smytynge aboue dried barli; his foli
23 schal not be don awei fro him. Knowe thou diligentli the
24 cheere of thi beeste; and biholde thou thi flockis. For thou

schalt not haue power contynueli; but a coroun schal be
25 3ouun to thee in generacioun and in to generacioun. Medew-
is ben openyd, and greene eerbis apperiden; and hey is
26 gaderid fro hillis. Lambren be to thi clothing; and kidis *be*
27 to the prijs of feeld. The mylke of geete suffice to thee for
thi meetis; in to the necessarie thingis of thin hous, and to
lijflode to thin handmaidis.

Cap. XXVIII.

1 A WICKID man fleeth, whanne no man pursueth; but
a iust man as a lioun tristynge schal be with-out ferd-
2 fulnesse. For the synnes of the lond *ben* many princis
therof; and for the wisdom of a man, and for the kunnyng
of these thingis that ben seid, the lijf of the duyk schal
3 be lengere. A pore man falsli calengynge pore men,
4 is lijk a grete reyn, wherynne hungur is maad redi. Thei
that forsaken the lawe, preisen a wickid man; thei that kepen
5 *the lawe*, ben kyndlid a3ens hym. Wickid men thenken not
doom; but thei that seken the Lord, perseyuen alle thingis.
6 Betere is a pore man goynge in his sympilnesse, than a riche
7 man in schrewid weies. He that kepith the lawe, is a wijs
8 sone; but he that fedith glotouns, schendith his fadir. He
that gaderith togidere richessis bi vsuris, and fre encrees,
9 gaderith tho togidere a3ens pore men. His preyer schal be
maad cursid, that bowith awei his eere; that he here not
10 the lawe. He that disseyueth iust men in an yuel weye,
schal falle in his perisching; and iuste men schulen welde
11 hise goodis. A ryche man semeth wijs to him silf; but
12 a pore man prudent schal serche him. In enhaunsing of
iust men is miche glorie; whanne wickid men regnen, fall-
13 yngis of men ben. He that hidith hise grete trespassis,
schal not be maad ri3tful; but he that knoulechith and
14 forsakith tho, schal gete merci. Blessid *is* the man, which is

euere dredeful; but he that is harde of soule, schal falle in to
15 yuel. A rorynge lioun, and an hungry bere, *is* a wickid
16 prince on a pore puple. A duyk nedi of prudence schal
oppresse many men bi fals chalenge; but the daies of hym
17 that hatith aueryce, schulen be maad longe. No man susteyneth a man that falsly chalengith the blood of a man, if he
18 fleeth til to the lake. He that goith simpli, schal be saaf;
19 he that goith bi weiward weies, schal falle doun onys. He
that worchith his lond, schal be fillid with looues; he that
20 sueth ydelnesse, schal be fillid with nedynesse. A feithful
man schal be preisid myche; but he that hastith to be maad
21 riche, schal not be innocent. He that knowith a face in
doom, doith not wel; this man forsakith treuthe, 3he, for
22 a mussel of breed. A man that hastith to be maad riche,
and hath enuye to othere men; woot not that nedinesse
23 schal come on hym. He that repreueth a man, schal fynde
grace aftirward at hym; more than he that disseyueth bi
24 flateryngis of tunge. He that withdrawith ony thing fro his
fadir and fro his modir, and seith that this is no synne,
25 is parcener of a manquellere. He that auauntith hym silf,
and alargith, reisith stryues; but he that hopith in the Lord,
26 schal be sauyd. He that tristith in his herte, is a fool;
27 but he that goith wiseli, schal be preysid. He that 3yueth to
a pore man, schal not be nedi; he that dispisith *a pore man*
28 bisechynge, schal suffre nedynesse. Whanne vnpitouse men
risen, men schulen be hid; whanne tho *vnpitouse men* han
perischid, iust men schulen be multiplied.

Cap. XXIX.

1 Sodeyn perischyng schal come on that man, that with hard
2 nol dispisith a blamere; and helth schal not sue hym. The
comynalte schal be glad in the multipliyng of iust men;

whanne wickid men han take prinshod, the puple schal
3 weyle. A man that loueth wisdom, makith glad his fadir;
4 but he that nurschith an hoore, schal leese catel. A iust
king reisith the lond; an auerouse man schal destrie it.
5 A man that spekith bi flaterynge and feyned wordis to his
6 frend; spredith abroad a net to hise steppis. A snare schal
wlappe a wickid man doynge synne; and a iust man schal
7 preise, and schal make ioye. A iust man knowith the cause
8 of pore men; an vnpitouse man knowith not kunnyng. Men
ful of pestilence distryen a citee; but wise men turnen awei
9 woodnesse. If a wijs man stryueth with a fool; whether he
10 be wrooth, ether he leiȝith, he schal not fynde reste. Menquelleris haten a simple man; but iust men seken his soule.
11 A fool bringith forth al his spirit; a wise man dilaieth, and
12 rescrueth in to tyme comynge afterward. A prince that
herith wilfuli the wordis of a leesyng; schal haue alle
13 mynystris vnfeithful. A pore man and a leenere metten
14 hem silf; the Lord is liȝtnere of euer ethir. If a kyng
demeth pore men in treuthe; his trone schal be maad stid-
15 fast with-outen ende. A ȝerde and chastisyng schal ȝyue
wisdom; but a child, which is left to his wille, schendith his
16 modir. Grete trespassis schulen be multiplied in the multipliyng of wickid men; and iust men schulen se the fallyngis
17 of hem. Teche thi sone, and he schal coumforte thee; and
18 he schal ȝyue delicis to thi soule. Whanne prophesie faylith,
the puple schal be distried; but he that kepith the lawe, is
19 blessid. A seruaunt may not be tauȝt bi wordis; for he
vndirstondith that that thou seist, and dispisith for to an-
20 swere. Thou hast seyn a man swift to speke; foli schal be
21 hopid more than his amendyng. He that nurschith his seruaunt delicatli fro childhod; schal fynde hym rebel aftir-
22 ward. A wrathful man territh chidingis; and he that is liȝt
to haue indignacioun, schal be more enclynaunt to synnes.

23 Lownesse sueth a proude man; and glorie schal vp take
24 a meke man of spirit. He that takith part with a theef,
hatith his soule; he herith a man chargynge greetli, and
25 schewith not. He that dredith a man, schal falle soon; he
26 that hopith in the Lord, shal be reisid. Many men seken the
face of the prince; and the doom of alle men schal go forth
27 of the Lord. Iust men han abhomynacioun of a wickid man;
and wickid men han abhomynacioun of hem, that ben in a
riȝtful weye. A sone kepynge a word, schal be out of perdicioun.

Cap. XXX.

1 The wordis of hym that gaderith, of the sone spuynge.
The prophesie which a man spak, with whom God was, and
which *man* was coumfortid bi God dwellyng with hym, and
2 seide, Y am the moost fool of men; and the wisdom of men
3 is not with me. Y lernede not wisdom; and Y knew not
4 the kunnyng of hooli men. Who stiede in to heuene, and
cam doun? Who helde togidere the spirit in hise hondis?
who bonde togidere watris as in a cloth? Who reiside alle
the endis of erthe? What is name of hym? and what is the
5 name of his sone, if thou knowist? Ech word of God *is*
6 a scheld set afiere, to alle that hopen in hym. Adde thou
not ony thing to the wordis of hym, and thou be repreued,
7 and be foundun a liere. I preiede thee twei thingis; denye
8 not thou to me, bifor that Y die. Make thou fer fro me
vanyte and wordis of leesyng; ȝyue thou not to me beggery
and richessis; ȝyue thou oneli necessaries to my lijflode;
9 lest perauenture Y be fillid, and be drawun to denye, and
seie, Who is the Lord? and lest Y compellid bi nedynesse,
10 stele, and forswere the name of my God. Accuse thou not
a seruaunt to his lord, lest perauenture he curse thee, and
11 thou falle doun. A generacioun that cursith his fadir, and

12 that blessith not his modir. A generacioun that semeth cleene to it silf, and netheles is not waischun fro hise 13 filthis. A generacioun whose iȝen ben hiȝ, and the iȝe-14 liddis therof ben reisid in to hiȝ thingis. A generacioun that hath swerdis for teeth, and etith with hise wank-teeth; 15 that it ete nedi men of erthe, and the porails of men. The watir-leche hath twei douȝtris, seiynge, Brynge, bringe. Thre thingis ben vnable to be fillid, and the fourthe, that 16 seith neuere, It suffisith; helle, and the mouth of the wombe, and the erthe which is neuere fillid with watir; but 17 fier seith neuere, It suffisith. Crowis of the stronde picke out thilke iȝe, that scorneth the fadir, and that dispisith the child beryng of his modir; and the briddis of an egle ete 18 that iȝe. Thre thingis ben hard to me, and outirli Y knowe 19 not the fourthe thing; the weye of an egle in heuene, the weie of a serpent on a stoon, the weie of a schip in the myddil of the see, and the weie of a man in ȝong wexynge 20 age. Siche is the weie of a womman auowtresse, which etith, and wipith hir mouth, and seith, Y wrouȝte not yuel. 21 The erthe is moued bi thre thingis, and the fourthe thing, 22 which it may not susteyne; bi a seruaunt, whanne he regneth; 23 bi a fool, whanne he is fillid with mete; bi an hateful womman, whanne sche is takun in matrymonye; and by an 24 handmaide, whanne sche is eir of hir ladi. Foure ben the leeste thingis of erthe, and tho ben wisere than wise men; 25 amtis, a feble puple, that maken redi mete in heruest to hem 26 silf; a hare, a puple vnmyȝti, that settith his bed in a stoon; 27 a locust hath no kyng, and al goith out bi cumpanyes; 28 an euete enforsith with hondis, and dwellith in the housis 29 of kingis. Thre thingis ben, that goon wel, and the fourthe 30 thing, that goith richeli. A lioun, strongeste of beestis, schal 31 not drede at the meetyng of ony man; a cok gird the leendis, 32 and a ram, and noon is that schal aȝenstonde him. He that

apperith a fool, aftir that he is reisid an hiȝ; for if he hadde
33 vndurstonde, he hadde sett hond on his mouth. Forsothe
he that thristith strongli teetis, to drawe out mylk, thristith
out botere; and he that smytith greetli, drawith out blood;
and he that stirith iris, bringith forth discordis.

Cap. XXXI.

1 The wordis of Lamuel, the king; the visioun bi which
2 his modir tauȝte hym. What my derlyng? what the derl-
3 yng of my wombe? what the derlyng of my desiris? Ȝyue
thou not thi catel to wymmen, and thi richessis to do awei
4 kyngis. A! Lamuel, nyle thou ȝiue wyn to kingis; for no
5 pryuete is, where drunkenesse regneth. Lest perauenture
thei drynke, and forȝete domes, and chaunge the cause of
6 the sones of a pore man. Ȝyue ȝe sidur to hem that
7 morenen, and wyn to hem that ben of bitter soule. Drinke
thei, and forȝete thei her nedinesse; and thenke thei no
8 more on her sorewe. Opene thi mouth for a doumb man, and
9 opene thi mouth for the causes of alle sones that passen
forth. Deme thou that that is iust, and deme thou a nedi
10 man and a pore man. Who schal fynde a stronge wom-
11 man? the prijs of her *is* fer, and fro the laste endis. The
herte of hir hosebond tristith in hir; and sche schal not
12 haue nede to spuylis. Sche schal ȝelde to hym good, and
13 not yuel, in alle the daies of hir lijf. Sche souȝte wolle
14 and flex; and wrouȝte bi the counsel of hir hondis. Sche
is maad as the schip of a marchaunt, that berith his breed
15 fro fer. And sche roos bi nyȝt, and ȝaf prey to hir mey-
16 neals, and metis to hir handmaidis. Sche bihelde a feeld,
and bouȝte it; of the fruyt of hir hondis sche plauntide
17 a vyner. Sche girde hir leendis with strengthe, and made
18 strong hir arm. Sche taastide, and siȝ, that hir marchaundie

was good; hir lanterne schal not be quenchid in the nȝt.
19 Sche putte hir hondis to stronge thingis, and hir fyngris
20 token the spyndil. Sche openyde hir hond to a nedi man,
21 and stretchide forth hir hondis to a pore man. Sche schal
not drede for hir hous of the cooldis of snow; for alle hir
22 meyneals ben clothid with double *clothis*. Sche made to
23 hir a ray cloth; bijs and purpur *is* the cloth of hir. Hir
hosebonde *is* noble in the ȝatis, whanne he sittith with the
24 senatours of erthe. Sche made lynnun cloth, and selde;
25 and ȝaf a girdil to a Chananei. Strengthe and fairnesse
is the clothing of hir; and sche schal leiȝe in the laste dai.
26 Sche openyde hir mouth to wisdom; and the lawe of merci
27 *is* in hir tunge. Sche bihelde the pathis of hir hous; and
28 sche eet not breed idili. Hir sones risiden, and prechiden
29 hir moost blessid; hir hosebonde *roos*, and preiside hir. Many
30 douȝtris gaderiden richessis; thou passidist alle. Fairnesse is disseiuable grace, and veyn; thilke womman, that
31 dredith the Lord, schal be preisid. Ȝyue ȝe to hir of the
fruyt of hir hondis; and hir werkis preise hir in the ȝatis.

ECCLESIASTES.

Cap. I.

1 The wordis of Ecclesiastes, sone of Dauid, the kyng of
2 Jerusalem. The vanyte of vanytees, seide Ecclesiastes; the
3 vanyte of vanytees, and alle thingis *ben* vanite. What hath
a man more of alle his trauel, bi which he traueilith vndur
4 the sunne? Generacioun passith awei, and generacioun
5 cometh; but the erthe stondith with-outen ende. The

sunne risith, and goith doun, and turneth aȝen to his place;
6 and there it risith aȝen, and cumpassith bi the south, and
turneth aȝen to the north. The spirit cumpassynge alle
thingis goith in cumpas, and turneth aȝen in to hise cerclis.
7 Alle floodis entren in to the see, and the see fletith not
ouer *the markis set of God;* the floodis turnen aȝen to the
8 place fro whennus tho comen forth, that tho flowe eft. Alle
thingis *ben* hard; a man may not declare tho thingis bi
word; the iȝe is not fillid bi siȝt, nether the eere is fillid
9 bi hering. What is that thing that was, that that schal
come? What is that thing that is maad, that that schal
10 be maad? No thing vndir the sunne *is* newe, nether ony
man may seie, Lo! this thing is newe; for now it ȝede
11 bifore in worldis, that weren bifore vs. Mynde of the formere thingis is not, but sotheli nether thenkyng of tho
thingis, that schulen come afterward, schal be at hem that
12 schulen come in the last tyme. I Ecclesiastes was king
13 of Israel in Jerusalem; and Y purposide in my soule to
seke and ensserche wiseli of alle thingis, that ben maad
vndur the sunne. God ȝaf this werste ocupacioun to the
sones of men, that thei schulden be ocupied therynne.
14 I siȝ alle thingis that ben maad vndur the sunne, and lo!
15 alle thingis *ben* vanyte and turment of spirit. Weiward
men ben amendid of hard; and the noumbre of foolis is
16 greet with-outen ende. I spak in myn herte, and Y seide,
Lo! Y am made greet, and Y passide in wisdom alle men,
that weren bifore me in Jerusalem; and my soule siȝ many
17 thingis wiseli, and Y lernede. And Y ȝaf myn herte, that
Y schulde knowe prudence and doctryn, and errours and
foli. And Y knew that in these thingis also was trauel and
18 turment of spirit; for in myche wisdom is myche indignacioun, and he that encressith kunnyng, encreessith also
trauel.

Cap. II.

1 Therfor Y seide in myn herte, Y schal go, and Y schal flowe in delicis, and Y schal vse goodis; and Y siȝ also 2 that this was vanyte. And leiȝyng Y arrettide errour, and 3 Y seide to ioye, What art thou disseyued in veyn? I thouȝte in myn herte to withdrawe my fleisch fro wyn, that Y schulde lede ouer my soule to wisdom, and that Y schulde eschewe foli, til Y schulde se, what were profitable to the sones of men; in which dede the noumbre of daies of her lijf vndur 4 the sunne is nedeful. Y magnefiede my werkis, Y bildide 5 housis to me, and Y plauntide vynes; Y made ȝerdis and orcherdis, and Y settide tho with the trees of al kynde; 6 and Y made cisternes of watris, for to watre the wode of 7 trees growynge. I hadde in possessioun seruauntis and handmaidis; and Y hadde myche meynee, and droues of grete beestis, and grete flockis of scheep, ouer alle men 8 that weren bifore me in Jerusalem. Y gaderide togidere to me siluer and gold, and the castels of kingis and of prouyncis; Y made to me syngeris and syngeressis, and delicis of the sones of men, and cuppis and vessels in 9 seruyce, to helde out wynes; and Y passide in richessis alle men, that weren bifor me in Jerusalem. Also wisdom 10 dwellide stabli with me, and alle thingis whiche myn iȝen desiriden, Y denyede not to hem; nether Y refreynede myn herte, that ne it vside al lust, and delitide it silf in these thingis whiche I hadde maad redi; and Y demyde 11 this my part, if Y vside my trauel. And whanne Y hadde turned me to alle werkis whiche myn hondys hadden maad, and to the trauels in whiche Y hadde swet in veyn, Y siȝ in alle thingis vanyte and turment of the soule, and that 12 no thing vndir sunne dwellith stabli. I passide to biholde wisdom, errours, and foli; *Y seide*, What is a man, that he

13 may sue the king, his maker? And Y si3, that wisdom
3ede so mych bifor foli, as miche as li3t is dyuerse fro
14 derknessis. The i3en of a wijs man *ben* in his heed, a fool
goith in derknessis; and Y lernede, that o perisching was
15 of euer either. And Y seide in myn herte, If o deth schal
be bothe of the fool and of me, what profitith it to me,
that Y 3af more bisynesse to wisdom? And Y spak with
16 my soule, and perseyuede, that this also was vanyte. For
mynde of a wijs man schal not be, in lijk maner as nether
of a fool with-outen ende, and tymes to comynge schulen
hile alle thingis togidere with for3etyng; a lerned man dieth
17 in lijk maner and an vnlerned man. And therfor it anoiede
me of my lijf, seynge that alle thingis vndur sunne ben
yuele, and that alle thingis *ben* vanyte and turment of
18 the spirit. Eft Y curside al my bisynesse, bi which Y
19 trauelide moost studiousli vndur sunne, and Y schal haue
an eir after me, whom Y knowe not, whether he schal be
wijs ether a fool; and he schal be lord in my trauels, for
whiche Y swatte greetli, and was bisi; and is ony thing
20 so veyn? Wherfor Y ceesside, and myn herte forsook for
21 to trauele ferthere vnder sunne. For-whi whanne another
man trauelith in wisdom, and techyng, and bisynesse, he
leeueth thingis getun to an idel man; and therfor this *is*
22 vanyte, and greet yuel. For-whi what schal it profite to
a man of al his trauel, and turment of spirit, bi which he
23 was turmentid vndur sunne? Alle hise daies ben ful of
sorewis and meschefs, and bi ny3t he restith not in soule;
24 and whether this is not vanyte. Whether it is not betere
to ete and drynke, and to schewe to hise soule goodis of
25 hise trauels? and this *thing is* of the hond of God. Who
schal deuoure so, and schal flowe in delicis, as Y *dide*?
26 God 3af wisdom, and kunnyng, and gladnesse to a good
man in his si3t; but he 3af turment, and superflu bisynesse

to a synnere, that he encreesse, and gadere togidere, and ȝyue to hym that plesith God; but also this *is* vanyte, and veyn bisynesse of soule.

Cap. III.

1 Alle thingis han tyme, and alle thingis vndur sunne
2 passen bi her spaces. Tyme of birthe, and time of diyng; tyme to plaunte, and tyme to drawe vp that that is plauntid.
3 Tyme to sle, and tyme to make hool; tyme to distrie, and
4 tyme to bilde. Tyme to wepe, and tyme to leiȝe; tyme to
5 biweile, and tyme to daunse. Tyme to scatere stoonys, and tyme to gadere togidere; tyme to colle, and tyme to be fer
6 fro collyngis. Tyme to wynne, and tyme to leese; tyme to
7 kepe, and tyme to caste awei. Tyme to kitte, and tyme to
8 sewe togidere; tyme to be stille, and tyme to speke. Tyme of loue, and tyme of hatrede; tyme of batel, and tyme of
9, 10 pees. What hath a man more of his trauel? I siȝ the turment, which God ȝaf to the sones of men, that thei be
11 occupied therynne. God made alle thingis good in her tyme, and ȝaf the world to disputyng of hem, that a man fynde not the werk which God hath wrouȝt fro the bigynnyng
12 til in to the ende. And Y knew that no thing was betere *to a man*, no-but to be glad, and to do good *werkis* in his lijf.
13 For-whi ech man that etith and drinkith, and seeth good of
14 his trauel; this is the ȝifte of God. I haue lerned that alle werkis, whiche God maad, lasten stidfastli til in to with-outen ende; we moun not adde ony thing to tho, nether take awei
15 fro tho *thingis*, whiche God made, that he be dred. That thing that is maad, dwellith perfitli; tho thingis that schulen come, weren bifore; and God restorith that, that is goon.
16 I siȝ vndur sunne vnfeithfulnesse in the place of doom; and
17 wickidnesse in the place of riȝtfulnesse. And Y seide in myn herte, The Lord schal deme a iust man, and an vnfeithful

18 man ; and the tyme of ech thing schal be thanne. I seide in myn herte of the sones of men, that God schulde preue hem, 19 and schewe that thei ben lijk *vnresonable* beestis. Therfor oon is the perisching of man and of beestis, and euene condicioun *is* of euer eithir; as a man dieth, so and tho *beestis* dien; alle *beestis* brethen in lijk maner, and a man hath no 20 thing more than a beeste. Alle thingis ben suget to vanyte, and alle thingis goen to o place ; tho ben maad of erthe, and 21 tho turnen aȝen togidere in to erthe. Who knowith, if the spirit of the sones of Adam stieth vpward, and if the spirit of 22 beestis goith dounward? And Y perseyuede that no thing is betere, than that a man be glad in his werk, and that this be his part; for who schal brynge hym, that he knowe thingis that schulen come after hym?

Cap. IV.

1 I turnede me to othere thingis, and Y siȝ fals chalengis, that ben don vndur the sunne, and the teeris of innocentis, and no man coumfortour; and that thei forsakun of the help 2 of alle men, moun not aȝenstonde the violence of hem. And 3 Y preiside more deed men than lyuynge men; and Y demyde hym, that was not borun ȝit, and siȝ not the yuels that ben 4 don vndur the sunne, *to be* blisfulere than euer eithir. Eft Y bihelde alle the trauelis of men, and bisynesses ; and Y perseyuede that tho ben opyn to the enuye of neiȝbore ; and 5 therfor in this is vanyte, and superflu bisynesse. A fool foldith togidere hise hondis, and etith hise fleischis, and seith, 6 Betere is an handful with reste, than euer either hondful with 7 trauel and turment of soule. I bihelde and foond also 8 another vanytee vndir the sunne ; oon is, and he hath not a secounde ; not a sone, not a brother ; and netheles he cecsith not for to trauele, nether hise iȝen ben fillid with

S

richessis; nether he bithenkith, and seith, To whom trauele Y, and disseyue my soule in goodis? In this also is vanyte, 9 and the worste turment. Therfor it is betere, that tweyne be togidere than oon; for thei han profite of her felouschipe. 10 If oon fallith doun, he schal be vndurset of the tothere; wo to hym that is aloone, for whanne he fallith, he hath noon 11 reisynge him. And if tweyne slepen, thei schulen be nurschid 12 togidere; hou schal oon be maad hoot? And if ony man hath maistri aȝens oon, tweyne aȝen-stonden hym; a thre- 13 folde corde is brokun of hard. A pore man and wijs is betere than an eld kyng and fool, that kan not bifore-se in to 14 tyme to comynge. For sum tyme a man goith out bothe fro prysoun and chaynes to a rewme; and anothir borun in to a 15 rewme is wastid bi nedynesse. I siȝ alle men lyuynge that goen vndur the sunne, with the secounde ȝong wexynge man, 16 that schal rise for hym. The noumbre of puple, of alle that weren bifore hym, is greet with-outen mesure, and thei that schulen come aftirward, schulen not be glad in hym; but 17 also this *is* vanyte and turment of the spirit. (V). Thou that entrist in to the hous of God, kepe thi foot, and neiȝe thou for to here; for-whi myche betere is obedience than the 1 sacrifices of foolis, that witen not what yuel thei don. Speke thou not ony thing folily, nether thin herte be swift to brynge forth a word bifore God; for God *is* in heuene, and thou art 2 on erthe, therfor thi wordis be fewe. Dremes suen many 3 bisynessis, and foli schal be foundun in many wordis. If thou hast avowid ony thing to God, tarie thou not to ȝelde; for an vnfeithful and fonned biheest displesith hym; but 4 ȝelde thou what euer thing thou hast avowid; and it is myche betere to make not a vowe, than aftir a vowe to ȝelde not 5 biheestis. Ȝyue thou not thi mouth, that thou make thi fleisch to do synne; nether seie thou bifor an aungel, No puruyaunce is; lest perauenture the Lord be wrooth on thi

6 wordis, and distruye alle the werkis of thin hondis. Where ben many dremes, *ben* ful many vanytees, and wordis with-
7 out noumbre; but drede thou God. If thou seest false chalengis of nedi men, and violent domes, and that riȝtfulnesse is distried in the prouynce, wondre thou not on this doyng; for another is hiȝere than an hiȝ man, and also
8 othere men ben more hiȝe aboue these men; and ferthermore the kyng of al erthe comaundith to the seruaunt.

Cap. V (V, *continued*).

9 An auerouse man schal not be fillid of monei; and he that loueth richessis schal not take fruytis of tho; and ther-
10 for this *is* vanyte. Where ben many richessis, also many men *ben*, that eten tho; and what profitith it to the haldere,
11 no-but that he seeth richessis with hise iȝen? Slepe is swete to hym that worchith, whether he etith litil ether myche; but the fulnesse of a ryche man suffrith not hym
12 to slepe. Also anothir sijknesse is ful yuel, which Y siȝ vndur the sunne; richessis *ben* kept in to the yuel of her
13 lord. For thei perischen in the worste turment; he gen-
14 dride a sone, that schal be in souereyn nedynesse. As he ȝede nakid out of his modris wombe, so he schal turne aȝen; and he schal take awei with hym no thing of his trauel.
15 Outirli *it is* a wretchid sijknesse; as he cam, so he schal turne aȝen. What therfor profitith it to hym, that he tra-
16 uelide in to the wynde? In alle the daies of his lijf he eet in derknessis, and in many bisinessis, and in nedynesse, and
17 sorewe. Therfor this semyde good to me, that a man ete, and drynke, and vse gladnesse of his trauel, in which he trauelide vndir the sunne, in the noumbre of daies of his
18 lijf, which God ȝaf to hym; and this is his part. And to ech man, to whom God ȝaf richessis, and catel, and ȝif power to

hym to ete of tho, and to vse his part, and to be glad of his
19 trauel; this is the ʒifte of God. For he schal not bithenke
miche on the daies of his lijf, for God ocupieth his herte with
delicis.

Cap. VI.

1 Also another yuel is, which Y siʒ vndur the sunne; and
2 certis *it is* oft vsid anentis men. A man *is*, to whom God
ʒaf richessis, and catel, and onour; and no thing failith to his
soule of alle thingis which he desirith; and God ʒyueth not
power to hym, that he ete therof, but a straunge man shal
3 deuoure it. This is vanyte, and a greet wretchidnesse. If
a man gendrith an hundrid fre sones, and lyueth many ʒeris,
and hath many daies of age, and his soule vsith not the
goodis of his catel, and wantith biriyng; Y pronounce of
4 this man, that a deed borun child is betere than he. For he
cometh in veyn, and goith to derknessis; and his name schal
5 be don awei bi forʒetyng. He siʒ not the sunne, nether
6 knew dyuersyte of good and of yuel; also thouʒ he lyueth
twei thousynde ʒeeris, and vsith not goodis; whether alle
7 thingis hasten not to o place? Al the trauel of a man *is*
in his mouth, but the soule of hym schal not be fillid with
8 goodis. What hath a wijs man more than a fool? and what
9 hath a pore *man*, no but that he go thidur, where is lijf? It
is betere to se that, that thou coueitist, than to desire that,
that thou knowist not; but also this is vanyte, and presump-
10 cioun of spirit. The name of hym that schal come, is clepid
now, and it is knowun, that he is a man, and he mai not
11 stryue in doom aʒens a strongere than hym silf. Wordis
1 ben ful manye, and han myche vanyte in dispuytinge. What
nede is it to a man to seke grettere thingis than hym silf;
sithen he knowith not, what schal bifalle to hym in his lijf, in
the noumbre of daies of his pilgrimage, and in the tyme that

passith as schadowe? ether who may schewe to hym, what thing vndur sunne schal come aftir hym?

Cap. VII.

2 A GOOD name is betere than preciouse oynementis; and
3 the dai of deth *is betere* than the dai of birthe. It is betere to go to the hous of morenyng, than to the hous of a feeste; for in that *hous of morenyng* the ende of alle men is monestid,
4 and a man lyuynge thenkith, what is to comynge. Yre is betere than leiȝyng; for the soule of a trespassour is amendid
5 bi the heuynesse of cheer. The herte of wise men *is* where
6 sorewe is; and the herte of foolis *is* where gladnesse is. It is betere to be repreued of a wijs man, than to be disseyued
7 bi the flateryng of foolis; for as the sown of thornes
8 brennynge vndur a pot, so *is* the leiȝyng of a fool. But also this *is* vanyte. Fals chalenge disturblith a wijs man, and it
9 schal leese the strengthe of his herte. Forsothe the ende of preyer is betere than the bigynnyng. A pacient man is
10 betere than a proud man. Be thou not swift to be wrooth;
11 for ire restith in the bosum of a fool. Seie thou not, What gessist thou is of cause, that the formere tymes weren betere
12 than ben now? for-whi siche axyng is fonned. Forsothe wisdom with richessis is more profitable, and profitith more
13 to men seynge the sunne. For as wisdom defendith, so money *defendith?* but lernyng and wisdom hath this more,
14 that tho ȝyuen lijf to her weldere. Biholde thou the werkis of God, that no man may amende hym, whom *God* hath
15 dispisid. In a good day vse thou goodis, and bifore eschewe thou an yuel day; for God made so this dai as that dai, that
16 a man fynde not iust playnyngis aȝens hym. Also Y siȝ these thingis in the daies of my natyuyte; a iust man perischith in his riȝtfulnesse, and a wickid man lyueth myche

17 tyme in his malice. Nyle thou be iust myche, nether vndurstonde thou more than is nedeful; lest thou be astonyed.
18 Do thou not wickidli myche, and nyle thou be a fool; lest
19 thou die in a tyme not thin. It is good, that thou susteyne
a iust man; but also withdrawe thou not thin hond from
hym; for he that dredith God, is not necligent of ony thing.
20 Wisdom hath coumfortid a wise man, ouer ten pryncis of
21 a citee. Forsothe no iust man is in erthe, that doith good,
22 and synneth not. But also ȝyue thou not thin herte to alle
wordis, that ben seid; lest perauenture thou here thi seruaunt
23 cursynge thee; for thi conscience woot, that also thou hast
24 cursid ofte othere men. I asayede alle thingis in wisdom;
Y seide, I schal be maad wijs, and it ȝede awei ferthere fro
25 me, myche more than it was; and the depthe *is* hiȝ, who
26 schal fynde it? I cumpasside alle thingis in my soule, to
kunne, and biholde, and seke wisdom and resoun, and to
knowe the wickidnesse of a fool, and the errour of vnprudent
27 men. And Y foond a womman bitterere than deth, which is
the snare of hunteris, and hir herte *is* a net, and hir hondis
ben boondis; he that plesith God schal ascape hir, but he
28 that is a synnere, schal be takun of hir. Lo! Y foond this,
seide Ecclesiastes, oon and other, that Y schulde fynde
29 resoun, which my soule sekith ȝit; and Y foond not. I
foond o man of a thousynde; Y foond not a womman of
30 alle. I foond this oonli, that God made a man riȝtful; and
he medlide hym silf with questiouns with-out noumbre.
1 (VIII). Who is siche as a wijs man? and who knowith the
expownyng of a word? The wisdom of a man schyneth
in his cheer; and the myȝtieste schal chaunge his face.

Cap. VIII (VIII, *continued*).

2 I kepe the mouth of the kyng, and the comaundementis
3 and sweryngis of God. Haste thou not to go awei fro his

face, and dwelle thou not in yuel werk. For he schal do al
4 thing, that he wole; and his word is ful of power, and no
5 man mai seie to hym, Whi doist thou so? He that kepith
the comaundement *of God in this lijf*, schal not feele ony
thing of yuel; the herte of a wijs man vndurstondith tyme
6 and answer. Tyme and cesoun is to ech werk; and myche
7 turment *is* of a man, for he knowith not thingis passid, and
8 he mai not knowe bi ony messanger thingis to comynge. It
is not in the power of man to forbede the spirit, nethir he
hath power in the dai of deth, nethir he is suffrid to haue
reste, whanne the batel neiȝeth; nethir wickidnesse schal
9 saue a wickid man. I bihelde alle thes thingis, and Y ȝaf
myn herte in alle werkis, that ben don vndur the sunne.
10 Sum tyme a man is lord of a man, to his yuel. Y siȝ wickid
men biryed, which, whanne thei lyueden ȝit, weren in hooli
place; and thei weren preisid in the citee, as *men* of iust
11 werkis; but also this is vanyte. Forsothe for the sentence
is not brouȝt forth soone aȝens yuele men, the sones of men
12 doon yuels with-outen ony drede. Netheles of that, that
a synnere doith yuel an hundrid sithis, and is suffrid bi
pacience, Y knew that good schal be to men dredynge God,
13 that reuerensen his face. Good be not to the wickid man,
nethir hise daies be maad longe; but passe thei as schadewe,
14 that dreden not the face of the Lord. Also another vanyte
is, which is don on erthe. Iust men ben, to whiche yuels
comen, as if thei diden the werkis of wickid men; and
wickid men ben, that ben so sikur, as if thei han the dedis
15 of iust men; but Y deme also this moost veyn. Therfor
Y preysid gladnesse, that no good was to a man vndur the
sunne, no-but to ete, and drynke, and to be ioiful; and that
he schulde bere awei with hym silf oneli this of his trauel, in
the daies of his lijf, whiche God ȝaf to hym vndur the sunne.
16 And Y settide myn herte to knowe wisdom, and to vndur-

stonde the departing, which is turned in erthe. A man is, that bi daies and niȝtis takith not sleep with iȝen. And Y vndurstood, that of alle the werkis of God, a man may fynde no resoun of tho thingis, that ben don vndur the sunne; and in as myche as he traueilith more to seke, bi so myche he schal fynde lesse; ȝhe, thouȝ a wijs man seith that he knowith, he schal not mow fynde.

Cap. IX.

I tretide alle these thingis in myn herte, to vndirstonde diligentli. Iust men, and wise men ben, and her werkis ben in the hond of God; and netheles a man noot, whether he is worthi of loue or of hatrede. But alle thingis ben kept vncerteyn in to tyme to comynge; for alle thingis bifallen euenli to a iust man and to a wickid man, to a good man and to an yuel man, to a cleene man and to an vnclene man, to a man offrynge offryngis and sacrifices, and to a man dispisynge sacrifices; as a good man, so and a synnere; as a forsworun man, so and he that greetli swerith treuthe. This thing is the worste among alle thingis, that ben don vndur the sunne, that the same thingis bifallen to alle men; wherfor and the hertis of the sones of men ben fillid with malice and dispisyng in her lijf; and aftir these thingis thei schulen be led doun to hellis. No man is, that lyueth euere, and that hath trist of this thing; betere is a quik dogge than a deed lioun. For thei that lyuen witen that thei schulen die; but deed men knowen no thing more, nether han meede ferthere; for her mynde is ȝouun to forȝetyng. Also the loue, and hatrede, and enuye perischiden togidere; and thei han no part in this world, and in the werk that is don vndur the sunne. Therfor go thou, *iust man*, and ete thi breed in gladnesse, and drynke thi wiyn with ioie; for thi

8 werkis plesen God. In ech tyme thi clothis be white, and
9 oile faile not fro thin heed. Vse thou lijf with the wijf which
thou louest, in alle the daies of lijf of thin vnstablenesse, that
ben ȝouun to thee vndur sunne, in al the tyme of thi vanyte;
for this is thi part in thi lijf and trauel, bi which thou
10 trauelist vndur the sunne. Worche thou bisili, what euer
thing thin hond mai do; for nether werk, nether resoun,
nethir kunnyng, nether wisdom schulen be at hellis, whidir
11 thou haastist. I turnede me to another thing, and Y siȝ
vndur sunne, that rennyng is not of swift men, nethir batel *is*
of stronge men, nether breed *is* of wise men, nether richessis
ben of techeris, ne grace *is* of crafti men; but tyme and hap
12 *is* in alle thingis. A man knowith not his ende; but as
fischis ben takun with an hook, and as briddis ben takun
with a snare, so men ben takun in yuel tyme, whanne it
13 cometh sudeynli on hem. Also Y siȝ this wisdom vndur the
14 sunne, and Y preuede *it* the mooste. A litil citee, and a
fewe men ther-ynne; a greet kyng cam aȝens it, and
cumpasside it with palis, and he bildide strengthis bi cumpas;
15 and bisegyng was maad perfit. And a pore man and a wijs
was foundun ther-ynne; and he delyuerede the citee bi his
wisdom, and no man bithouȝte aftirward on that pore man.
16 And Y seide, that wisdom is betere than strengthe; hou
therfor is the wisdom of a pore man dispisid, and hise wordis
17 ben not herd? The wordis of wise men ben herd in silence,
more than the cry of a prince among foolis.

Cap. X.

18 Betere is wisdom than armuris of batel; and he that
1 synneth in o thing, schal leese many goodis. (X). Flies that
dien, leesen the swetnesse of oynement. Litil foli at a tyme
2 is preciousere than wisdom and glorie. The herte of a wijs
man *is* in his riȝt side; and the herte of a fool *is* in his left

side. But also a fool goynge in the weie, whanne he is
vnwijs, gessith alle men foolis. If the spirit of hym, that
hath power, stieth on thee, forsake thou not thi place; for
heeling schal make gretteste synnes to ceesse. An yuel is,
which Y siʒ vndur the sunne, and goith out as bi errour fro
the face of the prince; a fool set in hiʒ dignyte, and riche
men sitte bynethe. I siʒ seruauntis on horsis, and princes
as seruauntis goynge on the erthe. He that diggith a diche,
schal falle in to it; and an eddre schal bite hym, that
distrieth an hegge. He that berith ouer stoonys, schal be
turmentid in tho; and he that kittith trees, schal be woundid
of tho. If yrun is foldid aʒen, and this *is* not as bifore, but
is maad blunt, it schal be maad scharp with myche trauel;
and wisdom schal sue aftir bisynesse. If a serpent bitith, *it
bitith* in silence; he that bacbitith priueli, hath no thing lesse
than it. The wordis of the mouth of a wijs man *is* grace;
and the lippis of an vnwijs man schulen caste hym doun.
The bigynnyng of hise wordis *is* foli; and the laste thing of
his mouth *is* the worste errour. A fool multiplieth wordis;
a man noot, what was bifore hym, and who mai schewe to
hym that, that schal come aftir hym? The trauel of foolis
shal turment hem, that kunnen not go in to the citee.
Lond, wo to thee, whos kyng is a child, and whose princes
eten eerli. Blessid *is* the lond, whos kyng is noble; and
whose princis eten in her tyme, to susteyne the kynde, and
not to waste. The hiʒnesse of housis schal be maad low in
slouthis; and the hous schal droppe in the feblenesse of
hondis. In leiʒyng thei disposen breed and wyn, that thei
drynkynge ete largeli; and alle thingis obeien to monei. In
thi thouʒt bacbite thou not the kyng, and in the priuete
of thi bed, curse thou not a riche man; for the briddis of
heuene schulen bere thi vois, and he that hath pennys, schal
telle the sentence.

Cap. XI.

1 SENDE thi breed on watris passynge forth, for aftir many
2 tymes thou schalt fynde it. ȝyue thou partis seuene, and
also eiȝte; for thou woost not, what yuel schal come on
3 erthe. If cloudis ben filled, tho schulen schede out reyn
on the erthe; if a tre fallith doun to the south, ether to
the north, in what euer place it fallith doun, there it schal
4 be. He that aspieth the wynd, sowith not; and he that
5 biholdith the cloudis, schal neuere repe. As thou knowist
not, which is the weye of the spirit, and bi what resoun
boonys ben ioyned togidere in the wombe of a womman
with childe, so thou knowist not the werkis of God, which
6 is makere of alle thingis. Eerli sowe thi seed, and thin
hond ceesse not in the euentid; for thou woost not, what
schal come forth more, this ethir that; and if euer eithir
7 *cometh forth* togidere, it schal be the betere. The liȝt *is*
8 sweet, and delitable to the iȝen to se the sunne. If a man
lyueth many ȝeeris, and is glad in alle these, he owith to
haue mynde of derk tyme, and of many daies; and whanne
tho schulen come, thingis passid schulen be repreued of
9 vanyte. Therfor, thou ȝonge man, be glad in thi ȝongthe,
and thin herte be in good in the daies of thi ȝongthe, and
go thou in the weies of thin herte, and in the biholdyng
of thin iȝen; and wite thou, that for alle these thingis God
10 shal brynge thee in to doom. Do thou awei ire fro thin
herte, and remoue thou malice fro thi fleisch; for-whi
ȝongthe and lust ben veyne thingis.

Cap. XII.

1 HAUE thou mynde on thi creatour in the daies of thi
ȝongthe, bifore that the tyme of thi turment come, and the
ȝeris *of thi deth* neiȝe, of whiche thou schalt seie, Tho plesen

2 not me. *Haue thou mynde on thi creatour*, bifor that the sunne be derk, and the liȝt, and sterrys, and the mone;
3 and cloude turne aȝen after reyn. Whanne the keperis of the hous schulen be mouyd, and strongeste men schulen tremble; and grynderis schulen be idel, whanne the noumbre schal be maad lesse, and seeris bi the hoolis schulen wexe
4 derk; and schulen close the doris in the street, in the lownesse of vois of a gryndere; and thei schulen rise at the vois of a brid, and alle the douȝtris of song schulen wexe
5 deef. And hiȝ thingis schulen drede, and schulen be aferd in the weie; an alemaunde-tre schal floure, a locuste schal be maad fat, and capparis schal be distried; for a man schal go in to the hous of his euerlastyngnesse, and weileris
6 schulen go aboute in the street. *Haue thou mynde on thi creatour*, byfore that a siluerne roop be brokun, and a goldun lace renne aȝen, and a watir pot be al to-brokun on the welle, and a wheele be brokun togidere on the
7 cisterne; and dust turne aȝen in to his erthe, wherof it
8 was, and the spirit turne aȝen to God, that ȝaf it. The vanyte of vanytees, seide Ecclesiastes, the vanyte of vanytees,
9 and alle thingis *ben* vanyte. And whanne Ecclesiastes was moost wijs, he tauȝte the puple, and he telde out the thingis
10 whiche he dide, and he souȝte out *wisdom*, and made many parablis; he souȝte profitable wordis, and he wroot moost
11 riȝtful wordis, and ful of treuthe. The wordis of wise men *ben* as prickis, and as nailis fastned deepe, whiche ben ȝouun
12 of o scheepherde bi the counsels of maistris. My sone, seke thou no more than these; noon ende is to make many
13 bookis, and ofte thenkyng is turment of fleisch. Alle we here togydere the ende of spekyng. Drede thou God, and kepe hise heestis; that is *to seie*, ech man. *God* schal brynge alle thingis in to dom, that ben don; for ech thing don bi errour, whether it be good, ether yuel.

SONG OF SOLOMON.

Cap. I.

1, 2 Kisse he me with the cos of his mouth. For thi tetis ben betere than wyn, and ȝyuen odour with beste oynementis. Thi name *is* oile sched out; therfor ȝonge dame- 3 sels loueden thee. Drawe thou me after thee; we schulen renne in to the odour of thin oynementis. The kyng ledde me in to hise celeris; we myndeful of thi teetis aboue wyn, schulen make ful out ioye, and schulen be glad in thee; 4 riȝtful men louen thee. Ȝe douȝtris of Jerusalem, Y am blak, but fair, as the tabernaclis of Cedar, as the skynnes 5 of Salomon. Nyle ȝe biholde me, that Y am blak, for the sunne hath discolourid me; the sones of my modir fouȝten aȝens me, thei settiden me a kepere in vyners; Y 6 kepte not my vyner. *Thou spouse*, whom my soule loueth, schewe to me, where thou lesewist, where thou restist in myddai; lest Y bigynne to wandre, aftir the flockis of thi 7 felowis. A! thou fairest among wymmen, if thou knowist not thi silf, go thou out, and go forth aftir the steppis of thi flockis; and feede thi kidis, bisidis the tabernaclis of 8 scheepherdis. Mi frendesse, Y licnede thee to myn oost 9 of knyȝtis in the charis of Farao. Thi chekis ben feire, 10 as of a turtle; thi necke *is* as brochis. We schulen make to thee goldun ournementis, departid and maad dyuerse 11 with silver. Whanne the kyng was in his restyng-place, 12 my narde ȝaf his odour. My derlyng is a bundel of myrre 13 to me; he schal dwelle bitwixe my tetis. My derlyng *is* to me a cluster of cipre tre, among the vyneres of Engaddi.

14 Lo! my frendesse, thou art fair; lo! thou *art* fair, thin iȝen
15 *ben the* iȝen of culueris. Lo, my derling, thou art fair, and
16 schapli; oure bed *is* fair as flouris. The trees of oure housis
1 *ben* of cedre; oure couplis *ben* of cipresse. (II). I *am* a flour
2 of the feeld, and a lilye of grete valeis. As a lilie among
3 thornes, so *is* my frendesse among douȝtris. As an apple-tre
among the trees of wodis, so my derlyng among sones.

Cap. II (II, *continued*).

I sat vndur the shadewe of hym, whom Y desiride; and
4 his fruyt *was* swete to my throte. The king ledde me in
5 to the wyn celer; he ordeynede charite in me. Bisette ȝe
me with flouris, cumpasse ȝe me with applis; for Y am
6 sijk for loue. His left hond *is* vndur myn heed; and his
7 riȝt hond schal biclippe me. Ȝe douȝtris of Jerusalem, Y
charge ȝou greetli, bi capretis, and hertis of feeldis, that ȝe
reise not, nether make to awake the dereworthe *spousesse*,
8 til sche wole. The vois of my derlyng; lo! this *derlyng*
cometh leepynge in mounteyns, and skippynge ouer litle
9 hillis. My derlyng is lijk a capret, and a calf of hertis;
lo! he stondith bihynde oure wal, and biholdith bi the wyn-
10 dows, and lokith thorouȝ the latisis. Lo! my derlyng
spekith to me, My frendesse, my culuer, my faire *spousesse*,
11 rise thou, haaste thou, and come thou; for wyntir is passid
12 now, reyn is goon, and is departid awei. Flouris apperiden
in oure lond, the tyme of schridyng is comun; the vois of
13 a turtle is herd in oure lond, the fige tre hath brouȝt forth
hise buddis; vyneris flourynge han ȝoue her odour. My
frendesse, my fayre *spousesse*, rise thou, haaste thou, and
14 come thou. My culuer *is* in the hoolis of stoon, in the
chyne of a wal with-out morter. Schewe thi face to me,
thi vois sowne in myn eeris; for thi vois is swete, and thi

15 face is fair. Catche ȝe litle foxis to vs, that destrien the
16 vyneris; for oure vyner hath flourid. My derlyng *is* to me,
17 and Y *am* to hym, which is fed among lilies; til the dai
sprynge, and schadewis be bowid doun. My derlyng, turne
thou aȝen; be thou lijk a capret, and a calf of hertis, on the
hillis of Betel.

Cap. III.

1 In my litle bed Y souȝte hym bi niȝtis, whom my soule
2 loueth; Y souȝte hym, and Y foond not. I shal rise, and Y
schal cumpasse the citee, bi litle stretis and large stretis; Y
schal seke hym, whom my soule loueth; I souȝte hym, and
3 Y foond not. Wakeris, that kepen the citee, founden me.
4 Whether ȝe sien hym, whom my soule loueth? A litil whanne
Y hadde passid hem, Y foond hym, whom my soule loueth;
Y helde hym, and Y schal not leeue *hym*, til Y brynge him in
5 to the hous of my modir, and in to the closet of my modir. Ȝe
douȝtris of Jerusalem, Y charge you greetli, bi the capretis, and
hertis of feeldis, that ȝe reise not, nether make to awake the
6 dereworthe *spousesse*, til sche wole. Who is this *womman*, that
stieth bi the deseert, as a ȝerde of smoke of swete smellynge
spices, of mirre, and of encence, and of al poudur of an oyne-
7 ment-makere? Lo! sixti stronge men of the strongeste men
8 of Israel cumpassen the bed of Salomon; and alle thei holden
swerdis, and *ben* moost witti to batels; the swerd of ech man
9 *is* on his hipe, for the drede of nyȝtis. Kyng Salomon made to
10 hym a seete, of the trees of Liban; he made the pilers therof
of siluer; *he made* a goldun restyng-place, a stiyng of purpur;
and he arayede the myddil thingis with charite, for the douȝ-
11 tris of Jerusalem. Ȝe douȝtris of Sion, go out, and se kyng
Salomon in the diademe, bi which his modir crownede hym,
in the dai of his spousyng, and in the dai of the gladnesse of
his herte.

Cap. IV.

1 Mı frendesse, thou art ful fair; thin iȝen *ben* of culueris, with-outen that that is hid with-ynne; thin heeris *ben* as the 2 flockis of geete, that stieden fro the hil of Galaad. Thi teeth *ben* as the flockis of clippid sheep, that stieden fro waischyng; alle *ben* with double lambren, and no bareyn is among tho. 3 Thi lippis *ben* as a reed lace, and thi speche *is* swete; as the relif of an appil of Punyk, so *ben* thi chekis, with-outen that, 4 that is hid with-ynne. Thi necke *is* as the tour of Dauid, which is bildid with strengthis maad bifore for defense; a thousynde scheldis hangen on it, al armure of stronge men. 5 Thi twei tetis *ben* as twey kidis, twynnes of a capret, that ben 6 fed in lilies, til the dai sprynge, and shadewis ben bowid doun. Y schal go to the mounteyn of myrre, and to the litil hil of 7 encense. My frendesse, thou art al faire, and no wem is in 8 thee. My spousesse, come thou fro the Liban; come thou fro the Liban, come thou; thou schalt be corowned fro the heed of Amana, fro the cop of Sanyr and Hermon, fro the 9 dennys of liouns, fro the hillis of pardis. My sister spousesse, thou hast woundid myn herte; thou hast woundid myn herte, 10 in oon of thin iȝen, and in oon heer of thi necke. My sistir spousesse, thi tetis ben ful faire; thi tetis ben feirere than wyn, and the odour of thi clothis *is* aboue alle swete smel- 11 lynge oynementis. Spousesse, thi lippis *ben* an hony-coomb droppynge; hony and mylk *ben* vndur thi tunge, and the 12 odour of thi clothis *is* as the odour of encence. Mi sister spousesse, a gardyn closid togidere; a gardyn closid togidere, 13 a welle aseelid. Thi sendingis out *ben* paradis of applis of 14 Punyk, with the fruytis of applis, cipre-trees, with narde; narde, and saffrun, *an erbe clepid* fistula, and canel, with alle trees of the Liban, myrre, and aloes, with alle the beste oyne-

15 mentis. A welle of gardyns, a pit of wallynge watris, that
16 flowen with fersnesse fro the Liban. Rise thou north wynd,
and come thou, south wynd; blowe thou thorouȝ my gardyn,
and the swete smellynge oynementis therof schulen flete.

Cap. V.

1 Mi derlyng, come in to his gardyn, to ete the fruyt of hise
applis. Mi sister spousesse, come thou in to my gardyn. Y
have rope my myrre, with my swete smellynge spices; Y
haue ete an hony combe, with myn hony; Y haue drunke
my wyn, with my mylk. Frendis, ete ȝe, and drynke; and
2 derewortheste *frendis*, be ȝe fillid greetli. Y slepe, and myn
herte wakith. The vois of my derlyng knockynge; my sister,
my frendesse, my culuer, my *spousesse* vnwemmed, opene thou
to me; for myn heed is ful of dew, and myn heeris *ben* ful of
3 dropis of niȝtis. I have vnclothid me of my coote; hou schal
Y be clothid ther ynne? I haue waische my feet; hou schal
4 Y defoule tho? Mi derlyng putte his hond bi an hoole;
5 and my wombe tremblide at the touchyng therof. Y roos, for
to opene to my derlyng; myn hondis droppiden myrre, and
6 my fyngris *weren* ful of myrre moost preued. Y openede the
wiket of my dore to my derlyng; and he hadde bowid awei,
and hadde passid. My soule was meltid, as the derlyng spak;
Y souȝte, and Y foond not hym; Y clepide, and he answerde
7 not to me. Keperis that cumpassiden the citee founden me;
thei smytiden me, and woundiden me; the keperis of wallis
8 token awey my mentil. Ȝe douȝtris of Jerusalem, Y biseche
ȝou bi an hooli thing, if ȝe han founde my derlyng, that ȝe
9 telle to hym, that Y am sijk for loue. A! thou fairestc of
wymmen, of what manner condicioun is thi derlyng of the
louede? of what manner condicioun is thi derling of a der-
10 ling? for thou hast bisouȝt vs bi an hooli thing. My derling

T

11 *is* whyt and rodi; chosun of thousyndis. His heed *is* best gold; hise heeris *ben* as the bowis of palm trees, *and ben*
12 blake as a crowe. Hise iȝen *ben* as culueris on the strondis of watris, that ben waischid in mylk, and sitten besidis fulleste
13 ryueris. Hise chekis *ben* as gardyns of swete smellynge spices, set of oynement makeris; hise lippis *ben* lilies, droppynge
14 doun the best myrre. Hise hondis *ben* able to turne aboute, goldun, and ful of iacynctis; his wombe is of yuer, ourned
15 with safiris. Hise lippis *ben* pilers of marble, that ben foundid on foundementis of gold; his schapplinesse *is* as of the Liban,
16 *he is* chosun as cedris. His throte *is* moost swete, and he *is* al desirable. Ȝe douȝtris of Jerusalem, siche is my derlyng,
17 and this is my freend. Thou faireste of wymmen, whidur ȝede thi derlyng? whidur bowide thi derlyng? and we schulen seke hym with thee.

Cap. VI.

1 My derlyng ȝede doun in to his orcherd, to the gardyn of swete smellynge spices, that he be fed there in orcherdis, and
2 gadere lilyes. Y to my derlyng; and my derlyng, that is fed
3 among the lilies, be to me. Mi frendesse, thou art fair, swete and schappli as Jerusalem, *thou art* ferdful as the scheltrun of
4 oostis set in good ordre. Turne awei thin iȝen fro me, for tho maden me to fle awei; thin heeris *ben* as the flockis of
5 geet, that apperiden fro Galaad. Thi teeth as a flok of scheep, that stieden fro waischyng; alle *ben* with double lambren,
6 *ether twynnes*, and no bareyn is among tho. As the rynde of
7 a pumgranate, so *ben* thi chekis, without thi priuytees. Sixti ben queenys, and eiȝti ben secundarie wyues; and of ȝong
8 damesels is noon noumbre. Oon is my culuer, my perfit *spousesse*, oon is to hir modir, and *is* the chosun of hir modir; the douȝtris of Syon sien hir, and prechiden *hir* moost blessid; queenys, and secundarie wyues preisiden hir. Who is this,

that goith forth, as the moreutid risynge, fair as the moone, chosun as the sunne, ferdful as the scheltrun of oostis set in
10 good ordre? Y cam doun in to myn orcherd, to se the applis of grete valeis, and to biholde, if vyneris hadden flourid,
11 and if pumgranate trees hadden buriowned. Y knew not;
12 my soule disturblide me, for the charis of Amynadab. Turne aȝen, turne aȝen, thou Sunamyte; turne aȝen, turne aȝen, that we biholde thee. What schalt thou se in the Sunamyte, no but cumpenyes of oostis?

Cap. VII.

1 Douȝtir of the prince, thi goyngis ben ful faire in schoon; the ioyncturis of thi heppis *ben* as brochis, that ben maad bi
2 the hond of a crafti man. Thi nawle *is* as a round cuppe, and wel formed, that hath neuere nede to drynkis; thi
3 wombe *is* as an heep of whete, biset aboute with lilies. Thi
4 twei teetis *ben* as twei kidis, twynnes of a capret. Thi necke *is* as a tour of yuer; thin iȝen *ben* as cisternes in Esebon, that ben in the ȝate of the douȝter of multitude; thi nose *is* as the
5 tour of Liban, that biholdith aȝens Damask. Thin heed *is* as Carmele; and the heeres of thin heed *ben* as the kyngis
6 purpur, ioyned to trowȝis. Dereworthe *spousesse*, thou art ful
7 fair, and ful schappli in delices. Thi stature is licned to
8 a palm tree, and thi tetis to clustris of grapis. I seide, Y schal stie in to a palm tree, and Y schal take the fruytis therof. And thi tetis schulen be as the clustris of grapis of a vyner; and the odour of thi mouth as the odour of
9 pumgranatis; thi throte *schal be* as beste wyn. Worthi to my derlyng for to drynke, and to hise lippis and teeth to
10 chewe. Y *scha cleue by loue* to my derlyng, and his turnyng
11 *schal be* to me. Come thou, my derlyng, go we out in to the
12 feeld; dwelle we togidere in townes. Ryse we eerli to the

vyner; se we, if the vyner hath flourid, if the flouris bryngen forth fruytis, if pumgranatis han flourid; there I schal ȝyue to thee my tetis. Mandrogoris han ȝoue her odour in oure ȝatis; my derlyng, Y haue kept to thee alle applis, new and elde.

Cap. VIII.

1 Who mai grante to me thee, my brother, soukynge the tetis of my modir, that Y fynde thee aloone without forth, 2 and that Y kisse thee, and no man dispise me thanne? Y schal take thee, and Y schal lede *thee* in to the hous of my modir, and in to the closet of my modir; there thou schalt teche me, and Y schal ȝyue to thee drink of wyn maad swete, and of the must of my pumgra- 3 natis. His lefthond vndur myn heed, and his riȝthond 4 schal biclippe me. Ȝe douȝtris of Jerusalem, Y charge ȝou greetli, that ȝe reise not, nether make the dereworthe *spousesse* 5 to awake, til sche wole. Who is this *spousesse*, that stieth fro desert, and flowith in delices, and restith on hir derlynge? Y reiside thee vndur a pumgranate tre; there thi modir was 6 corrupt, there thi modir was defoulid. Set thou me as a signet on thin herte, as a signet on thin arm; for loue is strong as deth, enuy *is* hard as helle; the laumpis therof *ben* 7 laumpis of fier, and of flawmes. Many watris moun not quenche charite, nether floodis schulen oppresse it. Thouȝ a man ȝyue al the catel of his hous for loue, he schal 8 dispise that *catel* as nouȝt. Oure sistir *is* litil, and hath no tetys; what schulen we do to oure sistir, in the dai whanne 9 sche schal be spokun to? If it is a wal, bilde we theronne siluerne touris; if it is a dore, ioyne we it togidere with tablis 10 of cedre. I *am* a wal, and my tetis *ben* as a tour; sithen 11 Y am maad as fyndynge pees bifore hym. A vyner was to the pesible; in that *citee*, that hath puplis, he bitook it to

keperis; a man bryngith a thousynde platis of siluer for
12 the fruyt therof. The vyner is bifore me; a thousynde *ben*
of thee pesible, and two hundrid to hem that kepen the
13 fruytis therof. Frendis herkene thee, that dwellist in or-
14 chertis; make thou me to here thi vois. My derlyng; fle
thou; be thou maad lijk a capret, and a calf of hertis, on the
hillis of swete smellynge spices.

GLOSSARY.

In the Glossary as printed in the quarto edition, some of the words appear in slightly different forms. In the present reprint, only those forms are retained which occur in the *later* version.

The abbreviations will be readily understood. Thus *adj.* = adjective; *adv.* = adverb; *prep.* = preposition; *pr. t.* = present tense; *p. t.* = past tense; *pr. p.* = present participle; *p. p.* past participle; *pl.* = plural; *s.* = substantive or singular; *v.* = verb (infinitive mood).

A.

Abac, *adv.* back, backwards, Ps. ix. 4; xlii. 2; *i.e.* to flight, Ps. xvii. 41.

Abiden, *pr. t. pl.* wait on, Ps. ciii. 27; *p. t.* **Abood,** waited, waited for, Job xxx. 26; Ps. xxxix. 1; liv. 9; cxviii. 166; remained, Ps.cv.11; *pl.* **abididen, aboden,** Ps. cv. 13; cxviii. 95.

Abiding, *s.* expectation, Ps. xxxviii. 8.

Afer, *adv.* afar, Job ii. 12.

Aferd, *p. p.* afraid, Job iv. 14; xi. 19.

A-fiere, *adv.* on fire, Prov. xxx. 5.

Agreggid, *p. p.* made heavy, Job xxiii. 2.

Aisch, aische, *s.* ashes, Job xiii. 12; xxx. 19; *pl.* **aschis,** Ps. ci. 10.

Alargidist, *p. t. 2 p.* madest large, Ps. xvii. 37; *p. p.* **alargid,** Ps. iv. 2.

Alemaunde-tre, *s.* almond-tree, Eccles. xii. 5.

Almeest, almest, *adv.* almost, Ps. lxxii. 2; xciii. 17.

Altherhiȝeste, *adj.* most high, very high, Ps. lvi. 3; lxxxvi. 5; xc. 9.

Al to-breke, *v.* to break in pieces entirely, Job ix. 17; *imp.* Job vi. 9; *p. t.* **al tobrak,** Job xxix. 17; *p. p.* **al to-broke, al to-brokun,** Job iv. 10; Ps. iii. 8.

Al to-brese, *v.* to break utterly in pieces, Ps. xlv. 10.

Amendide, *p. t.* amended, set right, Ps. xvii. 36; *p. p.* **amendid,** Ps. xcv. 10.

Amte, *s.* ant, Prov. vi. 6; *pl.* **amtis,** Prov. xxx. 25.

Anefeld, *s.* an anvil, Job xli. 15.

Anentis, *prep.* with, at, before, Job xxv. 2; Ps. xxxvi. 23; cviii. 20.

Angwisch, *s.* anguish, Job vi. 7.

Anoon, *adv.* presently, as soon as, Job iii. 11; Ps. xxxvi. 20.

Anoye, *s.* annoyance, Ps. cxviii. 28.

Anoye, *v.* to grieve, trouble, Job ix. 21; *pr. t. pl.* **anoien,** Ps. xxxiv. 1.

Anyntische, *imp. pl.* bring to nought, destroy, Ps. cxxxvi. 7; *p. p.* **anyntischid,** brought to nought, *i.e.* emptied out, Ps. lxxiv. 9.

Applis, *s. pl.* apples, Ps. lxxviii. 1 (Lat. *pomorum*).

Arerid, *p. p.* raised up, Ps. cvi. 25.

Arette, *v.* to reckon, charge, Job

xli. 18; *p. t.* **arrettide**, Ps. xxxi. 2; *pl.* **arettiden,** Job xxx. 7; *p. p.* **arettid, arrettid,** Job xviii. 3; Ps. cv. 31.
Arewis, arowis, *s. pl.* arrows, Job vi. 4: Ps. vii. 14.
Armeris, armuris, *s. pl.* armour, Ps. xxxiv. 2; xlv. 10.
As . . . so and, as . . . even so, Prov. xix. 12.
Asaie, *imp.* try, prove, Ps. xxv. 2.
Ascapide, *p. t.* escaped, Job i. 15, 16, 17.
Aschis, *s. pl.* ashes, Ps. ci. 10. See **aisch**.
Aseelid, *p. p.* sealed, S. Sol. iv. 12.
Aslepid, *p. p.* asleep, Prov. xxiii. 34.
Aspie, *v.* to lay wait for, watch privily, Ps. xxxvi. 12.
Aspies, *s. pl.* spies, ambush, Job xxxi. 9; Ps. ix (x). 8.
Astorid, *p. p.* made ready, Job xxix. 20 (Lat. *instaurabitur*).
Auauntith, *pr. t.* boasts, Prov. xxviii. 25.
Auerouse, *adj.* avaricious, Prov. i. 19; xxix. 4.
Avoidid, *p. p.* made void, done away, Job xv. 4.
Avouter, *s.* adulterer, Job xxiv. 15.
Auowis, avowis, *s. pl.* vows, Ps. xlix. 14; lv. 12.
Avowtreris, *s. pl.* adulterers, Ps. xlix. 18.
Auter, *s.* altar, Ps. xxv. 6; xlii. 4.
Axe, *v.* to ask, seek out, Job xxxi. 14; *pr. t. pl.* **axen,** Ps. x. 5; *p. t. pl.* **axiden,** Ps. xxxiv. 11; civ. 40; *imp.* **ax,** Job xii. 7.
Axere, *s.* asker, Job iii. 18; xxxix. 7.
Axyng, *s.* a petition, Job vi. 8; *pl.* **axyngis,** Ps. xix. 7; xxxvi. 4.
Aȝen, *adv.* again, Job i. 21.
Aȝenbiere, *s.* redeemer, Job xix. 25; Ps. xviii. 15.
Aȝenbieth, *pr. t.* redeems, Ps. vii. 3; *imp.* **aȝenbie, aȝeyn-bie,** Ps. xxv. 11; cxviii. 134; *p. p.*

aȝenbouȝt, aȝen-bouȝt, Job xv. 31; Ps. xxx. 6.
Aȝenclepe, *imp.* call again, Ps. ci. 25.
Aȝens, aȝenus, *prep.* against, Job i. 22; xxxiii. 13; Ps. ii. 2.
Aȝenseie, *v.* to contradict, Job xi. 10.
Aȝenseiyngis, *s. pl.* contradictions, Ps. xvii. 44.
Aȝenstood, *p. t.* withstood, resisted, Job ix. 4; *pr. p.* **aȝenstondynge,** Ps. xvi. 8.

B.

Bareyn, *adj.* childless, Job xxiv. 21.
Bedstre, *s.* bed, couch, Ps. vi. 7; xl. 4.
Been, *s. pl.* bees, Ps. cxvii. 12.
Beete, *v.* to beat, Ps. cxxviii. 4; *pr. t.* **betith,** Job ix. 23; *p. t. pl.* **beeten,** Prov. xxiii. 35; *p. p.* **betun,** Ps. lxii. 5.
Ben, *pr. t. pl.* are, Job iii. 8; Ps. ix. 21; xxxvii. 5; lxxii. 1; *p. p.* **be,** Job xviii. 3.
Bere, *pr. t.* bear, Job xiii. 14; *pl.* **beren,** Job ix. 13; *p. t.* **bar,** Job iii. 10; ix. 5; *pr. p.* **berynge,** Job ix. 26; *p. p.* **borun,** Job i. 2; xi. 12.
Bernacle, *s.* a bit or snaffle for a horse (Lat. *camus*), Ps. xxxi. 9; Prov. xxvi. 3.
Bernes, *s. pl.* barns, Prov. iii. 10.
Betyngis, *s. pl.* stripes, blows, plagues, Job xix. 6; xlii. 15; Ps. xxxi. 10; xxxvii. 18; lxxxviii. 33.
Biclippe, *imp. pl.* embrace, Ps. xlvii. 13; *pr. t. pl.* **biclippen,** Job xxiv. 8.
Bie, *s.* a necklace, Prov. i. 9.
Bie, *v.* to buy, Prov. xvii. 16.
Biere, *s.* a buyer, Prov. xx. 14.
Bifelde, *p. t.* befell, Job iii. 25; *p. p.* **bifelde,** Job ii. 11.
Bifor-come, *imp.* anticipate, Ps. xvi. 13; *p. p.* **bifor-come,** Ps. xx. 4.

GLOSSARY. 281

Bifore ocupie, v. to pre-engage, Ps. xciv. 2.
Bifore-se, v. to foresee, Eccles. iv. 13; p.p. bifor seien, Ps. cxxxviii. 4.
Bifore synge, v. to lead the chant, Ps. cxlvi. 7.
Bifore take, imp. take first or beforehand, Ps. lxxviii. 8; p.t. bifore took, Ps. lxxvi. 5.
Biheest, s. a promise, command, Ps. lv. 10; Eccles. iv (v). 3.
Bihetith, pr. t. promiseth, Job xvii. 5; Prov. xii. 18; p. p. bihi3t, Prov. vi. 1.
Biholde, p. p. beheld, Job i. 8.
Bihynde, adv. backwards, Ps. xliii. 11.
Bijs, s. silk, Prov. xxxi. 22.
Bikenen, pr. t. pl. beckon, make signs, Ps. xxxiv. 19.
Bilden, p. t. pl. built, Job iii. 14.
Bimowe, v. to mock, Ps. ii. 4.
Biriels, s. pl. tombs, burying-places, Job xv. 28 (*Biriels* is properly a sing. form, but is here used to translate Lat. *tumulos*. A. S. *burgels*, a burying-place).
Biriede, p. t. buried, Ps. lxxviii. 3.
Birthe, s. increase, Ps. cvi. 37 (Lat. *nativitatis*).
Birthun, s. a burden, Ps. xxxvii. 5.
Bisched, p. p. covered, Ps. lxxxviii. 46 (Lat. *perfudisti*).
Bisegiden, p.t. pl. besieged, Ps. xxi. 13.
Bisi, adj. careful, Ps. xxxix. 18 (Lat. *solicitus*).
Bisynesse, s. business, care, Eccles. iv. 4; pl. bisynesses, Eccles. iv. 4.
Bispreynt, p. p. sprinkled, Prov. vii. 17.
Bitake, v. to deliver, give up, Job xxx. 23; p. t. bitook, Ps. lxxvii. 48; p. p. bitakun, Ps. lxii. 11.
Bithenke, v. to meditate, recollect, Ps. i. 2; xxi. 28; xxxiv. 28; p.t. bithou3te, Ps. xli. 5.
Bitternessis, s. pl. bitter sorrows, Job xiii. 26.

Biwlappe, v. to wrap, Job xviii. 11.
Blisfulere, adj. comp. happier, Eccles. iv. 3.
Bloodis, s. pl. bloody deeds, cruelties, Ps. xxv. 9; cv. 39.
Blosme, v. to blossom, Ps. lxxi. 16.
Bolis, s. pl. bulls, Job xlii. 6; Ps. xxi. 13.
Bolneth, pr. t. becomes puffed up or swoln, Job xv. 13; p. t. bolnyde, Job xvi. 17; pr.p. bolnynge, Job xxxviii. 11.
Boon, s. bone, Ps. ci. 6; cxxxviii. 15; pl. bonys, boones, boonys, Job x. 11; Ps. vi. 3; lii. 6; cxl. 7.
Boor, s. a boar, Ps. lxxix. 14.
Boord, bord, s. a table, Ps. xxii. 5; lxxvii. 19.
Borewe, s. surety, Prov. xx. 16; pl. borewis, Prov. xxii. 26.
Borewe, v. to borrow, Ps. xxxvi. 21.
Botche, s. a boil, Job ii. 7.
Botere, s. butter, Job xxix. 6; Prov. xxx. 33.
Bouwe, bowe, s. an arch, a bow, Ps. vii. 13; lxiii. 5; Prov. xx. 26.
Bouwe, v. to bend, turn away, Ps. xlviii. 5; p.t. bowide, poured (Lat. *inclinavit*), Ps. lxxiv. 9; pl. bowiden, directed (Lat. *declinaverunt*), Ps. xx. 12; boweden, bowiden, Ps. xiii. 3; lii. 4; p. p. bowid, Ps. xxxvii. 7; xliii. 19; xlv. 7.
Bowge, s. a bottle, Ps. cxviii. 83.
Bowiden, p. t. pl. directed, Ps. xx. 12 (Lat. *declinaverunt*). See under Bouwe.
Breed, s. bread, Ps. xxxvi. 25; ciii. 14.
Breede, s. breadth, Ps. xvii. 20.
Breide, v. to draw, pull, Ps. xxiv. 15.
Brekyng, s. breach, gap, Ps. cv. 23 (Lat. *in confractione in conspectu ejus*).
Brenneth, pr. t. burns, Ps. ii. 14; imp. brenne, Ps. xxv. 2; p. t.

brente, Ps. cv. 18; *pl.* **brenten,** Ps. lxxiii. 7; *pr. p.* **brennynge, brynnynge,** Job xxvii. 21; Ps. lxxxii. 15; ciii. 4; *p. p.* **brent,** Job i. 5; Ps. ix (x). 2.
Brere, *s.* a briar, Job xxxi. 40.
Brid, *s.* a bird, a young bird, Job v. 7; *pl.* **briddis, briddys, bryddis,** Job xxxv. 11; xxxviii. 41; Ps. lxxxiii. 4; cxlvi. 9.
Briȝtnessis, *s. pl.* splendors, Ps. cix. 3.
Brochis, *s. pl.* brooches, S. Sol. i. 9.
Broddeste, *adj. superl.* broadest, Job xxxvi. 16.
Bruk, *s.* a locust, Ps. civ. 34 (Lat. *bruchus*).
Brymston, *s.* brimstone, Job xviii. 15: Ps. x. 7.
Buckis of geet, *s. pl.* he-goats, Ps. lxv. 15. See under **Geet.**
Buriowne, *v.* to produce, germinate, Job xiv. 9.
Buschis, *s. pl.* bushes, Job xxx. 7.
Buylith, *pr. t.* boileth, Prov. xv. 2; *p. t. pl.* **buyliden,** Job xxx. 27.
Bythenke, *v.* to meditate on, recollect, Ps. xxxvii. 1. See **Bithenke.**

C.

Caitifte, *s.* captivity, Ps. xiii. 7; lii. 7; lxvii. 19.
Calengynge, *pr. p.* accusing, Prov. xxviii. 3.
Canel, *s.* cinnamon, Prov. vii. 17.
Capparis, *s.* the caper-shrub (Lat. *capparis*), Eccles. xii. 5.
Capret, *s.* a wild goat, S. Sol. ii. 9; *pl.* **capretis,** S. Sol. ii. 7.
Careyn, *s.* a carcase, Job xxxix. 30.
Castels, *s. pl.* tents, camp, Ps. lxxvii. 28; cv. 16.
Castyng afore, *s.* forethought, Job xxxiv. 27.
Catel, *s.* substance, goods, Ps. cviii. 11; Prov. i. 13.
Caudron, *s.* cauldron, Ps. cvi. 9.
Cautelouse, *adj.* cautious, crafty, Job v. 13.

Celeris, *s. pl.* cellars, S. Sol. i. 3.
Cesoun, *s.* season, Eccles. viii. 6.
Chaier, *s.* chair, seat, Ps. cvi. 32.
Chalenge, *s.* accusation, Prov. xxviii. 16; *pl.* **chalengis,** Eccles. iv. 1.
Chalengere, *s.* accuser, Ps. lxxi. 4; *pl.* **chalengeris,** Job xxxv. 9.
Chare, *s.* chariot, Ps. lxvii. 18; *pl.* **charis,** Ps. xix. 8.
Chargiden, *p. t. pl.* regarded, Prov. i. 25.
Chariouse, *adj.* chargeable, burdensome, Prov. xxvii. 3.
Chaungyng, *s.* changing, Ps. lxxxviii. 52 (Lat. *commutationem*); *pl.* **chaungyngis,** exchangings, Ps. xliii. 13.
Cheer, chere, *s.* countenance, face, Job iv. 16; Ps. iv. 7; x. 8; *pl.* **cheris,** looks, Ps. liv. 22.
Chees, *p. t.* chose, Job vii. 15; Ps. xxiv. 12; xxxii. 12; *pl.* **cheesiden,** Job vii. 15; *p. p.* **chose,** Ps. lxiv. 5.
Chere, *s.* face, Job iv. 16. See **Cheer.**
Childith, *pr. t.* bringeth forth children, Job xxiv. 21; *p. t.* **childide,** Ps. vii. 15.
Chirche, *s.* assembly, Ps. xxxix. 10; lxxxviii. 6; cvi. 32; *pl.* **chirchis,** Ps. lxvii. 27.
Chyne, *s.* an opening, chink, breach in a wall, S. Sol. ii. 14.
Clees, *s. pl.* hoofs, *lit.* claws, Ps. lxviii. 32.
Clei, *s.* clay, Job xiii. 12.
Clenner, *adj. comp.* cleaner, purer, Job iv. 17; *superl.* **clenneste,** Prov. iii. 14.
Clennesse, *s.* cleanness, Ps. xvii. 21.
Clepe, *v.* to call, Job xii. 4; *p. t. pl.* **clepiden,** Job i. 4; *pr. p.* **clepynge,** Job ix. 16.
Clere, *adj.* splendid, bright, Ps. xv. 6.
Cleuede, *p. t.* cleaved, Ps. lxii. 9.
Closyngis, *s. pl.* leaves of a gate, Prov. viii. 3.

GLOSSARY. 283

Clothide, *p. t.* put on, Ps. cviii. 18.
Clottis, *s. pl.* clods, Job xxviii. 6 ; xxxviii. 38 ; xxxix. 10.
Cocatrice, *s.* a basilisk, Ps. xc. 13.
Coffyn, *s.* a basket (Lat. *cophinus*), Ps. lxxx. 7.
Colle, *v.* to embrace, Eccles. iii. 5.
Collyngis, *s. pl.* embraces, Prov. vii. 18 ; Eccles. iii. 5.
Comelyng, *s.* a stranger, Ps. xxxviii. 14; xciii. 6 ; pl. **comelingis,** Ps. civ. 12.
Compunct, *p. p.* filled with compunction, Ps. iv. 5 ; xxix. 13.
Comun, *p. p.* come, Job i. 6.
Comynalte, *s.* community, state, Prov. xxix. 2.
Comyne, *v.* to commune, Ps. cxl. 4.
Comynte, *s.* commonalty, community, Job xxiv. 9.
Coniectere, *s.* diviner, Prov. xxiii. 7.
Consuls, *s. pl.* chief men, Job iii. 14.
Conuenticulis, *s. pl.* conventicles, Ps. xv. 4.
Coolis, *s. pl.* coals, Ps. xvii. 13.
Coordis, *s. pl.* lines, Ps. xv. 6. See **Corde.**
Coostis, *s. pl.* coasts, Ps. vii. 7.
Coote, *s.* coat, Job xxx. 18.
Cop, coppe, *s.* top, Job xxii. 13 ; Ps. lxvii. 22 ; *pl.* **coppis,** Prov. viii. 2.
Corde, *s.* line, Ps. cxxxviii. 3 (Lat. *funiculum*); **cord of delyng,** line of separation, Ps. lxxvii. 54 ; *pl.* **coordis,** Ps. xv. 6.
Corour, *s.* a courier, runner, Job ix. 25. See **Currour.**
Cos, *s.* a kiss, S. Sol. i. 1; *pl.* **cossis,** Prov. xxvii. 6.
Coueitiden, *p. t. pl.* lusted, Ps. cv. 14.
Couenable, *adj.* suitable, Ps. ix (x). 1 ; xxxi. 6.
Couent, *s.* assembly, Ps. lxiii. 3 ; *pl.* **couentis,** Ps. xv. 4.
Coumfortid, *p. p.* strengthened, Ps. cxxxviii. 6, 17 ; cxli. 7 ; cxlvii. 13.

Couplis, *s. pl.* beams, rafters, S. Sol. i. 16.
Cratche, *s.* stall, crib, Job vi. 5 ; xxxix. 9.
Crist, *adj.* anointed, Ps. xvii. 51 ; xix. 7 ; xxvii. 8 ; *pl.* **cristis,** anointed ones, Ps. civ. 15.
Cristal, *s.* ice, Ps. cxlvii. 17.
Critouns, *s. pl.* refuse of the frying-pan, Ps. ci. 4. ' *Cretons,* the crispie pieces or mammocks, remaining of lard, that hath been first shred, then boyled, and then strained through a cloath ;' Cotgrave. The Vulgate has *cremium,* firewood.
Crokid, *adj.* curved, Job xxvi. 13.
Crokiden, *p. t. pl.* turned away, Ps. xvii. 46.
Cruddid, *p. p.* clotted, *lit.* curded, Job x. 10 ; Ps. lxvii. 16, 17 (Lat. *coagulatos*).
Culuer, *s.* a dove, Ps. liv. 7 ; lv. 1.
Cumpas, in his, our, &c. round about him, us, &c., Ps. xvii. 12 ; xliii. 14.
Cumpas, *v.* to go about, Ps. lviii. 7.
Currour, *s.* a runner, courier, Prov. xxiv. 34. See **Corour.**
Cursidnesse, *s.* misery, Ps. xiii. 3.

D.

Dai sterre, *s.* the morning-star, Job xxxviii. 32.
Dameselis, *s.* damsels, Ps. lxvii. 26.
Dampne, *v.* to condemn, Job ix. 20 ; Ps. xxxvi. 33.
Dasewide, *p. t.* grew dim, Job xvii. 7.
Deboner, *adj.* mild, meek, Ps. xxiv. 9.
Deedli, *adj.* mortal, Job xxxvi. 31.
Defautis, *s. pl.* faults, Ps. xviii. 14.
Defoule, *v.* to tread down, destroy, defile, Ps. cxxxviii. 11 ; *p. p.* **defoulid,** Job xiv. 2 ; Ps. ix (x). 5.
Delices, *s. pl.* delights, luxuries, Job xxx. 7.
Delitable, *adj.* delightful, Ps. lxvi. 1 ; Eccles. xi. 7.

Delite, *v.* to delight, Ps. xxxiv. 9.
Delitingis, *s. pl.* delights, Ps. xv. 10.
Delueden, *p. t. pl.* dug, pierced, Ps. xxi. 17; lvi. 7.
Deme, *v.* to judge, Ps. ix (x). 18; *pr. t. pl.* **demen**, Ps. ii. 10; *p. t.* **demyde**, Eccles. iv. 3; *p. p.* **demyd**, Ps. ix. 20.
Departe, *v.* to divide, Job xxi. 17; *p. t.* **departide**, parted, distinguished, Ps. cv. 33 (Lat. *distinxit*); *pr. p.* **departynge**, Ps. xxviii. 7.
Departyngis, *s. pl.* divisions, Ps. cxxxv. 13.
Depraueden, *p. t. pl.* turned to evil, Prov. i. 30.
Dereworth, **dereworthe**, *adj.* precious, Prov. v. 19; S. Sol. ii. 7; *superl.* **derewortheste**, S. Sol. v. 1.
Derlyng, *s.* darling, S. Sol. ii. 9; *pl.* **derlyngis**, Ps. lix. 6.
Destrie, *pr. t. subj.* mayst destroy, Ps. viii. 3; *p. p.* **distried**, **distryed**, Job iv. 11; Ps. x. 4.
Deuel, *s.* devil, Ps. cviii. 6.
Diseseful, *adj.* troublesome, Ps. xxxiv. 13.
Dispisable, *adj.* worthy to be despised, Prov. xviii. 1.
Disseit, *s.* deceit, Ps. xl. 10.
Disseruyng, *s.* deserving; **bi disseruyng**, deservedly, Ps. vii. 5.
Dissymelith, *pr. t.* dissembles, Prov. xii. 16; *p. t.* **dissymilide**, Job iii. 26.
Distried, **distryed**, *p. p.* destroyed, Job iv. 11; Ps. x. 4. See **Destrie**.
Distriyng, *s.* destruction, Job v. 21.
Disturble, *v.* to disturb, confound, Job xiii. 11; Ps. ii. 5; xx. 10; *p. p.* **disturblid**, Job iv. 5; Ps. vi. 11.
Disturblyng, *s.* a disturbance, Ps. xxx. 21.
Diyngis, *s. pl.* dyes, colours, Job xxviii. 19.

Doen, *pr. t. pl.* do, Ps. lxxii. 27; *p. t. pl.* **diden**, Ps. v. 11; *p. p.* do, **doon**, Job x. 7; xx. 18; Ps. xl. 14.
Dom, doom, *s.* judgment, Job xxxvi. 6; Ps. ix. 8; *pl.* **domes**, Ps. ix. 17.
Domesmen, *s. pl.* judges, Ps. cxl. 6.
Doo, *s.* a doe, Prov. vi. 5.
Douȝter, *s.* daughter, Ps. ix. 15; *pl.* **douȝtris**, Job i. 2.
Draft, *s.* dregs, Ps. xxxix. 3. [*Read* drast; draft *is a false form*].
Drast, *s.* dregs, Ps. lxxiv. 9.
Drawith, *pr. t.* draws towards him, Ps. ix (x). 9; *p. t.* **drouȝ**, **drow**, drew, Job xxiv. 22; Ps. cxviii. 131; Prov. vii. 21; 2 *p.* **drowist**, Ps. xxi. 10; *pl.* **drowen**, Ps. xxxvi. 14.
Drede, *s.* disgrace, Ps. lxxxviii. 41 (Lat. *opprobrium*).
Dresse, *v.* to direct, guide, prepare, Ps. v. 9; vii. 10; xxiv. 9; *p. t.* **dresside**, Ps. xxxix. 3; lviii. 5; *p. p.* **dressid**, Ps. xxxvi. 23.
Dressyngis, *s. pl.* guidances, Ps. xcviii. 4.
Drit, *s.* dirt, Ps. cxii. 7.
Droof, *p. t.* drove, Ps. xxxiii. 1; *pl.* **driueden**, Job xxiv. 3; *p. p.* **dryuun**, Job xiii. 12.
Duellen, *pr. t. pl.* dwell, Ps. lxxiv. 4.
Duyk, *s.* leader, prince, Job xxix. 10; Prov. ii. 17; *pl.* **duykis**, Ps. lxvii. 28.
Dyuerseli, *adv.* in diverse directions, apart, Ps. xliii. 11.
Dyuersitee, *s.* divers colours, Ps. xliv. 10; *pl.* **dyuersitees**, Ps. xliv. 14.
Dyuynyng, *s.* a divination, Prov. xvi. 10.

E.

Eddre, *s.* an adder, Eccles. x. 8.
Eeld, eld, elde, *adj.* old, Job xiv. 8; Ps. vi. 8; xxxi. 3; xxxvi. 25; *comp.* **eldre**, Ps. cvi. 32.
Eelde, *s.* age, Ps. xci. 11.
Eerbe, *s.* an herb, Ps. lxxxix. 6; *pl.* **eerbis**, Ps. xxxvi. 2.

GLOSSARY. 285

Eere, s. the ear, Ps. xvi. 6; pl. eeris, Ps. v. 2.
Eere ring, s. earring, Job xlii. 11.
Eete, ete, v. to eat, Ps. ci. 5; cxxvii. 2; p.t. eet, Ps. xl. 10; lxxvii. 45; pl. eeten, Job xlii. 11; pr. p. etynge, Ps. cv. 20; p. p. etun, Job vi. 6.
Eft, adv. again, Job vii. 4; Ps. xxvi. 8.
Eir, s. air, sky, Job xii. 7; xxxv. 5.
Eirun, s. pl. eggs, Job xxxix. 14.
Eiʒte, eiʒthe, eighth, Ps. vi. 1 (Vulg. pro octava); xi. 1.
Eiʒtetithe, eightieth, Ps. lxxx. 1.
Eld, adj. old, Ps. xxxvi. 25. See Eeld.
Ellis, else, but, Job ii. 5.
Enclynaunt, pr. p. disposed, Prov. xxix. 22.
Enerite, v. to inherit, Ps. xxiv. 13; xxxvi. 9.
Enforsen, pr.t.pl. endeavour, strive, Job vi. 27; xiii. 8.
Enhaunse, v. to exalt, lift up, Ps. xxix. 2; p.t. enhaunside, Ps. xxvi. 6; pr.p. enhaunsyng, Ps. iii. 4; p.p. enhaunsid, Ps. xxxvi. 35; lxxi. 16.
Enquere, v. to inquire into, Job x. 6; p. p. enquerid, Ps. cxxxviii. 3.
Enserche, v. to search into, Job x.6.
Ententif, adj. bent upon, attentive, Job xxix. 21; Ps. cxxix. 2.
Ere, v. to plough, Job xxxix. 10; p. t.pl. eriden, Job i. 14.
Erthe-tileris, s. pl. tillers of land, Job xxxi. 39.
Eschewith, pr. t. avoids, Prov. xi. 15; xvii. 16.
Etere, s. eater, Ps. xli. 5.
Ether, conj. or, Ps. xvii. 40; xxxii. 17.
Euel, iuel, iuele, yuel, adj. evil, Job i. 1, 8; Ps. lxxvii. 49; cxviii. 101; Prov. xv. 26.
Euene, adj. equal, Ps. lxxxviii. 7; Eccles. iii. 19.
Euene sterre, s. evening-star, Job xxxviii. 32.
Euene worth, adj. of like value, Job xxviii. 19.
Euenli, adv. equitably, Job ix. 32.
Euennesse, s. justice, Ps. x. 8.
Euer ethir, euer either, euer eithir, euere eithir, each, either, both alike, Job ix. 33; Prov. xvii. 15; xx. 12; Eccles. ii. 14; iv. 3; xi. 6.
Euete, s. a lizard, Prov. xxx. 28.

F.

Failide on, p. t. was weak against, Ps. cxxxviii. 21.
Fallinge-ax, s. a felling-axe, Ps. lxxiii. 6.
Fallyngis, s. pl. ruins, Ps. cix. 6 (Lat. ruinas).
Falsnessis, s.pl. frauds, Job xiii. 9.
Fauʒte, p. t. fought, Ps. lix. 2.
Feeld-asse, s. wild ass, Job vi. 5.
Feerdful, ferdful, adj. terrible, Job xvi. 10; Ps. xlvi. 3; cv. 22.
Feersnesse, fersnesse, s. force, assault, fierceness, Job xxii. 11; Ps. xlv. 5.
Fel, felle, adj. subtle, Prov. xii. 23; xiii. 16; xiv. 15.
Felde, p. t. fell, Job i. 19; xvi. 15; pl. felden, fellen, Job i. 15; Ps. xv. 6; lviii. 4; p.p. fallun, Prov. vi. 3.
Felnesse, s. astuteness, Job v. 13; Prov. i. 4 (Lat. astutia).
Felonye, s. great wickedness, Job xxxv. 15.
Felouschipid, p. p. associated, joined, united in, Prov. xxvi. 23.
Fendis, s. pl. fiends, Job xx. 25.
Fetheris, s.pl. wings, Ps. cxxxviii. 9.
Feynere, s. a feigner, Prov. xi. 9; pl. feyneris, Job xxxvi. 13.
Fille, v. to fulfil, fill, replenish, satisfy, Job v. 12; Ps. cix. 6 (Lat. implebit); Prov. v. 19; pr. p. fillynge, Prov. xxv. 14.
Fischis, s. pl. fishes, Ps. viii. 9.
Fitchid, p. p. fixed, Ps. xxxvii. 3.
Flei, fley, p. t. flew, Ps. xvii. 11.

GLOSSARY.

Fleischis, *s. pl.* flesh, Job xiii. 14.
Flete, *v.* to flow, float, melt, S. Sol. iv. 16; *pr. t.* **fletith,** Ps. lxvii. 3; *p. t. pl.* **fletiden,** Ps. xcvi. 5; *pr. p.* **fletinge, fletynge,** Ps. xxi. 15; Prov. xviii. 4.
Flotering, *s.* violent movement, Ps. liv. 23.
Floure, flowre, *v.* to flourish, Ps. xci. 13, 14; cii. 15; *p. t.* **flouride,** Ps. xxvii. 7,
Flowe, *v.* to abound, Job xxii. 26.
Flowing, *s.* a flood, Job xxi. 17.
Folc, *s.* people, Ps. xlii. 1.
Fonned, *adj.* foolish, Job i. 22; ii. 10.
Forsake, *p. p.* forsaken, Ps. ix. 11.
Forseid, *pp.* aforesaid, Ps. xviii. 14.
For-whi, forwhi, for-whi and, *conj.* because, for, wherefore, Job xiii. 16; xxi. 21; Ps. ix (x). 3; xxxix. 3; Prov. iv. 3.
Forʒaten, *p. t. pl.* forgot, Ps. xliii. 21; *p. p.* **forʒete,** Job xix. 14; Ps. ix (x). 11; xliii. 18.
Forʒoue, *p. p.* forgiven, Ps. xxxi. 5.
Foulere, *s.* a taker of birds, Prov. vi. 5.
Frendesse, *s.* a female friend, Prov. vii. 4; S. Sol. i. 8.
Fresche, *adj.* strange, new, Ps. lxxx. 10.
Fruyt, *s.* fruit, Ps. xx. 11.
Ful, *adj.* full, great; **ful out ioiyng,** i.e. **ful out-ioiyng,** great exultation, Ps. xli. 5.
Ful, *adv.* very, Ps. xv. 6.
Ful out, *adv.* completely, Ps. xx. 2.
Fulli, *adj.* extreme (lit. full-like), Ps. xxxi. 7, 11.
Fyndyngis, *s. pl.* inventions, Ps. xcviii. 8.

G.

Gadire, *v.* to gather, Ps. xv. 4.
Geet, geete, *s. pl.* goats, Job xxxix. 1; Prov. xxvii. 27; **geetbuckis,** he-goats, Ps. xlix. 9.
Gendrith, *pr. t.* begets, Eccles. vi. 3; *p. p.* **gendrid,** Job i. 13; Ps. ii. 7.

Gendrure, *s.* engendering, Job xl. 12.
Gerfawcun, gerfaukun, *s.* a kind of falcon, Job xxxix. 13; Ps. ciii. 17.
Gesse, *v.* to reckon, suppose, Job xli. 23; *pr. t.* **gessith,** Job xi. 12; *p. p.* **gessid,** Job xiii. 5.
Gestis, *s. pl.* deeds, Prov. ix. 18.
Giaunt, *s.* a giant, Job xvi. 15.
Gileful, *adj.* deceitful, Ps. v. 7.
Gilefuli, gylefulli, *adv.* deceitfully, Ps. v. 11; xiii. 3; Prov. xx. 19.
Gilis, giles, *s. pl.* guiles, Job xiii. 7; Prov. xxvi. 24. See **Gyle.**
Gilours, *s. pl.* guileful men, deceivers, Ps. liv. 24.
Gird, *p. p.* girt; Ps. xvii. 33; **gird the leendis,** girt round the loins, Prov. xxx. 31.
Gladith, *pr. t.* maketh glad, Ps. xlii. 4.
Glotouns, *s. pl.* gluttons, Prov. xxviii. 7.
Gnaste, *v.* to gnash, Ps. xxxvi. 12; *p. t. pl.* **gnastiden,** Ps. xxxiv. 16.
Gnawiden, *p. t. pl.* gnawed, Job xxx. 3.
Gobelyn, *s.* a goblin, demon, Ps. xc. 6.
Goen, goon, *pr. t. pl.* go, Job xxiv. 5; Ps. xi. 9; lxxxvii. 5; *p. t.* ʒede, Job i. 12; Ps. xviii. 5; *pl.* ʒeden, Job i. 4; *p. p.* **go, goon,** Job ii. 2; Ps. xxxvii. 5.
Goteris, *s. pl.* droppings, drops, Ps. lxiv. 11; lxxi. 6.
Gouernails, gouernals, *s. pl.* government, Prov. i. 5; xx. 18.
Gouernour, *s.* a steersman, Prov. xxiii. 34.
Greces, *s. pl.* steps, degrees, Ps. cxix. 1.
Grettere, *adj. comp.* greater, Ps. cxiii (cxv). 13.
Greuousere, *adj. comp.* more grievous, Job vi. 3.
Grutche, *v.* to grumble, Ps. lviii. 16; *p. t. pl.* **grutchiden,** Ps. cv. 25.

GLOSSARY. 287

Gryndere, *s.* a grinder, Eccles. xii. 4; *pl.* grynderis, Eccles. xii. 3.
Gyle, *s.* guile, Ps. ix (x). 7; *pl.* gilis, giles, Job xiii. 7; Prov. xxvi. 24.

H.

Haburioun, *s.* a breastplate, Job xli. 17.
Haldere, *s.* possessor, Eccles. v. 10.
Halewide, *p. t.* sanctified, Job i. 5; *p.p.* halewid, Ps. xlv. 5.
Halewyng, *s.* sanctifying, Ps. xxix. 1.
Han, *pr. t. pl.* have, Job xviii. 3; xxii. 15; Ps. v. 11.
Hap, *s.* chance, Job iv. 2.
Hardi, *adj.* bold, Job xxxvii. 24.
Heed, *s.* the head, Job i. 20; *i.e.* heading, beginning, Ps. xxxix. 9 (Lat. *capite*).
Heelthe, *s.* salvation, Ps. lix. 13. See Helthe.
Heep, *s.* a heap, S. Sol. vii. 2.
Heer, hair, *i.e.* foliage (Lat. *comam*), Job xiv. 9; *pl.* heeris, heiris, hairs, Job iv. 15; Ps. xxxix. 13.
Heestis, *s. pl.* commands, Ps. cxviii. 4, 6.
Hegge, *s.* a hedge, Eccles. x. 8; *pl.* heggis, Ps. lxxxviii. 41.
Heire, *s.* sackcloth, Ps. xxxiv. 13; lxviii. 12.
Hei3, an hei3e. See Hi3.
Hele, *v.* to conceal, cover, Prov. xxv. 2; *pr.t.* helith, Job xlii. 3; Prov. xi. 13; *p.p.* hilid, Job vi. 21; x. 22.
Helpide, *p. t.* helped, Ps. xciii. 17; *p.p.* helpid, Ps. lxxxv. 17; Prov. xviii. 19.
Helthe, heelthe, *s.* safety, salvation, Ps. xvii. 36; xx. 2; xxxiv. 3; xxxvi. 39; lix. 13.
Hem, *pron.* them, Job i. 4; ii. 11; hem silf, themselves, one another, Ps. lxxii. 27; Prov. xxii. 2.
Hemmes, *s. pl.* hems, borders, Ps. xliv. 14.

Hengis, *s. pl.* hinges, Prov. xxvi. 14.
Her, *adj. pron.* their, Job xxi. 8; Ps. xxvii. 4; *gen.* hern, theirs, of them, Job xxiv. 6; Prov. xi. 24.
Herie, *v.* to praise, Ps. xxxiv. 18; *imp. pl.* Ps. xxviii. 2; *p. t. pl.* herieden, Job xxxviii. 7.
Heriyng, *s.* praise, Ps. viii. 3; xxv. 7.
Herris, *s. pl.* hinges, Job xxii. 14; Prov. viii. 26.
Hert, *s.* a hart, Job vii. 2; *pl.* hertis, Ps. ciii. 18.
Hertid, *p. p.* wise, intelligent, Job xxxiv. 10.
Hertles, *adj.* foolish, Prov. xii. 8.
Hertli, *adj.* joyous, Job viii. 21; Ps. xlvi. 6.
Heuyli, *adv.* heavily, Job iv. 2.
Hey, *s.* grass, Ps. xxxvi. 2; lxxi. 16; Prov. xxvii. 25.
Hiddlis, *s.* secret, Job xiii. 10. (*Hiddlis* is a sing. form; A. S. *hýdels*.)
Hidousnesse, *s.* horror, Job iv. 13, 15; xxviii. 20.
Hilid, *p.p.* covered, Job x. 22. See Hele.
Hiling, hilyng, *s.* a covering, tent, Job xxiv. 7; Ps. xxxv. 8.
Hirt, *p.p.* hurt, Job xv. 33.
Hirtith, *pr. t.* stumbles, strikes against, Prov. xix. 2.
Hirtyng, *s.* stumbling, Prov. iv. 12.
Hise, *pl.* his, Ps. lxi. 13.
Hi3, hi3e, hei3, *adj.* high, exalted, Ps. xli. 8; lxxvii. 56; Prov. viii. 2; *comp.* hi3er, hi3ere, Job xxxi. 21; Ps. ciii. 3; *superl.* hi3este, Ps. ix. 3; xlv. 5; an hi3, an hei3e, on high, Job v. 11; Ps. vii. 9; lxxii. 11.
Hool, *s.* a whole condition, soundness, Job xii. 23.
Hool, *adj.* whole, Job v. 18.
Hooli, hooly, *adj.* holy, Ps. ii. 6; xix. 7.
Hoolis, *s. pl.* holes, Eccles. xii. 3.
Hoond, *s.* hand, Ps. lxx. 4.
Hoore, *s.* a whore, Prov. v. 3.

Hoornesse, s. hoariness, Prov. xx. 29.
Hoose, *adj.* hoarse, Ps. lxviii. 4.
Hoot, hoote, *adj.* hot, Job vi. 17; Ps. xxxviii. 4.
Hous-coppis, s. *pl.* house-tops, Ps. cxxviii. 6.
Hurlid, *p. p.* dashed down, Ps. cxvii. 13.
Hurtle, *v.* to dash down, hurl, Ps. cxxxvi. 9; *p. p.* hurtlid, Ps. xxxvi. 24; Prov. xxi. 6.
Hynd, s. (?) meaning uncertain, Ps. xxi. 1 (Lat. *susceptione*). (Two MSS. have a gloss: *hynd, that is, manheed of Crist, that roos aȝen in the morowtijd.*)
Hynderere, hyndrere, *adj.* hinder, Ps. lxvii. 14; lxxvii. 66.
Hyȝnessis, s. *pl.* heads, tops, Job xxiv. 24.

I.

Iacynctis, s. *pl.* hyacinths, S. Sol. v. 14.
Ianglere, s. a brawler, wrangler, Ps. cxxxix. 12; Prov. vii. 11.
Impugnyde, *p. t.* fought against, Ps. lv. 2.
Ioien, *pr. t. pl.* rejoice, Job iii. 22.
Ioli, *adj.* wanton, Prov. vii. 22.
Irchouns, s. *pl.* hedgehogs, Ps. ciii. 18.
Iris, s. *pl.* anger, Prov. xxvi. 10; xxx. 33.
Irun, s. iron, Job xxviii. 2; Ps. civ. 18.
Iubilacioun, s. a rejoicing, Ps. cl. 5.
Iuel, iuele. See Euel.
Iys, s. ice, Job xxxviii. 29.
Iȝe, yȝe, s. eye, Job xiii. 1; xxiv. 15; *pl.* iȝen, Job ii. 12; x. 4; Ps. v. 6.

K.

Kauȝt, *p. p.* caught, Ps. ix. 16.
Kepith, *pr. t.* heedeth, Prov. xv. 5.
Keping, kepyng, s. a watch, Ps. xxxviii. 2; lxxxix. 4; cxxix. 6.
Kerue, *v.* to cut, Job xl. 25; *pr. p.* keruynge, Prov. v. 4.
Keuere, *imp.* cover, Ps. xvi. 8; *p. p.* keuered, Ps. lx. 5.

Keueryng, kyueryng, s. covering, Ps. xvii. 36; lxii. 8.
Kien, s. *pl.* cows, cattle, Ps. lxvii. 31.
Kitte, *imp.* let him cut, Job vi. 9; *p. p.* kit, Job iv. 20; vii. 6.
Knouleche, knowleche, *v.* to confess, acknowledge, Ps. vi. 6; vii. 18; xxvii. 7.
Knoulechyng, s. confession, acknowledgment, Ps. xl. 5.
Knowe, knowun, *p. p.* known, Ps. xix. 7; xxxviii. 5; *i. e.* persons known, acquaintance, Job xix. 13; Ps. xxx. 12.
Knyȝthod, s. warfare, Job vii. 1; x. 17.
Knyȝtis, s. *pl.* soldiers, Job xxv. 3; S. Sol. i. 8.
Koude. See Kunne.
Kunne, *v.* to know, Prov. i. 2; Eccles. vii. 26; *pr. subj.* Job xxiii. 5; Prov. i. 2; *pr. t.* kan, Job xiii. 2; Ps. lxxxviii. 16; *pl.* kunnen, Job viii. 9; *p. t.* koude, Job xix. 4.
Kunnyng, s. knowledge, Job xiii. 2; Ps. xviii. 3; xciii. 10.
Kynrede, s. kindred, Ps. lxxiii. 8.
Kyueryng. See Keueryng.

L.

Ladde. See Lede.
Lambre, lambren. See Lomb.
Latijs, s. a lattice, Prov. vii. 6; *pl.* latisis, S. Sol. ii. 9.
Lede, *v.* to lead, Ps. cvii. 11; *p. t.* ladde, ledde, lede, Ps. lxxx. 11; civ. 37; cv. 9.
Leechis, s. *pl.* physicians, Ps. lxxxvii. 11.
Leendis, s. *pl.* loins, Job xxi. 14; Ps. xxxvii. 18; Prov. xxx. 31.
Leeneth, *pr. t.* lendeth, Ps. xxxvi. 26; cxi. 5.
Leep, s. a basket, Job xl. 26.
Leese, lese, *v.* to destroy, lose, Job xiv. 19; Ps. xx. 11; xciii. 23; *pr. t.* leesith, Job xii. 23; *p. t.* lost, loste, Ps. xliii. 3;

GLOSSARY. 289

lxxvii. 45; *pl.* losten, Ps. cv. 34; *p. p.* lost, Ps. lxxii. 27.
Leesewe, lesewe, *s.* pasture, Job xxxix. 8; Ps. lxxiii. 1; xciv. 7.
Leesyng, *s.* lying, falsehood, Ps. iv. 3; v. 7; lviii. 13; *pl.* lesingis, Prov. vi. 19.
Leeues, *s. pl.* leaves of a gate, Prov. i. 21.
Legatis, *s. pl.* ambassadors, Ps. lxvii. 32.
Leiden, *p. t. pl.* laid, Ps. cxxxix. 6; *p. p.* leid, Ps. cxix. 3.
Leie to, *v.* add thereto, Ps. xl. 9 (Lat. *adjiciet*); Ps. lxxvi. 8 (Lat. *apponat*); Prov. xix. 19; ley to, continue, Ps. lxxxviii. 23; *p. t. pl.* leiden to, added thereto, Ps. lxxvii. 17; *pr. subj.* leie to, attempt, Ps. ix (x). 18.
Leȝt, *s.* lightning, Job xx. 25; *pl.* leitis, leytis, Job xxxviii. 35; Ps. xvii. 15.
Leite, *v.* to lighten, Job xxxvi. 30; *imp.* Ps. cxliii. 6.
Leiȝe, *v.* to laugh, Job v. 22; Prov. i. 26; xxxi. 25; *imp.* Job ix. 23; *p. t.* leiȝide, Job xxix. 24.
Leiȝtir, *s.* laughter, Job viii. 21.
Lerne, *v.* to teach, Ps. civ. 22.
Lerud, *p. p.* learned, Ps. ii. 10; Prov. xvii. 27.
Lese. See Leese.
Lesewe. See Leesewe.
Lesewid, *p. p.* pastured, Job i. 14.
Lesingis. See Leesyng.
Lettide, *p. t.* hindered, Ps. lxxvii. 31.
Lettrure, *s.* learning, Ps. lxx. 15.
Ley to. See Leie to.
Leytis. See Leit.
Lie, *v.* lie, tell lies, Ps. lxv. 3 (Lat. *mentientur*); *p. t. pl.* lieden, Ps. xvii. 46; lxxx. 16.
Lifthalf, *s.* left side, Prov. iii. 16.
Lijflode, *s.* livelihood, Prov. xxvii. 27.
Lijk, lyik, *adj.* like, Job i. 8; xvi. 4.
Likyng, *s.* a delight, Ps. xxxv. 9.

Liȝt, *adj.* quick, ready, Prov. xxix. 22.
Liȝtne, *imp.* enlighten, Ps. xii. 4; *pr. p.* liȝtnynge, Ps. xviii. 9.
Liȝtnere, *s.* an enlightener, Prov. xxix. 13.
Liȝtnyng, *s.* illumination, Ps. xliii. 4.
Lokide, *p. t.* looked, Ps. ci. 20.
Lomb, *s.* a lamb, Prov. vii. 22; *pl.* lambre, lambren, Ps. lxxvii. 70; cvi. 41; cxliii. 13.
Loof, *s.* loaf, Prov. vi. 26; *pl.* looues, Ps. xli. 4.
Loore. See Lore.
Lordschipe, *s.* dominion, Ps. cii. 22; cxliv. 13.
Lore, loore, *s.* learning, Ps. ii. 12; xlix. 17; cxviii. 66.
Lorun, *p. p.* lost, i. e. broken, Ps. xxx. 13.
Loside, *p. t.* loosed, Job xxxix. 5.
Lost, loste, losten. See Leese.
Lottis, *s. pl.* lots, Prov. xvi. 33.
Lymes, *s. pl.* limbs, Job xvi. 8.
Lynage, *s.* tribe, race, kindred, Ps. lxxvii. 67, 68; *pl.* lynagis, Ps. lxxi. 17; lxxvii. 55.

M.

Mai, *pr. t.* can, Prov. iii. 27; *2 p.* maist, Job xxxiii. 5; xlii. 2; *p. t. pl.* miȝten, myȝten, could, prevailed, Ps. xx. 12; cxxviii. 2.
Maistri, maistrie, maistrye, *s.* mastery, Ps. xii. 5; li. 9; lxiv. 4.
Maistris, *s. pl.* masters, Prov. v. 13.
Manaasside, *p. t.* threatened, Job xvi. 10.
Mandrogoris, *s. pl.* mandrakes, S. Sol. vii. 13.
Mannus, *gen.* man's, Prov. xviii. 20; *gen. pl.* mennus, Ps. cxiii (cxv). 4.
Manquellere, *s.* a murderer, Ps. v. 7; *pl.* menquelleris, Ps. liv. 24.
Mansleere, *s.* a murderer, Job xxiv. 14.

U

GLOSSARY.

Margarite, s. pearl, Prov. xxv. 12.
Mawe, s. stomach, Prov. vii. 22.
Me, man (*used impersonally*), Job xxxix. 28; Ps. lxxi. 15; Prov. xvi. 6.
Meddling, s. mixture, Ps. lxxiv. 9.
Mede, s. reward, Prov. xi. 18.
Medlen, *pr. t. pl.* mix, Prov. xviii. 6; *p. t.* **meddlide, medlide,** Ps. ci. 10; Prov. ix. 2; *p. p.* meddlid, Ps. cv. 35.
Meete, v. to measure, Ps. lix. 8.
Mekith, *pr. t.* humbleth, Ps. lxxiv. 9; *p. t.* mekide, Ps. xxxiv. 13; *p. p.* mekid, Ps. xxxviii. 3; cv. 42.
Mentil, s. mantle, Prov. xxv. 20.
Merow3, s. marrow, Ps. lxv. 15; *pl.* merowis, Job xxi. 24.
Merueilis, merueiylis, merueylis, s. *pl.* marvels, Ps. lxxi. 18; lxxiv. 3; civ. 2, 5.
Merye, myrie, *adj.* merry, happy, Job xxi. 23; Ps. lxxx. 3; cxi. 5.
Mete, s. meat, Ps. lii. 5; *pl.* meetis, Ps. xliii. 12 [of meetis = for meat].
Meyneal, *adj.* of one's household, Job vi. 13; *pl.* meyneals, they of the household, Prov. xxxi. 15.
Meynee, s. household, family, Job i. 3; *pl.* meynees, Ps. xxi. 28; cvi. 41.
Miche. See **Myche.**
Modirles, *adj.* motherless, Ps. ix (x). 18.
Monestid, *p. p.* targht, Eccles. vii. 3.
Monestyngis, s. *pl.* admonitions, Prov. xii. 11.
Moore trees, s. *pl.* mulberry-trees, Ps. lxxvii. 47 (Lat. *moros*).
More, *adj. comp.* greater, Ps. lxxxix. 10; *superl.* mooste, Ps. xviii. 14.
More, *adv.* very much, thoroughly, Ps. l. 4.
Morenen, *pr. t. pl.* mourn, Job v. 11; *p. t. pl.* **morenyden,** Job xxix. 25.

Mouth, s. face, countenance, Ps. xxxiii. 1 (Lat. *vultum*).
Moreutid, morewtid, morutid, morwetid, s. morrow, morning, Job iii. 9; xxiv. 17; Ps. xxi. 1; lxxiii. 16; c. 8; *pl.* **morewtidis, morutidis,** Ps. lxii. 7; lxxii. 14.
Mouwyng, mowyng, s. mockery, Ps. xxxiv. 16; xliii. 14.
Mou3te, s. a moth, Job iv. 19; xiii. 28.
Mow, mowe, v. to be able, Job xi. 15; Ps. xvii. 39; Eccles. viii. 17; *pr. t. pl.* moun, Job v. 12; ix. 10.
Mussel, s. a morsel, Job xxxi. 17; *pl.* mussels, Ps. cxlvii. 17.
Must, s. new wine, Job xxxii. 19.
Myche, miche, *adj.* much, great, Ps. xxxv. 7; lxvii. 12; cxviii. 165.
Myche, *adv.* much, greatly, very, Ps. xlvii. 2; cii. 8.
Mychilnesse, s. greatness, Ps. xxxii. 16; xlix. 3.
Myddis, mydis, s. middle, Ps. lxxiii. 11, 12.
Myist, s. mist, Job iii. 5.
Mynde, s. remembrance, memory, memorial, Ps. ix. 13; xxiv. 7; xxix. 5; xxxiii. 17.
Mynen, *poss. pron. pl.* my, Ps. xxx. 16.
Mynen, *pr. t. pl.* dig through, undermine, Job xxiv. 16.
Myrie. See **Merye.**
Myseiste, s. poverty, need, Job v. 21.
Mys turne, v. to pervert, Prov. xvii. 23.

N.

Naile, *imp.* transfix, fasten, Ps. cxviii. 120 (Lat. *confige*).
Nappe, v. to sleep, Ps. cxx. 4; *p. t.* nappide, Ps. cxviii. 28.
Napping, s. slumber, Ps. cxxxi. 4.
Nawle, s. the navel, Job xl. 11; Prov. iii. 8.
Ne, nor, Eccles. ix. 11.

GLOSSARY.   291

Neisch, neische, *adj.* soft, delicate, Job xxiii. 16; Prov. xviii. 9.
Neiyng, s. a neighing, Job xxxix. 19.
Neiȝe, *v.* to approach, Job xxxiii. 22; Ps. xxxi. 6; *pr. t. pl.* neiȝen, Ps. xxvi. 2; *p. t.* neiȝede, l's. liv. 22; *pl.* neiȝden, neiȝeden, neiȝiden, Ps. xxxvii. 12; cvi. 18; cxviii. 150; *imp.* neiȝhe, Ps. lxiii. 8; *pr. p.* neiȝynge, Job xxiii. 17.
Nile. See Nyle.
Niȝ, *prep.* near, Ps. lxxxiv. 10.
No but, no-but, *conj.* except, Ps. xciii. 17; cxviii. 92; Prov. iv. 16.
Noiful, *adj.* hurtful, injurious, Ps. xxvi. 2.
Nol, *s.* head, neck, Job xv. 26; xvi. 13; *pl.* nollis, Job xiii. 12; Ps. cxxviii. 4.
Nolde. See Nyle.
Noon, no, Ps. iii. 3.
Noot, *pr. t.* knows not, Job xxviii. 13; Ps. xxxviii. 7.
Nosethirlis, nose-thurls, *s. pl.* nostrils, Job xxvii. 3; xxxix. 20; Ps. cxiii (cxv). 6.
Noumbriden, *p. t. pl.* counted, Ps. xxi. 18.
Nouȝt, nothing, Job vii. 16; xvi. 8; Ps. xxxii. 9.
Nurische, *v.* to nourish, Ps. xxx. 4; *p. t.* nurschide, Ps. xxii. 2.
Nyle, *pr. t.* will not, am unwilling, Job xxiii. 6; *pl.* nylen, Job xxi. 14; *p. t.* nolde, Job vi. 7; Ps. xxxv. 4; 2 *p.* noldist, Ps. xxxix. 7; *pl.* nolden, Job xxxiv. 27; Ps. lxxvii. 10; *imp.* nile, nyle, Job x. 2; Ps. xxxi. 9; xxxvi. 1, 8.
Nyȝ, *adj.* near, Ps. xxxiii. 19.
Nyȝ, *adv.* near, nearly, Job xiv. 8; Ps. xxxv. 5; xliv. 10.
Nyȝtis, *s. pl.* nights, Job ii. 13.

O.

O, oon, one, Job ix. 22; xi. 10; Ps. xiii. 1; xxi. 21.

Oblischen, *pr. t. pl.* bind, Prov. xxii. 26.
Occian, *s.* ocean, Job xxxviii. 30.
Of hard, *adv.* with difficulty, Eccles. i. 15; iv. 12.
Oldli, *adj.* old, Job xli. 23.
Onourid, *p. p.* honoured, Ps. xxxvi. 20.
Ony, any, Ps. xii. 4.
Onys, *adv.* once, Job ix. 23; Ps. lxi. 12.
Oon. See O.
Oost, *s.* army, force, host, Job xxix. 25; S. Sol. i 8; *pl.* oostis, S. Sol. vi. 3.
Orguns, *s. pl.* harps, Ps cxxxvi. 2.
Orrour, *s.* fear, horror, Job vii. 14.
Ostrigis, *s. pl.* ostriches, Job xxx. 29.
Ouercomynge, *pr. p.* surpassing, Job xxxvi. 26.
Ouerer, *adj. comp.* upper, Job xxxviii. 30.
Ourne, *v.* to adorn, Prov. xxvi. 23; *p. t.* ournede, Job xxvi. 13; *p. p.* ourned, Ps. cxliii. 12.
Ournement, *s.* ornament, Prov. vii. 10.
Out-takun, outakun, *prep.* except, Ps. xvii. 32; Prov. vii. 1.
Out ioiyng, i.e. out-ioiyng, *s.* extreme joy, exultation, Ps. xlvi. 2.
Ouȝte, *p. t.* owed, Prov. vii. 14.

P.

Paddok, *s.* a frog, Ps. lxxvii. 45; *pl.* paddoks, Ps. civ. 30.
Parcener, *s.* partner, Ps. cxviii. 63; *pl.* parceneris, Prov. v. 17.
Parfit, perfite, *adj.* perfect, Ps. lix. 2; lxvii. 10; lxxvii. 2.
Partie, *s.* part, portion, Job xxvi. 14; *pl.* partis, Ps. lxii. 11.
Passyng, *s.* surpassing feeling, overpowering agony, Ps. xxx. 23 (Lat. *excessu*).
Pees, *s.* peace, Job v. 24; Ps. xii. 3.

Peesid, *p. p.* appeased, Ps. lxxxii. 2.
Peiside, *p. t.* weighed, Prov. viii. 29; *p. p.* peisid, Job vi. 2.
Pennes, pennys, *s. pl.* wings. Ps. xvii. 12; Prov. xxiii. 5; Eccles. x. 20.
Perse, *v.* to pierce, penetrate, Job xl. 19; *p. p.* persid, Job xxx. 17.
Pesible, *adj.* peaceful, appeasable, Job v. 23; viii. 6.
Pissemyre, *s.* ant, Prov. vi. 6.
Plauntidist, *p. t.* 2 *p.* didst plant, Ps. xliii. 3.
Pleiede, *p. t.* played, delighted, Prov. viii. 30.
Pollid, *p. p.* cropped, clipped, Job i. 20.
Pomel, *s.* a head, hilt, or capital like an apple, Prov. xxv. 11.
Porails, *s. pl.* the common people, Prov. xxx. 14.
Pouert, *s.* poverty, Job xxxvi. 8; Ps. xxx. 11.
Poyntil, *s.* a style to write with, Job xix. 24.
Pressours, *s. pl.* winepresses, Ps. viii. 1; lxxx. 1; Prov. iii. 10.
Preye, *imp.* pray, Ps. xxxvi. 7.
Priue, priuy, *adj.* secret, Job iv. 12; Ps. civ. 30.
Priued, *p. p.* deprived, Job xxi. 10.
Priuetees, priuytees, pryuytees, *s. pl.* secrecy, mysteries, Ps. ix. 1; ix (x). 8; lxiii. 5.
Pryuyli, *adv.* secretly, Ps. xl. 8.
Puple, *s.* people, Job xii. 24; *pl.* puplis, Ps. ii. 1.
Purueide, *p. t.* provided, Ps. xv. 8. (Lat. *providebam,* saw before).
Puruyaunce, *s.* foresight, a providing, Eccles. iv (v). 5.

Q.

Queer, *s.* choir, Ps. cxlix. 3; cl. 4; quere, lii. 1.
Quemeful, *adj.* placable, Job xxxiii. 26.
Quenchid, *p. p.* overpowered by sleep, Ps. iii. 6.
Querels, *s. pl.* complaints, Job xxxiii. 10.
Quik, quyk, *adj.* living, Ps. xli. 3; liv. 16; lxxxiii. 3.
Quikene, quykene, *v.* to make alive, Ps. lxxix. 19; cxxxvii. 7; *imp.* quikene, quykene, quykine, Ps. cxviii. 25, 38, 40; *p. p.* quykenyd, Ps. lxx. 20.
Quytere, *s.* filth, corruption, Job ii. 8.

R.

Ramne, *s.* a bramble, Ps. lvii. 10.
Raueische, *imp. pl.* snatch, Ps. lxxxi. 4; *p. t. pl.* rauyschiden, took the spoil, Ps. xliii. 11.
Raueyns, *s. pl.* robbery, Ps. lxi. 11.
Rauynour, *s.* a robber, Job v. 15.
Ray-cloth, *s.* a striped cloth, Prov. xxxi. 22.
Reed, *adj.* red, Ps. cv. 7, 9.
Rehed, reheed, *s.* a reed, rush, Job xl. 16; Ps. lxvii. 31.
Refuit, refute, refutt, refuyt, *s.* refuge, Ps. ix. 10; lxx. 3; ciii. 18.
Reise, *v.* to raise, Job iii. 8; *p. p.* reisid, Job ii. 12; Ps. xix. 9.
Relifs, relifis, *s. pl.* fragments, remains, remnants, Job xviii. 19; Ps. xvi. 14.
Relikis, *s. pl.* remains, Ps. xxxvi. 37.
Renne, rennen, *v.* to run, Ps. xviii. 6; Prov. iv. 12; *pr. t.* renneth, Job xxxiv. 9.
Rennyngis, *s. pl.* runnings, streams, Ps. i. 3.
Renule, *v.* to renew, Ps. ciii. 30; *p. p.* renulid, Job xxix. 20; Ps. xxxviii. 3.
Repen, *pr. t. pl.* reap, Job iv. 8; *p. p.* rope, S. Sol. v. 1.
Repreue, *imp.* reprove, Job v. 17.
Repreuyngis, *s. pl.* reproofs, Ps. xxxvii. 15.
Repugne, *v.* to fight against, Job xxi. 34.

GLOSSARY. 293

Rewme, s. kingdom, Ps. xxi. 29; xliv. 7.
Reyn, s. rain, Ps. lxvii. 10.
Rikynyd, p. p. reckoned, Job iii. 6.
Riȝthalf, s. right hand, Ps. xv. 8, 10.
Riȝtwisnesse, s. righteousness, Ps. cxviii. 160.
Rooch, rooche, s. rock, Job xiv. 18; Ps. cxiii (cxv). 1.
Roose, s. praise (?), Ps. lix. 1 [sense quite uncertain]; pl. roosis, Ps. lxviii. 1.
Roouys, s. pl. roofs, Prov. xxvii. 15.
Rope. See Repen.
Rote, s. root, Job v. 3.
Rotun, p. p. rotten, Ps. xxxvii. 6.
Ruschyngli, adv. violently, Job vi. 15.
Ryuelyngis, s. pl. wrinkles, Job xvi. 9.

S.

Sad, adj. firm, fixed, Ps. lxxiii. 13.
Sadnesse, s. solidity, firmness, Prov. xxii. 21.
Sak, s. sackcloth, Ps. xxix. 12.
Salewis, s. pl. sallows, willows, Job xl. 17; Ps. cxxxvi. 2.
Saumple, s. example, pattern, copy, Job xvii. 6.
Sautere, sautre, sautree, sautrie, s. psaltery, Ps. xxxii. 2; xlvii. 5; lvi. 9; lxxx. 3.
Schamede, p. t. was ashamed of, Job iii. 25; imp. pl. schame, shame, Ps. xxxiv. 26; lxix. 3, 4.
Schap, s. shape, Ps. xlix. 3.
Schaplynesse, s. beauty, Ps. xliv. 5.
Schauyde, p. t. shaved, Job ii. 8.
Schodith, pr. t. poureth, Job xii. 21; imp. schede, draw, Ps. xxxiv. 3.
Scheld, s. a shield, Ps. xc. 5.
Scheltrun, s. array, squadron, S. Sol. vi. 3, 9.
Schende, v. to reprove, confound, put to shame, Ps. cxviii. 31; p. p. schent, Job vi. 20; Ps. xiii. 6.
Schendschipe, schenschip, schenschipe, s. reproach, disgrace, Job viii. 22; Ps. xliii. 14, 16; lxviii. 21; pl. schenschipis, Ps. lxviii. 10.
Schete, v. to shoot, Ps. x. 3; lxiii. 5.
Schittith, pr. t. shutteth, Job xii. 14.
Scho, s. shoe, Ps. lix. 10; cvii. 10.
Schrewe, s. a depraved person, Job ix. 20; pl. schrewis, Job v. 13.
Schrewid, adj. deceitful, Ps. lxxvii. 8, 57.
Schrewidnesse, s. depravity, wickedness, Job iv. 18.
Schridyng, s. a cutting of herbs, S. Sol. ii. 12.
Schuldris, s. pl. shoulders, Ps. xc. 4.
Schulen, pr. t. pl. shall, Ps. xviii. 15.
Schynyng, s. lightning, Ps. cxliii. 6.
Sculptilis, s. pl. idols, Ps. xcvi. 7.
Se, v. to see, Job x. 4; p. t. siȝ, siȝe, Job iv. 8; v. 3; Ps. cv. 44; 2 p. siest, siȝest, Job xxxviii. 18; Ps. xlix. 18; pl. sien, siȝen, Job ii. 13; Ps. lvii. 9; pr. p. seynge, Ps. xlvii. 6; p. p. seyn, sien, Ps. xxxiv. 21; lxxiii. 9.
Seeld, p. p. sold, Ps. xliii. 13; civ. 17.
Seeling, s. sealing, Job xxxviii. 14 (Lat. signaculum).
Seie, v. to say, Ps. xlix. 12; pr. t. pl. seien, Job xix. 28; Ps. iii. 3.
Seke, v. to search out, seek, Ps. xliii. 22; lxxxii. 17; p. t. souȝte, Ps. xxvi. 8; pr. p. sekyng, Ps. vii. 10; p. p. souȝt, Job ix. 10, 19; Ps. lxxxv. 14.
Selors, s. pl. cellars, Ps. cxliii. 13.
Semeli, adj. seemly, Ps. lvi. 1.

Sercle, *s.* ring, Prov. xi. 22.
Sete, *p. p.* sat down, Ps. cxxvi. 2.
Sewide, *p. t.* stitched, sewed, Job xvi. 16.
Seyntis, *s. pl.* saints, Ps. xxxvi. 28.
Sidur, *s.* cider, Prov. xxxi. 6.
Sien, siest. See **Se.**
Sikir, sikur, *adj.* secure, Prov. xi. 15; xv. 15.
Sikurli, *adv.* securely, Job xi. 18.
Silleris, *s. pl.* sellers, Prov. xi. 27.
Singuler, *adj.* dwelling alone, wild, Ps. lxxix. 14 (Lat. *singularis*).
Siouns, *s. pl.* branches, Ps. lxxix. 12.
Sithen, since, Job xxxiv. 29.
Sithis, *s. pl.* times, Job xix. 3; Ps. cxviii. 164.
Siʒ, siʒe, siʒen, siʒest. See **Se.**
Siʒt, *s.* sight, Job ii. 1; iv. 3.
Siʒhe, *pr. t.* sigh, Job iii. 24.
Skilfuli, *adv.* rightfully, Job xxi. 4.
Sle, slee. *v.* to slay, Ps. ix (x). 8; xxxvi. 32; lviii. 1.
Sleyng, *s.* slaying, slaughter, Ps. xliii. 22.
Slide, *p. p.* slipped, Prov. xxiv. 10.
Slidir, *adj.* slippery, Prov. xxvi. 28.
Slow, *adj.* slothful, Prov. xix. 24.
Slydirnesse, *s.* slipperiness, Ps. xxxiv. 6.
Snapere, *v.* to stumble, trip, Prov. iii. 23.
Soleyn, *adj.* solitary, Job iii. 14.
Sope, sopun vp. See **Soupe.**
Souereyneste, *adj. superl.* highest, Prov. viii. 2.
Souken, *pr. t. pl.* suck, suckle, Job xxxix. 30; *pr. p.* **soukynge,** Ps. viii. 3.
Soun, sown, *s.* sound, Job xv. 21; xxi. 12; Ps. ix. 7.
Soupe, *v.* to swallow up, sup up, Job xl. 18; *p. p.* **sope, sopun vp,** Ps. cxxiii. 4; cxl. 6.
Souʒt, souʒte. See **Seke.**
Sowneden, *p. t. pl.* sounded, Ps. xlv. 4.
Sparcle, *s.* a spark, Job xxi. 18; xxx. 19.

Spedith, *pr. t.* is expedient, profits, Job xv. 3.
Spete, *v.* to spit, Job xxx. 10.
Spier, *s.* a reed, rush, Job viii. 11.
Spirit, *s.* wind, breath, Ps. xlvii. 8; cxviii. 131.
Spotele, *s.* spittle, Job vii. 19.
Sprenge, *imp.* sprinkle, Ps. l. 9; *p. t. pl.* **spreynten,** Job ii. 12.
Sprenges, *s. pl.* branches, shoots, Ps. cxxvii. 3.
Spue, *v.* to vomit, Job xx. 15.
Spuylid, *p. p.* spoiled, Job xix. 9; xxii. 6.
Spuylis, *s. pl.* spoils, Ps. lxvii. 13.
Steef, *adj.* strong, Ps. xxxv. 9.
Steere, *s.* rudder, Prov. xxiii. 34.
Stide, *s.* place, Job xxxix. 22.
Stie, *v.* to go up, ascend, Ps. xxiii. 3; *p. t.* **stiede,** Ps. xvii. 9; xlvi. 6; *pr. p.* **stiynge,** Ps. cv. 7.
Stiriden, *p. t. pl.* moved, shook, Ps. xxi. 8.
Stiryng, *s.* shaking, Ps. xliii. 15.
Stiyng, *s.* an ascent, S. Sol. iii. 10; *pl.* **stiyngis,** goings, paths, Ps. lxxxiii. 6.
Stobil, *s.* stubble, Job xiii. 25.
Stok, *s.* the stocks, Job xiii. 27; xxxiii. 11.
Stoon, *s.* a stone, rock, Ps. xviii. 11; xxvi. 6.
Stoonde, *imp.* stand, Job xxxiii. 5; *p. t. pl.* **stoden,** Ps. xxxvii. 12, 13.
Streiʒte, *p. t.* stretched, Ps. lxxix. 12.
Stremed, *p. p.* poured out as a stream, Prov. v. 16
Strengere, *adj. comp.* stronger, Ps. xxxiv. 10.
Streyne, *v.* to draw tight, bind, Job xxvii. 23; *pr. t.* **streyneth,** Job xl. 12.
Stronde, *s.* a torrent, stream, Job vi. 15; *pl.* **strondis,** Ps. xvii. 5.
Studyes, *s. pl.* praises, Ps. ix. 12.
Sue, *v.* to follow, Job xxxvi. 21; Ps. xxii. 6; *pr. t.* **2 *p.* suest,** Job xv. 5; *p. t.* **suede,** Job xxxi. 7; Ps. xxxvii. 21.

GLOSSARY. 295

Suffre, *imp.* submit to, endure, Ps. xxvi. 14; cxlvii. 17.
Suget, *adj.* subject, Ps. viii. 8; xvii. 48.
Sum, *adj.* a certain, some, Job i. 6, 13; v. 1.
Sumdeel, *adv.* in some degree, Ps. lxxxix. 13.
Superfluli, *adv.* superfluously, Ps. xxiii. 4; xxx. 7.
Suyng, *s.* following, Prov. xi. 19.
Swagith, *pr. t.* assuageth, Prov. xv. 18.
Swatte, *p. t.* sweated, Eccles. ii. 19.
Sweren, *pr. t. pl.* swear, Ps. lvii. 12; *p. t.* swoor, Ps. xxiii. 4; lxxxviii. 4; *p. p.* swore, Ps. lxxxviii. 50.
Swettere, *adj. comp.* sweeter, Ps. xviii. 11.
Swolowe, *imp.* swallow, Ps. lxviii. 16; *p. t.* swolewid, Ps. cv. 17.
Swolowe, *s.* a gulf, Prov. xiii. 15.
Symelacris, symulacris, *s. pl.* idols, Ps. xcvi. 7; cxiii (cxv). 4.
Syngulerli, *adv.* alone, only, Ps. iv. 10; xxxii. 15.

T.

Takyng, *s.* a snare, Ps. xxxiv. 8.
Tapetis, *s. pl.* carpets, Prov. vii. 16.
Tarie, *imp.* delay, tarry, Ps. xxxix. 18.
Tau3te, *p. t.* taught, Prov. iv. 4; *p. p.* tau3t, Job iv. 3.
Teetis, *s. pl.* teats, Job iii. 12.
Telle, *imp. pl.* number, count, Ps. xlvii. 13.
Temperid, *p. p.* directed, ordered, Prov. xvi. 33.
Tent, tente, *s.* attention, heed, Ps. v. 3; lxviii. 19.
Termes, *s. pl.* ends, boundaries, Ps. ii. 8; Prov. xxiii. 10.
Terren, *pr. t. pl.* provoke, Job xii. 6; *p. t.* terride, Ps. ix (x). 3; *pl.* terreden, Ps. cv. 7; *pr. p.* terrynge, Ps. lxxvii. 8; *p. p.* terrid, Ps. v. 11.

Terryng, *s.* a provoking, Ps. xciv. 9.
Than, thanne, *adv.* then, Ps. xviii. 14; lxviii. 5.
Thenke, *v.* to think, medita*te*, thenke for, to meditate on, Ps. xxxvii. 20; *pr. t. pl.* thenken, think, Ps. ix (x). 2; *p. t. pl.* thou3ten, Ps. ii. 1.
Theueli, *adv.* in a thief-like manner, furtively, Job iv. 12.
Theues, *s. pl.* thieves, robbers, Job xix. 12.
Thicke, *adj.* crowded, Ps. cxvii. 27.
Thilke, that, Job iii. 14; Ps. civ. 26; *pl.* Ps. lxxii. 12; Prov. viii. 3.
Thes, these, Ps. xix. 8.
Tho, thoo, those, they, them, Job i. 15; Ps. xviii. 12; lxxvii. 4; Prov. iv. 22.
Thoru3, thur3, *prep.* through. Job ii. 2; Ps. cxxiii. 5.
Thou3, *conj.* though, Job viii. 4; Ps. xxii. 4.
Thou3ten. See Thenken.
Thretne, *inf.* to threaten, Ps. cii. 9.
Threttenthe, thirteenth, Ps. xiii. 1.
Threttithe, thrittithe, thirtieth, Ps. xxx. 1; xxxii. 1.
Thridde, third, Ps. iii. 1.
Thur3. See Thoru3.
Til in to, *prep.* until, unto, Ps. xvii. 51.
Til to, *prep.* unto, until, Ps. xiii. 1; xv. 7.
Tilid, *p. p.* tilled, Prov. xiii. 23.
Tirauntrie, *s.* tyranny, Job xv. 20.
Tiyl-stoon, *s.* brick, Ps. xxi. 16.
To comyng, *ger.* to come, future, Ps. xxi. 32.
To-fore, *prep.* before, Ps. lxxvi. 3.
Token, *p. t. pl.* took, Ps. xxxix. 12.
Toord, *s.* dung, Ps. lxxxii. 11.
To-rende, *pr. t.* tear in pieces, Job xiii. 14; *p. p.* to-rent, Ps. xxix. 12.
Touris, *s. pl.* towers, Ps. xlvii. 13.

Translatiden, *p. t. pl.* copied out, Prov. xxv. 1 (Lat. *transtulerunt*).
Trauailous, *adj.* laborious, troublesome, Job vii. 3.
Trauel, *s.* labour, toil, Ps. xxiv. 18; lxxii. 5.
Trauele, *v.* to labour, toil, Ps. xlviii. 10; *p. t.* traueilide, trauelide, Job xxxix. 16; Ps. vi. 7; *p. p.* trauelid, Job ix. 29; Ps. cv. 32.
Tre, *s.* wood, a tree, Job xli. 18; Ps. i. 3; li. 10.
Trewe, *adj.* true, Ps. xviii. 10.
Trist, *s.* trust, Job xi. 18.
Trist, triste, *ger.* to trust, Ps. cxvii. 8; *pr. t.* triste, Ps. x. 2; *pl.* tristen, Ps. ii. 14.
Tristili, *adv.* trustfully, confidently, Ps. xi. 6; Prov. iii. 23.
Trodun, *p. p.* trodden, Job xxiv. 11.
Tungis, *s. pl* tongues, Ps. v. 11.
Twei. *num.* two, Ps. lxi. 12.
Tympan, *s.* a timbrel, Job xxi. 12.

V.

Veer-tyme, *s.* spring, Ps. lxxiii. 17.
Veniaunce, *s.* vengeance, Job ix. 5; Ps. xxxvii. 2.
Venym-makere, *s.* charmer, Ps. lvii. 6.
Ver, *s.* a glass cup, Prov. xxiii. 31.
Vertu, *s.* power, Ps. xx. 14; xxviii. 4, 11; *pl.* vertues, powers, mights, armies, Ps. xxiii. 10; xliii. 10.
Vndirnyme. *v.* to rep̄ *v.* ix. 8.
Vndursette, *v.* to prop up, Job viii. 15; *pr. t.* vndursettith, placeth beneath, Ps. xxxvi. 24; *p. p.* vndurset, supported, Eccles. iv. 10.
Vndurstoden, *p. t. pl.* stood under, Ps. lvii. 10.
Vnknew, *p. t.* knew not, was ignorant, Job vi. 24.
Vnknyt, *p. p.* loosed, unbound, Job vi. 17.
Vnkunnynge, *pr. p.* ignorant, Ps. xxxviii. 9.
Vnkunnyngis, *s. pl.* ignorances, Ps. xxiv. 7.
Vnnethe, vnnethis, *adv.* scarcely, Job xxvi. 14; Prov. vi. 26.
Vnnoble, *adj.* ignoble, Job xxx. 8.
Vnperfit, *adj.* imperfect, Ps. cxxxviii. 16.
Vnpite, *s.* impiety, Job xxxiv. 10; Prov. iv. 17.
Vnpitouse, *adj.* merciless, impious, Job xxxiv. 18; Ps. xvi. 9.
Vnri3tfulnesse, *s.* unrighteousness, Job xi. 14.
Vnwemmed, *adj.* without blemish, Ps. xvii. 24; xxxvi. 18; lxiii. 5.
Voide, *adj.* empty, despoiled, Ps. vii. 5.
Volatils, volatilis, *s. pl.* birds, Job xii. 7; Ps. xlix. 11.
Vp, vpe, *prep.* after, according to, on account of, Ps. v. 11; ix (x). 4; xxvii. 4; lxxviii. 11.
Vpsedoun, *adv.* upside down, Job xxx. 12; Ps. cxvii. 13.
Vttermere, *adj.* outer, Ps. lxii. 6.
Vynegre, *s.* vinegar, Ps. lxviii. 22.
Vyner, *s.* a vineyard, Job xxiv. 6; S. Sol. i. 5; *pl.* vyneris, Job xxiv. 18.

W.

Waische, *v.* to wash, Ps. xxv. 6; *p. t.* waischide, Job xxix. 6.
Wank-teeth, *s. pl.* molar teeth, Prov. xxx. 14.
Wannesse, *s.* lividness, Prov. xx. 30.
War, *adj.* wary, prudent, wise, aware, Job xxxvi. 20.
Wed, *s.* a pledge, Job xxii. 6; Prov. xx. 16.
Weeten, *pr. t. pl.* make wet, Job xxiv. 8.
Weilen, *pr. t. pl.* wail, mourn, Job xxv. 5.
Wei3te, *s.* weight, Job xxviii. 25.

Welde, v. to possess, obtain, Prov. xxviii. 10; pr. t. pl. welden, Prov. i. 19; imp. welde, Ps. lxxviii. 11; Prov. iv. 3; p. t. weldide, established, Prov. viii. 22; pl. weldiden, obtained, Ps. xliii. 4.
Weldere, s. possessor, Eccles. vii. 13.
Wellid, p. p. welded, Job xxviii. 1.
Wellyng-place, a smelting-place, a furnace, Prov. xxvii. 21.
Wem, s. stain, blemish, Ps. xviii. 8; cxviii. 1.
Wengis, wyngis, s. pl. wings, Ps. xxxv. 8; lx. 5; lxii. 8.
Wenyde, p. t. weaned, Ps. cxxx. 2.
Were, p. t. 2 p. wert, Ps. xliii. 4.
Werk-beeste, s. beast of burden, Ps. lxxii. 23.
Werst, adj. worst, very bad, Ps. xxxiii. 22.
Wexe, s. wax, Ps. lvii. 9.
Wexe, v. to grow, Job viii. 11; pr. t. wexeth, Job viii. 12; p. t. wexide, Ps. xxxvi. 25; pr. p. wexynge, Job xiii. 26.
Whal, s. a whale, Job vii. 12.
Whannus, whennus, adv. whence, Job i. 7; Ps. cxx. 1.
What, wherefore, why, Job xv. 12, 13; xxvii. 12.
Whele, s. a wheel, Ps. lxxxii. 14.
Whiche, which; whiche heriyngis, which as praise, Ps. lv. 12.
Wielde, wyelde, adj. wild, Job xxiv. 5; xxxix. 1; Ps. xlix. 10, 13.
Wilful, adj. willing, gracious, Ps. lxvii. 10.
Wilne, v. to will, desire, Job xxxix. 9; Ps. xxxvi. 23; cxi. 1; pr. t. wole, Job ix. 20; xxxvi. 29; Ps. xxi. 9; pl. wolen, Ps. xxxiv. 27; xxxix. 15; p. t. wolde, Ps. xvii. 20; xxxix. 9; 2 p. woldist, Ps. xl. 12; p. p. wold, Ps. l. 18.
Wite, v. to know, Job v. 24; Ps. lii. 5; pr. t. woot, Job ix. 2; xxx. 23; Ps. lxxii. 11; 2 p.

woost, Job xxxvii. 15; p. t. wiste, Ps. lxxii. 22; 2 p. wistist, Job xxxviii. 21; Ps. xxxix. 10; imp. pl. wite, Ps. iv. 4; ix. 21.
With-out, with-outen, withouten, prep. without, Job iv. 20; viii. 11; Ps. v. 11; ix. 7; xxxvi. 18.
With-outforth, with-out-forth, adv. outwardly, without, Ps. xxx. 12; xl. 8.
With-ynne, prep. within, Ps. xxxiv. 13; xxxviii. 4.
Witti, adj. skilful, S. Sol. iii. 8.
Wlappynge, pr. p. wrapping, Job xxxviii. 2; p. p. wlappid, Job iii. 5.
Wlatide, p. t. hated, Job xix. 17; Ps. cvi. 18.
Wold, wolde, woldist, wole, wolen. See Wilne.
Wombe, s. belly, Job xl. 11; Ps. xvi. 14.
Wondirli, adv. wonderfully, Job x. 16.
Wood, adj. mad, Prov. xxii. 24.
Woost, woot. See Wite.
World. s. age, everlasting, Ps. xx. 5; world of world, ever and ever, Ps. xx. 5, 7; xxi. 27; xxxvi. 27; til in to the world, for ever, Ps. xvii. 51; in to worldis, for ever, Ps. xlvii. 15; fro the world, from everlasting, Ps. xxiv. 16; xl. 14.
Wortis, s. pl. herbs, Ps. xxxvi. 2; Prov. xv. 17.
Wᵒ   ᵒ, pr. p. wooing, Prov.
‾ _   nide, p. t. angered, Ps. ix (x). 4; pl. wraththiden, Ps. lxxvii. 41.
Wraththis, s. pl. anger, Ps. lxxxvii. 17.
Wroot, p. t. wrote, Eccles. xii. 10.
Wrouȝte, p. t. worked, made, Job xxxi. 15; p. p. wrouȝt, Job xxxvi. 23.
Wyelde. See Wielde.

Wyndewe. *v.* to winnow, Ps. xliii. 6.
Wyngis. See **Wengis.**

Y.

Ymage, *s.* a shadow, vain thing, vanity, Ps. xxxviii. 7.
Ympnes, *s. pl.* hymns, Ps. xcix. 4.
Ynneste, *adj. superl.* innermost, Prov. xxvi. 22.
Yreyne, *s.* a spider, Ps. xxxviii. 12; lxxxix. 9; *pl.* **yreyns,** Job viii. 14.
Yrun, iron, Job xix. 24; Ps. ii. 9.
Ysope, *s.* hyssop, Ps. l. 9.
Yuel. See **Euel.**
Yuer, ivory, Ps. xliv. 9; S. Sol. vii. 4.
Yȝe. See **Iȝe.**

Ȝ.

Ȝaf, ȝauen, ȝauest. See **Ȝyue.**
Ȝate, *s.* a gate, Ps. cxvii. 20; *pl.* **ȝatis,** Ps. cxvii. 19.
Ȝe, you, Job vi. 22.
Ȝeer, *s.* year, Ps. lxiv. 12; lxxxix. 4; *pl.* **ȝeeris, ȝeris,** Job xxxvi. 26; Ps. lxxxix. 10; ci. 25, 28.
Ȝelde, *v.* to yield, render, pay, repay, Job ix. 19; Ps. xxi. 26; *p. t.* **ȝeldide,** Job xxix. 11; Ps. vii. 5; *pr. subj.* **ȝelde,** Job xli. 2; *pr. p.* **ȝeldynge,** Ps. vii. 5; *p. p.* **ȝolde, ȝolden, ȝoldun,** Job xxi. 19; Ps. lxiv. 2; Prov. vii. 14.
Ȝelding, ȝeldyng, *s.* reward, retribution, Ps. xviii. 12; cxxxvi. 8; *pl.* **ȝeldyngis,** Ps. lxviii. 23.
Ȝerde, *s.* rod, staff, Job ix. 34; Ps. ii. 9.
Ȝeris. See **Ȝeer.**
Ȝhe, yea, Job vi. 7; xiii. 15.
Ȝistirdai, yesterday, Job viii. 9.
Ȝit, yet, Job i. 16; Ps. xxxvi. 11.
Ȝiueth. See **Ȝyue.**
Ȝok, *s.* yoke, Ps. ii. 3; *pl.* **ȝockis,** Job i. 3; xlii. 12.
Ȝolde, ȝolden, ȝoldun. See **Ȝelde.**
Ȝong, ȝonge, *adj.* young, Job xiii. 16; Ps. viii. 3; *comp.* **ȝongere,** Ps. xxxvi. 25.
Ȝougthe, *s.* youth, Job xxix. 4; Ps. xlii. 4; *pl.* **ȝongthis,** Ps. xlv. 1.
Ȝotun, *p. p.* molten, Job xli. 6; Ps. cv. 19.
Ȝoue, ȝouun. See **Ȝyue.**
Ȝyue, *v.* to give, Job xxii. 3; Ps. xx. 7; *pr. t.* **ȝiueth, ȝyueth,** Job vi. 8; xiv. 13; *p. t.* **ȝaf,** Job i. 21; Ps. xxxix. 2; 2 *p.* **ȝauest,** Job xxii. 8; *pl.* **ȝauen,** Job xlii. 11; Ps. lxviii. 22; *imp. pl.* **ȝiue,** Job vi. 22; *p. p.* **ȝoue, ȝouun,** Job iii. 20, 23; x. 12; Ps. xxix. 8; xxx. 13.

INDEX TO THE PSALMS.

It is not uncommon in old authors to find the Psalms quoted by their Latin names, such as *Beati quorum* (Ps. xxxii), and the like; we still speak of *Venite* (Ps. xcv). The following index to the Psalms, made for my own use many years ago, has often proved of service; and it is here printed, in the hope that it may be of service to others.

The references are to the *English* numbering of the Psalms, mostly indicated, in the present volume, by being placed within marks of parenthesis. The various parts of Psalm cxix are denoted by the usual Hebrew letters; thus *Beati immaculati* is Psalm cxix, *aleph*. W. W. S.

Ad Dominum, 120.
Ad te, Domine, 28.
Ad te, Domine, levavi, 25.
Ad te levavi, 123.
Adhæsit, (*daleth*) 119.
Afferte Domino, 29.
Appropinquet, (*tau*) 119.
Attendite, popule, 78.
Audite hæc, 49.

Beati immaculati, (*aleph*) 119.
Beati omnes, 128.
Beati quorum, 32.
Beatus qui intelligit, 41.
Beatus vir, 112.
Beatus vir, qui non, 1.
Benedic, anima mea, 103, 104.
Benedicam Domino, 34.
Benedictus Dominus, 144.
Benedixisti, Domine, 85.
Bonitatem fecisti, (*teth*) 119.
Bonum est confiteri, 92.

Cantate Domino, 96, 98, 149.
Clamavi in toto, (*koph*) 119.
Cœli enarrant, 19.
Confitebimur tibi, 75.
Confitebor tibi, 9, 111, 138.
Confitemini, 105, 106, 107, 118, 136.
Conserva me, 16.
Cum invocarem, 4.

De profundis, 130.
Defecit anima, (*caph*) 119.

Deus, auribus, 44.
Deus deorum, 50.
Deus, Deus meus, 22, 63.
Deus, in adjutorium, 70.
Deus, in nomine, 54.
Deus, judicium, 72.
Deus laudum, 109.
Deus misereatur, 67.
Deus noster, 46.
Deus, quis similis, 83.
Deus, repulisti, 60.
Deus stetit, 82.
Deus ultionum, 94.
Deus, venerunt, 79.
Dilexi quoniam, 116.
Diligam te, 18.
Dixi, custodiam, 39.
Dixit Dominus, 110.
Dixit injustus, 36.
Dixit insipiens, 14, 53.
Domine, clamavi, 141.
Domine Deus, 88.
Domine, Deus meus, 7.
Domine, Dominus, 8.
Domine, exaudi, 102, 143.
Domine, in virtute, 21.
Domine, ne in furore, 6, 38.
Domine, non est, 131.
Domine, probasti, 139.
Domine, quid, 3.
Domine, quis, 15.
Domine, refugium, 90.

INDEX TO THE PSALMS.

Domini est terra, 24.
Dominus illuminatio, 27.
Dominus regit me, 23.
Dominus regnavit, 93, 97, 99.

Ecce nunc, 134.
Ecce, quam bonum, 133.
Eripe me de inimicis, 59.
Eripe me, Domine, 140.
Eructavit cor, 45.
Et veniat super me, (*vau*) 119.
Exaltabo te, Deus, 145.
Exaltabo te, Domine, 30.
Exaudi, Deus, 55, 61, 64.
Exaudi, Domine, 17.
Exaudiat te, 20.
Expectans expectavi, 40.
Exsurgat Deus, 68.
Exultate Deo, 81.
Exultate, justi, 33.

Feci judicium, (*ain*) 119.
Fundamenta ejus, 87.

In æternum, (*lamed*) 119.
In convertendo, 126.
In Domino confido, 11.
In exitu Israel, 114.
In quo corriget, (*beth*) 119.
In te, Domine, 31, 71.
Inclina, Domine, 86.
Iniquos odio, (*samech*) 119.

Jubilate Deo, 66, 100.
Judica, Domine, 35.
Judica me, Deus, 43.
Judica me, Domine, 26.
Justus es, (*tsaddi*) 119.

Lætatus sum, 122.
Lauda, anima mea, 146.
Laudate Dominum, 117, 147, 148, 150.
Laudate nomen, 135.
Laudate, pueri, 113.
Legem pone, (*he*) 119.
Levavi oculos, 121.
Lucerna pedibus, (*nun*) 119.
Magnus Dominus, 48.

Manus tuæ, (*yod*) 119.
Memento, Domine, 132.
Memor esto, (*zain*) 119.
Mirabilia, (*pe*) 119.
Miserere mei, 51, 56, 57.
Misericordiam, 101.
Misericordias, 89.

Nisi Dominus, 127.
Nisi quia Dominus, 124.
Noli æmulari, 37.
Non nobis, Domine, 115.
Nonne Deo, 62.
Notus in Judæa, 76.

Omnes gentes, plaudite, 47.

Paratum cor, 108.
Portio mea, (*cheth*) 119.
Principes persecuti, (*shin*) 119.

Quam bonus Israel, 73.
Quam dilecta, 84.
Quare fremuerunt, 2.
Quemadmodum, 42.
Qui confidunt, 125.
Qui habitat, 91.
Qui regis Israel, 80.
Quid gloriaris, 52.
Quomodo dilexi, (*mem*) 119.

Retribue servo, (*gimel*) 119.

Sæpe expugnaverunt, 129.
Salvum me fac, 12, 69.
Si vere utique, 58.
Super flumina, 137.

Te decet hymnus, 65.

Usque quo, Domine, 13.
Ut quid, Deus, 74.
Ut quid, Domine, 10.

Venite, exultemus, 95.
Verba mea auribus, 5.
Vide humilitatem, (*resh*) 119.
Voce mea, 77, 142.

www.ingramcontent.com/pod-product-compliance
Lightning Source LLC
Chambersburg PA
CBHW022049230426
43672CB00008B/1118